QUESTIONS OF ANTHROPOLOGY

Edited by
RITA ASTUTI, JONATHAN PARRY AND
CHARLES STAFFORD

LONDON SCHOOL OF ECONOMICS MONOGRAPHS ON SOCIAL ANTHROPOLOGY

Volume 76

BERG
Oxford • New York

First published in 2007 by
Berg
Editorial offices:
1st Floor, Angel Court, 81 St Clements Street, Oxford, OX4 1AW, UK
175 Fifth Avenue, New York, NY 10010, USA

Berg is the imprint of Oxford International Publishers Ltd.

Library of Congress Cataloguing-in-Publication Data

Questions of anthropology / edited by Rita Astuti, Jonathan Parry, and Charles Stafford.
p. cm. — (London School of Economics monographs on social anthropology ; v. 76)
Includes bibliographical references and index.
ISBN-13: 978-1-84520-749-6 (cloth)
ISBN-10: 1-84520-749-1 (cloth)
ISBN-13: 978-1-84520-748-9 (pbk.)
ISBN-10: 1-84520-748-3 (pbk.)
1. Anthropology—Philosophy. I. Astuti, Rita. II. Parry, Jonathan P. III. Stafford, Charles.
GN33.Q84 2007
301.01—dc22

2007011919

British Library Cataloguing-in-Publication Data

A catalogue record for this book is available from the British Library.

ISBN 978 184520 749 6 (Cloth)
978 184520 748 9 (Paper)

Typeset by JS Typesetting Ltd, Porthcawl, Mid Glamorgan
Printed in the United Kingdom by the MPG Books Group.

www.bergpublishers.com

QUESTIONS OF ANTHROPOLOGY

LONDON SCHOOL OF ECONOMICS MONOGRAPHS ON SOCIAL ANTHROPOLOGY

The Monographs on Social Anthropology were established in 1940 and aim to publish results of modern anthropological research of primary interest to specialists.

The continuation of the series was made possible by a grant in aid from the Wenner-Gren Foundation for Anthropological Research, and more recently by a further grant from the Governors of the London School of Economics and Political Science. Income from sales is returned to a revolving fund to assist further publications.

The Monographs are under the direction of an Editorial Board associated with the Department of Anthropology of the London School of Economics and Political Science.

CONTENTS

PREFACE

Anthropologists are heirs to an intellectual tradition that has directly and self-consciously attempted to address some of the central questions arising from human existence and social experience. In its earliest days, the enquiry focused, for example, on the extent to which human behaviour is natural and innate, and the extent to which it is learned and culturally constructed; on questions about the evolution of society, and about the way in which the whole range of existing societies might be related to each other in an evolutionary scheme of things. A generation or so on, and though the questions might have somewhat narrowed and had certainly changed in focus, much of their ambition remained. What is the relationship between the way in which we understand the natural world and the kind of society we live in? Is marriage, the family or incest avoidance universal? From where do taboos come? What is the significance of exchange in social life and how is order possible in stateless societies?

This collection responds to a growing sense of unease, at least on the part of some, that in our own day socio-cultural anthropology has become increasingly narrowly focused, self-referential and abstruse. In the process, the discipline has progressively lost sight of those large general questions that had earlier inspired it, and about which ordinary people all over the world are spontaneously curious. This has happened at its peril since it is that curiosity that prompts many students to study it, colleagues in neighbouring subjects to turn to it for insights, and at least some outside academia to read it for interest and enlightenment.

The contributors to *Questions of Anthropology* were invited to start from a general question that was raised by their own field research, but one that also has wide human resonance. At least implicitly, this question was to be addressed in a comparative frame and in as non-technical and accessible a manner as possible. Most of those that they have come up with – 'What happens after death?'; 'What is going to happen next?'; 'What makes people work?' – are ones which most people in nearly all human cultures must at some point in their lives have reflected on. Some – 'Why, exactly, is the world as it is?'; 'How do we know what is true?' – may appear to be of a more philosophical character, and perhaps of a sort calculated to encourage most ordinary people to heed Charlie Brown's advice: 'No problem is too big or too complicated to be run away from.' But in many cultures, many ignore that wisdom; in most there are some who refuse to run and a majority who can relate to the question even if they are too modest to suppose that they have an answer. It is true that by the time we get to the question that Michael Stewart poses – 'How does genocide happen?' – we are well outside the direct experience of most human populations, though in the contemporary world not outside that of a distressingly large number. And in the contemporary world, most are at least aware of the phenomenon and likely to ask what everybody asks, 'How can it happen?' In short, each of the essays published here addresses an issue of real importance to human beings generally, and regardless of their culture; an issue for which it does not require a professional training in anthropology to see the significance. Paradoxically, however, these are also the kinds of issues that today professional anthropologists seldom explicitly formulate or directly address.

One reason we think it important to make the attempt is that, while most conventional introductions to the subject provide a broad survey of the history and development of the field, outline its major theories and summarise the findings of particular case studies, they often seem to lose sight of the questions with which non-anthropologists come to it and that give it excitement and promise. By putting these back at the centre of the enquiry, we would like to try to recapture at least some of that. The intention is not, of course, to attempt to provide a substitute for these broad surveys, but rather a complement to them that might usefully be read in conjunction.

With the exception of the Afterword, the papers collected here were originally presented at a workshop held at the London School of Economics in June 2005.[1] This was immodestly entitled, 'What is anthropology? … and other "Zafimaniry" questions', and was held in honour of Maurice Bloch whose work has provided the direct inspiration for this volume (though he was at no stage directly involved in it and is in no way responsible for its defects or for what some will undoubtedly regard as its hubris).[2] More about the background to this endeavour is explained in the Afterword, which sets it in the context of Bloch's theoretical project as it has developed over the years. There are, however, two preliminary points that require some brief explanation at the outset.

The first is the reference to 'Zafimaniry questions' in the workshop title and in some of the papers that follow. The Zafimaniry are one of the two Malagasy groups with whom Bloch has done intensive and prolonged fieldwork. Though few of them have had much formal education, and a good many are illiterate, Bloch has been at pains to point out in a couple of recent publications (2000, 2005: ch.1) that they are often intensely interested in, and spontaneously speculate about, anthropological questions of a general theoretical sort – questions, for example, about what aspects of human behaviour are learned and what is innate ('Is it natural for men to want more than one wife?'; 'Do all people in all cultures love their kinsmen equally?'); questions about the relationship between language and culture, and about whether human beings are fundamentally the same despite the fact that they speak very different languages and have very different customs. In this, the Zafimaniry are probably no different from people in any other society; and Bloch's message has been that it is to these fundamental questions that ordinary people ask that anthropology must return if it is to rediscover its original inspiration. It is in this spirit that we collectively came to refer to this volume as a project in 'Zafimaniry anthropology' and to our questions as 'Zafimaniry' ones.

In nearly all of the essays that follow these are questions that concern the anthropologist's informants themselves; but in a few cases their concern is implicit and inferred, rather than overt and explicitly articulated. Cannell, for example, takes an issue – 'How does ritual matter?' – that her Bicolano informants (in the central Philippines) and her Mormon informants (in the United States) do not formulate in quite those terms, but which is nevertheless clearly central to the way in which they talk about religious experience. Lambek's contribution goes a good deal further in inferring the question ('How do women give birth?') from the 'mythopraxis' of the Malagasy people he studied – that is, from episodes in the mythic-history of Sakalava monarchs that are acted out during healing rituals that centrally involve the possession of mediums by ancestors of the ruling dynasty. This mythopraxis, he argues, offers a kind of commentary on the dangers of childbirth in the 'pre-modern' world, and celebrates the fortitude of women (though there may, perhaps, be a case for suggesting that they are equally about the very particular problems of royal succession). Toren's chapter provides what might appear to be the limiting case. On fundamental matters, her Fijian Christian informants just *know* what is true, and the problem she poses seems to emerge less from *their* troubled questioning than from the *anthropologist's* encounter with their certainties.

However that may be, the chapters by, for example, Keller and Stafford differ from those just mentioned in that they deal with issues with which their informants are openly and explicitly concerned on an almost daily basis. What seems to motivate their questions turns out, however, to be not at all the same. Keller looks at the way in which the different Christian fundamentalist groups she discusses see religion as a *scientific* quest to *understand* God's creation. Understanding is a moral obligation, a religious duty; and religion is inseparable from 'science'. For Stafford's informants, by contrast, it is immediately plain that the point of attempting to predict the future has rather less to do with trying to get an intellectual purchase on the world than it has to do with *controlling* it. Calling on Kierkegaard (rather than Charlie Brown), he nonetheless ends by suggesting that it might have been best not to bother, that the attempt might well create more anxiety than it assuages.

Carsten's question, 'How do we know who we are?', is prompted by her study of the experiences of young adult adoptees in Scotland who have sought out their birth parents. What is at stake here is the *past* rather than the future, and it is the desire to establish some measure of control over it, she suggests, that motivates their search. The comparison is with her field experience on the island of Langkawi in Malaysia, where fostering is extremely common but where everybody knows who their birth parents are and parental roles are a lot less exclusive. In that context, the problem that preoccupies her Scottish informants – 'Who, really, am I?' – has little resonance. The initial question turns out to be rather less general than we might perhaps have supposed. Allerton's issue about loneliness is different. It is as much, if not more, of a problem for her Manggarai friends and informants (on the Indonesian island of Flores) as for people in the West. The circumstances that create it are not, however, similar. Specifically, 'spinsterhood' is not – for reasons she explains – the source of anything like the same angst in Manggarai society as it is for the likes of Bridget Jones.

Perhaps predictably, even in the same society the way in which people think about the big questions discussed in this volume is often strongly dependent on context. In Rival's essay on sexuality, for example, the fantasy sex portrayed in myth and ritual is one thing, the sex that is expected to take place with exciting strangers from other long houses is another, and the domestic sex that occurs within the safety of one's own long house community is something else again. One of the central contentions of Astuti's chapter about the understandings that her (Malagasy) Vezo informants have about the continued existence of some aspect of the person after death is that these vary significantly according to whether the event is placed within or outside a ritual frame. To most anthropologists, however, this is likely to come as less of a revelation than the way in which Astuti is able to document the difference with some precision with the help of methods borrowed from cognitive psychology. It is difficult to imagine that it would have emerged so clearly from more conventional kinds of interview data, or even from endless overheard conversations during the course of prolonged periods of participant observation.

Issues of method are once again raised in Freeman's piece on 'Why are some people powerful?' Though he writes here about the time that he spent as a speech-writer for the President of Madagascar, it is on his earlier experiences as an ethnographer that his analysis relies. He takes, that is, a bottom-up view of politics to focus on the way in which the subjects of power think about and experience it, rather than looking at the personal qualities of the leader himself or at the socio-economic conditions that underwrite his political influence.

So although each of these essays proposes a 'Zafimaniry'-type question, the kinds of data that our authors draw on to answer it are sometimes derived from very different types of sources – mythopraxis, methods borrowed from cognitive science, verbatim transcripts of long conversations, as well as the more conventional anthropological method of just hanging out over long periods of time. But nor is it only the methods that vary, and this brings me to the second necessary preliminary. This is to say that despite the common inspiration of this volume, and despite the fact that all of the contributors have at one time or another been closely associated with the anthropology department at the London School of

Economics, readers will search in vain for a unified theoretical position that runs through all of these essays. Neither does it exist, nor have the editors made any attempt to impose one. As is, again, discussed more fully in the Afterword, several of the chapters take positions that are not only at variance with each other but are also at variance with positions taken by Bloch. Not that his writings significantly figure in the chapters that follow. It was never the intention to produce a volume that directly starts out from his work or provides a commentary and reflection on it. In fact, apart from the Afterword, the only chapter that makes more than passing reference to it is the one by Cannell. What we have rather aimed to produce is a collection that addresses the kinds of questions in which he – and we hope student and non-specialist readers, as well as some of our professional colleagues – might be interested. We hoped, that is, to get back to talking about the kind of questions that anthropologists have recently tended to ignore – to questions of 'Zafimaniry anthropology'.

Jonathan Parry

ACKNOWLEDGEMENTS

The editors are grateful to Oliver Woolley for help in preparing the final manuscript for the press.

NOTES

1. The only paper presented at the workshop that is not published here is one by Dan Sperber whose other commitments prevented him from revising it for this volume.
2. The workshop was held to mark Bloch's formal retirement from the Department of Anthropology at the LSE where he had taught since 1968. He nevertheless remains closely associated with the department and continues to teach in it.

REFERENCES

Bloch, M. 2000. 'Postmodernism – The nature/culture debate in just another guise?', *Irish Journal of Anthropology* 5(1): 111–15.
—— 2005. *Essays on cultural transmission*, Oxford: Berg.

CHAPTER 1

WHAT DOES IT MEAN TO BE ALONE?

Catherine Allerton

In this paper I want to discuss what it means to be 'alone' in particular ethnographic and historical contexts by considering the status of unmarried women. As countless instances in music, film and literature indicate, the spinster is often viewed as an icon of loneliness. Indeed, despite (as we shall see) fairly high and consistent rates of non-marriage amongst both men and women, the never-married woman has long held a problematic status in much of Euro-American culture. Images associated with the word 'spinster' are largely negative (Franzen 1996), perhaps explaining why the term is to no longer appear in official British marriage registers.[1] In literature, spinsters are 'old maids' who were never chosen, portrayed by poets as 'maidens withering on the stalk' with a 'tasteless dry embrace' (Linn 1996: 70). Perhaps the best-known recent example of the 'problematic spinster' genre is *Bridget Jones's Diary*, the book and film of which have both been enormously popular. The eponymous heroine is a thirty-something single woman, who sings along desperately to 'All By Myself' and can't wait to get hitched to save herself from an overbearing mother and a faltering career. Contemporary Bridgets who need a little self-help in finding their man can choose from an array of popular books, where titles aimed at single women eclipse those aimed at men. These include: *Why men marry some women and not others: how to increase your marriage potential by up to 60 per cent*; *The rules: time-tested secrets for capturing the heart of Mr Right*; and the intriguingly academic sounding *Find a husband after 35: using what I learned at Harvard Business School.*

But why should this be? Why should an unmarried woman be considered more 'alone' than an unmarried man? Why, in the words of the historian Olwen Hufton, should a spinster be seen as a 'sempiternal spoilsport in the orgy of life' (1984: 356)? Do all cultures see unmarried women as problematic? What does it mean to say that someone is 'alone' in different cultural and historical contexts?

My ethnographic point of contrast with the popular Euro-American view of the bitter 'old maid' is the region of southern Manggarai, in the west of the Indonesian island of Flores. In the two connected villages where I have carried out fieldwork,[2] there are large numbers of older women who have never married or had children and who, I am quite sure, have no intention of ever doing so. These women vary enormously in appearance, health, personality, family set-up and socio-economic position. However, they are never the subject of ridicule within the village, nor are they considered frigid busybodies or women in a dangerous, anomalous position. Although people talked about marriage proposals that these women might have received in the past, they did not think that they *ought* to be married. Very few of these women ever expressed to me any kind of yearning for the married state and neither did their parents hope they would find (in the words of many worried British mothers) a 'nice young man' to 'settle down' with. If there was a Manggarai version of 'All By Myself', these women would not be found singing it.

In this paper, I want to try to do two different things. Firstly, I want to try and make sense of why so many women who I know in southern Manggarai have chosen to remain single, and why for the most part this is an unproblematic choice. Secondly, I want to compare this contemporary situation with a range of ethnographic, historical and demographic literature in order to think about the status of unmarried women across time and space. Why do some societies have near universal rates of marriage? Why, in other societies, do 20 per cent or 30 per cent of the population remain unmarried? What factors influence the acceptance, rejection or ridicule of unmarried women? Are unmarried women everywhere thought to be *alone* and *lonely*, awaiting the arrival of Mr Right?

Anthropology has spawned various 'classic' debates on marriage, including of course the issue of the impossibility (in the face of the levirate, female-only and ghost marriage) of ever coming up with a definition in the first place. However, whilst the latter debate focused on the question of whether, once marriage *had* been defined, it could be said to exist in that form across all societies, anthropology has rarely asked the question of whether marriage is universal *within* particular societies. One notable exception is the work of Jack Goody, particularly in *Production and Reproduction* (1976), where he compares a situation of near-universal marriage in Africa with historically high rates of non-marriage in (Western) Europe, linking the latter with the existence of distinct economic or religious roles for the unmarried as well as Europe's system of 'preferential primogeniture'. The impact of such a system of inheritance, in particular with regard to the creation of a class of permanent bachelors, has been explored by anthropologists both ethnographically (cf. Arensberg 1937; Bourdieu 1962; Scheper-Hughes 2001) and historically (Goody 1983: 183–4). Nevertheless, in non-European settings, it has still often been assumed that unmarried adults are 'almost entirely limited to the widowed, the maimed, the deformed, the diseased, the insane and the mentally deficient' (Mead 1934: 53). I wish to contend that this is very far from the case, and that we need to be careful about assuming that marriage is always an essential rite of passage on the road to non-European adulthood, or that high rates of marriage necessarily correlate (as many demographers assume) with 'traditional', agrarian or even 'patrilineal' societies.

THE 'UNIVERSALITY' OF MARRIAGE

To the anthropologist accustomed to fine-grained distinctions between different groups living on one smallish Indonesian island there is something rather bracing about demography and 'population studies', where the nation-state and its statistics reign supreme. However, demography, backed up with a judicious dose of ethnography, does provide a useful starting-point for showing the cross-cultural variation in the 'universality' of marriage. The broadest contrast drawn in the demographic literature is between a 'European' versus an 'Eastern European' or simply a 'non-European' marriage pattern. J. Hajnal (1965) was the first to note this contrast, arguing that the 'European pattern' was marked by, firstly, a high age at marriage, and, secondly, a high proportion of people who never marry at all. To take a random, alliterative example, in Sweden in 1900, 80 per cent of women were still single at age twenty to twenty-four, with 19 per cent remaining single at ages forty-five to forty-nine (the time at which Hajnal considers a woman to be *permanently* unmarried). By contrast, in Serbia at the same time, only 16 per cent of women were still unmarried at ages twenty to twenty-four, and by ages forty-five to forty-nine the proportion had dropped to only 1 per cent.

The 'European' pattern that Hajnal and others note is interesting for a number of reasons. Firstly, it disproves the assumption that lower rates of marriage in Europe are the result of urbanisation or industrialisation. The high proportion of unmarried persons in Western Europe seems to extend back at least as far as the seventeenth century and possibly even earlier (Hajnal 1965: 134; cf. Goody 1983). Secondly, it is intriguing that spinsters have frequently been the target of suspicion, derision and witchcraft accusations (Bennett and Froide 1999: 14) *despite* the fact that unmarried women and men have long been a feature of the European kinship landscape. Thirdly, from roughly 1940 onwards, this 'European pattern' changed dramatically, with both men and women marrying more frequently and at an earlier age than in previous recorded periods (Hajnal 1965: 104; Dixon 1971: 230). This was also true of the United States, where the generations of women born between 1865 and 1895 had the highest proportion of single women in US history, a situation that had changed significantly by the late 1920s (Franzen 1996: 5–6).

In both Hajnal's and other related work, the 'Eastern European' pattern of lower age at, and near universality of, marriage, is extended to most non-European countries. Dixon reports that, based on data from around 1960, South Korea, India, Pakistan and Libya in particular all showed an 'amazing facility for marrying off their female populations', with other Asian and Middle Eastern societies not far behind (1971: 217). However, Hajnal's link between age at marriage and rates of marriage has been disproved by the example of Japan, which for over 400 years has had a pattern of relatively late age at marriage combined with very low rates of unmarried persons (Cornell 1984: 327). At the other end of the scale, Ireland continually reappears as a country with low rates of marriage, particularly for men: in 1960, 33.6 per cent of men aged forty to forty-four remained bachelors, compared to only 0.3 per cent in South Korea (Dixon 1971: 217). Nancy Scheper-Hughes has described how, in 1960s and 70s Ireland, these bachelors were recognised as 'saints' for looking after the family farm and their parents, but also how they were highly susceptible to being institutionalised with schizophrenia (Scheper-Hughes 2001).

To what extent is Hajnal right to extend the 'Eastern European' pattern to Asian countries? Certainly, the apparent universality of marriage in Asia seems to be backed up by the ethnographic literature. Rozario (1986) argues that rural Bengali women not married by the time they turn twenty are considered unmarriageable; these women then exist in a permanently liminal, ambiguous state since they have not been through the rite of passage which transforms a 'girl' into a 'woman'. In Japan, failure to marry has carried 'severe implications of immaturity and lack of moral responsibility' (Goldman 1993: 196), and in Taiwan, the ghosts of young women who die unmarried are thought to cause misfortune for their families until granted proper status as a wife and mother through marriage to a living man (Harrell 1986).

However, it is interesting that the most striking of these ethnographic cases should come from East and South Asia. More recent demographic literature has stressed the considerable variation concealed by any idea of an 'Asian marriage pattern' (Smith 1980). In particular, there seems to be a notable difference between South and Southeast Asia, two regions that mark, respectively, the earliest and latest average female ages at marriage of the 'developing world' (Jensen and Thornton 2003: 10). In Bangladesh, India, Nepal and Pakistan, marriage remains virtually universal for women (Dube 1997: 109). The notable exception here is Sri Lanka (the 'Ireland of Asia'), which has long had a far lower marriage prevalence than its South Asian neighbours (Jones 1997: 73). In Southeast Asia, the marriage pattern is more varied, both within and between nations. The Philippines, Thailand and Burma have higher than average celibacy levels for women (Smith 1980: 75), partly because both Buddhism and Christianity have allowed for the theoretical possibility of a woman remaining single (Dube 1997: 109), also a relevant factor in the Sri Lankan case. By contrast, the statistics for Indonesia have tended to report close to universal marriage rates (Jones 1997: 74).

In the case of Indonesia, though, it seems likely that national figures mask considerable regional variation, and tend to be skewed by the particular marriage pattern on Java, which has historically been characterised by early and universal marriage (Boomgaard 2003: 203). The eastern and southeastern islands of Indonesia have long had a higher female age at marriage than Java (Smith 1980: 69) and Boomgaard has concluded that outside of Java, marriage in Indonesia was probably not universal before 1850 (2003: 197). This suggests that significant numbers of women not marrying is not necessarily a new phenomenon in the region. However, what is interesting is that, since 1960, Southeast Asia has seen ever-rising rates of non-marriage, with far greater proportions of unmarried people in cities (Jones 1995: 192).

WHO IS AN UNMARRIED WOMAN?

As anthropologists know, defining the married and unmarried in any one society may sometimes be tricky. Defining such categories cross-culturally is even more difficult. Although in certain societies, widowed, divorced and never-married people face similar stigmas (Krishnakumari 1987), in others there are clear differences between these statuses. In this paper, I am concerned only with women who have never been married, not with widows or the divorced (who, in any case, are fairly thin on the ground in Catholic Flores). What term to give such women is clearly a problem, given the pejorative connotations of the word 'spinster'. The precise technical term for the unmarried state is 'celibacy', deriving from the Latin *caelebs*, meaning 'alone or single' (Bell and Sobo 2001: 11). However, the everyday usage of 'celibacy' implies abstention from sexual relations, something clearly not the case for all single people, although definitely relevant to the unmarried on Flores. In this paper, when I refer to the 'unmarried' I mean those single people who have never married; I also sometimes use 'singlewomen' to refer to never-married rather than widowed or divorced women. I should stress that I am also speaking of women who have no children, although I recognise that in many societies unmarried women can be mothers too. Indeed, this raises serious issues of the comparability of the unmarried in different contexts since, in the West, the declining incidence of marriage has been largely offset by '*de facto* relationships', something that does not yet appear to be the case for Southeast Asia (Jones 1997: 70; cf. Tan 2002).

Perhaps the most crucial issue with regard to defining singlewomen is the age at which 'spinsterhood' can be said to be permanent. Although Hajnal takes the numbers remaining single at ages forty-five to forty-nine as an indication of the numbers who never marry at all (1965: 102), in many societies the age that marks the onset of permanent single status may be considerably younger. This age is also frequently lower for women than for men. Rozario reports that while a man in rural Bangladesh can remain unmarried until he is thirty-five or even forty, women should be married by the time they are twenty (1986: 262). Similarly, Sa'ar argues that whilst demographers sometimes use twenty-five as the age from which a woman is considered unmarried, for Israeli-Palestinian girls twenty is a better marking point (2004: 16). In Manggarai, people have to be eighteen before they can be married in church, though priests say they prefer couples to be in their mid-twenties, something which is generally the case. Some women even marry as late as twenty-eight or twenty-nine. However, I do not know any cases of women who have married once they are over thirty and I have therefore taken this age as a rough cut-off point between what Bennett and Froide (1999) term 'life-cycle singlewomen' (those who do eventually marry) and 'lifelong singlewomen'. I should stress, though, that since very few people know their date or even year of birth, I have had to estimate many women's ages.

SINGLEWOMEN IN MANGGARAI

My fieldwork in western Flores has been conducted with a community of subsistence cultivators and coffee farmers split between a highland, origin village called Wae Rebo and a lowland, road-side village called Kombo. In 1997, the population of this dual-sited community was roughly 480, although it has grown considerably since then. In 1997, there were 147 adult women in the community (defined as those over sixteen), of whom roughly 44 per cent were unmarried (sixty-five individuals). Some of these unmarried women were, and others probably still are, 'life-cycle singlewomen', that is, women who will eventually marry. Between 1997 and 2005, six of these women married (one of whom subsequently died in childbirth). A few others have temporarily left the village, either to move to look after the children of their white-collar brothers, or to work in shops in the towns of Flores. However, in 2005, thirty-seven of these original sixty-five women were over the age of thirty and could be said to be permanently single. In addition, a number of women who in 1997 were in their late teens or early twenties are now approaching the age by which, if they have not married, they are likely to remain single. When I returned to the community in 2001, Les, a woman in her mid-twenties, referenced her single status by exclaiming: 'Oh, Auntie Kata, you come back to see us and here I still am!' When I saw her again in 2005, she seemed to have accepted that she might not marry, and made no such jokes about it.

Rather like late-seventeenth- and early-eighteenth-century England, then (Sharpe 1999: 209), roughly 25 per cent of the adult women in this community could be said to be 'lifelong singlewomen'. However, this high rate does *not* extend to adult men, for whom marriage, even though it may be delayed to their thirties, is nearly universal. Wae Rebo-Kombo has only three true bachelors and of these, only Agus, a man in his late forties or early fifties, seems to have consciously chosen not to marry. The other two men have moderate to severe learning difficulties and are not expected by their families to marry. There is also a widower in his fifties whose wife died childless soon after their marriage and who, unusually, never remarried. What is significant is that both this childless widower and Agus are seen as rather odd individuals, either (in the case of the widower) inappropriately lewd with women or (in the case of Agus) impossibly shy and nervous. Actually, I think that Agus, although he is mocked for being 'scared of women', is well liked in the community. He is an extremely gentle and polite man, and treats his hunting dogs with the sort of kindness that is normally absent from Manggarai–canine relations. However, he is undoubtedly a 'loner', never joining in with older men as they sit chewing betel quids together or drinking coffee at meetings. The widower is similarly absent from everyday communal life and I have never met him personally.

By contrast, Wae Rebo-Kombo's large population of unmarried older women are extremely visible and vocal in communal life, and are rarely subject to the kind of whispered ridicule reserved for these two older unmarried men. Unlike the 'somber mass' of Béarnais bachelors described by Bourdieu, these women do not necessarily feel themselves to be 'unmarriageable' (2002: 111; translation in Reed-Danahay 2005: 122–3). The oldest women in this group are in their fifties, and are addressed using the Indonesian term *Tanta* ('Aunt'), since their lack of children prevents them from taking on the teknonyms used to address other older women. Significantly, there are no unmarried women in their sixties, seventies or eighties, and the narratives of older women reveal a past situation where women married at a younger age and had to accept the choices of their elders. This suggests that a once-universal female marriage rate has undergone significant change in the last thirty or forty years, prompting two key questions: why should this change have occurred, and how does this situation square demographically with universal marriage for men? Undoubtedly, a key influence has been the Catholic Church, which has pushed for marriage at a later age, stressed the necessity of a free choice for both bride and groom, and which has discouraged practices familiar to anthropologists as the 'levirate' and the 'sororate' (marriage to a deceased spouse's sibling). At the same time, the creation of universal primary schooling has also opened up new opportunities for women, particularly bearing in mind the very strong relationship between improved education and female marriage patterns in Indonesia (Jones 1997: 60). Economic factors are also relevant: the introduction of machine-spun, synthetically-dyed cotton in markets in Manggarai removed the necessity to engage in lengthy processes of hand-spinning and dyeing and meant that women could concentrate on weaving, producing increasing numbers of textiles for sale. Male (but not female) migration is also becoming more common, reducing the number of potential marriage partners for women of marriageable age.

EXPLANATIONS OF WHY WOMEN REMAIN SINGLE

Despite the broader demographic trends that have influenced the contemporary situation of singlewomen in this community, I want to devote some time to exploring local-level explanations of why so many women remain single. This is not only because these explanations are extremely revealing, but also because even more general demographic trends cannot explain why the percentage of singlewomen appears to be so high in this case.

One issue, of course, is the extent to which this village is something of a freak. This was suggested to me by various outsiders, who argued that it was the remoteness of Wae Rebo that had caused its high rates of unmarried women. Indeed, one outsider described these women as having 'crippled blood' (*dara péku*), an image which conveys both the criticism that these women do not travel to enough social events to meet men, and the general sense that their blood will not 'walk' down to the next generation. However, I am inclined to treat the 'freak' view with considerable scepticism. Wae Rebo is no more isolated than many other villages in rural eastern Indonesia, and I was certainly always aware of unmarried women when visiting other Manggarai villages. Older, unstigmatised, unmarried women also seem to be common in other areas of eastern Indonesia, such as among the Lio of east-central Flores

(Willemijn de Jong, personal communication), and amongst weavers on the island of Sumba (Forshee 2001).

Unmarried women in this community are, of course, aware of external critiques of their position. Indeed, the suggestion that Wae Rebo women might have 'crippled blood' was recounted to me in a suitably outraged fashion by my friend Nina, an attractive woman in her late thirties whose comments that she felt 'sick to her stomach' (*luék tuka*) in contemplating a particular man's moustache were a reflection of her decidedly misanthropic tendencies rather than any general antipathy to men. Like many unmarried women, Nina was happy to reflect on her own life choices, and to joke about being a 'nun' or preferring a radio to a husband, but was never very interested in more sociological reflection on unmarried women as a 'category'. Those within the village who *do* engage in such reflection tend to be married women who have moved to Wae Rebo-Kombo to live with their husbands. These women, who are usually very fond of, and grateful to, their husband's unmarried sisters and aunts, will sometimes speculate on possible explanations for these women never having married. Had people made a kind of anti-love magic to prevent men wanting to marry these women? Had their fathers prevented them marrying because they wished them to stay at home? Or were these women, quite simply, scared of childbirth?

Other explanations as to why these women never married betray a tension between the idea of 'singledom' as an unfortunate fate of particular women versus the notion that these women have consciously rejected marriage. Certain women were thought to have remained single because of ill health, appearance or mental instability. However, Tanta Tina, an extremely striking and industrious woman in her late forties, was said to have had many different marriage offers, but to have been reluctant to accept any of them. In reflecting on their position, many unmarried women do themselves move between seeing their single status as either a fate beyond their control, or a definite choice that they have made. Two sisters, Anna and Regi, both described to me unwanted attentions they had received from men in the past, and yet both seemed agnostic regarding their single status. As Regi herself summed it up: 'Well, if a husband arrives, that's fine, if a husband doesn't arrive, that's fine too'. Nina had also received marriage proposals in the past. She once stated, quite categorically: 'I don't want to receive anyone's letter [of proposal]'; on another occasion, though, she said she would quite like to have children, but 'the problem is there's no father for them' (*masalah toé manga amén*) and women, unlike men, 'cannot go looking' (*toe ngangseng kawé*) for a spouse. This final point is crucial, and points to the fact that changes in the arrangement of marriages have left women in a somewhat ambivalent position, no longer forced into unions they object to, but also lacking sexual independence or the ability to seek their own spouse in a situation where young men and their families are responsible for initiating the marriage process.

Interestingly, Nina's own mother had been forced to marry her husband, and their marriage, which has produced four children, was a tense and argumentative one. It has always been my impression that both Nina and Meren, her older, also-unmarried sister, have been profoundly influenced by their mother's forced marriage. They are both close to their mother but openly dismissive of their elderly father's opinions, and they would frequently ask me questions about whether women in the United Kingdom were forced to marry against their will. Meren, who is in poor health and chooses to live on her own in a field-hut away from the village centre, was perhaps troubled by their common single status, confiding to me that she had told Nina: 'Don't feel you have to follow me.' However, the phenomenon of more than one sister remaining single was not confined to this family, but is also found in families where the parents had a more compatible marriage. Thus, amongst the community's unmarried women, there are fourteen cases where at least two, and sometimes three or four, sisters have remained single together. In others, the presence of an older, unmarried aunt seems to have influenced the decision of at least one of her brother's daughters to remain single. Indeed, what Hufton (1984) calls 'spinster clustering' – the cohabitation of at least two unmarried women – is a common phenomenon in Wae Rebo-Kombo. The house of Tanta Tina in Wae Rebo contains five older, unmarried women and at least three younger, unmarried women. In this instance, the presence of industrious and successful unmarried aunts undoubtedly encourages young women to consider both marriage *and* spinsterhood as possible future roles.

The idea that being a spinster can be a kind of successful career is an intriguing one, unexpected in the ethnography of Asia, but well described in the historical literature on European 'singlewomen', contradicting 'the demographer's belief that the spinster would only too readily change her status' (Sharpe 1999: 209). Manggarai singlewomen may state that they cannot marry and leave the village because they 'love my mother' (*momang ende*) or 'love the land' (*momang tana*); just as frequently, though, they say that they need to 'protect the economy' (*jaga ekonomi*). *Ekonomi*, an English loan-word to Indonesian, is used here to refer to cash-crop farming, particularly of coffee, rather than subsistence agriculture. Several unmarried women have been given land by their fathers where they have planted their own coffee trees. When Anna and Regi did this during my fieldwork, I felt they were signalling a decision to invest in their unmarried future in the community. One singlewoman in her fifties, Tanta Tin, ran a rather profitable business selling paraffin carried over the mountains by her older sister's son. Other unmarried women sell highland fruit at lowland markets, and most, as throughout Eastern Indonesia, have an important ritual and economic role to play in the production of woven textiles. Indeed, the significance of weaving in this region, where women's role as cloth producers is at least as highly valued as their role as wives and mothers (de Jong 2002: 272) is undoubtedly a key factor influencing the high status of unmarried women. Although married women do weave, once they have had a certain number of children, they often become too tired or busy to involve themselves in textile production, and it is, therefore, no coincidence that Wae Rebo's most original and accomplished weavers were Tanta Tin and another unmarried woman in her fifties.

Unlike the more heavily-policed situation of unmarried women in some Muslim areas of Southeast Asia, singlewomen in Manggarai have a great deal of independence and freedom, a situation which only becomes easier as they age. By contrast, unmarried Manggarai men lack a clear role. Unlike his industrious spinster sisters, a man's rejection of marriage is seen as evidence of his laziness, his fear of working to support a family. In many respects, unmarried women also have far more freedom, and are far less subject to the control of others, than in-married young wives. Unmarried women have control over the fruits of their own labour, and many stressed to me that if married, things would be far less 'safe/quiet' (*aman*), since they would have to worry about their husband gambling or spending all of their money on cigarettes. The possibility of ending up unhappily married, saddled with a gambling man, is undoubtedly a major disincentive for these women to marry, given that in rural Manggarai divorce is impossible.

However, whilst such women may be critical of men as husbands, they have a somewhat different view of men as brothers. The comments of these women on the changes in kinship status that marriage brings have led me to conclude that these women would rather remain part of their brother's family, working together with him, than experience the inevitable alienation involved in becoming a *woé*. *Woé* is a term that denotes both a 'married sister or daughter' *and* her husband's family, the kind of term that is normally translated by anthropologists as 'wife-takers'. Those who are *woé* remain permanently indebted to the natal families of their wives and mothers. However, the ultimate irony of the system is that, although it is the 'gift' of a woman that creates this debt, after marriage the woman herself becomes part of the group that must repay it. When her real or classificatory brothers decide to marry, she and her husband receive 'requests for money' (*sida*) and other assistance that they must always meet. Such requests are also made at the rituals that follow a death, irrespective of whether a group of *woé* have paid off their bridewealth or not.

One hot day in the highlands, during a siesta on my bed, Nina chatted to me again about why she didn't want to marry. She said:

> Life is different for married women, they are always really busy [*sibuk-sabuk*], they always have to find money to marry their brothers [*laki nara*]. Whenever I hear a tape playing for a *kémpu*,[3] I feel really sad, because I think it could be mine, my own *kémpu*. A man has to treat his sister and mother well, but he can treat his wife how he likes – she is someone who has already been bought [*ata poli weli*].

Similarly, when I went with her sister to bathe at a river in the lowlands, Meren said:

> After you are married, when your brother decides he wants to get married, you have to give a buffalo. But if you aren't married, then you can just search together [*kawé sama*] with your brother, so that he can get a wife.

At the heart of this and other statements by singlewomen lies the profound understanding that a woman's relationship with her brother (and, by implication, with her natal family) becomes quite different once she marries and becomes *woé*. If women remain unmarried, they do not experience such alienation but remain a key part of their parents' and brother's household. Certainly, it has always seemed to me that there are great advantages to a man in having one or two unmarried sisters in his house, and the relationship between children and their aunts can be extremely close, dispelling any assumption that unmarried women experience their situation as one of 'childlessness'.

After she had told me about preferring to 'search together' with a brother rather than marry, I asked Meren, 'Don't you feel sad that you don't have any children of your own?' She replied: 'No, because you can care for your brother's children. Look at Tanta Tina in Wae Rebo. All of her brother's children see her as just like a mother, because she has brought them up.'

Tanta Tina, to whom Meren refers, had provided a highland home to all of her brother's children, in the periods both before and after primary schooling (her brother lived in the lowlands and took care of the school-age children). Her role in the family was confirmed when one of these children, a young woman called Kris, sought to marry a man from the same community. Although Kris's own mother was in favour of the match, Tanta Tina objected and it was, therefore, abandoned. This example shows that unmarried women's roles in their brother's children's lives goes beyond matters of practical childcare and even extends to the negotiation of marriage. They are, therefore, very unlike the European 'maiden aunts' who historically constituted a 'reserve of domestic service' associated with 'female renunciation' (Goody 1976: 59). Some older unmarried Manggarai women exert a powerful influence on family decision-making. One such example was Tanta Tin, who, since her elder brother's death, had become the *de facto* household head of an extended family unit consisting of herself, her brother's widow, his unmarried daughter and his two married sons. Tanta Tin once spoke to me about the love she felt for Maka, the youngest son of her deceased brother:

> [When I look at him] it's just like looking at my own brother. Ai, that's still my brother. Yes, he's replaced his father's face. So I'm like this with him. If he is going far away and I don't see him go, I feel very sad. Yes ... very sad when he goes.

For Tanta Tin, Maka represents the living embodiment of his father, and her closeness to him means that she feels sad when he goes away. However, it also means that when the time came for Maka to find a wife, it was Tanta Tin who went to ask for a *tunkgu* or 'joining' match with Maka's classificatory mother's brother's daughter, Sisi. Whilst Maka may have taken the place of her deceased brother in Tanta Tin's affections, in ritual and alliance matters concerning the family, that place has been taken by Tanta Tin herself.

WOMEN, SIBLINGS AND BEING 'ALONE'

Although this is clearly a very small sample of people from which to make generalisations for Manggarai as a whole, it would seem that women remain unmarried in this context for a range of different reasons. Fate certainly plays a part, as does a recent increase in male migration. I do want to stress, though, that for many women, remaining single is an active choice, motivated partly by a desire to retain an economically independent existence in their natal village, as well as a dislike of the possible implications of becoming *woé* to their natal kin. Of course, it is only a minority (25 per cent or so) of women who reject such alienation. Most are happy to embrace it, for the pleasures that sexual intimacy, children and life in a different village may bring. I realise that, by largely focusing on the reasons that women give *against* marriage, I have neglected the positive factors that motivate most of them to marry. However, this is partly because married women, even obviously happy ones, tend to have very little to say on this subject, no doubt reflecting the fact that, in some respects, marriage still remains a 'given' of social life. In particular, there is very little discussion of sex, unlike in the West, where Bridget Jones and other 'problematic spinsters' are often explicitly interested in problems of sexual availability and frustration. I do not profess to know how my unmarried Manggarai friends, living in a deeply prudish society, feel about a life without sexual intimacy, but my suspicion is that it is not foremost amongst their concerns.

The unproblematic status of unmarried women in this context, as well as the emphasis they themselves give to their role as sisters, brings to mind Sherry Ortner's famous article on the sex/gender system in hierarchical societies (1981). Put very briefly, Ortner's argument is that the apparently 'high status' of women in the cognatic/endogamous societies of Polynesia and Southeast Asia is because of the 'encompassing' nature of kinship in these societies, and the resulting fact that women are primarily defined as kinswomen (daughters, sisters and aunts). By contrast, she argues, in the patrilineal systems of India and China, women have a generally lower status since cultural emphasis is placed on their role as wives and mothers, and they tend not to be seen in terms of their ongoing value as kinswomen (1981: 399–400). Now, certainly, cultural definitions of female adulthood in terms of marriage and motherhood may well account for the almost universal rates of marriage in India and China. In the South Asian context, in particular, the problematic status of unmarried women is often expressed in terms of the dangerous and polluting nature of their uncontrolled sexuality (Rozario 1986: 261). However, in the Southeast Asian context, the 'high status' of women as kin does not necessarily mean that a woman can remain unmarried. Strong ideological preferences for marriage are not necessarily the result of gendered concepts of purity and pollution. Nor, interestingly enough, does the high prevalence of marriage in South Asia necessarily result in marital stability (Parry 2001).

In many Southeast Asian societies, the sexes are frequently seen as 'complementary' rather than 'opposite', and married couples may therefore be seen as the basic productive units of society. For example, amongst the Buid of Mindoro, marriage is the ideal social relationship and forms the basic domestic unit; this means that although divorce is frequent, ideally no adult should remain single for more than a few weeks at a time (Gibson 1986). Similarly, amongst the Wana of Sulawesi, the conjugal couple is central to everyday and ritual life, and the assumption that people will marry is almost automatic (Atkinson 1990). Now, both these societies are cognatic and endogamous, conforming to Ortner's vision of Southeast Asian (and Polynesian) social structure. However, although such systems are common across Southeast Asia, the region is also home (most notably in Eastern Indonesia) to societies that emphasise exogamous marriage and an ideology of patrilineal descent. Manggarai is one such society. What is interesting about Manggarai is that, although women share a characteristically Southeast Asian 'high status', and although they are highly valued as sisters and daughters, the exogamous nature of marriage means that it displaces them from their home. Indeed, it may well be the fact that women are valued *both* as wives/mothers (who leave their natal home) *and* as daughters/sisters (who remain in their natal home), that makes *both* marriage *and* singledom attractive prospects for a young woman. In this context, patrilineality does not necessarily lead to universal marriage.

Kinship is, of course, only one of the factors that may influence the perception of unmarried women. Another is the extent to which they are able to occupy a specific economic role (cf. Goody 1976: 58). It is worth remembering that the very term 'spinster' originally meant a female spinner of wool, and that it was only in the seventeenth century that it came to refer to a singlewoman, largely because many such women earned their living working as 'spinsters' (Bennett and Froide 1999: 2). Similarly, another term frequently used to refer to singlewoman, 'maid', references the frequent link between single status and employment as a servant (ibid., p.16). Throughout Eastern Indonesia, weaving offers women a ritually and economically important role that they can undertake independently of any male (de Jong 2002; Forshee 2001). The introduction of cash crops such as coffee, and the inheritance of land by Manggarai daughters from their fathers also gives unmarried women independent economic roles. Certainly, when viewed cross-culturally, the move away from an agrarian, subsistence economy does frequently open up new opportunities for women that may make 'singledom' a more attractive prospect. However, the extent to which men may feel threatened by this new independence varies. Allman describes how during the colonial period in the former Gold Coast the introduction of cocoa as a cash crop led many women to establish their own farms, rather than labouring on the farm of a husband. This resulted in a temporary chaos in gender relations, with chiefs rounding up unmarried women over fifteen and not releasing them from prison until a man was named as their potential husband (Allman 1996). In the contemporary context, Ashante women traders may briefly marry and have children, but still express preference for independent trading, declaring that 'onions are my husband' (Clark 1994). Again, this raises the issue of the comparability of unmarried women cross-culturally, since apparently high marriage rates may conceal large numbers of women who effectively act as singlewomen. Ashante traders may be 'married' and have children but in many respects they act as independent single women. Similarly, in many different cultural contexts, uxorilocal marriages provide a way for a woman to remain in her natal village and retain a great deal of independence (Bloch 1978).

Having considered the differing status of singlewomen cross-culturally, and the complex economic, historical, religious and kinship factors that may or may not make marriage universal, I now want to shift the focus back to the nature of 'alone-ness'. As the testimonies of my single friends have hopefully shown, unmarried Manggarai women are not perceived by others as 'alone', nor do they experience their situation as one of loneliness. When I tried to provoke a reaction in Nina, Meren, Anna or Regi by telling them of single British friends of mine who experienced 'singledom' as a somewhat lonely state, who wondered how they would meet 'the one', and who worried they would never have children, my Manggarai friends all looked rather blank and told me this was very strange. Singlewomen in this contemporary Indonesian context do not flinch at news of weddings and babies, they do not cry themselves to sleep listening to sentimental ballads, they are not the object of witchcraft accusations or undisguised contempt. They, thus, provide an interesting contrast with Western Europe where, despite a long history of high numbers of unmarried women, singlewomen are still often seen as both 'alone' and 'lonely'. However, this does not mean that being 'alone' (*hanang-koé* or 'only-little') is not an extremely important Manggarai notion. Indeed, as I shall briefly describe, Manggarai people share what seems to be a general Southeast Asian fear and dislike of being alone (Cannell 1999: 153, 159).

Now, obviously, in the course of everyday, productive life – when a woman goes to collect vegetables from her field, for example – people may sometimes have to be alone, and this is accepted. However, there are certain activities that should never be performed alone. Perhaps the most important of these is sleeping, since the sleeping person is vulnerable to disturbing dreams or visitation by spirits. This is particularly the case immediately after a death, when the soul of the deceased may still visit its relatives at home. Bereaved houses are therefore always full of people, including young men who gamble all night to keep the house 'lively' (*ramé*). Those who make noises or talk in their sleep are always immediately woken up by others, and it is partly because of this that no-one should ever sleep in a house alone. If the absence of other household members leaves a person alone in their house, other friends or relatives will always turn up at dusk to cook supper and sleep together with them. Indeed, it is almost as important not to eat alone as it is not to sleep alone. A wife will always wait for her husband to return to the house from work in the fields, however late he is, before dishing up their shared meal, and a visitor will be saved the embarrassment of eating alone by a household member joining them, even if only to eat a small amount. Once, when I was visiting their house, two small boys were whingeing quietly about being hungry. In response, their great-aunt, Tanta Tin, dished them up rice and vegetables on two separate plates. However, the boys refused to eat. Tanta Tin then picked up the two plates and unceremoniously sloshed their contents onto a third, whereupon the boys ate happily using individual spoons. 'Ah,' she said indulgently, 'they don't want to eat alone.'

By contrast with the West, where the capacity to be alone is considered crucial to mature emotional development (Winnicott 1958), people in Manggarai view being alone as, at best, a temporary inconvenience and, at worst, a spiritually and emotionally dangerous state. This also links with a general negative evaluation of solitariness as a character trait. In particular, those who walk around alone at night are viewed as extremely suspicious, since shape-changing sorcerers operate during the dark, turning themselves into cats or other creatures in order to harm others. However, like those in Britain, Manggarai people do not apply the term 'alone' (*hanang-koé*) merely to actual, physical circumstances, but also use it as a more emotion-laden term to describe the more general situation of certain individuals. When used in this way, there are definite categories of people who stand out as being 'alone'.

The most obvious of these categories might appear to be childless married couples. Certainly, in many ethnographic contexts, including amongst the Zafimaniry (Bloch 1993), it may not be a marriage ceremony as such which cements a couple together, but the birth of one or more children. Indeed, in many parts of the world, infertility may be a prime reason for divorce. Across Southeast Asia, children of both sexes are extremely highly valued and infertility is taken very seriously. However, the specific ways in which childlessness is dealt with vary. In Pulau Langkawi, childless couples frequently foster a child given to them by a sibling (Carsten 1997: 247). However, in Manggarai, neither divorce nor fostering are options for childless couples. This seems to suggest that the 'alone-ness' of childless couples is not so extreme or so threatening that it needs to be solved by other mechanisms. The childless couples that I knew in Wae Rebo-Kombo, with one significant exception, were not stigmatised or viewed as less-than-adult. They were fully involved with community life and, though they did not foster children, had an important role in the care of children of relatives or fellow house-members. The exception to this rule was an elderly couple who were spoken of antagonistically. However, this was not primarily due to their childlessness (indeed, the man was rumoured to have fathered various illegitimate children) but because of what people saw as their failure to contribute to collective funds for funerary and other rituals.

Two types of individual who *are* spoken of more frequently as being 'alone' are orphans and only children. An 'orphan' is considered someone who has lost either a mother or a father whilst young, and may be vulnerable to sickness caused by the love or interference of this parent from beyond the grave. Only children are, actually, extremely rare in Manggarai, partly because of high fertility rates, and partly because a man will tend to marry again if his wife dies whilst he is still young. One woman, Agnes, an in-married mother of seven, *was* an only child and this was repeatedly pointed out to me both by Agnes and others. Despite her seven children, Agnes would say 'I'm really very alone' (*hanang-koé kéta kaku ga*), as if stressing the poignancy of her lack of siblings in a situation where siblings are highly valued. Interestingly, within larger families, a single brother would also be considered 'alone', whereas a single sister would not. This is because, within a broadly patrilineal context, a man's same-sex siblings (*ahé-ka'é*) are crucially important both in everyday life and in the context of marriage negotiations and rituals.

A final category of people who are considered 'alone' are those who are outside of reciprocal exchange obligations. Within Wae Rebo-Kombo, villagers operate a system of pooling money and foodstuffs at certain ritual events, on the understanding that co-villagers share the responsibility for, for example, providing coffee to guests after a death, or cooked rice to accompany the meat at marriage rituals. There are also more specific obligations that operate between groups of male (real and classificatory) 'siblings' (*ahé-ka'é*). However, one family – an elderly man and his three adult sons – were considered to have 'broken' (*biké*) their connections with their wider *ahé-ka'é* because of a particular argument between two individuals in the past. This family no longer makes contributions towards events of their *ahé-ka'é* (any contributions they do attempt to make are always 'pushed away', *tolak*), nor do they receive help from others at the time of weddings, funerals or other rituals within their own family. Within the Manggarai context, then, it is people such as this who are considered to be most profoundly 'alone'. Moreover, the crucial thing about this category is that the people in it are considered to have somehow *chosen* to be 'alone', unlike those others mentioned above, whose 'alone-ness' is largely a result of fate.

Being 'alone' is obviously a complexly gendered notion in many societies. As indicated at the beginning of this paper, in British society, it is frequently those who are 'single' (without a partner, whether or not they are married), and particularly single women, who are thought to be most 'alone'. However, there is a kind of problem with the way in which using 'single' to refer to unmarried people in other cultural contexts somehow implies that they are *on their own*. I prefer to follow Goffman (1971), who uses the terms 'singles' and 'withs' to reference interactional units. Whereas a 'single' is a party of one, a person 'by himself', a 'with' is part of a party of more than one, whose members are perceived to be 'together' (Goffman 1971: 19). If we follow Goffman's definition, we can help to see why unmarried women are not a problem, even in a context where (as for much of Southeast Asia) 'alone-ness' *is* problematic. The simple reason is that, although unmarried women may have a 'single status' with regard to marriage, in terms of wider social life they are most definitely 'withs', whether connected with another unmarried sister, their parents, or their brother and his children.

In Manggarai, as in much of Southeast Asia, it might be said that to be alone is not to be without a spouse but to be without a sibling. As we have seen, it is not the unmarried, or even the childless, who are thought to be most alone but those who, whether through fate or because of their own actions, are excluded from the benefits of siblingship. Male siblingship is, within this patrilineal context, particularly stressed. However, the examples of 'spinster clustering' amongst unmarried sisters, as well as the explanations that unmarried women give regarding their reluctance to become *woé* to their brothers, also show the significance of female and mixed siblingship. Interestingly, siblingship is also represented in another register in Manggarai, through various ideas about 'body siblings' (*ahé-ka'é weki*), also known as 'spirits of the nape of the neck' (*déwa du'ang*) or 'angels' (*malaikat*). Each individual is thought to have such a guardian spirit, and they are closely connected with that individual's health, fate and happiness. On a number of occasions, I also heard unmarried women refer to such guardian spirits as their 'husband from the other side' (*rona palé-sina*), that is their spirit spouse. Not only does this connect with more general Southeast Asian tendencies to equate spouses with siblings (Carsten 1997: 92–4; Cannell 1999: 54–9), but it also suggests something of a paradox. In this context, 'body siblings' ensure that no one is ever totally 'alone', as well as ensuring that even unmarried women do have some kind of spouse.

What, finally, of the issue of 'loneliness'? Are those who are defined as 'alone' always 'lonely'? This is clearly not always the case, as my example of the orphan Agnes, happily surrounded by her seven children, should prove. However, as I have discovered, 'loneliness' is a hard concept to research from a cross-cultural, anthropological perspective. A search of literature and internet sites overwhelmingly leads to two kinds of information: self-help and practical tips for university students and self-help and spiritual guidance for those of single status. A third area of concern appears to be the extent to which modern technologies, such as the internet, are actually increasing the incidence of loneliness in many societies. Perhaps, then, loneliness is not a cross-cultural notion of any value, but the product of specific historical and technological circumstances? In Manggarai, though people talk of themselves and others being alone, they do not talk of feeling 'lonely'. Indeed, as I discovered during fieldwork bouts of homesickness, expressing 'loneliness' in this context is extremely difficult. There are simply not the words. However, does this mean that people never feel lonely? During my fieldwork of 2001, the wife of the elderly, childless couple I mentioned above died. Since this old woman had been the target of much suspicion, and since the couple were outside of reciprocal exchange obligations, very few people went to cry over the corpse, or to visit the house after the death, a terrible symbol of the couple's social isolation. Shortly after this, though, people commented that her husband had started to make more social visits within the village. Was it possible, after all, that he was motivated to do so by loneliness?

CONCLUSION: MARRIAGE AND 'ADULTHOOD'

Gossip about forthcoming, previously scandalous or indefinitely postponed marriages must be one of the staples of fieldwork, wherever it is carried out. Equally, most societies would seem to be somewhat intrigued, surprised or disgusted by the marriage customs of their neighbours, provoking all manner of 'Zafimaniry questions' (see Preface). People in Manggarai, though unaware of anthropological literature on the 'matrilineal puzzle', often chatted – with equal quantities of puzzle and amusement – about the marriage practices of the Ngada people to the east. How odd that it was men rather than women who had to leave their natal home after marriage… How strange that women could inherit land and houses… Side-by-side with talk about marriage histories and customs always went some speculation on the *lack* of opportunity or desire for marriage of certain individuals. As this paper has tried to show, there are several key questions that may motivate such speculation across human societies. Why don't some women want to marry? Is that a natural thing or an abhorrence? Should women be forced to marry? Are unmarried women polluting? Are they alone? Should we pity them?

Although it is demographic literature that provides us with broad comparisons in the cross-cultural 'universality' of marriage, we can question many of the reasons that demographers give for such universality. Dixon, for example, argues that it is 'clan or lineage systems and ancestor worship' and an attendant compulsion to produce children to 'strengthen the clan' that causes the 'stigma and shame' attached to non-marriage and childlessness in 'many non-Western countries' (1971: 226). As this paper has shown, the existence of an emphasis on patrilineality, as well as a concern with the ancestors, does not necessarily lead to the stigmatisation of the unmarried state. However, lest I be drawn into too much demographer-bashing, let me end by making some criticisms of anthropology and, in particular, that area of the discipline concerned with 'personhood'.

The influence of van Gennep's (1977) model of rites of passage in the anthropology of personhood seems to have created a kind of unspoken assumption that, in many non-Western societies, marriage is an essential rite in turning people into full 'adults'. This can be seen quite explicitly in certain comments of Margaret Mead:

> While primitive societies vary in the degree to which they explicitly emphasise the point, to be socially mature is to be, among other things, married. Therefore, in most primitive societies such individuals are definitely social deviants … so that a discussion of their rather bizarre situation is irrelevant… (Mead 1934: 53)

Mead's language here may be outdated, but I would argue that her assumptions are not. Anthropologists still frequently make over-hasty assertions that unmarried women are 'anomalies' or exist in a permanent state of 'liminality', somehow never reaching full adulthood. Yet why should we assume that all societies conceive of the road to adulthood as a kind of single, van Gennep-like progression? After all, the ethnographic literature is full of powerful counter-examples to prevailing cultural emphases on marriage. In northwest India, and despite the strong cultural imperative to marry, girls may choose to become celibate *sadhins*, a name that associates them with a wider Hindu ascetic tradition, whilst they live in their natal homes as unmarried women (Phillimore 2001). Amongst Israeli-Palestinians, and despite the stigma associated with remaining unmarried, many unmarried females 'overcome the pitfalls set by the norm of marriage and do attain womanhood' (Sa'ar 2004: 2). Surely, given the diversity of human experience, it might make more sense to imagine that societies could conceive of a number of different ways to be an 'adult'? In each case where anthropologists assert that marriage and children are *the* way to achieve 'adulthood', it therefore seems important to ask about unmarried or childless individuals and how, *exactly*, they are not thought to be 'adult'. For, contrary to what we may assume for certain kinds of societies, marriage and the production of children may not be the only ways to live a fulfilled and valued life.

ACKNOWLEDGEMENTS

I am indebted to those Manggarai singlewomen who befriended me and who always discussed their lives with openness and humour. Thanks to Rita Astuti, Johnny Parry, Charles Stafford and other workshop participants for their astute comments on earlier drafts of this paper. Thanks also to Michelle Obeid and Simon Nicholson for their comments, and to Willemijn de Jong for providing me with information about unmarried women among the Lio. It 'goes without saying' that Maurice Bloch's ability to pose provocative questions has always been an inspiration.

NOTES

1. *The Guardian*, 'Spinsterhood bites the dust', 29 July 2005.
2. Doctoral fieldwork was conducted for twenty months in 1997–9 and sponsored by the British Economic and Social Research Council. Fieldwork in 2001 was for four months and sponsored by the British Academy Committee for South East Asian Studies and Wolfson College, Oxford. I also made a brief visit to the area in April 2005.

3. A *kémpu* is the marriage ritual at which the bridewealth is negotiated. In recent times, the potential groom and his party have carried a tape-recorder playing Manggarai pop songs as they travel to the bride's natal home.

REFERENCES

Allman, J. 1996. 'Rounding up spinsters: gender chaos and unmarried women in colonial Asante', *Journal of African History* 37: 195–214.

Arensberg, C.M. 1937. *The Irish countryman: an anthropological study*, London: Macmillan.

Atkinson, J.M. 1990. 'How gender makes a difference in Wana society', in J.M. Atkinson and S. Errington (eds), *Power and difference: gender in island Southeast Asia*, Stanford: Stanford University Press.

Bell, S. and E.J. Sobo (eds) 2001. *Celibacy, culture and society: the anthropology of sexual abstinence*, Madison: University of Wisconsin Press.

Bennett, J.M. and A.M. Froide. 1999. *Singlewomen in the European past 1250–1800*, Philadelphia: University of Pennsylvania Press.

Bloch, M. 1978. 'Marriage amongst equals: an analysis of the marriage ceremony of the Merina of Madagascar', *Man* 13(1): 21–33.

—— 1993. 'Zafimaniry birth and kinship theory', *Social Anthropology. The Journal of the European Association of Social Anthropologists* 1: 119–32.

Boomgaard, P. 2003. 'Bridewealth and birth control: low fertility in the Indonesian Archipelago, 1500–1900', *Population and Development Review* 29(2): 197–214.

Bourdieu, P. 1962. 'Célibat et condition paysanne', *Études Rurales* (Paris) 5/6: 32–136.

—— 2002. *Le bal des célibataires: Crise de la société paysanne en Béarn*, Paris: Points Seuil.

Cannell, F. 1999. *Power and intimacy in the Christian Philippines*, Cambridge: Cambridge University Press.

Carsten, J. 1997. *The heat of the hearth: the process of kinship in a Malay fishing community*, Oxford: Clarendon Press.

Clark, G. 1994. *Onions are my husband: survival and accumulation by West African market women*, Chicago: University of Chicago Press.

Cornell, L.L. 1984. 'Why are there no spinsters in Japan?', *Journal of Family History* 9: 326–39.

Dixon, R.B. 1971. 'Explaining cross-cultural variations in age at marriage and proportions never marrying', *Population Studies* 25: 215–33.

Dube, L. 1997. *Women and kinship: comparative perspectives on gender in South and South-East Asia*, Tokyo: United Nations University Press.

Forshee, J. 2001. *Between the folds: stories of cloth, lives and travels from Sumba*, Honolulu: University of Hawai'i Press.

Franzen, T. 1996. *Spinsters and lesbians: independent womanhood in the United States*, New York: New York University Press.

Gennep, A. van. 1977 (1908). *The rites of passage*, translated by M.B. Vizedom and G.L. Caffee, London: Routledge and Kegan Paul.

Gibson, T. 1986. *Sacrifice and sharing in the Philippine highlands: religion and society among the Buid of Mindoro*, London: Athlone Press.

Goffman, E. 1971. *Relations in public: microstudies of the public order*, London: Allen Lane.

Goldman, N. 1993. 'The perils of single life in contemporary Japan', *Journal of Marriage and the Family* 55: 191–204.

Goody, J. 1976. *Production and reproduction: a comparative study of the domestic domain*, Cambridge: Cambridge University Press.

—— 1983. *The development of the family and marriage in Europe*, Cambridge: Cambridge University Press.

Hajnal, J. 1965. 'European marriage patterns in perspective', in D.V. Glass and D.E.C. Eversley (eds), *Population in history: essays in historical demography*, London: Edward Arnold.

Harrell, S. 1986. 'Men, women and ghosts in Taiwanese folk religion', in C.W. Bynum, S. Harrell and P. Richman (eds), *Gender and religion: on the complexity of symbols*, Boston: Beacon Press.

Hufton, O. 1984. 'Women without men: widows and spinsters in Britain and France in the Eighteenth Century', *Journal of Family History* 9: 355–76.

Jensen, R. and R. Thornton. 2003. 'Early female marriage in the developing world', *Gender and Development* 11(2): 9–19.

Jones, G.W. 1995. 'Population and the family in Southeast Asia', *Journal of Southeast Asian Studies* 26(1): 184–95.

—— 1997. 'The demise of universal marriage in East and South-East Asia', in G.W. Jones et al. (eds), *The continuing demographic transition*, Oxford: Clarendon Press.

de Jong, W. 2002. 'Women's networks in cloth production and exchange in Flores', in J. Koning et al. (eds), *Women and households in Indonesia: cultural notions and social practices*, Richmond: Curzon Press.

Krishnakumari, N.S. 1987. *Status of single women in India; a study of spinsters, widows and divorcees*, New Delhi: Uppal Publishing House.

Linn, R. 1996. '"Thirty nothing": What do counsellors know about mature single women who wish for a child and a family?', *International Journal for the Advancement of Counselling* 18: 69–84.

Mead, M. 1934. 'The sex life of the unmarried adult in primitive society', in I.S. Wile (ed.), *The sex life of the unmarried adult: an inquiry into and an interpretation of current sex practices*, New York: The Vanguard Press.

Ortner, S.B. 1981. 'Gender and sexuality in hierarchical societies: the case of Polynesia and some comparative implications', in S.B. Ortner and H. Whitehead (eds), *Sexual meanings: the cultural construction of gender and sexuality*, Cambridge: Cambridge University Press.

Parry, J.P. 2001. 'Ankalu's errant wife: sex, marriage and industry in contemporary Chhattisgarh', *Modern Asian Studies* 35(4): 783–820.

Phillimore, P. 2001. 'Private lives and public identities: an example of female celibacy in Northwest India', in E. Sobo and S. Bell (eds), *Celibacy, culture and society: the anthropology of sexual abstinence*, Madison: University of Wisconsin Press.

Reed-Danahay, D. 2005. *Locating Bourdieu*, Bloomington and Indianapolis: Indiana University Press.

Rozario, S. 1986. 'Marginality and the case of unmarried Christian women in a Bangladeshi village', *Contributions to Indian Sociology* 20(2): 261–78.

Sa'ar, A. 2004. 'Many ways of becoming a woman: the case of unmarried Israeli-Palestinian "girls"', *Ethnology* 43(1): 1–18.

Scheper-Hughes, N. 2001. *Saints, scholars and schizophrenics: mental illness in rural Ireland*, Berkeley: University of California Press. Twentieth anniversary edition, updated and expanded, from the 1977 original.

Sharpe, P. 1999. 'Dealing with love: the ambiguous independence of the single woman in Early Modern England', *Gender and History* 11(2): 209–32.

Smith, P.C. 1980. 'Asian marriage patterns in transition', *Journal of Family History* 5(1): 58–97.

Tan, J.E. 2002. 'Living arrangements of never-married Thai women in a time of rapid social change', *Sojourn* 17(1): 24–51.

Winnicott, D.W. 1958. 'The capacity to be alone', in *The maturational processes and the facilitating environment: studies in the theory of emotional development*, (1965) London: The Hogarth Press.

CHAPTER 2

HOW DO WE KNOW WHO WE ARE?

Janet Carsten

When I think about doing fieldwork in a Malay fishing village, and about the kinds of conversations I have had there (mainly in the 1980s, but off and on over the last twenty-five years), I have some difficulty recalling any occasion on which the people I lived with spontaneously philosophised about what one might regard as the fundamental questions of life: who we are, why we are here, and what the meaning of it all is. I can, however, recall hundreds of occasions on which people sat around discussing who was going to join a rice-harvesting party, the details of a forthcoming wedding feast and its finances, the distribution of some form of government loan, the price of fish and so on.

Probably all this says quite a lot about my deficiencies as an ethnographer, but it may also reflect the kinds of topics with which the women and men I knew best were at ease. I think they would have been somewhat baffled, as well as amused, if I had asked them the questions we have set ourselves in this volume. Although my Malay friends and informants might agree that these are questions that matter, I suspect they would either regard many of the answers as given by their Islamic faith, or be bemused at the idea that they could possibly have the answers. Underlying this, I suggest in this essay, is perhaps a more robust certainty about some of these important questions than is available to many people in the West, who seem particularly plagued by the uncertainties of their own existence, including the question of who exactly they are.

In this chapter, I discuss material drawn from a set of interviews that I conducted in the late 1990s with adult adoptees in Scotland on the specific topic of their meetings with the birth parents, from whom they had been separated in early infancy. I frame this discussion partly against the backdrop of earlier work on kinship on the island of Langkawi, Malaysia. Because I have discussed the Malay material in detail elsewhere (Carsten 1991, 1997), my descriptions here are rather brief. I focus on the narratives of family history that I collected in Scotland, and delineate some of the differences that have struck me between these and those I was told in Malaysia in the 1980s. This endeavour raises some important issues of comparison and comparability.

In Scotland in the late 1990s, I was engaged in a narrowly defined project designed to find out what happened when adult adoptees searched for, and met up with, their birth kin.[1] The study was, thus, concerned with the experiences of a particular set of adults who had been adopted in childhood, and who had engaged in searches for their birth kin. Working through interviews only, I had very little access to the everyday encounters and conversations of people's lives. This project was certainly not designed to give a complete picture of 'kinship in Scotland', still less of kinship in the United Kingdom. My work in Malaysia amongst a population of villagers, by contrast, had been concerned with received ideas and practices concerning kinship more generally. I lived for eighteen months in the house of a family in the village I studied and, over time, became very familiar with everyday practices of kinship, and particularly with the network of kin, friends and associates of the family with whom I lived (see Carsten 1997). While the Malay practices of kinship I have written about would definitely not apply to all Malays (in particular, urban middle- and upper-class practices are excluded, as are those of non-Malays in Malaysia), they may to some extent be used to generalise about other rural and coastal communities.

There are certainly limits, then, to the extent to which either study can appropriately be generalised within its particular national context, and also further limits to the extent to which one would make comparative claims between them. As I have indicated, this in part results from the very different methodologies on which they are based. Issues of comparison, however, framed the later project in two ways.

First, it was explicitly conceived to compare aspects of the Malay fostering practices that I had studied in Langkawi with adoption in the UK. I was interested in how, in this particular context of relatedness, people in Britain thought about and dealt with the juxtaposition between 'social' and 'biological' kinship. Here David Schneider's discussion

(1980) of the opposition between the 'order of nature' and the 'order of law', or substance and code, as central to North American notions of kinship, seemed obviously pertinent. It was partly with his analysis in mind, as well as my earlier work on Malay kinship, that I embarked on this small study of the experiences of a few adoptees in Scotland. Because I have discussed Schneider's work at length elsewhere (Carsten 1995a; 1997; 2000b; 2004), I do not elaborate as fully on this opposition here, or on Schneider's arguments, as I did in these earlier writings.

Second, when I came to analyse the interview transcripts, I was struck by the way that, although they dealt with rather unusual aspects of kinship experience that might be thought relevant only to adoptees who engage in such searches, those I interviewed highlighted concerns and practices, which, in different ways, were also recognisable in a much wider culture of kinship and personhood (Carsten 2000a). I return to this aspect of the interviews towards the end of this chapter. And in reflecting on the ways in which the material I gathered echoed, or reproduced, elements of a broader culture of kinship in Britain or the United States, I have of course drawn on an enormous body of ethnographic and historical scholarship, some of which I cite here (Edwards 2000; Davidoff et al. 1999; Schneider 1980).

I begin, however, with the sense of certainty, which, it seemed to me, grounded the perceptions that villagers in Langkawi had of themselves and which, I suggest here, is partly rooted in particular practices of kinship in which their lives are deeply embedded. In Langkawi, I could with reasonable certainty predict the questions that, on meeting me or any other passing stranger from the city for the first time, most people would spontaneously articulate.[2] They would ask where I was from, how many siblings I had, were my parents still alive, was I married, and, sometimes, whether I had children. Nowadays, chronologies having shifted slightly, people certainly ask about children, and they often enquire about grandchildren too. I quickly learned that when I collected detailed family histories, these were the questions that mattered. Where someone lives, their siblings and parents, spouse, children and grandchildren are the key elements out of which one can build a picture of who they are, and of the things that matter about their identity.

To a considerable extent, one could say that, in Scotland too, people who meet each other for the first time are likely to ask similar and predictable kinds of questions, although here work probably features more prominently as a defining facet of identity. In the interviews that I conducted, other differences emerged too. Notwithstanding the peculiar features of these conversations, I was very struck by the insistence with which, when asked why they had been motivated to carry out a search for their birth parents, those I interviewed said 'to find out who I am', or 'you've got to know where you came from'. Such assertions were striking not just in the regularity with which they were made, but also for the implied self-evidence of the idea that previously hidden knowledge about one's birth parents could, when revealed, have the power to reshape a person's sense of self, to tell them who they were (see Strathern 1999; Carsten 2000b; 2004; forthcoming).

In Langkawi, although short- and long-term fostering is a very frequent feature of family relations, it would be hard to imagine people undertaking such searches, or that the facts, or people, brought to light in this way would be thought to have this kind of import. This state of affairs is connected to the high frequency of fostering, the lack of secrecy surrounding birth parents and the fact that parental relations tend to be cast in less exclusive terms than those in Britain.[3] I will return to the significance of revealing previously hidden knowledge about family relations below, but thinking about the differences in these two scenarios, one might very broadly say that people in Langkawi seemed, on the whole, to have a fairly secure sense of who they were, whereas those I interviewed in Scotland were apparently more unsure about fundamental questions of their identity. It was this uncertainty that set them off on their quests to find out about their birth parents.

The idea that the question of identity, or who we are, apparently has a looming importance in contemporary Western cultures, an importance which might look a bit bizarre to many people elsewhere, is hardly controversial (see Lambek and Antze 1996). In any case, that the small and unmarked details of people's everyday lives may be the details that matter, and that they can be steadily placed in a larger picture that reveals some more profound things about the differences and similarities of different cultures, is a lesson that, in part at least, I learned in the 'longeurs' inside Malay houses as I listened to not always fascinating conversations about the price of fish, or waited for something more interesting to happen than drinking coffee, peeling onions or minding a baby.

But what does kinship have to do with it? In the next section I consider what kinship does more broadly, before tracing in detail the kinds of kinship knowledge that seem important to how we know who we are.

WHAT'S KINSHIP GOT TO DO WITH IT?

In thinking about what kinship does, I have been inspired by a recent article by Robert McKinley (2001) on 'The Philosophy of Kinship', in which he offers a trenchant critique of the work of David Schneider by arguing for the importance of kinship as a moral system, a 'philosophy of moral obligation' (2001: 138). McKinley's argument, which, as he makes clear, owes a great deal to Meyer Fortes, is that what kinship does is to provide a non-negotiable moral frame of reference for people's actions. One of several points that Schneider got stunningly wrong was, he suggests, to assert that kinship only exists in Europe and North America. In fact, the opposite is true. The problem with Westerners is that they have too little kinship in the sense of a moral universe in which this philosophy of obligation holds. Everywhere else has far more, and is better off for that. If Westerners have restricted the field of kinship too far, so that they are engulfed by choice and uncertainty, in other places the kind of certainty provided by the unconditional precepts of kinship (however variable these may be) prevails.

As a fellow Malaysianist, the sorts of example that McKinley has in mind are ones with which I am very familiar. I can think of several instances from my return visits to the village where I have worked that exemplify the sense of an extended moral universe governed by the norms of kinship obligation. A few months ago, when I arrived in Langkawi after an absence of six years (and partly as a gesture of solidarity in the aftermath of the Tsunami), I was quite surprised to find the entire village engaged in preparations for a rather more important visit. The recently elected Prime Minister of Malaysia, Abdullah Badawi, was coming to Langkawi on the following day to make his post-Tsunami gesture of solidarity. Pak Lah, as he is affectionately known in a common avuncular mode, had called a feast, *kenduri*, for the entire population of Langkawi, and it was to be held in the grounds of the village elementary school. And so villagers were doing the necessary work of killing water buffalo; chopping and slicing vegetables; erecting a temporary marquee; and cooking vegetable and meat curries, as well as rice, in vast cauldrons and pans, much as they would do for any large wedding feast, but on an immensely bigger scale. The altogether familiar elements of this kind of preparation struck me in a new light as women and men of the village gave their labour for two days: the deployment of this type of extended free labour, normally dictated by the moral universe of kinship, was here being co-opted for a ritual that was fundamentally political.

This rather flamboyant and public instance brings to mind other more domestic ones, such as the time when, on returning to the village after an even longer absence, I was, within hours of arrival, put to plucking chickens on the ground with a small group of related women for a much smaller feast. In fact, I had so thoroughly internalised these kinds of labour and kinship practices that I doubt I would have been struck by any incongruity, had not a friend from the local town, who happened to be visiting, expressed his amusement at the circumstances in which he found me. The rather obvious point I am trying to make is that these examples illustrate the way in which the certain obligations of kinship have a long reach – they apply after absences of many years, and they can be used to mobilise labour to feed thousands in a merging of kinship idioms with a political event.

In the West, McKinley argues (following many others), things are done differently. The very narrow field to which the unconditional demands of kinship apply is now so shrunk that it hardly extends beyond the individual herself. I am not sure I follow him in this part of his argument, for several reasons, including the fact that many of those I know best seem rather heavily weighted by the unconditional demands of kinship. More importantly, I think, McKinley's discussion ignores the force of religion in the kind of moral discourse he describes. The Malay world of kinship can hardly be extricated from the precepts of Islam, and here of course there is a disjunction with Western cultures (though, significantly, this may apply very differently in the US and Europe).

If societies in the West are plagued by what seems, to many commentators, to be a dearth of kinship, how do we explain the enormous desire to find out about ancestors that is expressed in a great variety of phenomena, including the popularity of websites for genealogical searches, the extraordinary interest provoked by the publication of successive sets of UK census data from the nineteenth and early twentieth century on the Web, and the success of the recent BBC series *Who Do You Think you Are?*, which itself generated a remarkable surge in interest in tracing family histories? Surely, whatever else they may be about, these phenomena are about finding out who we are and, in some way at least, they are also about kinship. But just what kinds of knowledge are generated by genealogical searches, and where do they fit in amidst other forms of kinship?

GENEALOGICAL KNOWLEDGE

I focus here on two cases from the interviews I conducted in Scotland in 1998–9 with adult adoptees, who had in the previous few years engaged in searches for, and met up with, their birth parents.[4] I should emphasise that it is difficult to gauge exactly what proportion of adult adoptees engage in such searches, and that available estimates are based on the number of adoptees seeking access to their birth records – which may not be a reliable guide (see Carsten, forthcoming). John Triseliotis, who conducted the most authoritative study of adopted people's search for their origins in Scotland in the 1970s, suggests that only a small minority of adoptees seek access to their birth records (Triseliotis 1973, 1984). He estimates an annual rate of enquiries of 0.6 per cent in England and Wales, and of 0.9 per cent in Scotland (Triseliotis 1984: 47–8). There is, however, evidence to suggest that these numbers have risen since this research was conducted.[5]

The interviews took place in people's homes, so that although I did not have access to the daily lives of those I met, I did gain a brief impression of their current circumstances. In the set of thirteen interviews I conducted, it is difficult to find an altogether typical pattern. The stories I was told were, by their nature, quite variable due to a mixture of chance and differing life circumstances and personal histories. Some common features do emerge, however, and the two stories I discuss here have been chosen with this in mind. The first is, in various ways that I will explain, a more typical scenario; the second struck me as being more unusual. I juxtapose them here in order to highlight the kinds of knowledge that may be gained through genealogical searches and the uses to which they may be put.

At the time I interviewed her in January 1999, Sam was a young woman in her late twenties with a partner and a baby. She described her adoptive family of parents and an older brother who was also adopted with great warmth, saying she had 'wonderful memories of childhood' and that her 'mum and dad were brilliant'. As she put it, 'I couldn't have been more loved ever, from anybody.' Sam had always known she was adopted and, like many adoptive parents, her mum and dad had made her feel specially chosen in this way. Occasionally, like many children, she would have a falling out with her parents, and fantasise about her 'real mum', and about 'being a princess or something'. Increasingly, as she got older, Sam has come to see herself as quite similar to her adoptive father and rather unlike her adoptive mother: 'I don't think I'm like my mum whatsoever. She's quite a timid person, and I'm a lot stronger than that.'

In spite of her happy childhood, Sam told me that she 'had always, always wanted to' institute a search:

> I needed to know about me, because I knew I didn't look anything like my mum or dad, and for some reason it really, really bothered me ... I needed to know who I was really, and I was also very intrigued at what my name would have been, because I never really liked Samantha. Silly things like that. It makes you wonder. People take it for granted that when they look in the mirror they generally know that there's somebody they look like, and I think I just needed to know that, and I also needed to know why. I really, really wanted to know why I had been given up for adoption.

All of these elements – physical appearance, feelings about a personal name, the sense of not knowing who she was and the desire to know why she was given up for adoption – recurred in almost all the interviews I carried out. Indeed, I might say that Sam's story was, in many ways, so typical that it hardly stood out from the others.

When she was about nineteen, Sam decided to look up her birth certificate. Initially, like many adoptees, she was more interested in finding her birth mother than her birth father, and had not really thought much about the possibility of finding siblings. Gradually, however, she became more interested in finding her birth father. When she did discover what her original name had been, Sam phoned her adoptive mother to tell her that she would never complain about her name again. Sam described to me her strong emotional reaction on seeing her birth records, the names of her birth mother and grandparents: 'even though it was just names on a bit of paper, it was like discovering that these are the people, that this was my family, this was who I came from'.

A surprising number of those I interviewed discovered that their birth mother lived, or had connections, quite locally, and this was true in Sam's case. By looking up a name in the phone book, Sam was able to make contact with a friend of her birth mother's with whom the latter had lived during her pregnancy. And so she simply turned up at the friend's house and, through the friend, made contact and eventually went to meet her birth mother.

Sam described how she had gone to meet her birth mother, Jane, and how Jane had described to her how she had met her father who, as she put it, was 'a bit of a Jack the lad'. As well as hearing the story of their relationship, Sam had on that occasion met her half-brother and -sister: 'and that was quite strange, knowing they were my half-brother and -sister but I didn't feel anything towards them'. On a second occasion, she went with her boyfriend to meet her birth mother:

> I liked that because I'd felt very much on my own, because I was in this woman's house, and Jane had her children there and her friend there, and I was totally like an outsider. So it was quite nice to have somebody of mine there, of my life, and I wanted him to meet her to see what he thought.

Sam's adoptive mother had given her some photographs from her childhood to take with her for Jane, but 'She didn't accept them. She just kind of looked at them and gave them back... She didn't really seem all that interested.'

Again, like many of those I interviewed, Sam had not discovered any striking physical resemblance to her birth mother: 'The only thing in common ... is that we both blush very easily, and it annoys me because it generally isn't because I'm embarrassed. I just go bright red at the slightest thing, and she's exactly the same.'

Sam told me how, although she had thought they would be in regular contact, in fact, meetings with Jane had been quite far apart and had eventually come to a halt, although Jane did continue to send birthday cards. Sam had tried to find out from Jane about her birth father but she 'seemed to have a selective memory or she just didn't want to remember'. She has, however, kept in touch with her half-brother and -sister, with whom she described having become 'really good friends' and who lived not too far away. Sam did eventually manage to trace her birth father,

Mike, who had been working abroad. She described her first meeting with him in vivid terms:

> I met him, and he was standing there with grey hair swept back in a ponytail, a Hawaiian shirt cut down to practically his navel with a tan and a big anchor medallion … and a massive beer belly … and I thought 'Oh, what a character.'

Once again, there was no obvious physical resemblance. After their initial meeting, Mike had gone back to working abroad. 'So I didn't see him for a while. I occasionally got a postcard. But then he just turned up. He basically just turns up. You never know when he's going to appear.' Sam had also met Mike's brother on one occasion. She had not established relations with her half-siblings on her father's side, and she found it hard to imagine Mike together with her adoptive parents.

As was the case with most of those I interviewed, Sam's experiences confirmed, for her, that she had been better off with her adoptive parents. Relations with her birth mother had, at least at the time I interviewed her, petered out, as Jane failed to show any interest in seeing her. As for her birth father, 'I know he's glad that I found him, and as much as he can he wants to be around, but … he's not a family man.' What was important to Sam was discovering that she was pregnant and starting her own family. 'Jack is part of me, which is wonderful … It feels nice to have, I suppose, my blood, my kin, and start my own little family.' These feelings counterbalanced her sense of having been rejected for a second time by her birth mother. As she put it, 'I'm lucky to have not wanted to find her just because I needed a mum, but just because I needed to know who I was.' Like the majority of those whose stories I was told, Sam said she had no regrets about having undertaken her search:

> All of a sudden you do know where you come from, and you do know what you should have, what you would have been called, and things like that, and you do know how you've ended up where you are. Things that people generally take for granted, all of a sudden you know it after twenty-odd years or whatever.

As I have indicated, many of the elements of Sam's story can be taken as representative of the kinds of scenarios that unfold when adoptees try to find their birth parents. The chronologies of the stories I was told, of course, differ, as do the personalities of the people involved, but in re-reading the interview transcript again, I have been struck by the resonance of Sam's story, which was also one of the less melodramatic or flamboyant of the narratives to which I listened. The second narrative that I examine here had several unusual aspects, and these were apparent both to me as I listened and to Elaine as she recounted her story to me. But there are also aspects of these two stories that overlap, and we can see congruencies between them.

Like Sam, Elaine was in her late twenties when I interviewed her in May 1999. She had a long-term partner, and talked with a warm and vivacious manner. Once the interview got going, she needed very little prompting to recount the story of her search. Elaine too spoke with great warmth about her adoptive parents: 'We get on very well and always have ... I really have got a very good relationship with them.' Of course, like all parents and teenage children, they had had their fallings out, and Elaine admitted these too, saying she had 'thought a lot of that was probably just rebellious'. She also spoke of a strained relationship with an older sister who, like herself, had been adopted. Elaine, like most of those I interviewed, said that she had always been told she was adopted. But by the way she described this, it became clear that being told as a young child one is adopted does not necessarily mean that one really understands what this means:

> I remember, my memory is sitting, it must have been pre-school days, watching television, and I think it was the news, and I don't know when the law was changed for adopted things, but I remember it was an article about being adopted and turning round to my mum and saying 'What does adopted mean?' 'Well, that's what you are, we've always told you that, but what it means, I'll tell you when you are older.' So I think, from that age, I sort of sensed that I was adopted but I didn't want to know what it was. And I was ten or eleven. I was either at primary 6 or primary 7, we had a spelling book and one of the words we had to do for spelling was adopted, and at that point I remember the teacher saying 'Is there anybody in the class adopted?' And Tom was adopted, and I thought, 'Oh my God, I am as well!' But of course I hadn't been told what the word meant. And I was like, oh yes, I remember that day in March. I mean that is a vivid

> memory, because I remember thinking I'd been at the dentist about a week before, and the dentist had said that my teeth were similar to my sister's, and my mum had said, 'Well, I don't know how that could be because they are both adopted.' Because I was sitting there thinking, 'Well my mum's said adopted, she said I was adopted.' You know, I just didn't want to be the adopted one. And I went home that night, and it was my dad's birthday, and I remember saying to my mum 'Am I adopted?' and she said, 'Yes, I've always told you that.' And I remember going up to my bedroom and just howling my eyes out. But I think I'd always known that there was something that I wasn't going to like about it, and I had stuck my head in the sand hoping it would go away. So I would say I was about ten or eleven when I fully understood, they never sat me down and sort of said 'By the way…'

Elaine, as she said, had been 'upset for a long time', and although she did know about her adoption, like many adoptees, she hesitated to bring up the subject with her parents, not wanting to upset her mother and, likewise, her parents had hesitated to bring up the topic too: 'They were probably just waiting for me… They've always just waited for us to ask, and then you don't want to ask because you don't want to upset them. It's just a vicious circle.' But as a teenager, she had been troubled by how her birth mother could have given her up as a baby, and by the idea that her birth might have been the result of violence or rape. At this point her adoptive parents had settled these doubts by showing her the documents they had:

> Yes, they brought them down. They didn't have my natural mother's name or my natural father's name on it, but we had a bit of paper from this foster family that I was in for two months, and that was changed because my name was Lorraine, so I didn't realise that I'd – I just assumed that my mum and dad had got me from day one, so that was a bit of a shock. Then I found out my name was Lorraine, so that was strange having a second name…

Not wanting to 'hurt her mum and dad', Elaine had let the matter rest until after she had completed her education. And then, once she had established herself independently, she decided to search for her original birth records. She told me:

> Nothing triggered it off. It was just getting older, more curious. I wasn't in a relationship, and I don't think I could have ever gotten in a serious relationship. I never felt complete. I never felt whole. I always needed to know and I think maybe that was it. I think time was going on, maybe you should know, put your mind at rest and take it from there.

Like other adoptees, Elaine, after looking up her birth records, placed information on herself on a national register for those wishing to make contact with birth kin. At this point, events began to take their own course. She received a letter that informed her that her birth mother had also put her name on the register some years previously. This meant that the social worker she subsequently spoke to on the phone could immediately give Elaine information about her birth mother, including the fact that she had married and gone on to have four more children. Elaine told me that she 'was quite delighted to have these half-brothers and -sisters'. The social worker also told her that her mother had been widowed:

> And then she just said that, and we talked about something else, and I said, 'She must have been awfully young to be widowed.' And there was just a stony silence, and the social worker said, 'Well there's something else I have to tell you. They're not your half-brothers and -sisters, they are your full brothers and sisters.' So at that point, it's like, oh my God, this is fantastic. Then the penny drops that my natural father is dead, and I'll never get to meet him.

At this point, Elaine accepted the social worker's offer to facilitate a correspondence with her birth mother. An initial exchange of letters revealed that her birth mother, Kate, had put herself on the register soon after becoming a widow, and that she had since remarried. Kate also sent photographs of Elaine's siblings which:

> was absolutely amazing because I have a little sister that is me. So, she's identical to me, so it's like, 'Oh my God'. Whenever I showed these photographs to my mum and dad, Mum, she's like 'I can't believe it.' Two very much like me but one just identical to me, and I wrote back…

After this, Elaine and Kate spoke to each other on the phone, and they arranged to meet.

> Everything had happened so quickly, I hadn't really – I don't think you can be prepared for something like that, but it just sort of happened. And I got off the train, and I had my head down, and I thought, I can't do it. I'd seen a photo of Kate, and it wasn't like not having a clue, and she'd had a photo of me, but apparently – and this is a big standing joke – she had her head down, and Mike [her husband] said, 'Look for her. You know who she is, look for her.' All she could apparently see was from there down, and she goes, 'I don't need to look up, that's her there.' Just identical legs, identical walk, knees together, ankles out. She goes, 'I know that's my daughter there.'

Unlike many of those I interviewed, Elaine and Kate's first meeting went well, and was quite relaxed.

> It was all very matter of fact ... we went for a coffee in the station, sat down and did some general gabbing, nothing too heavy, and went shopping, got Christmas presents, went for lunch, and we did this. It was very weird; it was 'Oh, I've known you all my life. No I haven't, I've only known you today.' There was no awkward silences, there was, I don't know, it was just very, very strange. It just seemed a very natural and very relaxed day.

In meeting Kate, Elaine said she hadn't felt that she was meeting a stranger – as several of those whom I interviewed clearly did – but that she was more like someone she already knew. There were some other unusual aspects to Elaine's story, which emerged more clearly as she spoke about these events. She had been surprised and delighted to discover that she had several full siblings and, as she told her story, it became clear that the most striking feature of all was the way that she eventually managed to establish warm and positive relationships with her brothers and sisters, and how, as a consequence of this, she had been inserted into a whole new nexus of kin relations which hinged on these siblings. Interestingly, Elaine also likened her relationship with Kate to a relationship between sisters rather than one between mother and daughter:

> She's sort of, I'd say more than a mother-daughter relationship, a more big sister-sister relationship. She'll talk to me, and she'll tell me things that she won't tell the others, and stuff like that. She starts confiding with me about the family ... she would talk to me and vice versa. I just had no qualms from the word go, it was like boyfriend trouble, phone and tell her...

While this might have been expected to drive a wedge between Elaine and her adoptive mother, this was far from being the case. Although Elaine had, like many adoptees, been quite nervous of broaching the topic of her search, particularly with her adoptive mother, the latter had obviously tried to remain as open and supportive as possible. Elaine described how her mother had offered to accompany her on the train journey to meet Kate for the first time, saying she would simply disappear for a day out somewhere along the way. In fact, Elaine had made this journey by herself, but had appreciated the offer, and described to me how, on her return, her mum had met her off the train: 'and we went for a pizza, and I told her all about it, and everything I had been told, and I think Kate had given me a few more photos of people, and it was all fine.' As far as Elaine is concerned, the fact that she told Kate things that she hadn't spoken to her mum about eventually led to telling her mum about those things too because, as she put it: 'I'd do anything that would get me and my mum closer together rather than putting a wedge between us.'

Elaine's first meeting with her siblings evoked an immediate and striking sense of kinship:

> and then the amazing thing was we both started to talk, and we all seemed to be talking at the same time and the hands were doing the same things, and we were coming out with the same things, and at that point it was great hilarity because, from that moment on, with everything I did, one of them would burst out laughing and say, oh, no, so and so does that, and so and so does that. So I think we went round a few shops, then we went and met Fay and that's when I got my fright because Fay, that was me walking off that bus at that age. That was strange, that was really strange. But the rest of the afternoon, there was great hilarity at how alike we all were, and all sort of walking together, that was quite amusing because we all had this stupid walk, and we went for lunch, but again by the time I left,

> from the word go it was 'Oh right, OK, big sister' ... and from then on the phone calls just started...

Elaine described how the continued involvement of her adoptive parents in these new relationships had allowed good relations with both sets of kin to be maintained:

> My mum and dad said, 'Tell us all the stories,' but I think, looking back on it, that was the best thing I could have done. Keep them involved in everything. And then Susie [one of her birth sisters] got a camcorder, so you know, I would come home with videos of us and everything. My mum loved watching the videos... And as time went on I think she started to relax more and I think the crunch came when the two lots met.

This interview came towards the end of those I carried out, and I had learnt over the course of the preceding months to expect the unexpected, but at this point I was brought up short. No one else I had interviewed had managed to integrate their birth kin with their adoptive kin; it was rare enough just to be able to establish smooth relations with a birth mother. Elaine described how Kate and her second husband, and Elaine's birth siblings had come to her wedding the previous year. In order for that to happen, they had decided it would be good for everyone to meet at least once beforehand. In fact, this had all gone well, and the two mothers had established an amiable and independent relationship. As Elaine readily acknowledged, this made things very much easier for herself.

SHARED KINSHIP

Elaine's story falls at the positive end of a continuum in which, at the other (and more frequently recounted) extreme, it proved impossible to establish any kind of relations with birth parents. The relationships that Elaine had set in train had already persisted for some years, and there were no obvious signs that they would be liable to break down in the future. Sam's somewhat different story might be taken as falling roughly mid-way in this continuum. In her case, relations with her birth mother had been difficult, and were eventually broken off – although the sending of birthday cards suggests at least some possibilities left open for the future. But she had managed to establish an amiable, if rather occasional, relationship with her birth father, and good relations with her half-siblings on her birth mother's side. And this was the case in several other stories I was told, in which it seemed friendly and ongoing contacts with half-siblings were often the unlooked-for result of searches that had not produced viable relations with birth parents. Siblingship, one might say, was less freighted by guilt or blame on either side, and thus perhaps more amenable to positive outcomes – though I was struck by the apparent lack of jealousy or rivalry in these encounters.

One theme which emerges from both these stories, and that I suspect connects with siblingship, is that, where positive relations with birth parents were instituted, these relationships did not exist in isolation. In the stories I was told, the degrees to which those I interviewed described others being involved in their searches was very variable. However, the most successful outcomes, in terms of instituting relationships, tended to be achieved, no doubt for a mixture of reasons, by those who did not undertake their searches entirely alone but, rather, with the close support of others. Thus Elaine's story is very striking in that she described not only her adoptive parents' support, but also how their continued involvement had been actively sought and encouraged on her, and also her birth mother's, part. Sam, too, had extremely good relations with her adoptive parents, though in her narrative their involvement in her search emerged less prominently. She did, however, speak about how important her partner's support had been to her. And this was mentioned, too, by others whom I interviewed, for whom the involvement of a partner meant that they felt less isolated during the anxious times of tracing, and then meeting, birth parents. Conversely, those who had undertaken their searches alone, as most did, were more vulnerable when they encountered difficulties.

Elsewhere (2000a; 2004) I have suggested that one important theme in these narratives is the attempt, on the part of adoptees, to exert agency in the present over events over which they had no control in the past. This was achieved in a variety of ways – partly by simply going back over past events and reinserting oneself in them as an adult rather than as a child. This involved proactively seeking out knowledge, and arranging meetings with birth kin, as well as sharing new knowledge and the experience of meetings with a partner or spouse. While as infants their participation had been inherently passive, as adults, adoptees initiated events and attempted to keep control of how they unfolded.[6] It was an achievement of some sense of agency which, I suspect, led all those whom I interviewed to reflect positively on how their searches had gone, even when, as happened in many cases, they had not been able to establish relations with their birth kin. But being supported by partners or by adoptive parents was not simply a matter of lessening the considerable anxiety involved in these discoveries about ones origins. The involvement of partners or parents provided a conduit for voyages of self-discovery to be transformed into shared kinship even when this was through listening, rather than through an active engagement in the new relationships (see Das 1997). This was apparent in several of the narratives to which I listened, but it emerges most clearly, I think, in Elaine's story. As she described it, her relationship with her adoptive mother, far from being damaged, had actually improved as Elaine had initiated relations with her birth mother and siblings. And this process was heightened as the two mothers engaged with each other directly.

But there was another interesting facet to Elaine's story. At the time she began her search, Elaine had not been involved with a partner. As she said of herself at the time: 'I wasn't in a relationship, and I don't think I would ever have gotten a serious relationship. I never felt complete. I never felt whole. I always needed to know, and I think that was maybe it.' Elaine had, in fact, met the man she later went on to marry at around the same time that she began her search and, in her description of these events, it was clear that she linked her engagement and marriage with finding her birth family. It was the fact that: 'before we started going out officially, he was there from the word go, which is good, and he gets on brilliantly with them', that had made everything seem to come together for her over a period of about a year. In the rather extraordinary conjunctures of these relationships, Elaine vividly conveyed the importance that siblingship held for her:

> I just sort of feel an instant closeness with them ... this definite bonding that was there from the word go. I think that's what I like so much about it. They are my sisters and brothers. Kate will always be my natural mother, but maybe more like a sister relationship than a mother relationship, but my sisters and brothers, they are like my sister and brothers. I don't try and get away from that relationship at all.

Her husband had been part of this bonding too, partly through the good relationship that he had formed with her younger brother who, as Elaine said, had always wanted a big brother.

KNOWING WHO WE ARE

In setting out to find out about their origins, some of the adoptees I interviewed had encountered half-siblings or siblings with whom there seemed to be more possibilities, or easier ones, for forming ties of relatedness than was the case with their birth parents. The idioms of kinship between siblings, resting as they do more on equality and sharing than hierarchy, exclusivity and unconditional care may, in these contexts, lend themselves better to the creation of new kinship than parental relations. Where explorations into one's origins could also be shared with adoptive kin, or with a spouse or partner, it seems that the outcomes for all of those involved, in terms of making or breaking relations, was more likely to be positive.

It might be said that I have shifted the focus of this paper from 'How do we know who we are?' to 'What does kinship do?' Many people in the West apparently find that it takes a considerable amount of work to discover who they are. Whether this work is undertaken through psychotherapy, genealogical research or writing memoirs, it appears to be undertaken in the spirit of a voyage of self-discovery rather than through any particular assumptions about the perceived certainties of kinship relations. Several of those whom I interviewed specifically told me that they weren't in search of new relationships: 'I don't need another mother; I already have one.' But of course the realities may be more complex. The searches I have discussed here were, for most of those I interviewed, more in the nature of internal journeys of self-discovery than attempts to find ready-made kinship relations. The experiences I was told about had not necessarily been shared, and, if they were, then sometimes only to a very limited degree. They undoubtedly reflected the importance of creating one's own origin story, or being the author of one's own life, to a Western sense of self (Lambek and Antze 1996). And here the inevitable retrospective orientation in time of such endeavours is significant. It was through assuming a greater sense of control over their past that those I interviewed apparently also gained a sense of who they were.

The foregrounding of issues of identity and memory is perhaps surprising in a context where one might expect interviewees to speak more about the importance of genetic inheritance. I have discussed elsewhere how those I interviewed did not spontaneously filter their experiences in this way. Even when specifically asked a question which invited reflection on the relative importance of nature versus nurture in their stories, responses were extremely variable – attributing similarities with adoptive or birth families to upbringing or to inheritance, or to a combination of these, in a manner which was almost certainly as diverse as those of a more general population (Carsten 2000a, 2004). This may be partly the result of the fact that these interviews were carried out after adoptees had engaged in searches, rather than when they were still in prospect. It may be that adoptees only minimised the significance of genetic inheritance having discovered the limits to the connections their searches revealed – both in terms of the relationships that were likely to ensue, and the sense of similarity to birth relatives. Without having conducted research among those who were contemplating embarking on searches, it is difficult to assess this possibility but, on the whole, those I spoke to regarded their present identity as a result of a mixture of environmental and genetic factors.

The motives behind searches involved a perceived need among these adoptees to discover the facts of their own histories – histories which could then be refracted through the lens of either environmental or genetic factors, with either being given more weight, depending partly on what was revealed, and partly on their own prior experiences and attitudes. Thus, in the rare case of being able to make a firm and positive connection with birth relatives, it is perhaps not surprising to find that Elaine's account refers several times to an uncanny sense of physical similarity with her sisters or her birth mother. In contrast, other adoptees might either stress a lack of physical similarity, such as Sam's depiction of her birth father, or note a physical resemblance, but use it to underline a sense of emotional estrangement, as in her comment on her birth mother's similar tendency to blush easily (Carsten 2000a). The range of possibilities that are open under these circumstances suggests that Schneider's assertions about the symbolic importance of blood or biogenetic inheritance in American kinship merits quite a lot more investigation (see Edwards 2000).

And this brings us back to the comparison with Malay kinship in Langkawi with which I began this essay. As I have discussed elsewhere, in conversations about the effects of long-term fostering or about the nature of kinship connection, those I knew well in Langkawi tended to emphasise how physical appearance and kin relatedness were more the result of living together in the same house, and of eating food cooked in the same hearth, than of ties of sexual procreation. Those who are thought to be most alike are those who are nurtured in the same womb, and brought up together in the same house, sharing food as well as procreative links; in other words, full siblings. Siblingship is at the heart of Malay kinship. It provides the model for moral quasi-kinship relations among those who are not related, and for marriage. In this sense Malay kinship can be viewed as an elaboration on the theme of expanded siblingship (Carsten 1997; McKinley 1981).

Furthermore, like Rita Astuti's beautifully evoked figure of the aged Dadilahy among the Vezo of Madagascar (Astuti 2000), these Malays tend to map out kinship in front of them, seeing it produced in the future, in a succession of children, grandchildren and great grandchildren. Rather than tracing ties of origin to particular ancestors, it is being part of an extended network of siblings and cousins, and having children and grandchildren, that ensures the certainties of who they are in the present. Nor, I think, is a sense of agency or control over past events central to those Malays who I know well. The certainties of political marginality in the past do not provide a fertile ground for this (Carsten 1995b).[7] Knowing who you are is, at least in part, grounded in the assumptions of present and future kinship relations that can be called on to produce a feast for thousands in a matter of days, or to shore up temporary financial insecurity by means of a simple phone call. Here identity is not in question, and what one would mean by asking, 'How do we know who we are?' would itself be a bit of a puzzle. The important thing about kinship in this context is not to provide answers to these kinds of question but to live out properly the moral obligations that kinship sets in train – and also constantly to create more kinship in the form of sibling sets who go on to intermarry and produce more sibling sets in the future.

This sounds like something very much like McKinley's characterisation of kinship as moral philosophy. But McKinley also suggests that the 'many reductions in the scope of kinship within Euro-American society' have left Western culture with 'no effective equivalent to kinship'.

What is taken for kinship in the West is merely a penumbra of bonds surrounding individual social life, with the value of individual autonomy always pushing such attachments very near to their vanishing point (2001: 138).

Here, I am not sure that I would follow him. Although, the adoption narratives I have presented here could, in many ways, be said to epitomise an individual quest for identity that is characteristic of a lack of kinship in the West, nevertheless, I think there are some elements of these stories that would be immediately recognisable to my Malay friends. It is true that the idea of a search for one's birth parents would seem rather alien because of the way that Malay fostering occurs alongside a network of other ties that does not exclude those with birth kin. Nevertheless, the idea that one might discover siblings rather than birth parents would certainly be appreciated because it accords so very well with the logic of Malay kinship, operating as an expanded system of siblingship. Following from this, and thinking further about the importance of the two stories I have related here, the idea that successful marital relations are in a fundamental way linked to positive sibling relations would also be very familiar in Malay terms. Most important of all, perhaps, the sense that kinship relations are proved in the doing, and that their viability rests, at least in part, in openness to future possibilities would be immediately comprehensible.

Although I have suggested that, from this Malay point of view, as from many others, the question 'How do we know who we are?' might not necessarily be either pressing or relevant in the terms it presented itself to those I interviewed in Scotland, and that origin stories may not be thought of as providing the key to identity, I think that, above all, the people I know in Langkawi would immediately recognise Elaine's desire 'to be part of a huge family', and her delight now that she feels she is.

NOTES

1. This research was funded by a Nuffield Foundation Social Science Research Fellowship. I am grateful to the Scottish NGO that helped me make contact with adoptees, and to Jennifer Speirs for her initial introduction.
2. Research in Langkawi from 1980–2 was funded by the Social Science Research Council (now ESRC). Subsequent research was funded by the Wenner-Gren Foundation and the British Academy. Return visits in 1999

and 2005 were supported by grants from the Munro Fund of the University of Edinburgh.

3. See Carsten 1991 for a detailed analysis of fostering patterns in Langkawi. Most cases of informal fostering involved children living for highly variable lengths of time with kin; they retained knowledge about, and relations with, their parents.
4. Names of interviewees and of their relatives, and some other identifying information, have been changed.
5. The Adoptions Unit of the office of the Registrar General in Scotland states that, in 2002, 454 people applied for access to their original birth certificate at the General Register Office for Scotland. This figure, which is substantially higher than the seventy-three adult adoptees Triseliotis records as seeking this information in the twelve months during 1969–70 when he conducted his research (Triseliotis 1973: 11), does not include those who, knowing their original birth name, apply directly for access to the Court Process of their adoption. Nor does it include those who, knowing their original name, directly place their name on a register for those seeking to make contact with birth kin. Composite figures are not available (Jennifer Speirs, personal communication).
6. In several cases, when birth mothers were felt to become overly demanding or assertive, those I interviewed described how they had withdrawn from contact.
7. I have previously discussed how an ongoing history of migration to Langkawi from peninsular Malaysia, as well as southern Thailand and Sumatra, has defined the contemporary population of Langkawi. Such demographic mobility is characteristic of many parts of Southeast Asia (Carsten 1995b). Although Langkawi villagers have a history of poverty, economic marginality and demographic mobility, they are nevertheless part of the politically dominant Malay Muslim majority in Malaysia, and this informs the sense they have of themselves in the contemporary Malaysian political landscape. The observations I make here would, of course, not apply to Malaysian Chinese or Indians, and one might also expect differences for middle- or upper-class urban Malays.

REFERENCES

Astuti, R. 2000. 'Kindreds and descent groups: new perspectives from Madagascar', in J. Carsten (ed.), *Cultures of relatedness: new approaches to the study of kinship*, Cambridge: Cambridge University Press.

Carsten, J. 1991. 'Children in between: fostering and the process of kinship on Pulau Langkawi, Malaysia', *Man* 26: 425–43.

—— 1995a. 'The substance of kinship and the heat of the hearth: feeding, personhood and relatedness among Malays of Pulau Langkawi', *American Ethnologist* 22(2): 223–41.

—— 1995b. 'The politics of forgetting: migration, kinship and memory on the periphery of the Southeast Asian state', *Journal of the Royal Anthropological Institute* 1: 317–35.

—— 1997. *The heat of the hearth: the process of kinship in a Malay fishing community*, Oxford: Clarendon Press.

—— 2000a. '"Knowing where you've come from": ruptures and continuities of time and kinship in narratives of adoption reunions', *Journal of the Royal Anthropological Institute* 6: 687–703.

—— 2000b. 'Introduction: cultures of relatedness', in J. Carsten (ed.), *Cultures of relatedness: new approaches to the study of kinship*, Cambridge: Cambridge University Press.

—— 2004. *After kinship*, New York and Cambridge: Cambridge University Press.

—— Forthcoming. 'Constitutive knowledge: tracing trajectories of information in new contexts of relatedness', *Anthropological Quarterly*.

Das, V. 1997. 'Language and body: transactions in the construction of pain', in A. Kleinman, V. Das and M. Lock (eds), *Social suffering*, Berkeley: University of California Press.

Davidoff, L., M. Doolittle, J. Fink and K. Holden. 1999. *The family story: blood contract and intimacy, 1830–1960*, London and New York: Longman.

Edwards, J. 2000. *Born and bred: idioms of kinship and new reproductive technologies in England*, Oxford: Oxford University Press.

Lambek, M. and P. Antze. 1996. 'Introduction: forecasting memory', in P. Antze and M. Lambek (eds), *Tense past: cultural essays in trauma and memory*, New York and London: Routledge.

McKinley, R. 1981. 'Cain and Abel on the Malay peninsula', in M. Marshall (ed.), *Siblingship in Oceania: studies in the meaning of kin relations* (ASAO Monographs No. 8), Lanham, Md.: University Press of America.

—— 2001. 'The philosophy of kinship', in R. Feinberg and M. Oppenheimer (eds), *The cultural analysis of kinship: the legacy of David Schneider*, Urbana and Chicago: University of Illinois Press.

Schneider, D.M. 1980. *American kinship a cultural account*, 2nd ed. Chicago: University of Chicago Press.

—— 1984. *A critique of the study of kinship*, Ann Arbor: University of Michigan Press.

Strathern, M. 1999. 'Refusing information', in *Property, substance and effect: anthropological essays on persons and things*, London and New Brunswick, NJ: Athlone Press.

Triseliotis, J. 1973. *In search of origins: the experiences of adopted people*, London and Boston: Routledge and Kegan Paul.
—— 1984. 'Obtaining birth certificates', in P. Bean (ed.), *Adoption: essays in social policy, law, and sociology*, New York: Tavistock Publishers.

CHAPTER 3

WHAT IS GOING TO HAPPEN NEXT?

Charles Stafford

In the early and mid-1990s, while conducting fieldwork in northeast China, I became friends with a farmer, Mr Zhang. Although he was only sixty-one when we met, I thought at first that he might be a good deal older. He had a nervous disposition, and I later learned that he suffered badly from insomnia. It seemed he was worried about many things – indeed, about almost everything – ranging from the rising price of fertilizer, to whether or not Taiwan might decide to separate from China, thus provoking war. I can't really hope to explain, based on a few months' fieldwork, exactly what generated Mr Zhang's various anxieties; but even a cursory glance at his life story may provide us with some clues.

He was born in 1932, and grew up during the Japanese colonial era in Manchuria, so-called. This may well have been a nervous-making time to be a child. He told me that, among other restrictions, the Japanese forbade local people to eat rice. It was also prohibited for the local population to give rice to their ancestors during the crucial New Year offerings. Some families dared to do so in secret anyway, but this could have dire consequences because there were informants in the countryside – 'running dogs' – who might tell the Japanese. When Mr Zhang was twelve years old, the colonial era collapsed around him, to be replaced by the further dangers and uncertainties of the Chinese civil war. Eventually, the Communists defeated the KMT, after which some of the 'running dogs' were killed.

During this same volatile period of modern Chinese history, the 1940s, Mr Zhang faced personal tragedy. The year before the Japanese defeat, when he was eleven, his mother died, to be followed by the death of his father four years later, when he was fifteen. My understanding is that both deaths were caused by illness, although I have not been able to confirm this.

Mr Zhang's story since then has been one of trying to establish networks of support, however fragile, against the odds. With no parents to handle the negotiations, he nevertheless secured a marriage agreement. Then, as his ties to his parents' village became increasingly tenuous, he and his wife moved to her natal community in order to receive help from her kin. This was an important consideration, not least because they had no children of their own. Eventually, however, they adopted a daughter who went on to marry a Chinese-Korean man. This new son-in-law, having come from a poor background, agreed to live in his wife's village, and in the home of Mr and Mrs Zhang. He was to be their *yanglaoxu* – 'support-the-elderly son-in-law' – but he did not take on Mr Zhang's surname, nor did he hand over his income to him, nor was he, in any meaningful sense, under his father-in-law's control. Still, everyone liked and respected him, especially after his wife gave birth to two rather wonderful grandchildren, a girl and a boy. At the time of my first visit to the village of Dragon Head in the early 1990s, these children were six years old and two years old, respectively.

It might be noted that Mr Zhang, when I met him, was living with a number of kinship arrangements which, although very common in China, would still be seen by many people in the countryside as nervous-making. He did not have the support, to any significant extent, of an existing patrilineal network, nor – in the absence of a son – could he be said to have put very reliable arrangements in place for his old-age security. Instead, he depended primarily on his wife's relatives, on an adopted daughter, on the adopted daughter's husband (who was an outsider in the community where they lived), on grandchildren who did not share his surname, on friends and on the state.

Nor had Mr Zhang exactly prospered under the post-Mao economic reforms. At an age when most people would like to stop worrying about such things, he faced considerable financial insecurity. When I met him, he was trying to figure out how to build a new house because his old one provided limited insulation against the bitter cold of the north China winters. As you might expect, this generated headaches for him, not least because the house would cost more than seven times his annual income. In order to start building he was obliged, in his mid-sixties, to borrow a significant amount of money from relatives and neighbours, money which would fall due within three years. What if he could not pay it back?

I could go on with this list of things that worried Mr Zhang. But let me stop there, because my focus in this chapter is not so much the particularities of Mr Zhang's life, interesting though these may be. What I really want to examine are his attempts, in the context of this life, to address what is presumably a very common type of human question, namely: what is going to happen next?

I take it for granted that most people in most societies are at least somewhat anxious not only (retrospectively) about things that have already happened, but also about what is waiting around the corner. Of course, many anthropologists, on hearing this, will think of the huge range of ways in which such concerns might be articulated and addressed. Consider, for instance, Weber's famous account of religious anxiety. He tells us, among other things, that Calvinists were concerned about being 'saved' – a prospect that, so far as I know, is a matter of total indifference to Mr Zhang. More to the point, given the beliefs of Weber's Calvinists about predestination (which, again, are very unlike Mr Zhang's ideas about 'fate'), they approached the present and the future in very particular ways. They believed that worldly success now – something that required careful planning and investment – could be taken as a sign of having been chosen by God. To put this differently: anxiety about a future that they could not, in any case, control (thanks to predestination) was sublimated through (controllable, future-oriented) activity in the present (Weber 2001).

Pierre Bourdieu, for his part, has written of people who face a very different kind of dilemma: those for whom the future is more or less without hope. Commenting on the uneven distribution of life-chances in society, he suggests that those with power over the world tend to have aspirations that are, in effect, 'adjusted to their chances of realisation'. By contrast, the relatively disempowered are more likely, he says, to come up with aspirations that are:

> detached from reality and sometimes a little crazy, as if, when nothing was possible, everything becomes possible, as if all discourses about the future … had no other purpose than to fill what is no doubt one of the most painful of wants: the lack of a future. (Bourdieu 2000: 226)

So although I've suggested that everyone worries about what will happen next, there is clearly a significant gap between the responses of Weber's Calvinists and Bourdieu's sub-proletarians to their respective predicaments.

By contrast with the enterprising hopefulness of the former, and the daydreaming hopelessness of the latter, there is also, perhaps, the possibility of indifference. And indeed we do have ethnographic accounts of societies in which relatively little emphasis – in some cases, almost none – is placed on thinking about or planning for the future (Day et al. 1999). Along these lines, my colleague Rita Astuti has described the 'short-termism' of the Vezo of Madagascar, a fishing people who claim to be constantly 'surprised' (*tseriky*) by much of what happens to them (Astuti 1995, 1999). Astuti describes the Vezo as 'present-oriented', and notes that they see themselves neither as heavily determined by the past, nor as capable of planning for the future. But perhaps in thinking this they are being a bit disingenuous, because they *do* sometimes plan and save – not least in order to be able to meet future ritual expenses (1995: 128). They also worry about some eventualities; for example, they speculate that the arrival of Japanese fishing vessels near Madagascar might cause the sea to run out of fish (1995: 48). And activities in the marketplace appear to compel at least some Vezo, some of the time, to try to predict the course of supply and demand (Astuti 1999).

So even in societies where a lack of concern about the future seems unusually marked, I assume there are at least a few mechanisms – historically and culturally variable ones, of course – for thinking and talking about what might happen next.

But let me stay for a moment with the Vezo. Astuti tells us that, when it comes to dealing with life, the Vezo describe themselves as 'lacking wisdom' (*tsy mahihitsy*), and this specifically means that they do not know how to *learn* from the past in order to deal with the uncertainties of the present and the future (1995: 51). Thus, as I've noted, they frequently express surprise at what happens to happen. A more rational way to proceed, as the Vezo themselves seem to know, would be to engage in a bit of learning.

When Mr Zhang thinks (with some anxiety) about what is going to happen next, he has the benefit of more than six decades of personal experience, some of it bitter and all of it presumably educational. But he can also draw on a Chinese tradition that – unlike the Vezo one – is very strongly oriented towards both the past and the future. That is to say, this tradition stresses not only the extent to which the historical past (including the history of kin relations within and across ancestral lines) weighs upon and determines the present, but also the extent to which the future may be predictable, and in some ways even controllable. To put this differently, this tradition holds that the sequence of events we confront in life is not entirely (or even predominantly) random. Those who can *see* the patterns in the sequences, and who can *learn* from observed regularities, have acquired a potentially important type of knowledge or, as the Vezo might have it, wisdom.

In what follows, I want to focus on two 'pattern-recognition exercises' of this kind, both of which are highly relevant to the case of Mr Zhang. The second, that I'll come to in a moment, has to do with patterns in interpersonal relations. But the first has to do specifically with predictions of the future, and is centred around China's cosmological scheme.

I should start by saying that soon after I met Mr Zhang he made it clear to me that he was against traditional Chinese 'superstitions', and that he had basically supported the Communist effort to root them out once and for all. He is certainly not religious in any observable way. So I was a little surprised to learn that he is personally very keen on *suan ming*, i.e. on 'calculating fate', and actually sees himself as something of an expert in it. In fact, this isn't entirely surprising because there is something proto-scientific about Chinese cosmology which makes it attractive to people who wouldn't be caught dead worshipping gods. In terms of comparisons across cultures, this is a very important point. One reason for Mr Zhang to concentrate on what will happen next is that quite a few bad things have, of course, already happened to him during his lifetime. However, because he does *not* believe in gods – unlike many people in the world, including many people in China – a theodicy, as such, isn't of much use to him. That is, he can't make use of a god-centred explanation of his (possibly unfair quota of) suffering. What he relies on instead is the naturalistic, or quasi-naturalistic, system for explaining fate that is found in Chinese cosmology/astrology.[1]

There isn't space here to go into the details of this system, but let me briefly explain its logic as understood by many ordinary people. Basically, what happens in the universe can be explained with reference to patterns. This is partly because the universe's temporal cycles repeat themselves: year follows year, etc. But it is also because many other transformative processes in the universe (e.g. the process whereby one natural element is transformed into another) have their own repetitive logics. An individual, born at a particular moment in time, acquires a certain destiny. One can predict this destiny through analysing the individual's position vis-à-vis the natural cycles of the universe; but one can also manipulate it in certain ways. For instance, one can reckon which days or years will be especially dangerous for certain types of activities, and then avoid them.

This Chinese way of comprehending things – which, I might note, is built significantly on 'structural logics' in the Levi-Straussian sense – may be characterised as mathematical in orientation, and it certainly has a numerological tendency.[2] For instance, fortune-tellers often simply manipulate numbers of years or days or hours in order to 'calculate' (*suan*) the significance of a particular moment in time for an individual. If you visit a *suanmingren*, literally a 'calculating destiny person', you're likely to find that, among other things, he writes down sequences of numbers and literally does some calculations, before discussing the possible course of events. As practices of this kind illustrate, within the Chinese cosmology, numbers are held to reveal something profound about the nature of the universe and the position of individuals in it. So this is one way of pondering the future, and even *quantifying* it.

But given that much of his life has already passed him by, what is its relevance for Mr Zhang? In his house, he keeps copies of several different lunar calendars (almanacs), which contain a good deal of information useful for calculating fate, along with at least one well-thumbed specialist book about fortune-telling. When he thinks of the future – e.g. when he sorts out his house-building plans – there's no question that the cosmological framework I've described comes into play. Outside experts may be consulted, especially when very serious matters are at stake. For instance, his wife's health was frail during my last visit, and everyone was, of course, taking incredibly seriously the news (from a 'calculating destiny person') that she might well die within the year.

Another matter of concern during the time I spent with him was the fact that one of his nephews (his wife's brother's son) was not yet engaged to marry. It drove Mr and Mrs Zhang to distraction that this young man was so nonchalant about finding a wife. Fortune-telling indicated that he had only two years within which to arrange a satisfactory match, after which the prospects for a happy outcome would dramatically decrease. On the one hand, I found it easy to sympathise with the nephew, who couldn't quite believe that things were so pressing. On the other hand, given Mr Zhang's own experience of the brutal fatefulness of life, it doesn't surprise me that he should be anxious about risk-taking – and turn to the cosmological system, i.e. the system for reading the patterns of the universe, for guidance.

Of course, Chinese cosmology is a very particular type of cultural-historical artefact, as is the more general 'numerical orientation' – in many respects very highly elaborated – within Chinese culture and thought (cf. Stafford 2003a). And yet some of the principles behind these things are, undoubtedly, widely shared across human cultures. So if, as I've been suggesting, it's a very human thing to ask questions about what is going to happen next, it is also a very human thing to seek answers through observing the patterns of reality in numerical or quasi-mathematical terms. Obeyesekere remarks, for instance, on the 'persistence and proliferation' of astrological practices (which have a numerological orientation) in South Asian lay Buddhism, and a great many other examples of this same tendency could be cited.[3] Indeed, when Astuti tells us about ritual planning amongst the Vezo – who, as I've indicated, are generally very un-Chinese in their approach to the past and the future – it turns out that they, too, care a good deal about the auspiciousness of certain days and times for key activities. They consult diviners (known as *ombiasa*) who are specialists in the difficult task of finding 'good days' within the flow of time on which important rituals can be safely held (Astuti 1995: 129). It happens that the *sikidy* techniques used by these Malagasy diviners draw directly upon Arabic influences, and that they are explicitly numerical and mathematical in orientation (Ascher 1997).

One attraction of this style of divination, I'd like to stress, is that it *might* just about be immune to human interference. That is, by using quantification and randomisation to try to gain direct access to the truth, one hopes – perhaps against hope? – that the messy business of human intentionality will be kept out of the process.[4] Given the tendency of humans to interfere in the plans and projects of others, perhaps this is a wise move.

Now let me turn to the second 'pattern-recognition exercise' I've referred to, the one that has to do with patterns in interpersonal relations. In thinking about this, it may help to draw on the notion of schemas as used by cognitive anthropologists. Schemas, in very simple terms, may be thought of as 'learned expectations regarding the way things usually go' (Strauss and Quinn 1997: 49). In terms of cognitive efficiency, the advantage of schemas is that they free us from the need to constantly rethink the fundamental categories and practices of life.

So: what is the schema in China for 'the way things usually go' in interpersonal relations? As you might expect, a proper answer to this would be hugely complex, not least because in China there are folk theories of many kinds about human relations, the life of the emotions and so on. Many of these, perhaps not surprisingly, are built around notions of *reciprocity*: for example, the idea that children should reciprocate for the love and care received from their parents, or that a family should reciprocate for the support given by neighbours and friends in times of need. Such ideas are hardly unique to China, and indeed the patterning of reciprocity across the range of human societies has been one of the main preoccupations of modern anthropology.

But how are such patterns – the stuff of interpersonal and collective relations – actually conceived and articulated by ordinary people in China? And what gives them emotional force? In previous work on China and Taiwan I've stressed the organising power of what might be called the 'separation and reunion' idiom or schema (Stafford 2000a, 2003b). To put it as simply as possible, this holds that the normal thing in life is for people (and spirits) to go away and then to return again. This doesn't sound very complicated, although of course the emotions connected with some of these arrivals and departures might be very complicated indeed.

But what I want to stress – and it relates closely to these psychological complications – is that patterns of 'coming and going' (*laiwang*) have a great *social* significance in rural China. This is not only because they are intimately linked to deep patterns of reciprocity between persons, but also because they fundamentally organise a substantial proportion of Chinese social life both inside and outside of families. Among many other examples I could give, the lunar calendar is centrally framed around idioms and practices of separation and reunion, e.g. in the 'sending away' (*song*) and 'welcoming' (*jie*) of gods and ancestors at crucial moments, or in the near-absolute requirement that children should return home before each new year arrives. This spatial logic genuinely matters because relationships of many kinds – including those between friends, between children and parents, between descendants and ancestors, and between communities and gods – are conceived, in great part, as *products* of separations and reunions. To put this differently: while reciprocity is seen as the foundation stone of proper relationships, without moments of separation and reunion such relationships might never be recognised or sustained – and could eventually fade away.[5] It's as if one needs a poignant departure (or at least a departure of some kind) in order to make a relationship real.

Perhaps anthropologists reading this (and then seeing the examples which follow in the next section) will ask why I should stress 'patterns of separation and reunion' as opposed to 'patterns of reciprocity', given that the former is surely only a local Chinese idiom for the latter. Briefly, I do so in order to relate my analysis to the psychology of attachment – something that arguably helps determine patterns of reciprocity in *all* human societies. From a developmental point of view (to which I'll return in a moment), the emotions of attachment arguably *prefigure* practices of reciprocity, and help to motivate them.

But before getting to that: how does the schema I'm describing relate to questions regarding what is going to happen next? First, as I've noted, the separation and reunion schema is a key organising principle behind the annual calendar of festivals and events, which means that anticipation of the future is closely linked to it. Second, the schema gives people strong expectations about the patterns that interpersonal relations will follow over time. For example, even when loved ones die, we can anticipate future reunions with them through the procedures for worshipping the dead. Third – and for me this is the most interesting point – because the practices of separation and reunion help to actually constitute relationships, they are one way of actively trying to make a particular future happen. That is, through making certain that given relationships will continue to exist into the future, one can attempt to control one's own destiny.

Now let me go back to the particularities of Mr Zhang's case. He once told me an interesting story about his '*taiye*' (the term means paternal grandfather, but here was a reference to an older male ancestor). This man had been one of the migrants who set out from Shandong for northeast China about 200 years ago. He and his younger brother hoped to escape the overpopulation and poverty of their native province. They went by boat and then foot, according to Mr Zhang, working and sometimes begging for food along the way. But, while travelling, the brothers became separated and tragically never managed to find each other again. Mr Zhang's '*taiye*' also never returned to Shandong. Knowing that the Chinese tradition strongly emphasises not only ancestral ties but also ties to the land from which the ancestors have come, I asked Mr Zhang whether or not he, the descendant, now had any links to Shandong. No, he said, that all ended a long time ago (*zao jiu meiyou*). He said that his '*taiye*' had no way of returning to worship his ancestors on occasions such as *qingmingjie*, so those ancestors were basically forgotten (*wang le*), and in his new home he simply 'started again from scratch' (*congxin kaishi*).

This story of separation – in which brothers are tragically lost, ancestors and homeland neglected – might almost serve as a parable for Mr Zhang's own life, which has been marked by various failures in terms of the Chinese separation and reunion schema. As I've explained, both of his parents died while he was a child, leaving him an orphan. After marriage, he left his natal village, to a great extent abandoning his ancestral and kinship connections there. And then he and his wife failed to have a son. This, in turn, makes it more likely – or so many people around them would think – that Mr and Mrs Zhang will be neglected in old age. It also makes it more likely that no one will bother, once they have died, to sustain the cycle of reunions with them that would provide their spirits with an ongoing connection, in the future, to the world of the living. What might happen next, in other words, is a final abandonment to mirror the parental abandonment of Mr Zhang's childhood.

But it is precisely in order to avoid a fate of this kind – both in life and after death – that Mr Zhang and his wife have actively pursued strategies for re-connecting themselves to the world. For example, I noted that the Zhangs, having realised that their ties to his community were of diminishing value, moved to her natal village. Mrs Zhang told me they moved there because she wanted 'to be around her own people'. Central to this was the fact that there were so many of her people – the Yangs – to be around. It was a big extended family, and as far as she is concerned 'the more people who are around the better' (*yue duo yue hao*). Living in that kind of situation, she said, the 'back and forth' (*laiwang*) is very intense. During the lunar New Year festivities – as she noted enthusiastically – the pigs and chickens she and her daughter had raised in the previous year were always quickly eaten up by the guests who crowded into their small home for reunion meals.

I should point out, however, that a move of the kind made by the Zhangs wasn't very straightforward at all when they made it, in the early 1970s. China's *hukou* system (a system of household registration) was at its most restrictive then, dramatically limiting mobility. Luckily, Mrs Zhang's younger brother was the village head, *cunzhang*, and he was able to smooth the way. But why would he bother to expend political capital in so doing? The simple answer is that he was heavily indebted to his sister. Mrs Zhang's mother died when she was eleven years old (exactly the same age that her husband was when his mother died). After this, it fell to her to take care of her younger siblings, including the brother who later became the village head. As a result, her siblings have always felt a stronger responsibility to Mrs Zhang than they would have felt had she simply lived amongst them and then 'married out' to another family. This principle of reciprocity may be (and is) formulated in terms of the separation and reunion schema. The sister who acts as a mother is entitled, in spite of marrying out, to the kind of ongoing care and *inclusion* (that is, non-abandonment) that would normally be given to a mother. And because the Zhangs live amongst her relatives, they constantly have the kind of 'back and forth' with them that is a prerequisite for strong relationships.[6] Mr and Mrs Zhang benefit hugely from this. It gives them an anchor, and helps them control, at least to some extent, an uncertain future.

Meanwhile, Mr Zhang has actively developed relationships of mutual support with others in the local community, and this is again described in terms of 'back and forth'. For example, I mentioned that when I first met him he was preparing to build a new home, and that it would cost roughly seven times his annual income. In some respects, this was a very risky undertaking. But in reality the risks were mitigated by the existence of a network of support, including his wife's relatives, his adopted daughter and her husband, and his neighbours. Especially with the latter, he knew that they would come to his assistance, either donating or lending money, because for many years he had been doing exactly the same kind of thing for them. He participated in, and financially supported, most of *their* key rituals of separation and reunion – the weddings, the funerals, the New Year banquets – and they were, therefore, obliged to provide support to him when it was needed. To put this differently: no matter what happened next, they would have to be there.[7]

Needless to say, the separation and reunion schema I've been describing is a cultural-historical artefact, with its own Chinese particularities. But I said earlier, with regard to 'calculating the future', that some of the principles behind Chinese cosmology are not unique to China. I noted that even the Vezo, who seem relatively indifferent to the future, nevertheless use mathematical divination to select auspicious days for important events. Similarly, features of the Chinese separation and reunion schema are undoubtedly widely shared across human cultures. Indeed, I've argued elsewhere that the 'separation constraint', i.e. the inevitability of separation and loss in spite of human needs for attachment and support, is a universal factor in human social life (Stafford 2000a, 2003b). Not surprisingly, the problems associated with this constraint – including the strongly ambivalent emotions it may inspire – are explored in rituals everywhere, and are closely tied, as I've just been saying, to underlying issues of human reciprocity.

This is strikingly so, for example, in the case of Vezo death practices, the logic of which would surely be very comprehensible to someone like Mr Zhang. It seems natural for the living to feel a sense of loss when loved ones die, and for them to try to maintain some kind of reciprocal attachment with loved ones beyond the grave. But one of the problems with dead people, the Vezo say, is that because they also 'feel a longing for the living' they may be inclined to return to them and, in some cases, create difficulties. Even the beloved dead are, therefore, a source of ambivalence. As Astuti notes:

> the living devote time and efforts to keep the dead away, raising a barrier (*hefitsy*) between life and death... Raising this barrier, however, is a paradoxical enterprise, for in order to keep the dead away, the living are forced to engage with them. The deal is straightforward: the dead will refrain from interfering with their descendants (by making them ill, appearing in their dreams, preventing them from having children, etc.), if their descendants will remember and care for them by staging complex and expensive rituals aimed at building solid and lasting tombs. (1999: 87)

Separating life from death, and ensuring that the dead only impact on the living in positive ways, are therefore central concerns of Vezo death practices, just as they are for the Chinese (cf. Watson and Rawski 1988).

At this stage, let me briefly recapitulate what I've been saying. I've sketched out two very different pattern-recognition exercises. In the first, the patterns of the universe, as seen from the framework of Chinese cosmology/numerology, are used to speculate about fate. (There is something rather logical about this, and it has the advantage of short-circuiting human intentionality.) In the second, patterns of interpersonal relations, as organised around the separation and reunion schema, give people strong expectations about how life will unfold – and how it can be *made* to unfold. (There is something rather emotional about this, and it is clearly immersed in the world of human intentionality.) But how are these two systems of patterns actually recognised and learned, in the first place, by individuals such as Mr Zhang? In order to consider this question, I'd like to shift focus and look at things, however briefly, from a developmental perspective.

It's relatively easy to imagine how Mr Zhang's grandchildren might learn the separation and reunion schema. For example, when their grandparents have gone away from the house and are about to return, the children are sometimes instructed by their parents to show respect by walking to the outside gate of the farmhouse complex in order to greet (*jie*) their elders. By means of a great variety of similar practices and injunctions, the importance of arrivals and departures, and their connection to patterns of reciprocity, is repeatedly stressed to children by the adults around them. They come to pay attention to situations of this kind. Of course, what they actually *learn* from particular experiences (e.g. from observing the noisy rituals for 'sending off' gods) is likely to be extremely subtle. But putting it all together into a recognisable pattern – that is, seeing that people and spirits go away and then return, and seeing that a fuss is often made about this – shouldn't be too complicated.

By contrast, learning the patterns of the universe seems a trickier business. Few people in the countryside, let alone children, would claim to be experts in calculating fate. And yet, quite early in life, they are exposed to what I would call the Chinese 'numericisation' of reality. Simply put, in this tradition there is a strong tendency to think about and talk about reality using numbers and numbered lists. So, when people discuss rituals or banquets, the talk is constantly of numbers: how many sticks of incense, how many times to bow, how many tables, how many guests, how many dishes. Politics and political education are similarly numericised: we should support the 'three represents' of Jiang Zemin, we should live in 'ten-star civilised households', and so on. Meanwhile, children learn that the Chinese language is, itself, conceivable in numerical terms. Written characters are made of brush-strokes that are counted (and indeed most dictionaries are organised in a stroke-count order). An extension of this is that every person's written name has numbers attached to it. In one popular type of fortune-telling, known as 'calculating the brushstrokes' (*suan bihua*), the number of strokes in an individual's written name, when related to the 'eight characters' of their date and time of birth, are said to hold vital clues to their fate. Mr Zhang's grandchildren, somewhat early in life – being constantly surrounded by talk of this kind – might reasonably decide that there is something numerical about the way the world is.

But let me push this question of learning a bit harder for a moment. How exactly is it possible for children to acquire knowledge of the patterns I've been discussing? We know from psychologists that becoming numerate isn't actually very easy, and that it takes children a long time to even use basic counting terms properly. However, we also know that processes of numerical learning among infants and children are assisted and guided by two things. On the one hand, there are cultural-historical artefacts (such as counting terms in particular languages) that heavily mediate the development of numeracy. On the other hand, there are evolved cognitive abilities and constraints specifically related to the domain of number. A great deal of evidence suggests that seeing and responding to 'numerosity' in the world – that is, observing numerical patterns – is an evolved disposition not only in humans, but also in many other species (including, as it happens, pigeons and horses). It has proved to be useful for humans to be able to differentiate numbers of objects, events, and so on.[8] Human infants are, therefore, able to manipulate 'number' long before they learn number words, and long before anyone teaches them anything at all about arithmetic.

Of course, there is a huge distance between the minimal numerical skills of infants and complex historical artefacts such as numeration systems, not to mention numerological divination techniques such as the ones used in Asia and elsewhere. But our evolved number abilities may help explain why it is that numerical representations of reality have a kind of 'catchiness' for humans, and are widely distributed among human populations.

One can make a similar argument, as it happens, concerning the separation and reunion schema. It may or may not be true, as some psychologists have argued, that human 'attachment behaviours' are a set of evolved dispositions. But human infants are of course highly dependent on their carers, and the argument – which I find plausible – is that we, as a species, have been selected to instinctively pay attention to the problem of abandonment. In short, this particular form of anxiety may be genuinely universal (Stafford 2000a). It also means that narratives of separation may have a natural resonance, both cognitive and emotional, for us. Mr Zhang's grandchildren, immersed in a social world where the coming and going of significant others is a matter of importance, have repeated opportunities to master such narratives and internalise them as part of their own understandings of how the world works.

My point, I should stress, is *not* that evolutionary adaptations somehow 'explain' why Mr Zhang is keen, for example, on using numbers to calculate the odds of his nephew achieving a good marriage or why his grandchildren are required, as a sign of politeness, to walk with guests all the way up to the main road outside of the village when seeing them off. Zhang might just as easily use non-numerical forms of divination and teach his grandchildren different rules of politeness. But the shared cognitive abilities and orientations of humans – including the ability to 'see number' in reality, and the tendency to have anxieties about separation – may help explain why, for instance, the practices of the Chinese and the Vezo, which by all odds should be strikingly different, instead share some interesting and potentially important family resemblances.

Of course, it takes a good deal of experience to make the change from being a grandchild – starting to see patterns in the world on the basis of intuitions and experiences – to being a grandparent like Mr Zhang. In his book *The wisdom paradox*, the neuro-psychologist Elkhonon Goldberg (a protégé of Aleksander Luria) characterises this process of growing older in the following terms:

> With age, the number of real-life cognitive tasks requiring a painfully effortful, deliberate creation of new mental constructs seems to be

> diminishing. Instead, problem-solving ... takes increasingly the form of pattern recognition. This means that with age we accumulate an increasing number of cognitive templates. Consequently, a growing number of future cognitive challenges is increasingly likely to be relatively readily covered by a pre-existing template, or will require only a slight modification of a previously formed mental template. Increasingly, decision-making takes the form of pattern recognition rather than problem solving. (Goldberg 2005: 20)

According to Goldberg, the empirical evidence for this change is found in its neuro-physiological correlates. Briefly, with age and experience we build up sets of neural networks in our brains, known as 'attractors'; and these are the basic mechanism through which we recognise patterns and make connections between past, present and future events (2005: 20–1). The activity of these pattern-recognition networks is located in the neo-cortical regions of the brain, and the evidence does indeed appear to show that cognition becomes 'increasingly neo-cortical in nature' as we get older.[9] In very simple terms, the change described by Goldberg is one in which our ability to solve problems efficiently is enhanced with age; he even suggests that competence of this kind, when taken to its extreme form, may be close to what we normally think of as 'wisdom'.

But if Mr Zhang has gone through this process, thereby becoming a wise old man, we are still left exactly where we started: with the problem of his anxiety. As I explained, he suffers from insomnia and everyone in the village of Dragon Head knows that he is an anxious type of person. He worries about money, about his wife's health, about China-Taiwan relations. He worries about his nephew's smoking, saying the young man should preferably restrict himself to just one cigarette per hour, no more. These days, he and his wife also worry about the fact that the Chinese government is insisting on the cremation of the dead. This costs quite a lot of money, he says, and is 'inconvenient' in various ways. In fact, the main inconvenience of cremation is that it threatens to complicate relations between the living and the dead, and to make it impossible, in the view of many, for proper ancestral rituals of reunion and separation to be held. Then what? It is yet another thing to worry about.

Nor does the Chinese tradition, with its wealth of mechanisms for recognising, and even controlling, the patterns of life, seem to have reduced Mr Zhang's sense of disquiet. Indeed, if anxiety is seen as a culturally constructed state, then one possibility is that the Chinese tradition is actually good at *inducing* it. At weddings I've attended in the northeast, for example, the bride and groom are sometimes made to eat what are known as 'broad-hearted noodles' (*kuanxinmian*). They are served precisely eight such noodles, which are very thick, and which are bound together in bundles of four tied up with red string. I was told that the numbers here – four and eight – stand for the expression *siping bawen*, literally 'four peace, eight stable'. According to my dictionary, this expression means 'steady and sure, over-cautious, and loathe to take the smallest risk'. As a recipe for life (and for marriage), this is surely a very nervous-making philosophy.

Perhaps more to the point, many Chinese people feel precisely that the two patterns I've outlined above – the numerical one and the relational one – can easily become too much of a good thing. That is, the obsession with reading numbers as indicators of fate, and with manipulating interpersonal relations in order to control the future, are explicitly seen by many people in China as a kind of unhealthy mania. Mayfair Yang has written of the post-Mao fascination, bordering on obsession, with the art of cultivating personal relationships for pragmatic ends (Yang 1994). Meanwhile, as I was writing this essay, I learned that taxi cabs in Shanghai with the number four on their licence plates were being taken off the streets during the period of college entrance exams. Parents – knowing that the word for 'four' sounds like the word for 'death' – were apparently worried that their children might accidentally ride in such taxis, thus fatally harming their chances of success.[10]

It is a bit hard to imagine a similar thing taking place in most other parts of the world. The Vezo and other peoples may very well use mathematical divination from time to time, but few cultures have anything to match the deep Chinese fascination with number meanings – which sometimes borders on genuine paranoia at what numbers might reveal and/or provoke.

But if anxiety can be seen as one product of Chinese culture, it undoubtedly also arises from personal experience, and from personal position. One can well imagine that as a young man Mr Zhang must have learned that life is filled with risks and is very fragile indeed. In this world, 'four peace, eight stable' is but a dream. As an old man, he reminds me of the typical ego in Alfred Gell's discussion of growing old in the flow of time, surrounded by the accumulated 'opportunity costs' of all the things which never happened (Gell 1992: 217–20). Mr Zhang's parents might have lived, he might still be in their village, he and his wife might have had a son, and so on. What, he might well ask himself late in life, could have made these things happen?

As a system for explaining what *does* happen there is, as I've said, something proto-scientific about Chinese cosmology: something rigorous, and empirical, and logical. It sets out to reveal the structure of the universe and the place of individuals in it, partly through quantification. Through 'calculating fortune', people like Mr Zhang may be able to take steps to control what happens to them and to others. But, in general terms, the unfolding of the patterns of the universe is simply something one has to live with, while tinkering around the edges. By contrast, patterns of separation and reunion are, by their very nature, a field for strategic action. It seems that one can work on and transform relationships in a way that one can't work on and transform the universe. And yet, what is often most anxious-making about relationships is precisely their contingent nature. The people around us have their own plans and intentions and understandings, which may or may not correspond to ours. And as Mr Zhang's unpredictable abandonment as a child reminds us, our lives always have the potential to change instantly and irrevocably. This is bound to be a matter of ongoing concern.

What we lack, it seems, is control. In his account of Chinese geomancy, Stephan Feuchtwang has suggested that geomantic practices are, at least in part, 'motivated by anxiety' linked very directly to this question of controllability:

> The anxiety is brought about by a situation in which the subject knows he is not in control of factors critically affecting the circumstances in which he finds himself. In [geomancy] the anxiety is related both to social factors out of the subject's control and to unpredictable and uncontrollable natural factors, such as the weather. (2002: 278)

The solution to these dilemmas, he suggests, is twofold: 'to fabricate a sense of control where there is no real control' and 'to regularise the making of decisions in an irregular and uncertain field of choice' (2002: 279). Regularisation of decision-making might, one supposes, calm us down.

But some philosophical discussions of anxiety – less optimistically – draw a contrast, following Kierkegaard, between the nervousness we feel because we cannot control what is happening to us and the nervousness we feel because we *can* control what is happening to us. Kierkegaard refers to the latter kind of anxiety as 'the dizziness of freedom', a nervous state brought on by the 'possibility of *being able*' to act (1980: 44; cf. 1980: 61). Anxiety of this kind is held, at least by some philosophers, to be fundamentally constitutive of the human condition, regardless of whether one lives in China or elsewhere.[11]

NOTES

1. I should point out that this system is also used by Chinese people who *do* believe in gods (including those who worship them fervently), and that even people like Mr Zhang – who, for their part, would stress the 'scientific' nature of fortune-telling activities – are inclined to shift back and forth between naturalistic and metaphysical explanations of events.
2. Cf., for instance, Stephan Feuchtwang's detailed discussion of geomancy (2002), which illustrates the numerological orientation of Chinese cosmology.
3. Obeyesekere points out that the explanation of what happens to individuals – including their sometimes unjustified suffering – should, in principle, be provided by the theory of *karma*. And yet: 'It is well known that, in all societies which have *karma*-type theories of predestination, horoscopy and other astrological beliefs have been elaborated to an exceptional degree despite the fact that these beliefs are strongly deprecated in the formal religious doctrine' (Obeyesekere 1968: 21–2).
4. I'm grateful to Maurice Bloch for drawing my attention to this important aspect of divinatory practices.
5. This is precisely what happens with gods if they are ignored by their worshippers, and not systematically invited to *return* to local communities: they actually lose their localised power/efficacy (*ling*) as their relationship with devotees fades.
6. One small, but important, manifestation of this is that the village head's youngest son – Mrs Zhang's nephew – was instructed by his father to visit his aunt and uncle *every evening* in order to make certain that they were well.
7. One shouldn't over-romanticise this schema, and pretend that it is always seen as a positive thing. The requirement to provide mutual support as and when necessary is often considered to be a huge burden (cf. Stafford 2000b).

Mr Zhang explicitly told me how troublesome and annoying it can be at times. There is, more generally, ambivalence about the burdens of close relations of many kinds, for example about those with one's parents and with the dead. Mr Zhang's relationships with his adopted daughter, with his 'support-the-elderly son-in-law', and with his wife's kin have sometimes been less than ideal. Some people even told me that this support network has actually treated Mr and Mrs Zhang rather shabbily at times. But the point I'm making here is simply that the separation and reunion schema gives people, including Mr Zhang, strong expectations about the likely pattern of interpersonal relations, about what *should* happen next, even if these expectations are sometimes confounded in practice.

8. Cf. Brian Butterworth (2000: 153 ff.) on why numerical cognition may have evolved.
9. There is also a shift towards 'increasing reliance on the left cerebral hemisphere' – i.e. on the part of our brains where understandings of how things work are largely situated (Goldberg 2005: 104–5).
10. 'Number up for unlucky China cabs', BBC News online, http://news.bbc.co.uk/go/pr/fr/-/1/hi/world/asia-pacific/4612869.stm
11. Patrick Gardiner explains the connection between Kierkegaard's conception of anxiety and his conception of the person thus: 'To be a person is to exist in the mode, not of being, but of becoming, and what every person becomes is his own responsibility, the product of his will, even if (as is frequently the case) this is something he does not want to confront and seeks to conceal from himself. Moreover, every individual can be held to be aware … of a tension between his current conception of his condition and the presence of alternatives that are in some sense available to him; as it is put at one point, there is not a living being who "does not secretly harbour … an anxiety about some possibility in existence or an anxiety about himself". Such disturbing intimations and attitudes … [are considered by Kiekegaard] to be revelatory of our intrinsic character and to feature, in one form or another, in the life-story of every individual. In this way they are constant and pervasive, endemic to the human condition' (Gardiner 2002 [1988]: 111).

REFERENCES

Ascher, M. 1997. 'Malagasy sikidy: a case in ethnomathematics', *Historia Mathematica* 24: 376–95.

Astuti, R. 1995. *People of the sea: identity and descent among the Vezo of Madagascar*, Cambridge: Cambridge University Press.

—— 1999. 'At the center of the market: a Vezo woman', in S. Day et al. (eds), *Lilies of the field: marginal people who live for the moment*, Boulder: Westview Press.

Bourdieu, P. 2000. 'Social being, time and the sense of existence', in *Pascalian meditations*, Cambridge: Polity Press.

Butterworth, B. 2000. *The mathematical brain*, London: Papermac (Macmillan).

Day, S., E. Papataxiarchis and M. Stewart (eds) 1999. *Lilies of the field: marginal people who live for the moment*, Boulder: Westview Press.

Feuchtwang, S. 2002. *An anthropological analysis of Chinese geomancy*, Bangkok: White Lotus Press.

Gardiner, P. 2002 (1988). *Kierkegaard: a very short introduction*, Oxford: Oxford University Press.

Gell, A. 1992. *The anthropology of time*, Oxford: Berg.

Goldberg, E. 2005. *The wisdom paradox*, New York: Gotham Books.

Kierkegaard, S. 1980. *The concept of anxiety*, Princeton: Princeton University Press.

Obeyesekere, G. 1968. 'Theodicy, sin and salvation in a sociology of Buddhism', in E. Leach (ed.), *Dialectic in practical religion*, Cambridge: Cambridge University Press.

Stafford, C. 2000a. *Separation and reunion in modern China*, Cambridge: Cambridge University Press.

—— 2000b. 'Chinese patriliny and the cycles of yang and laiwang', in J. Carsten (ed.), *Cultures of relatedness*, Cambridge: Cambridge University Press.

—— 2003a. 'Langage et apprentissage des nombres in Chine et a Taiwan', *Terrain* 40: 65–80

—— (ed.) 2003b. *Living with separation in China: anthropological accounts*, London: Routledge Curzon.

Strauss, C. and N. Quinn. 1997. *A cognitive theory of cultural meaning*, Cambridge: Cambridge University Press.

Watson, J.L. and E.S. Rawski. 1988. *Death ritual in late imperial and modern China*, Berkeley: University of California Press.

Weber, M. 1991. *The Protestant ethic and the spirit of capitalism*, London: Routledge.

Yang, M. 1994. *Gifts, favors and banquets: the art of social relationships in China*, Ithaca: Cornell University Press.

CHAPTER 4

WHY, EXACTLY, IS THE WORLD AS IT IS?

Eva Keller

In the field of social anthropology, there has been a long-standing interest in the relationship between 'science' and 'religion', an interest going back to the very beginnings of the discipline. However, in recent decades, this interest has dramatically waned. One important reason for this was anthropologists' recognition of the danger of assuming that those phenomena we label as 'religion' actually have anything particular in common with each other (Asad 1993). If there is no such thing as 'religion', then of course it makes little sense to compare 'religion' to 'science'. For this reason in particular the comparative project has largely been abandoned.[1] Moreover, philosophical and social scientific discussions have challenged many of the cherished assumptions regarding the nature of 'science' itself as well (especially Kuhn 1996 [1962] and Latour and Woolgar 1979).

In spite of these setbacks, which have to a great extent curtailed the anthropological research agenda concerning 'science and religion', many of our informants around the world continue to be interested in the relationship between particular 'religions' they are involved in, and in that which they understand 'science' to be. Indeed, I encountered a pronounced interest of that nature during my fieldwork amongst Seventh-day Adventists in Madagascar. So, although the discussion of how 'religion' may relate to 'science' is more or less dead in anthropology, it remains very much alive for many of those whose understanding of the world it is that anthropologists study. This is, I believe, not a state of affairs that we can afford to ignore. I therefore want to pick up the topic again, looking at it, however, from a different perspective to that of previous approaches. In order to outline how the approach I take in this essay differs from previous ones taken by social anthropologists, I will first briefly summarise the most important anthropological discussions of 'religion and science' to date. Although this essay does not engage directly in this discussion, what follows throws interesting light on its very nature.

From the list of anthropologists who have in the past offered a detailed analysis of the relationship between what they understood by 'religion' and 'science', one can distinguish two basic theoretical camps. In the first camp we find scholars like Tylor, Lévi-Strauss and Horton who, although their specific theories have little or nothing in common with one another, claim that 'science' and 'religion' are indeed related to each other and that, therefore, they can be analytically connected. Tylor linked 'religion' and 'science' in an evolutionary sequence (1994 [1871]). Lévi-Strauss interpreted 'science' and 'religion' as merely different manifestations of the universal mental activity of 'structuration' (1972 [1962]). For Horton (1970, 1982), 'science' and traditional African 'religion' represented expressions of the same intellectual processes, except for the fact that 'science' had an immanent scepticism towards its own theories and was, thus, open to change, while traditional 'religious' thought was closed.

In the second theoretical camp, one finds anthropologists like Evans-Pritchard and Tambiah who, although their specific theories, too, vary considerably, both claimed that 'science' and 'religion' had nothing to do with each other, except, possibly, as opposites. Evans-Pritchard, in his review of earlier anthropological attempts to discover the *origin* of 'religion' – an enterprise he considered both futile and methodologically flawed – held that 'religion', unlike 'science', was a matter of inner life (1965). For this reason it could only be understood from within, by those in whose inner life 'religion' actually played a part. Atheists or agnostics – like those whose work he reviews and whose motivation, according to Evans-Prichard, was to show that all 'religion' was an illusion – analyse 'religion' like a blind man talks about the beauty of colours (1965: 121). Thirty years later, Tambiah postulated the co-existence of 'two orientations to our cosmos': the 'scientific' orientation, or 'causality', which he said was concerned with examining the details of the cosmos, as opposed to the 'religious' orientation, or 'participation', which he suggested was about being part of the cosmos (1990: 105–6; ch.5, 7).

Despite these fundamental differences, however, the conclusions of all these scholars are based on the same analytical approach: namely the comparison of the *inherent qualities*, or *essence*, of 'religious' phenomena – such as their rationality or openness towards change – with the inherent qualities of 'science' (cf. Tambiah 1990: 2). In other words, the anthropological discussion has revolved around the examination of what 'religion' and 'science' *are*, and whether or not what they *are* can be compared in any meaningful way. For Tylor, Lévi-Strauss and Horton, the inherent qualities of 'science' and 'religion' can be analytically connected, while for Evans-Pritchard and Tambiah, 'religion' and 'science' are completely different, and thus incomparable, phenomena.

This discussion, concerned with the comparability of the essence of 'religion' with that of 'science', has been put on ice in anthropology, and, as briefly discussed above, for good reasons. This essay is, therefore, not intended to encourage the resurrection of the old anthropological question of whether or not 'religion' and 'science' *are* related phenomena. Nevertheless, twenty months of fieldwork among Seventh-day Adventists in Madagascar have forced me to think about 'religion' vis-à-vis 'science' all the same, though from a different perspective to that of previous approaches: the perspective of what involved practitioners perceive their 'religion' to offer them. I will argue that not only the Malagasy Adventists, but also other people involved in what one might call 'fundamentalist' Christianity, see in their 'religion' something very similar to what scientists see in 'science', namely a method to explain the world rationally and accurately, and that this is precisely what attracts them to these 'religions'.

In order to argue my point, I will present three ethnographic examples. The first refers to my own fieldwork in Madagascar; the second example concerns a contemporary Baptist church in Michigan; and the third example takes us back in time to the fundamentalist movement in the United States around the turn of the twentieth century. The choice of these examples is not arbitrary, rather it is intended to demonstrate that the theoretical considerations put forward in this essay neither specifically concern Madagascar or exclusively the Seventh-day Adventist church, nor are they necessarily limited to the modern world. The comparison of the Adventist, the Baptist and the early fundamentalist case is based on striking similarities in people's understanding of the nature of the 'religion' they have embraced.

After lengthy discussions in academia and elsewhere about the adequacy of the term 'fundamentalism' to describe a whole range of religious movements, defining what 'fundamentalists' do or think has proven not only an impossible, but also a questionable, enterprise. It is because of this that I am sympathetic to a very loose definition – or rather description – of the Christian 'fundamentalists' with which this essay is concerned. Adopting George Marsden's phrase, the term 'fundamentalist' is used here merely to vaguely describe 'people professing complete confidence in the Bible' (Marsden 1980: 3), that is people who believe that all the Books in the Bible are God's inerrant[2] word.[3]

MALAGASY SEVENTH-DAY ADVENTISTS

Seventh-day Adventism is a millenarian form of Christianity, with a theological focus on the struggle for power between God and Satan, the imminent return of Jesus Christ, the subsequent destruction of all evil and eternal life in paradise thereafter. Fieldwork[4] was conducted over a period of twenty months amongst two congregations both situated in a district on Madagascar's northeast coast: one in a town of roughly 20,000 inhabitants (Maroantsetra) and one in a nearby village (Sahameloka) where people live as rice farmers.[5] For the sake of simplicity, I will, however, simply refer to Seventh-day Adventism in Madagascar in the discussion that follows.

Bible study

The most frequent and prominent activity that Seventh-day Adventists in Madagascar engage in is the intense study of the Bible. Bible study happens in two contexts: at home, together with other household members, ideally every day of the week for about thirty minutes; and on the Sabbath (Saturday), in church, together with other Adventists of the same village or town, for between one and several hours. Besides these more institutionalised contexts of Bible study, church members often engage in 'reading' the Bible on the spur of the moment, alone or together with one or several other persons. I have seen almost illiterate people spending a good part of a free afternoon bent over their Bible trying to make sense of some of its text.

The importance of Bible study in the daily lives of church members in Madagascar would strike any casual observer as noteworthy. However, the activity in and of itself does not imply any particular orientation towards the studied text on the part of the student. Bible study can, for example, be a matter of memorisation and recitation, as is the case in Koranic schools (Eickelman 1978, Lambek 1993: 22–3). So, what exactly is the purpose of Bible study for the members of the Adventist church in Madagascar?

Both at home and in church, people engage with the Bible with the help of a booklet, called the 'Bible Study Guide', which provides a different lesson for each day. The original English version is produced in the United States and is then translated into hundreds of languages and distributed to Adventist communities around the world, including Madagascar. Each lesson is dedicated to a specific topic, drawing the attention of the readers to a selection of relevant Bible verses, and encouraging them to think about what these tell them about the day's topic. Lessons contain a number of questions to be thought about and discussed, and offer some answers and interpretations.

During fieldwork in Madagascar, I lived with two different, unrelated families, one in town, one in the village. My hosts in town led the lives of civil servants and were highly educated by local standards; in this respect, they were exceptional within the local Adventist church. My hosts in the village, on the other hand, were poor rice farmers with very little formal education, like the great majority of Adventists in the district. In both families, almost every day, the adults and the older children sat together after dinner in order to read and discuss the day's lesson from the 'Bible Study Guide'. The most literate person would read out the given text and then encourage everyone present to share their own thoughts about, and interpretation of, the relevant Bible verses and the accompanying text in the booklet. Although it would be an exaggeration to say that everyone always participated in daily Bible study with great enthusiasm it was taken very seriously in both households, and most days the lesson was studied attentively and with noticeable intellectual engagement on the part of the participants. Bible study was clearly undertaken in a spirit of learning, and the focus always lay on discussion and comprehension of the topic presented in the day's lesson.

Moving to activities in church, Bible study also occupies a remarkably prominent place there for both the congregation in the village and in the town. One of the most important parts of the day-long Sabbath service is what is referred to by Seventh-day Adventists worldwide as the Sabbath

School. The purpose of Sabbath School is to discuss, in small groups, the past week's lessons from the 'Bible Study Guide' – which ideally everyone has already read at home with their family – and to help each other clarify and understand their meaning. It is in particular the questions that have been asked but left unanswered in the Guide that the members of the church jointly explore during Sabbath School. People exchange, and argue about, divergent interpretations of the week's lessons. They discuss their respective points of view, cite biblical verses from across the Old and the New Testament as evidence for their opinions, and weave their own experiences from daily life into the discourse. They listen to each other attentively, and then make new comments that might support or question the previous speaker's point. As at home, one person, whose job it is to encourage everyone to participate, acts as chair during Sabbath School.

The leitmotif of Bible study, whether at home or in church, is clearly that everyone should reach an understanding of biblical truth for themselves through dialogue and intellectual exploration of the Bible and Bible-related text, rather than through a 'correct' reading delivered by experts. This emphasis on comprehension through careful study and reflection is also expressed in the following extract from the 'Bible Study Guide' of 9 February 1999:

> When we learn to take a single passage and find all that the Lord has put there for us to understand, there will be a deepening of our spiritual experience and a hunger for continued study. It's a blessing to listen to someone who is well versed in Bible study explain the Scriptures, but what greater blessing it is to personally experience the help of the Holy Spirit in discovering the deep significance of a Bible passage for ourselves.

Comprehension

The Malagasy Adventists not only study the Bible intensely, they also explicitly state that their religion is about *comprehension* of what the Bible says, and they define Adventists as 'people who know the Bible' (*ôlo mahay baiboly ny advantista*). They emphasise that knowledge of the Bible distinguishes them from the other Christian denominations with which they are familiar, and to which many of them used to belong. Catholics and Protestants are criticised by local Adventists for allegedly simply carrying the Bible to church and back without ever opening it and for consequently being totally ignorant of its content. Local Adventists would sometimes remark – with visible contempt on their faces – that other Christians 'just believe' (*mino fô zare*) without understanding *why* they believe what they believe. And they would add that this sort of religious conviction – based as it is, according to them, on blind faith rather than intellectual exploration – is clearly inferior to their own informed choice of God. Thinking back on their time as Catholics, one couple, for example, said: 'We used to be Catholics. But with the Catholics, one doesn't study the Bible very thoroughly. They simply say: "The Catholic religion is true." And that is that.'

Beyond deception

The Catholics and Protestants are considered ignorant by the Malagasy Adventists because they are thought of as failing to study the Bible and failing to intellectually engage with its content. At the same time, the Adventists also consider ancestor-related practices such as sacrifices to the dead – which underpin the foundations of the local society – as totally misguided, but for different reasons. While non-Adventist Christians' ignorance is considered to be due to a lack of intellectual effort on their part, ancestral tradition is interpreted to be the result of active deception by Satan. Satan is thought to be very clever in ways that local Adventists are explicit about. And it is because of his cleverness that he succeeds in making the Malagasy believe that the ancestors truly exist, and that they can bless or punish their descendants, while in reality, the ancestors are but the devil in disguise.

As a manifestation of Satan's power, ancestor-related practices are thought to be immoral, and any kind of participation in them is categorically rejected by Malagasy Seventh-day Adventists. The relevant point for the present discussion, however, is not that Satan is an evil-natured character, but that he deceives us, and, through various clever means, tricks us into accepting as true that which is, in fact, false. Thus through Satan's power, people's minds become shrouded in a layer of deception, their vision of empirical reality is distorted and their ability to think rationally is, according to the Malagasy Adventists, deactivated.

Adventism and 'science'

The Malagasy Adventist church members conceive of the nature of Adventism as necessarily and fundamentally linked to the study, and hence knowledge, of the Bible. This is in contrast to mainstream Christianity and 'ancestor worship', which they perceive to be a matter of deception and ignorance. In short, what they consider to characterise Adventism is its reliance on the rational analysis of the Bible and the rational enquiry into the empirical facts of the world. Moreover, they sometimes talk of Adventist practice as a *science*, in French, or as *siansa*, in Malagasy. In what sense do they consider this to be the case?

Before we move on, it is important to note that the Malagasy Adventists are perfectly aware that becoming a professional scientist involves a very high level of education and a long process of training, both unavailable to people like themselves in a remote Malagasy province. In what sense, then, do they think of themselves, as Adventists, as partaking in *siansa*? What do they understand *siansa* to be?

I have, in fact, never heard any of my informants make isolated statements about the nature of *siansa*. However, they sometimes use the expression *siansa* in ways which clearly establish a conceptual link between *siansa* and Adventism, and which allow us, indirectly, to understand what they consider *siansa* to be. For example, in a Sabbath service in town, a service dedicated to emphasising the importance of studying the Bible, one speaker had a child hold up a piece of paper on which was written in clear and bold capital letters: 'Books are the source of all *siansa*' (*Ny boky no fiandohan' ny siansa rehetra*). The overall message: 'Study the Bible, because books are the source of all *siansa*,' clearly construed *siansa* to be the same kind of activity as studying the Bible, which, as we have seen, represents a rational enquiry into the empirical facts of the world. In other words, both Adventism and *siansa* are perceived to offer the possibility of understanding the world rationally, in contrast to the kind of blind faith the Adventists consider to be dominant in mainstream Christianity, and from which they distance themselves so emphatically.

The Malagasy Adventists love in Adventism precisely what they also consider to be the approach of *siansa* towards discovering truth, namely an approach based on rational investigation. Indeed, *siansa* is perceived by local Adventists to *confirm* biblical truth. To be sure, the Adventists have no doubt that the Bible contains, for those who study it carefully, the truth about the entire history of the world and the forces at work in it. This, however, does not stop them from continuously looking for further confirmation of biblical truth beyond the Bible itself, because as I often heard in church: 'True things have proof' (*misy porofo ny zavatra marina*). Often people found such proof precisely in findings from *siansa* that they heard about through the global Adventist communication network, which carries news concerning fields such as geology or astronomy to places like rural Madagascar. One example concerned the development of the sun. The local pastor – and through him other church members in town and beyond – had heard of some apparently brand new discovery by (non-Adventist) scientists suggesting that the sun would grow to one hundred times its present size, and that eventually it would become so hot that all life on earth would become extinct. This piece of information, so local Adventists concluded, demonstrates the accuracy of the biblical prophecy foretelling the destruction of this earth by a 'lake of fire' (Book of Revelation 20: 9–15). *Siansa* had once again *confirmed* the Bible's inerrancy. Similarly, a black hole in the constellation of Orion, discovered by (non-Adventist) astronomers, was interpreted by local Adventists as the space where Christ would descend to earth prior to the impending millennium.

It is thus clear that the Adventists are not in the least against *siansa*, quite the contrary in fact. The only thing they oppose is what they consider bad *siansa*; that is *siansa* that contradicts or, worse, belittles the Bible, as is most famously exemplified by Darwin's theory of evolution. The rejection of evolutionism, however, is a rejection of what is considered to be an incorrect theory lacking any proof whatsoever, and not a rejection of *siansa* per se. Most Adventists in Madagascar were not familiar with the term *evolution*. However, because the content of the creation-evolution debate was regularly discussed in church, the majority of them were aware that there are learned people somewhere in the world, who claim that humankind was not created by God, but instead developed out of other species; and it was these learned people that local Adventists saw themselves as arguing against when defending the biblical story of creation.

In sum, Adventism and *siansa* are conceptually coupled within Adventist discourse in at least two ways. First, and most importantly, both are thought to be characterised by intellectual investigation, rationality and empirical proof, rather than blind faith. Second, Adventism is believed to have interesting things to say about such issues as the origin and history of humankind, issues the Malagasy church members recognise that scientists, such as astronomers and geologists, attempt to unravel too (although some of them come up with completely ludicrous theories such as evolutionism).

In fact, absorbing information from *siansa* and studying the Bible is, from the Adventists' perspective, essentially the same thing: it is working towards a better understanding of why, exactly, the world is as it is. Indeed, the very distinction between Adventism and *siansa* is problematic for the reasons outlined above. Nonetheless, for Seventh-day Adventists it is a necessary distinction, because in contrast to mainstream scientists they base their enquiry on the one key source of knowledge that is superior to all other means available to human beings in their search to discover the true facts about the world: they base their enquiry upon the Bible. Since the Bible contains the true story of our past, present and future – a story largely confirmed by mainstream *siansa* – to understand the Bible is to understand empirical reality. The cyclone that struck the area where I worked in April 2000 razed the Adventist church in the village to the ground, while the Catholic church was hardly damaged and the Protestant church only needed its roof repaired. This, the Adventists concluded among themselves, was clear evidence – and thus yet another piece of confirmation of biblical truth – that Satan had targeted *them* specifically, because they, unlike the other Christians, were not on his side.

From a secular perspective, it is of course precisely the Adventists' reliance on the Bible as the key to truth that renders their enquiry unscientific. However, in order to better understand how things look from their point of view, let us consider the following thought experiment. Imagine a native speaker of English who decides to learn Greek. Our hypothetical person knows of the existence of English-Greek dictionaries and trusts that these contain true statements about the Greek language. Would it not, therefore, be absurd for her *not* to use such a wonderful tool for achieving her goal of learning Greek? The dictionary won't actually teach her the Greek language, but it gives her the necessary building blocks which she can use to proceed smoothly in her learning process without making lots of totally unnecessary mistakes. It is very much the same, from the Adventists' perspective, when people use the Bible as a tool of enquiry to find out the true history and make-up of the world. To understand the truth is, even with the Bible, a long and difficult process – as, even with the use of the appropriate dictionary, learning Greek would be – because Adventism is not simply a matter of reproducing doctrine. But it would be extremely unwise, and indeed irresponsible, not to base one's enquiry into understanding why, exactly, the world is as it is, on the one source which one knows to contain all the codes. Questioning the authority of the Bible would be as nonsensical as questioning the authority of the dictionary (though, of course, dictionaries are not God given).

AMERICAN BAPTISTS

Turning to the second example of contemporary 'fundamentalist' Christianity, we encounter a totally different context. In his book called *How the Bible works. An anthropological study of Evangelical Biblicism* (2004), Brian Malley writes about a congregation of born-again Baptists in Michigan in the United States. The church is located in 'a relatively wealthy neighborhood in a fairly wealthy town' (ibid., p.21), and the members are predominantly white and 'unusually highly educated' (ibid., p.27). Most of them are professionals – 'teachers, engineers, computer programmers, nurses and small business owners' – and sixty-four per cent of the adults have 'completed postgraduate work', with some of them being 'current or former faculty members at the University of Michigan' (ibid., p.27).

This provides a stark contrast to the context in which I did fieldwork in Madagascar. The area where I worked is a remote part of the country difficult to access other than by airplane or else on foot. Most members of the local Adventist church lived in the countryside and even those in town remained closely linked with rural life. Most local people, including the Adventists, were poor also by Malagasy standards. But perhaps more importantly, and again in complete contrast to the situation discussed by Malley, most local Adventists, especially in the countryside, had very little formal education. After between two and five years at primary school – of which a substantial part tended to be cancelled due to teachers having obligations elsewhere – reading and writing were not skills that people, in general, tended to have totally mastered.

Despite these clear differences in context, however, when reading Malley's book I was struck by a number of similarities between the

American Baptists and the Malagasy Adventists in terms of the religious activities they engage in. Brian Malley was similarly struck by the similarities when he read my ethnography (personal communication). The most obvious similarity is the emphasis on, and the style of, Bible study. The members of the Baptist church regularly study the Bible at home, and Bible study sessions form a central part of the church service on Sunday. The parallel not only extends to the *fact* of Bible study, but also to the way it is conducted. The structure of, and the atmosphere during, the study sessions in Michigan appear to be extremely similar to what I encountered in Madagascar. Bible study sessions take place in small discussion groups with one person acting as chair. Sometimes these discussions are based on accompanying study guides, which most participants have to hand, and which, in terms of structure, appear to be highly reminiscent of Adventist Bible Study Guides, including empty spaces to insert one's own thoughts and answers to particular questions and conundrums found in the Bible.[6] On the basis of the same participatory principles found among the Adventists, the members of the Baptist church investigate the logic of the Bible and how it relates to empirical reality. Malley provides the example of a study session during which people discussed whether or not there are things that are *not* possible for God and, if so, whether this contradicts God's omnipotence (ibid., pp.74–81). The discussion revolved around apparent logical inconsistencies within the Bible – God is all-powerful, yet God is also said *not* to be able to lie or to die – and how such apparently contradictory statements might be interpreted. People seemed genuinely bothered by such inconsistencies, which they dealt with by carefully scrutinising the exact words used in the Bible, by speculating about possible translation errors or by suggesting alternative linguistic analyses of particular words, as well as by trying to understand the meaning of a particular statement within the historical context in which it was made (remember that many members of the congregation are professional scientists). Everyone present contributes, always citing a Bible verse in support of their opinion. If someone fails to do so, she or he is immediately reminded to provide a relevant Bible passage as proof of what they are saying. All of this adds up to a lively and engaged discussion of biblical texts, which are subjected to thorough analysis on the basis of the conviction that the Bible is God's inerrant word. Like the Adventists in Madagascar, the Michigan Baptists explicitly see the Bible as a book that invites active study, rather than the memorisation and recitation of its contents. In a sermon delivered in church, the Baptist pastor advised the congregation to buy Bibles that

> you can mark up. You can get your fancy Bible to bring to church if you want to impress everyone else, but for study purposes get something you can write in and underline and mess with. … Use it. You know, when something impresses you, write it in there. That's how you're going to learn, that's how it's going to come alive to you. Don't try to treat it as some sort of holy object that you dare not touch. (ibid., p.89)

Malley makes an analytical distinction between 'belief traditions and interpretive traditions' (ibid., pp.79–80). While a belief tradition emphasises the importance of *believing* certain propositions, in the interpretive tradition, beliefs must be *proven* to be correct by reference to a sacred text. 'In an interpretive tradition, the text is needed to stand above the beliefs – the text is the ground of their authority' (ibid., p.126). The Michigan Baptists clearly follow the interpretive tradition, as statements during Bible study sessions are only accepted as truthful if the speaker can connect them to biblical text. 'Have a verse for that?', the chairperson would often enquire. The Malagasy Adventists, too, follow the interpretive tradition in that they insist that 'true things have proof', with that proof being available both in the Bible itself, and also from other sources, notably *siansa* and the observation of empirical reality.

The interpretive principle demands of people that they provide *evidence* of beliefs. This implies another principle: that one must never accept anything as true unless one *understands why* it is true. The Adventists' contempt for the Catholic and Protestant alleged habit of 'just believing', and of not caring to study the Bible in order to fully comprehend its content, expresses this principle unequivocally. The Michigan Baptists are equally clear about this point. In the sermon from which I quoted above, the pastor goes on to say:

> [M]ake sure that whatever [Bible] you get allows you to do the discovery of truth, and isn't simply a regurgitation of somebody else's studies. (ibid., p.90)[7]

Like the Malagasy Adventists, the Baptists in Michigan see their religion primarily as a study effort to *comprehend* God's word as revealed in the Bible and to thus be able to understand the empirical reality that they experience day to day. To study the Bible, to intellectually explore every verse, and every combination of verses, is to search for evidence of the truth.

PRELIMINARY CONCLUSION

To sum up: The Malagasy Adventists and the American Baptists studied by Malley share adherence to the following propositions:

1. The whole of the Bible is God's inerrant word.
2. The foundation of Christianity is not unthinking faith, but the *comprehension* of God's inerrant word.
3. In order to comprehend God's word, it is of primary importance to carefully *study* and analyse the Bible's content, to relate it to empirical reality, which confirms biblical truth, and to thus find out the true facts about the world.
4. One should only accept facts to be true on the basis of *evidence*.
5. One should engage in Bible study in order to discover the evidence of true facts for oneself.

Both groups thus attribute enormous value to individual and collective Bible study. And in the Malagasy Adventists' and the Michigan Baptists' own understanding, the kind of intellectual exploration of biblical text they practise is a sincere attempt to understand why, exactly, the world is as it is, on the basis of rationality and empirical evidence. For the Adventists where I did fieldwork, it was not only the cyclone that hit the area that was an empirical phenomenon. Satan, who caused it to specifically target the *Adventist* church of the village, was also part of the objectively existing world. For those convinced of Satan's existence, then, studying and analysing his actions in the world is exactly the same sort of process as that undertaken by the geologist when studying the movement of the Alps.

EARLY FUNDAMENTALISM IN THE UNITED STATES

Both the Malagasy Adventists and the American Baptists consider their religion to be about understanding the world rationally and accurately through the intellectual exploration of the available data and the provision of evidence. This is also true for those people in the United States who, in the 1920s, were the first to proudly call themselves fundamentalists. In their case, their claim that *fundamentalism is science* (precisely because it is based on rationality and empirical evidence) became one of their most important trademarks.

In the historical outline of the emergence of early American fundamentalism which follows, my authority is George Marsden (1980, 1991), a much respected historian of American Christianity and, especially, fundamentalism. The term 'fundamentalist', as well as the movement which bore that name as a badge of pride, only emerged around 1920. However, the intellectual pedigree of those early fundamentalists goes back much further.

Before Darwin

In the first half of the nineteenth century, America experienced a period of religious revival, known as 'The Second Great Awakening'. For the revivalists, the only conceivable foundation of civilisation was Christianity in its Protestant tradition. As well as revivalism this period represented 'an age that reverenced science', so it was essential that confidence in the Bible should 'not be based on blind faith' (Marsden 1980: 16), but that biblical truth be demonstrated rationally and scientifically, on the basis of human common sense. The 'facts of Scripture' were to be merged with the 'facts of nature' (ibid., p.7). In the words of a contemporary scholar: 'The Bible is to the theologian … what nature is to the man. It is his store-house of facts' (Charles Hodge 1857, cited in Mardsen 1980: 113). No contradiction was perceived to exist between 'religion' and 'science'. On the contrary, both worked towards the same end and by the same means: the comprehension and thus glorification of God's creation by means of rational analysis. These views were commonly held and generally unchallenged.

After Darwin

Perhaps the most influential challenge to this happy marriage between 'science' and 'religion' came with the publication of Darwin's theory of evolution in 1859. Darwinian evolutionism caused a tremendous dilemma for contemporary scientists, because with Darwin, the Bible and science, which in earlier decades had been regarded as complementary, now came to appear contradictory, a contradiction which became increasingly apparent to many in the course of the second half of the nineteenth century. According to Marsden (1980: ch.1, 2, 3; 1991: ch.1, 5), there were two basic reactions to the post-Darwinian crisis among contemporary scientists.

The first was to accept Darwin, but to rescue the importance of 'religion' by moving it into a realm that was beyond the reach of 'science'. While 'science', in this new, dualistic view, continued to be concerned with the discovery of objectively provable facts through rational enquiry, 'religion' became the realm of the invisible, the spiritual, the emotional and of morality.

The second reaction to the intellectual crisis Darwin had triggered in the academic world was to reject evolutionism. It is important to note that this position was not justified on moral or ethical, but rather on scientific and rational, grounds. Rather than stressing the 'intuition of the heart "which reason does not know"' (Marsden 1991: 35), those who defended biblical truth against Darwin argued that evolutionism was a false pseudo-scientific theory based on speculation rather than fact. Was it not totally against reason to accept a theory suggesting that a system as complex and orderly as the world was the outcome of chance rather than the product of an intelligent designer? Was it not totally non-rational to refute the *hard facts* of scripture in favour of some speculative hypothesis? Surely, no true scientist would do such a thing. In an effort to prove their point that the Bible, by contrast, was truly scientific, the exact mathematical calculation of the dates of future events, especially the millennium, on the basis of the prophetic books in the Bible, became a preoccupation of many a Biblicist scholar. 'Science', said one leading interpreter of prophecy in 1889, has 'nothing more exact' (Nathanial West, cited in Marsden 1980: 57). Scripture was now seen as an 'encyclopaedic puzzle' (Marsden 1980: 58), to be researched and analysed according to the scientific principles of precision, classification and generalisation.

We might note here, in passing, a certain analogy between the theoretical camps I outlined at the beginning of this essay and the two major reactions to Darwin just described. While those continuing to adhere to the Biblicist paradigm emphasised, like Tylor, Lévi-Strauss and Horton, the continuity between 'science' and 'religion', for the dualists, as for Evans-Pritchard and Tambiah, 'religion' and 'science' came to represent totally different areas of experience that were simply incomparable. One wonders to what extent the 'science-religion' debate in anthropology has been influenced by the controversy among Christians concerning the nature of 'religion'.

By the 1870s, the debate between those scientists who had gone the dualist way, proclaiming the separation of the material and the spiritual, and those who had remained faithful to the old marriage of 'science' and 'religion' – or rather, to Biblicist 'science' – was in full swing. The debate was a genuine one, and neither side considered the other an unworthy opponent.

However, by the beginning of the twentieth century, the dualists had basically won and their views were widely accepted as the only scientific ones in intellectual and academic circles. From then on, those scientists still proclaiming the scientific nature of the Bible were ridiculed and intellectually discredited. 'Science' had won the territory of reason and rationality, 'religion' had become concerned with that which cannot be explained. When the last 'reconciler of evolution and early Genesis … died in 1921,' Marsden comments, '[he] was the last of a species' (1991: 147).

These debates had primarily been taking place in academic circles from the 1870s to the end of the century. Until at least the 1910s, the American general public remained largely untouched by the post-Darwinian crisis (Marsden: 1991: 38–9). And when, after that period, the debate entered the public awareness, many American people – in contrast to the new academic paradigm – continued to hold Biblicist views, but now as defenders of an old tradition against the challenge of secular science.

The rise and decline of early American fundamentalism

The emergence of Christian fundamentalism as a powerful popular movement in the United States was closely linked to the First World

War. Carried by the general patriotic mood that prevailed in America at that time, anti-evolutionist fundamentalists argued that the barbarism the world witnessed in Germany was a direct result of the Darwinian naturalisation of the might of the strong. The same would happen in America also if it did not turn its back on the law of the jungle. The danger of Darwinism for human civilisation was phrased in ethical terms, but the fundamentalists of the 1910s and 1920s attempted to demonstrate the falsity of evolutionist theory on *scientific* grounds, just as Biblicist scholars of the nineteenth century had done. Darwinism was not only considered deeply immoral, but also completely unscientific. Science, so everyone agreed, was about the rational explanation of facts. Biblical scholarship, argued the fundamentalists, provided precisely that, while Darwin had nothing to offer but a collection of wild guesses. True scientists, so everyone agreed, started their enquiry totally open-minded, without excluding any type of explanation on principle. The basis of evolutionism, however, argued the fundamentalists, was the *a priori* rejection of the possibility of supernatural intervention; hence Darwinism failed the scientific standard of impartiality.

These arguments were laid out, in particular, in 'The Fundamentals', a series of twelve widely distributed paperback volumes published between 1910 and 1915, in which numerous writers from America and Britain argued for the need to fight the secularisation of science and, especially, Darwinism. While Biblicist views no longer had a place within academia, by 1920 fundamentalism was a movement of considerable influence among the American general public. However, the success of fundamentalism was short-lived and was soon to totally collapse.

Because the theory of biological evolution had become the main target of the fundamentalists, its elimination from school curricula became one of their main objectives. In fact, by 1923 legislation directed against the teaching of evolution had been adopted in several Southern states (where public support for the fundamentalist cause was particularly strong) and 'similar bills were pending throughout the nation' (Marsden 1980: 185). In the state of Tennessee, the teaching of evolutionism was banned in all public schools. One young biology teacher, however, a man called John Scopes, set out to challenge the new law by teaching his pupils Darwin's theory. He was promptly brought to trial. The

'Scopes' or 'Monkey Trial', as it became known, received tremendous attention in the American press, and beyond. 'The event was comparable to Lindbergh's transatlantic flight in the amount of press coverage and ballyhoo' (Marsden 1991: 60). While the trial had been triggered by Scopes' illegal teaching of evolution in a high school in Tennessee, what it represented, in fact, was a far more general showdown between the fundamentalists and the modernists. On the side of the modernists, in defence of Scopes, stood one of the best contemporary lawyers. On the side of the prosecution stood a man called Bryan. Bryan was not only one of the leading fundamentalist campaigners against Darwinism, he had also been Democratic candidate for president three times, and was a well-known and respected public figure (ibid., p.59). However, in the course of the trial, Bryan, while being cross-examined by his rhetorically brilliant opponent, got caught up in a web of contradictions in his statements and ended up making a fool of himself.

Scopes, the biology teacher, was found guilty, as he had actually broken the law. However, the informal outcome of the trial, which had a much greater impact than the formal one, amounted to the fundamentalists being made a laughing stock by the press. After the Scopes Trial of 1925, public support for fundamentalism collapsed like a house of cards, and fundamentalists were, henceforth, associated in popular opinion with ignorance and intellectual backwardness – attributes many still associate with 'fundamentalism' these days.

While America and the rest of the world soon began to think of the fundamentalism of the 1910s and 1920s as little more than a bizarre, and somewhat embarrassing, episode, the fundamentalists themselves were deeply shocked by these developments, because in their understanding of things, they were the inheritors of a respectable and impeccable intellectual tradition. Marsden describes the conceptual transition that took place in American society between 1860 and 1925 as a Kuhnian paradigm shift (1980: 214–15): a shift from seeing the Bible as a store-house of facts to seeing it as a moral code. While academia, the theologians and the general public eventually all adopted the new paradigm, the fundamentalists did not. They continued to judge Darwin's evolutionism, and modernity, more generally, from the perspective of the old paradigm of Biblicist 'science', and from that perspective, evolutionism indeed looked unscientific.

Newton's descendants

The fundamentalists had good reason to be proud of their intellectual pedigree. In his account of the emergence of modern science in seventeenth-century England, Robert Merton (1970 [1938]) tells us a story that is almost identical to what we have encountered among the early American fundamentalists, as well as among the Malagasy Adventists and the group of Michigan Baptists studied by Malley.

According to Merton, the emergence of modern science is closely linked to the emergence of Puritan values, which were dominant among all Protestant groups of seventeenth-century England. Man's rational capacities were especially valued by the Puritans, because reason made it possible for man to *understand*, and thus to glorify, God's creation. The study of the divine laws immanent in nature became part and parcel of what religion was about. Hence, for the seventeenth-century scientists, there was no distinction between physics, or other emerging sciences, and 'religion'. In the view of these early scientists, as in the view of those who later opposed Darwin, *rationality* was the foundation of faith. In the words of a contemporary scholar writing in 1664:

> [F]aith is no unreasonable thing; … God requireth you to believe no more, than is your perception of the reasons why you should believe. … They that believe, and know not why, or know no sufficient reason to warrant their faith, do take a fancy, or opinion, or a dream for faith. (Richard Baxter 1664/65, cited in Merton 1970: 67)

Sir Isaac Newton (1642–1727) throughout his life spent as much time studying the Bible as he did studying natural law. He remained convinced until the end of his life that the Bible was literally true, and wrote extensively on the interpretation of the prophetic books of Daniel and Revelation, though much of the theological part of his work remains unpublished (Snobelen 2002; 2003). Indeed, throughout the controversies of the second half of the nineteenth and the early twentieth century regarding the 'scientific' nature of the Bible, those defending the old marriage between 'religion' and 'science' always claimed Newton as their hero. The thorough analysis of the Bible, so the early fundamentalists continuously stressed, was equivalent to Newtonian physics. Scripture, like nature, for them, 'was a perfect self-contained unity governed by exact laws which could be discovered by careful analysis and classification' (Marsden 1980: 57). So, who was Darwin to supposedly enlighten the great Newton?

I have no record in my field notes of any of my informants in Madagascar actually referring to Newton as their intellectual predecessor, but I am certain that if they had known who Newton was and how he had spent his days, they, too, would have done so. Indeed, to claim that they, and other Biblicist thinkers like them, are Newton's intellectual descendants is not unreasonable. Because like Newton, many of today's 'fundamentalists' are people who have complete trust in the inerrancy of the Bible and its compatibility with empirical science.

CONCLUSION

The Christian 'fundamentalists' presented in this essay think of the Biblicist approach to knowledge as an approach based on rational enquiry and empiricism rather than blind faith. For them it is an approach guided by the careful examination of biblical text, the connection of this text with empirical data and the attempt to establish generalising principles regarding the nature of the world. Furthermore, in the case of at least the Malagasy Adventists and the early American fundamentalists, this approach, precisely *because* of its perceived characteristics, is thought to be scientific, although obviously, the term '*siansa*' is bound to have shades of meaning for the Malagasy rice farmer that the term 'science' did not have for the early American fundamentalists, and vice versa.

Tambiah postulates a distinction between two orientations to the world: causality/science and participation/religion (1990). In his list of some representations of 'causality' and 'participation', we read that causality is represented by: 'the successive fragmentation of phenomena, and their atomisation, in the construction of scientific knowledge'. Participation, on the other hand, includes 'cosmic oneness', 'contiguity relations and the logic of interaction'. Tambiah then goes on to list a number of contexts typical for causality including 'pedagogic sessions at universities attempting to reduce complexity to elementary principles'. This is opposed to a number of contexts given as typical of participation that include 'church services' and 'millenarian movements' (ibid., p.109). Tambiah's model clearly is not borne out by a closer examination of 'fundamentalist' Christianity because, as I have tried to show, the Christians presented in this essay are not so much concerned with 'cosmic oneness' as with the detailed examination of the Bible, with linking biblical studies to 'science', and with analysing, classifying and generalising. These are precisely the characteristics Tambiah attributes to the 'scientific', rather than the 'religious', orientation.

The ethnographic examples discussed here also put into perspective Nicholas Humphrey's theory, which attempts to explain why modern people are increasingly attracted to all sorts of paranormal phenomena – telepathy, the bending of spoons by the force of thought – despite the fact that science has long since shown the trick nature of such phenomena (1996). Part of Humphrey's theory is that the world created by science is a cold world, in which a greater human purpose is missing. According to Humphrey, it is due to the fact that it is quite simply too disheartening for us to accept that we are little more than an ephemeral collection of atoms that many people, disenchanted by science, cling to something beyond material reality. *Knowledge* of what makes the world go round is, for them, not good enough. Indeed, they feel 'a thirst for things which are *contrary to reason*' (1996: 162, emphasis in the original).[8] For the Malagasy Adventists and the Michigan Baptists, it is quite the opposite. For them, as for the early American fundamentalists and their intellectual predecessors, emotional reassurance through religious faith – to 'just believe' – is not good enough. While people who are keen on the paranormal may be unhappy with the perceived lack of existential meaning in a world dominated by science, the Christian 'fundamentalists' described here are deeply unhappy with the 'unscientific' world of Catholicism and mainstream Protestantism. For them, modern mainstream Christianity is unsatisfactory precisely because it contents itself – following the dualist approach to 'science' and 'religion' which eventually won in the aftermath of the post-Darwinian crisis – with telling people to believe, to trust in God and to feel His presence, while failing to provide sufficient *knowledge* about the cosmos. I do not want to suggest that Seventh-day Adventism in Madagascar, for example, is simply a survival of a pre-Darwinian Euro-American intellectual tradition, however. 'Fundamentalists', whether in early-twentieth-century America or in the contemporary world, have not simply been left behind by the developments of the modern times.

Rather, they are people deeply dissatisfied with what modern mainstream Christianity has to offer.

Up to now, I have presented Biblicist Christians' own perception of the nature of the religions they are part of. However, I also want to put forward another argument, which is quite independent of 'the native's point of view', though derived from it. As I outlined at the beginning of this essay, I am not concerned with assessing the inherent quality of Christian 'fundamentalism', and it is therefore not my intention to comment on whether or not the kind of Biblicist Christianity discussed here *is* actually based on rationality and empiricism as its adherents claim. However, what the ethnography of practitioners' perception of the nature of Biblicist Christianity reveals, is the presence of a *desire* to understand the world intellectually by means of one's own rational examination of the available evidence – a way of understanding the world, which the Malagasy Adventists, the Michigan Baptists and the early American fundamentalists believe(d) they can (or could) access through Biblicist Christianity. It is this *desire* that I want to argue they share with scientists. Although, of course, the nature of the *practise* of science is not beyond dispute (Kuhn 1996 [1962]; Latour and Woolgar 1979), the *attraction* of the scientific enterprise as a means to understand the world rationally, and on the basis of the discovery of empirical facts, is, I believe, not controversial.

I have inserted the word 'exactly' into the title of this essay, because its heroes are not satisfied with just any kind of explanation of why the world is as it is. They want intellectually satisfying explanations that are exact to the final detail. Like scientists, they see the world as a massive jigsaw puzzle comprising millions of pieces, and like scientists, they are not satisfied with admiring the picture the puzzle reveals, wanting instead to understand how, exactly, piece A fits with piece B, and what, exactly, piece 93 has to do with piece 2110. Both practices involve the same scrutinising effort and both generate the same thrill when previously unknown links are discovered. In one case, it might be the discovery of a new archaeological site, in the other case it might be the discovery of the 'fact' that one can actually know from where in the sky Jesus will descend to earth, or an understanding of why the storm did not damage the Catholic church. Like scientists, the 'fundamentalists' of this essay want to understand the world through the accuracy of reason.

Indeed, it is because Biblicist Christians and scientists *share* a set of values – in particular rationality and the provision of proof in the process of discovering why, exactly, the world is as it is – that it is possible for them to be in mutual conflict (a state of affairs recognised by both sides) over such issues as the origin of species. It is because they share this set of values that they can argue about whose explanation is more rational and whose has most proof to support it, with both sides accusing each other of irrationality and the lack of evidence for their respective arguments.

If the kind of Biblicist Christianity this essay has been concerned with provides such a powerful explanatory tool for so many people across time and space – from Newton to rural people in contemporary Madagascar – its attraction cannot be reduced to any particular socio-political context, or, in fact, any particular type of context. At least part of the attraction of Biblicist Christianity must be culturally *non-*specific.

Indeed, if the desire to understand why, exactly, the world is as it is – on the basis of rational enquiry, the examination of the available evidence and the attempt to establish generalising principles – can be identified as one of the common motivating factors that leads people to engage in science and in Biblicist Christianity respectively (as I believe it can), then one surely has to pose a 'Zafimaniry question' (see Preface): could not *the desire to intellectually comprehend* the details of the workings of the cosmos be a convincing candidate element of human nature, manifesting itself, as it does, in such diverse contexts as science and certain forms of 'religion'?

Of course, this candidate element *alone* could not explain why Christian 'fundamentalism' or science become influential in certain contexts, but not in others, or among certain people, but not others (cf. Sperber 1996, Bloch and Sperber 2002). Obviously, many historical, cultural, political and other factors will play an important part in making Biblicist Christianity successful or unsuccessful in particular circumstances, just as a whole variety of aspects will influence whether a particular person becomes a physicist or a housewife. No single-factor explanation can do justice to the complexity of social life. The aim of this essay, however, has not been to provide a socio-historical explanation for the instances of Christian 'fundamentalism' discussed. Rather, its purpose has been to highlight the remarkable fact that people involved in the supposedly radically contradictory fields of Biblicist Christianity and science share the same desire to understand the world through the accuracy of reason, a desire which may be of a much more general nature than is often suggested.

ACKNOWLEDGEMENTS

For their constructive comments on earlier drafts of this essay, I would like to thank Maurice Bloch, Fenella Cannell, Matthew Engelke, Brian Malley and Joel Robbins, as well as the editors of this volume, Rita Astuti, Johnny Parry and Charles Stafford.

NOTES

1. Tambiah 1990 (see discussion below) is an exception.
2. The belief in the Bible's inerrancy does not necessarily imply its *literal* interpretation in all instances (cf. Malley 2004: 92–101).
3. This may also be true of other Christians, as indeed it is of many Catholics and Protestants who are members of the mainstream churches in Madagascar.
4. I am neither a member of the Seventh-day Adventist nor any other church.
5. For a full ethnographic account cf. Keller 2005.
6. These impressions are based on the study guide 'One Holy Passion. The Attributes of God. Study guide to accompany the audio/video series', by RC Sproul (1989), which the congregation in Michigan has used in the past and which Brian Malley kindly provided me with.
7. In fact, this links up with Malley's key argument. How does the Bible work? he asks. How does it succeed in being an important book for millions of people across time and space? The reason, he suggests, is to be found in the fact that there are no specific hermeneutic rules determining how exactly the Bible has to be interpreted. Thus, every generation of Christians, and indeed every individual, can interpret the Bible in such a way as to make it relevant to their own lives. This encourages intellectual exploration of the Bible's content. If there are no hermeneutic rules, however, the Bible might be interpreted as undermining its own authority. Malley suggests that this is prevented from happening by the fact that people following the interpretive tradition approach the Bible with all their thoughts directed towards discovering its relevance for their own lives.
8. This is, according to Humphrey, the main reason why people *desire* the existence of the paranormal. But how is it *possible* that people believe in such things as psycho-kinetics (moving an object by the force of thought)?

The most important reason for this, according to Humphrey, is to be found in Cartesian dualism, which makes possible the conceptual separation between the mind and the body (1996: ch.24, 26).

REFERENCES

Asad, T. 1993. 'The construction of Religion as an anthropological category', in *Genealogies of religion. Discipline and reasons of power in Christianity and Islam*, Baltimore and London: The Johns Hopkins University Press.

Bloch, M. 2001. 'Postmodernism – The nature/culture debate in just another guise?', *Irish Journal of Anthropology* 5(1): 111–15.

Bloch, M. and D. Sperber 2002. 'Kinship and evolved psychological dispositions. The Mother's Brother controversy reconsidered', *Current Anthropology* 43(5): 723–48.

Eickelman, D.F. 1978. 'The art of memory: Islamic education and its social reproduction', *Comparative Studies in Society and History* 20: 485–516.

Evans-Pritchard, E.E. 1965. *Theories of primitive religion*, Oxford: Clarendon Press.

Horton, R. 1970. 'African traditional thought and Western science', in B.R. Wilson (ed.), *Rationality*, Oxford: Blackwell.

—— 1982. 'Tradition and Modernity Revisited', in M. Hollis and S. Lukes (eds), *Rationality and relativism*, Oxford: Basil Blackwell.

Humphrey, N. 1996. *Leaps of faith. Science, miracles, and the search for supernatural consolation*, New York: Basic Books.

Keller, E. 2005. *The road to clarity. Seventh-day Adventism in Madagascar*, New York, Houndmills: Palgrave Macmillan.

Kuhn, T. 1996 (1962). *The structure of scientific revolutions*, Chicago: University of Chicago Press.

Lambek, M. 1993. *Knowledge and practice in Mayotte. Local discourses of Islam, sorcery, and spirit possession*, Toronto et al.: University of Toronto Press.

Latour, B. and S. Woolgar 1979. *Laboratory life: The social construction of scientific facts*, Los Angeles: Sage.

1993. *We have never been modern*, Cambridge, Mass.: Harvard University Press.

Lévi-Strauss, C. 1972 (1962). *The savage mind*, Oxford: Oxford University Press.

Malley, B. 2004. *How the Bible works. An anthropological study of Evangelical Biblicism*, Walnut Creek, Lanham, New York, Toronto, Oxford: Altamira Press.

Marsden, G.M. 1980. *Fundamentalism and American culture. The shaping of twentieth-century evangelicalism, 1870–1925*, Oxford et al.: Oxford University Press.

—— 1991. *Understanding fundamentalism and evangelicalism*, Grand Rapids, Michigan: William B. Eerdmans Publishing Company.

Merton, R.K. 1970 (1938). *Science, technology and society in seventeenth-century England*, New York: Howard Fertig.

Snobelen, S.D. 2002. 'Isaac Newton (1642–1727)', in *Oxford encyclopedia on the enlightenment*, published online: www.isaac-newton.org

—— 2003. 'Isaac Newton (1642–1727)', in *Oxford encyclopedia on the enlightenment*, Published online: www.isaac-newton.org

Sperber, D. 1996 (1985). 'Anthropology and psychology: towards an epidemiology of representations', in *Explaining culture: a naturalistic approach*, Oxford, Cambridge (Massachusetts): Blackwell.

Tambiah, S.J. 1990. *Magic, science, religion, and the scope of rationality*, Cambridge et al.: Cambridge University Press.

Tylor, E.B. 1994 (1871). *Primitive culture: researches into the development of mythology, philosophy, religion, art, and custom* (vol. 2), London: Routledge.

CHAPTER 5

HOW DOES RITUAL MATTER?

Fenella Cannell

For the purposes of this volume, a 'Zafimaniry question' (see Preface) is one which people with whom we have lived on fieldwork themselves ask, and which resonates widely in human experience. It is also, according to Maurice Bloch (2005), the sort of question that anthropology ought to be able to address better than other disciplines. Bloch's contention that all of us, everywhere, are intuitive anthropologists, is very appealing. Not all communities, however, seem to have the same taste for explicit abstract debate that Bloch reports for the Zafimaniry. As other contributions to this volume show, some of the questions that matter most at a local level are those that are only asked by implication.

When it came to thinking of examples from my own fieldwork, I encountered a different difficulty. My own periods of fieldwork, the first in the Catholic Philippines and the second with Latter-day Saints (Mormons or LDS) in America, were both conducted with Christian people. They do ask many explicit, existential questions; but most of these relate in some way to the particular traditions of Christian thinking that they have inherited and created. 'Are you a Catholic?' 'Do you have a testimony?' 'Shall we be able to talk to our children in heaven?' Such questions might require some glossing not only for outsiders but also for different Christian groups, and so sit uneasily with the idea of universally accessible human puzzles.

Given the possible misunderstandings even between my two sets of informants, one might want to ask what the category of 'Christianity' actually means (I have looked at some general aspects of this problem in other publications [Cannell 2005b; Cannell, 2006]). Suffice it to say here, that for anthropologists, the question cannot be answered by reference to a body of doctrine alone, but must take account of the self-understandings of the extremely diverse range of people who claim Christian identity. Here, I investigate one small element of those self-understandings, and look at a question that is certainly raised both by Filipino Catholics and American Latter-day Saints: the question of what is important about rituals.

By this, I do not simply intend the usual anthropological question about rituals; that is, what are they for or what do they do? Rather, I want to explain what people in my two different fieldwork locations say matters to them about taking part in ritual. I will then ask how well some dominant strands of anthropological thinking can allow for, and account for, these indigenous views.

TEMPLE RITUAL AND MORMON RELIGIOUS EXPERIENCE

Although Latter-day Saints attend regular Sunday School and Eucharistic services in their local meeting houses each week, these services are quite distinct from the special ceremonies which define the LDS religious imagination, namely the temple rituals. While meeting houses are architecturally low-key, Mormon temples are visually imposing and magnificent, often made of reflective materials or soaring out of the landscape on a scale to rival the great European Catholic cathedrals. But visitors cannot walk through the great Salt Lake City temple as they might walk through Chartres; LDS temples are generally closed to outsiders, and even church members must obtain an annual 'temple recommend' from their bishop, which is to be presented each time they attend.[1]

LDS church members do not pass through the whole temple and its ritual until they reach maturity; this is usually just before marriage for women, and just before leaving on mission for men, although some young women also serve a mission. For both sexes, this first adult participation is known as 'taking out your endowments' or 'first ordinances', and it is an event of major spiritual and emotional importance. Passing into this mature status could not have a greater religious importance, because for Latter-day Saints temple ritual is necessary for salvation. Mormons are promised that, if they lead a moral life and go to the temple, they can be inseparably linked with their parents, spouses, children and other loved ones, in the hereafter, as a 'forever family' capable of eternal increase and learning. The totality of rituals performed in the temples can also literally effect the salvation of others, including living converts and the vast legions of the dead, on whose behalf, in fact, the bulk of temple ritual is performed by proxy. As Latter-day Saints understand the matter, the dead, like the living, can exercise free choice as to whether or not to accept baptism into the LDS church, a decision that they may indicate to those acting for them in ritual through various signs and intimations. Although leading a Christ-centred daily life is important for Latter-day Saints, therefore, the role of the temple ritual in generating salvation for all mankind can hardly be exaggerated.

Exterior images of the individual temples are much-loved by Latter-day Saints and appear in many forms, as screen savers, programme covers for church services and so on. Some people also enjoy, and collect, interior views, but these are treated with more reserve. It is, actually, possible for visitors to see the inside of a Mormon temple, but only for one brief period, the so-called 'open house' between the completion of a new temple and its religious dedication, when tickets for a tour are available to non-members, and to members of all ages. The luxurious and often beautiful temple interiors are, therefore, not actually secret, but they are associated with the form and content of the temple rituals that take place there. And these are, as the church would have it: 'not secret, but sacred'. They are not to be lightly spoken of, and their details are never to be discussed with outsiders, not even with Latter-day Saints who have not yet taken out their endowments. It is worth noting that most of the rooms inside a LDS temple look, to the untutored eye, rather like public rooms from a deluxe hotel. They do not look like Catholic or Protestant churches, and the arrangement of most of the rooms gives few clues as to their liturgical functions. Thus, the most loved room of a temple, the Celestial Room, where Latter-day Saints will rest and feel close to the spirit of the divine at the conclusion of the ritual, looks like a particularly splendid drawing-room.[2]

One consequence of this taboo on the temple ritual is that it looms large in Mormonism's image in the outside world. Those hostile to Mormonism sometimes use the temple ritual to claim that Mormonism is a 'cult'.[3] This is not a position I endorse, although I do think that Douglas Davies (2000) is right to speak of Mormonism as, in some ways, a 'mystery religion'; that is, there are many layers of meaning in LDS doctrine, and it is not intended that they all be unfolded at once. Rather, the Latter-day Saint is meant to pass through successive and inexhaustible levels of religious knowledge and feeling in her lifetime and beyond mortal life. The temple ritual is key to this conception; by avoiding direct discussion of it, the space for that process of discovery and growth is retained.[4]

As an outsider, it nevertheless surprised me very much to find that even intimate family members, such as mothers and daughters, rarely discuss the temple ceremony in any explicit way. There may, sometimes, be a little discussion among those who are resting together in the Celestial Room (this being permitted by the church), but there should be no discussion of the ritual's details outside the temple itself.

Because of this careful avoidance, it is very rare for young people to know what to expect when they are about to take out their endowments for the first time. The effects of not knowing are unpredictable; the first experience of temple ritual may be disorienting in its strong contrast to the 'practical' face of meeting house Mormonism, and is sometimes powerfully upsetting. As one woman, whose experiences were rather typical, told me:

> I'm not really that... I'm not one of those people that has a wonderful experience with the endowment ritual... I had a few problems enjoying it... [My husband is] the same way ... going through the temple ... the first couple of times I did it, I thought, this is really *weird* ... it's so different from everything else in the Church.

The adjective 'weird' cropped up many times in my interviews in this context, along with comments such as: 'You go there for the first time and you think, you know, "Whoah! What's going on here?" You know?' For several people I met, the dislocating effects of the ritual had been so off-putting that they failed to return over many years, despite the advice of the Church that they should do so.

The shock of first temple ritual is a widely recognised phenomenon among Saints who have taken out their endowments. Although what happens in temple ceremony must not be discussed, the nature of emotional and spiritual *experiences* in the temple *is* a discussable topic. Indeed, while always being careful to avoid any inappropriate or disrespectful tone, many people I met were intensely interested in this subject, and were willing and even eager to think and talk about it.

The combination of the absolute avoidance of sacred detail with the high valuation of individual experiences within the temple creates a certain dilemma for the Church organisation. Latter-day Saints live within a Church that is now highly standardised and bureaucratised. Alongside the regular Eucharistic Sunday services, all observant Latter-day Saints also spend two more hours each Sunday, as a rule, at age-appropriate Sunday Schools (for adults and children), as well as special group meetings for youth, for adult men and for women. Adult Sunday School is taken by lay teachers and follows a curriculum defined centrally by the Church. This curriculum involves the study of the books of the sacred scriptures[5] in rotation over a period of years. The Church has a central distribution centre for supplies in Salt Lake City and its own publishing arm, and prepares and distributes both teachers' and students' manuals for the study of the given text each year. The special group meetings for women, adult men, youth and children are also based on centrally published Church textbooks and sourcebooks.

One intention of this system is to unify the worldwide Church in one programme of worship, and to prevent the development of local 'un-orthodoxies'. One effect of it, often noted by members and others, is that the content and conduct of individual meetings may become overly routine. 'You ask someone a question in Sunday School class and everybody's expecting a certain answer, we all know the answer, so it becomes very fixed and repetitive.'[6]

The Church does now offer some instruction for those planning to enter the temple for the first time. Teenagers, who may be preparing for mission and marriage, and adults, especially converts, who may be going to the temple later in life, are both given some 'temple preparation'. Temple ritual itself is not discussed. Instead, preparation concentrates on the effects and values that it is designed to promote: on the Mormon ideal of eternal marriage, for example, or on the spiritual benefits of assisting with ritual work on behalf of the dead. S. Michael Wilcox is an instructor at the institute of religion at the University of Utah[7] and author of the book *House of Glory; finding personal meaning in the temple* (Wilcox 1995), which is published by the orthodox Latter-day Saints press, Deseret Book, and which is available in its bookstores. Wilcox and the distinguished LDS Church Authorities from whom he quotes are clearly aware of the problems experienced by many members on first taking part in temple ritual:

> Elder Widtsoe cautioned that it is not fair 'to pass opinion on temple worship after one day's participation followed by an absence of several years. The work should be repeated several times in quick succession, so that the lessons of the temple may be fastened upon the mind.' (Wilcox 1995: 42)

Elsewhere, Wilcox notes that the authorities understand that people, especially the 'inexperienced' (ibid., p.31), may be troubled by many questions about details of temple worship: 'Is this or that thing reasonable?' 'Why should I do this or that?' In theory, these are needless questions. In practice, Wilcox (again citing Widtsoe) suggests that it is better to answer them, although such specific answers may only be given to those who have been through the temple rituals together and only during discussion in the Celestial Room. Even experienced Saints, however, will not have all the answers, and it is recognised that certain things may trouble them: 'As we pray for understanding, we can be assured that everything in the temple is beautiful. "No jot, iota or tittle of the temple rites is otherwise than uplifting and sanctifying," wrote Elder James E. Talmage.' (Wilcox 1995: 32)

In the temple, Wilcox tells us, we need to be open to hear the messages of the Holy Spirit. In order to be most receptive, we should prepare by avoiding all contact with anything which might be offensive or unholy, and by reading the scriptures, which provide many parables and metaphors for the temple as, for example: the place of 'living waters' in which heaven and earth can truly be said to meet, and from which an inexhaustible revelation will flow. We also need to be prepared to understand that this precious knowledge will be communicated in unfamiliar ways, and especially through symbols.

Wilcox uses the standard example of the temple's Sealing Rooms[8] as an illustration of the symbolic. Sealing Rooms are quite small, with a central dais at which the bride and groom will kneel to be married. Two walls of the room, opposite each other, are mirrored so that both bride and groom can see endless reflections of themselves as a joined pair, receding on either side into infinity. Since the purpose of temple marriage is, precisely, to make their partnership permanent through time so that it will last beyond death (and is also understood to have been chosen in a pre-mortal existence, although we cannot develop this here), the double mirrors eloquently express the unique and extraordinary powers of the temple to translate between the constraints of this world and the possibilities of eternity. This, as Wilcox notes, is understood by Mormons to be an 'easy' symbol; 'everything in the temple can teach us' (Wilcox 1995: 25) but many of its symbols require a lifetime of interpretation, contemplation and prayer, or may remain forever beyond our mortal comprehension.

The Church, therefore, remains poised between two imperatives here. Wishing to guide, and perhaps even to define, the reactions of its members to the temple ritual, it nonetheless studiously avoids the explicit account of that ritual which would render it available as a tool for the point-by-point direction characteristic of Church guidance on many other religious matters. One of my Latter-day Saint informants, himself a university professor, offered an acute insight into the implications of this from his own experience:

> I was talking to [my students] just on Tuesday, I asked them the question: 'Why don't we talk about what goes on in the temple?'... Now there's a stock answer to that, which is?
>
> 'We're told not to?' [Fenella]
>
> Yeah, 'We're told not to,' and we say, 'Well it's sacred!' And I say, 'But my wife is sacred and I talk about her all the time, and all sorts of things are sacred that we talk about, but we don't talk about the temple, why not?' Well they have no answer to that. But ... my thought about that is, well suppose we did have a Sunday School class which two or three times a year had a routine lesson called 'The temple and what it means'; then we start learning a bunch of stock answers about what that means, and the temple experience becomes rigidified, ordinary, standardised, institutionalised and it dies. But what is the temple, to Mormons? It's very alive. Why? Because we go there and we don't have any particular meanings established for us already about what this means and what does ... we're thinking for ourselves, and my way of thinking is that it allows the Holy Spirit to touch each person in whatever ways he or she can be touched at the time. And so the temple becomes a living experience for us, and we go back and back and back and back, and every time we go we learn different things,

> it becomes a spiritual experience throughout life because it has not become institutionalised. In fact, that's the only place I can think of in the Church that's untouched by these 'sociologisation' processes, by the bureaucracy. We just have decided not to talk about the temple. … My experience is that the temple is clearly a spiritual experience, because you can't go there expecting anything in particular. There are no stock answers.

If the placing of the temple beyond 'stock answers' makes it a place of intense religious potential, however, it also makes it a location of risk. Mormons are well taught, and they know why they are supposed to visit the temple, in terms of the blessings that can be made available to others including the dead. They also know, however, that attending the temple is supposed to make *them* feel a certain way. In particular, in the temple one should feel calm, serene, be able to overcome anger and bitterness and feel a sense of Christian, or even a foretaste of celestial, love for others. In addition, they may hope for and expect, although not demand, to receive insights and revelations of the Holy Spirit into the meaning of the ritual itself and other important issues in their lives or the lives of people with whom they may be concerned.

People consciously measure their own experiences in the temple according to these criteria. One woman I know, for example, had a hard time visiting the temple after her husband, whose courtship and early married years with her had been closely associated with their active partnership in genealogical and temple work, left her in very painful and humiliating circumstances. She described how, years later, she had been through the temple with one of her own sons on his return home from mission. Sitting in the Celestial Room, they met a young woman who had broken off a relationship with her son, while he was away, together with the man she had married instead and her parents. The end of this relationship had been the cause of sadness and pain. Yet sitting in the Celestial Room, Patricia felt the healing of resentment, and a peaceful and accepting sense that everything would be all right; and she admired, in her son's courtesy to his former fiancée, a manifestation of the same spirit.

At other times, people may experience great anxiety about the gap between their own experiences and the ideal of temple experience. One friend of mine commented that her own temple wedding 'was one time when I felt exactly what I was meant to feel' in the temple, whereas at other times this had not been so. A widow explained that she had felt 'angry with God' when her husband died, and *particularly* in the temple, where for five long years she had hoped for intimations of comfort or revelation that were withheld from her, although she felt that they had been granted to others. And, as noted above, it is extremely common for people to feel an adverse reaction to their first experience of the endowment ritual, and to be left with a sense that the ceremony was simply 'weird'.

For practising Mormons, the recommended course of action for those not feeling the 'right' thing in the temple is simply to wait, pray, read the Scriptures and keep going back to the temple. For many people this counsel of patience is a sufficient one, and this is particularly so for that group of Latter-day Saints who describe themselves as most attracted by the 'practical' aspects of their Church. It is possible to be an observant Mormon who attends the Sunday meetings and carries out all their duties, and yet not to have a particularly developed interest in attending the temple frequently.

Although this strategy may serve for the medium or even, occasionally, the long term, my sense, however, is that it only works if it can be thought of as, ultimately, a *temporary* condition. The work of salvation carried out in temple ritual is so central to Mormonism that personal indifference or antipathy to temple ritual is very difficult to reconcile with it. One has to cling to a sense that, *eventually*, one might feel at least some of what is meant by the richness of temple experience.

If a person decides this is never going to happen, or if (as happens in some cases) some aspect of temple ritual, or some particular incident within a temple ceremony, strikes a profoundly negative chord with someone, one of two things is likely to happen. Either the person will blame themselves and become deeply impressed with a sense of their own spiritual worthlessness, or else they will begin to be alienated from the whole notion of the temple ritual as truth and its spiritual value. Sometimes one reaction gradually turns into the other. In any case, the person for whom temple ritual remains inaccessible as meaningful spiritual experience may well eventually leave the Church. Thus, during the course of my fieldwork, I met many people for whom a banal or traumatic experience in the temple was cited as a pivotal element in what one might call their 'departure' or 'de-conversion' narratives (although it is not the only reason for leaving the Church). Former Mormons of course vary greatly in their attitudes, some feeling bitter, others mocking, others being quite comfortable with their shift into secular life or into a different and more compatible religious community. But it was noticeable that, in many cases, the intense importance given to temple experience still lingered in the language of ex-Latter-day Saints, giving a note of wistfulness or remembered joy for those for whom it had been a positive experience, and a note of sorrow, anger and confusion for those for whom it had not. Seldom was the temple remembered indifferently. And of course, for excommunicates such as Margaret Toscano, a devout Mormon whose published interpretations of LDS theology in relation to women were censured by the Church, the temple becomes the place from which, above all, one is in exile (Toscano and Toscano 1990: 279–91).

Thus far, I have argued that Mormon temple ritual combines a notion of ritual efficacy that it would be difficult to overstate, with a focused attention on the importance of interior experience by those who perform the rituals. One way to look at this would be to think of Mormonism as an unusual, possibly unique, confluence of two traditions that are usually kept separate, at least in Christianity.[9] Mormonism is not a Protestant tradition, but it does have Protestant historical antecedents. One could argue that the Mormon attention to interiority is part of what Webb Keane (2007: ch.7) has described as the defining Protestant commitment to the idea of '*sincerity*' and its entanglements with rhetorical constructions of 'modernity'. That is, the relationship between personal experience, thought of as interior, and its outward or public expressions, including expressions in speech, is a matter for the utmost anxiety and conscious self-monitoring, in part because an insincere articulation of the self blocks, or impedes, the action of the Holy Spirit in the world.[10]

These kinds of Protestant tradition, however, are most usually associated, as in Puritanism, with an aversion to ritual, an aversion based on the fear that ritual itself may be 'insincere', in the sense of tending innately towards a deflection of attention away from God and towards the objects, officiants or formal actions involved in ritual, who may become the idolatrous recipients of worship in God's place. This latter equation in no sense describes Latter-day Saint attitudes to the physical world or to the right relations between man and Heavenly Father; although in the plain speaking and acting of the Mormon ward Sunday Sacrament service (where, as in some low Church Protestant traditions, even the Eucharistic wine is replaced by water, where there is no priest but only lay officiants, etc) one can see perhaps the legacy of this way of thinking. The Sacrament Service exists in Mormonism in relation to the temple ritual, and in the temple ritual, although there is still no clerical elite,[11] all the other elements regarded with the gravest suspicion by Puritans (including heavy formalisation, complex symbolism, the use of costume, prescribed arcane speech and movements, etc.) are markedly present and elaborated.

It is, of course, inadequate to cast Mormonism as a variant form of Protestantism. For Latter-day Saints it is a poor account because they understand the temple ritual to be an ancient form of practice known at the time of Solomon, given originally by God to Adam, and restored in direct revelation to their Prophet. For historians, theologians and sociologists, it is a poor account because neither the complex origins of Mormonism nor the nuances of its doctrine are sufficiently described in this way. However, for the purposes of this paper, the notion of the unusual juxtaposition of a central emphasis on ritual, with a heavy stress on sincerity, may have some value, seen perhaps in relation to the question of ritual efficacy.

It is usual to contrast Roman Catholic notions of ritual efficacy with Protestant ones.[12] For Catholics, the sacraments are efficacious if, and only if, they are administered by an ordained priest of the church. This efficacy is not, however, compromised by the personal worthiness or unworthiness of the priest as an individual, however much the Church might enjoin the priest to be worthy. Ritual efficacy, once properly created, functions according to God's promise, through the performance of the correct actions alone.

For Protestants, stereotypically, the situation is very different. Ritual efficacy of the Roman Catholic kind is dismissed as 'magical' or 'superstitious' precisely because it is considered too independent of questions of personal accountability. Eucharistic sacraments are understood to be symbolic, with the emphasis falling on the intention and state of mind of the believer at the moment that he or she takes the Eucharist.

For Latter-day Saints, neither of these situations obtains. Instead, one could say that the efficacy of temple ritual has a dual aspect. On the one hand, the efficacy of (say) baptism for the dead is covenantal. It follows from the divine promise of certain powers to Joseph Smith and his followers, once instituted within a restored (universal, lay[13]) 'priesthood'. I do not think that most Saints would argue that the access of a deceased soul to membership of the church was compromised because the individual performing a baptism had allowed his mind to wander to a football game or things even less pleasing to the Holy Spirit. On the other hand, most Latter-day Saints highly value individual intimations or spiritual signs that such baptisms and other endowments on behalf of deceased persons have been effective and well received. People working in the temple may feel the dead person's relief and happiness, or may even, on occasion, see the deceased as a spirit. This kind of receptiveness, which underlines and reinforces ritual efficacy, is certainly thought to be dependent on the worthiness and spiritual state of the person carrying out the ritual work. And most Saints are, in fact, very uneasy about the idea that they or other people might go through the temple in an inappropriate state of mind, or that their concentration on the ritual might falter. In addition, there is the other side of ritual efficacy that we have outlined above – the question of whether temple ritual has been effective *for the performer of it* in creating that spiritual experience which will permit him to remain a Mormon.

We could compare this distinctively Latter-day Saints attitude to what ritual experience is like, and should be like, to that of my other group of Christian informants, rural Catholics in Bicol.[14] For Bicolano Catholics, too, the *experience* of taking part in ritual is important; indeed, one could say that all ritual activity is approached as an arena of transformative, healing participation for both individuals and groups. In the area in which I lived, the central religious figure is a miraculous statue of Christ laid out in death, known in Bicol as the *Amang Hinulid*.[15] Local people think of Christ not as an abstract and general figure, but as this particular Christ, who is personally and intimately known to them, and who often appears in dreams or shows himself in miraculous encounters, and talks to ordinary people about the 'help' they need. Most ritual activity is undertaken as the result of such conversations, in which someone will offer to carry out a 'devotion' to the *Ama* in return for help received or anticipated, particularly the curing of one's own sickness, or that of a child or other relative. The form that 'devotions' take is varied, but may typically include Lenten activities such as the 'reading' of the Bicol-language text of the *Pasion* (the story of Christ's life and death) during an all-night vigil, or else participation in one of the *tanggal* or

Passion plays. During the *tanggal*, one promises to enact, or else to have someone else, such as one's child, enact, a particular figure in the Christian story; again, this usually involves an all-night vigil and is a demanding process.

Bicolanos understand all these rituals as forms of 'sharing' in the feelings of the religious figure who is addressed. In the *tanggal* this sharing is especially vivid since one literally 'imitates' the holy person, thus drawing very close to them and their experiences. The process is sometimes described in Bicol by the Spanish loan-term '*sacrificio*', but it is not a sacrifice that involves death or even (usually) bloodshed or wounding.[16] Instead, it is the sacrifice of offering one's labour, and of sharing the painful feelings suffered by Christian figures, especially through the experience and expression of 'pity' (*herak)* for their sorrows. This plays out within wider Bicol idioms of loyalty, support for others and identification with them, which are characteristic of social relations in non-ritual contexts, including kinship and politics. The result of this voluntary 'accompanying' of Christ, Mary and the other figures from the Christian drama is that the person feels that they have also shared in their strength. Not only do people very frequently say that the *Ama* is responsible for recovery from illness; they also say that when they complete a vigil or other devotion, they do not feel drained and over-tired, but, on the contrary, experience a lightness of both body and of mood, and are able to carry on with their ordinary daily tasks as well.

Now, this attitude to what ritual should feel like has many aspects, only one of which is its obvious link to a wider corpus of Southeast Asian ascetic practices outside the Philippines (cf. Cannell 1999: 137 ff.; Cannell, 2006b). But what is of special note for our argument here is that, although Bicolanos are very clear about what ritual participation is like, they do not, to the best of my understanding, feel anything like the degree of anxiety about that experience expressed by American Mormons in relation to the temple ritual. I witnessed, many times, vigils that in one way or another were felt not to have gone ideally well – where people stumbled over lines, got interrupted, fell asleep in the middle, made silly jokes, developed head-colds (despite the ritual's healing powers), or felt they hadn't offered the right food to their guests, for example. But although everyone recognised that some occasions passed off with more élan, and some with a little less, I never heard anyone worry that their *attitude* was wrong, or that this might compromise the success of the ritual.[17] One's attitude, it seems, was 'good enough' almost by virtue of one's very participation.

This comparison, briefly sketched though the Bicol material is, may be helpful. It seems to support the idea that Latter-day Saints' anxiety levels about how one feels in ritual may be partly conditioned by the history of ideas about 'sincerity' which have figured especially prominently in Protestant times and places. At the same time, we should not elide this insight with the idea that concepts of interiority, and the crucial relevance of interior experience, are only found in that context (or, indeed, in association with Western modernity, however defined). Bicolano 'sharing' is premised on the distinctively pan-Filipino and Southeast Asian idea of the self in social exchange, for which the Tagalog term *loob* (literally 'inside') is sometimes used as a generic. This concept is not derived from, although it has interacted with, the history of Christian conversion (for example cf. Cannell 1999; Rafael 1988; Ileto 1979). For Bicolanos, too, local ideas about what it feels like to take part in ritual are clearly expressed, and are thought to be absolutely germane to how ritual works.

HOW RITUAL MATTERS FOR ANTHROPOLOGISTS

If a 'Zafimaniry question' is one asked by ordinary people, but also one asked by anthropologists, it now seems high time to consider what anthropologists think matters in ritual.

Again, my approach here will necessarily be selective, although not arbitrary. My main example will be the theory of ritual in the work of Maurice Bloch. This brilliant work has been enormously influential in British anthropology, and internationally, since the 1970s, and generates many powerful readings of ethnographies in a wide range of locales. Despite its undoubted originality, however, it also in some ways typifies, and in others extends, certain ways of thinking about ritual and experience that can be found very widely in anthropology today, as well as in the work of important predecessors, including Evans-Pritchard. It therefore constitutes an instance of attitudes in the discipline more generally.

Bloch's theory of ritual is well known, and its general outlines will be suggested here only in brief. As far back as 1974, Maurice Bloch famously proposed that ritual should be understood as a special form of communication, linked to the maintenance of 'traditional authority' (Bloch 1974). What was special about ritual communication was not its richness, as many had argued, but, on the contrary, its semantic impoverishment. Ritual language was distinguished by the vagueness of its propositional content and, at the same time, by the impossibility of engaging with it, as one might in ordinary conversation, in such a way as to be able to falsify its messages. In subsequent work, Bloch has developed these insights in many directions, while always maintaining that the semantic rigidity and propositional generality of ritual statements were the key to its effectiveness. These vague and rigid messages would, in fact, always fall into a rather narrow range of types, the central trope of which is an opposition between 'ordinary life' and 'real life' in which the biological conditions of human existence are, through the progression of the ritual, compared to some notion of a life after death or outside ordinary biological conditions, which is represented in the ritual as ultimately more real and more valuable. Thus, in Merina circumcision ritual ordinary human sex and birth are represented as less important in the creation of the life of a little boy than the blessing (*tsodrano*) that comes from the Merina ancestral dead. Indeed, for the Merina, all real life comes from the blessings of the unchanging ancestors. Ritual knowledge is essentially 'mystifying', and stands apart from the everyday understandings that people may hold. In almost all cases, the hierarchical opposition between 'ordinary life' and 'real life' supports, and stands for, hierarchical social domination of some kind. These ritual antitheses will in fact 'do for any domination' (Bloch 1986: 191). This partly accounted for the conclusion he reached in his long-term historical study of Merina ritual, *From Blessing to Violence*, in which he demonstrated that the basic ritual logic of Merina circumcision remained unchanged through considerable political and economic transformations, including the development of the Merina state, the colonial takeover of Madagascar and the achieving of independence.

Bloch's theory of ritual largely avoids the discussion of participants' experience. One of the reasons for this is that, for Bloch, individual responses to ritual, however interesting and important to the individuals who feel them (and even to the ethnographer), cannot significantly alter its effects so long as rituals continue, in fact, to be performed. If a Merina person feels bored during a circumcision ritual, or if they disliked the person for whom a secondary funeral is being performed, or even if they personally doubt the reality of post-mortem existence, this individual state of mind, according to Bloch, will not actually vitiate the ideological effect of Merina ritual, which is to ascribe the source of real fertility to Merina ancestors. Bloch, and Bloch and Parry (1982), in their important general discussion of funerary rituals, do not consider that ritual can be effectively approached through the question of what people feel when they are performing it. Indeed, they are more inclined, like Hertz, to invert the question and to concentrate on those aspects of apparently 'private' feeling which can actually be shown to be socially constructed, such as conventions of mourning.

In its reticence about individual experience, Bloch's theory partakes of a long anthropological tradition, a tradition perhaps most famously formulated by Evans-Pritchard. Evans-Pritchard responded positively (as do Bloch and Parry) to Durkheim's presentation of ritual as social and collective representation, but he criticised Durkheim's formulation of the general emotion that supposedly arises in rituals to renew social life, the so-called '*conscience collective*'. For Evans-Pritchard, this was no better than a crude theory of 'crowd psychology' and implied that religion's origins lay in psychology when, for Evans-Pritchard, the origins of religion cannot be known. 'Only chaos would result,' he argued, 'were anthropologists to classify social phenomena by the emotions which are supposed to accompany them, for such emotional states, if present at all, must vary not only from individual to individual, but also in the same individual on different occasions and even at different points in the same rite' (Evans-Pritchard 1965: 44).

According to Talal Asad (1993: 72–4), this line of argument can, in fact, be traced back to Hocart and then onward from Evans-Pritchard, by diffusion, into the disciplinary mainstream. Asad reasons that this argument drew strength historically from 'the Gibbonian attitude towards "enthusiastic religion", the emotional Christianity of classes who might be difficult to govern, as opposed to the polite, orderly, ceremonial Christianity favoured by Enlightenment rules' (ibid., p.72).[18]

This association seems plausible, and points moreover to an elite *Protestant* inflection in anthropology above all. But neither Evans-Pritchard – himself a Catholic convert for whom religious (mystical) experience, although not the subject of social science, was nevertheless supremely real (Evans-Pritchard 1960; Engelke 2002) – nor Bloch, whose theory is robustly atheistic, directly analysed this point.

Bloch, nonetheless, takes this mistrust of the experiential in ritual in a highly distinctive direction that becomes central to his work. That is, he proposes a particular kind of understanding of ritual as false consciousness; and in so doing it is arguable that he again weaves into his theory certain strands of Christian and Judeo-Christian thinking which have not been fully acknowledged.

As indicated above, Bloch's theory of ritual builds (despite many wide-ranging comparative discussions in *Prey into Hunter* and elsewhere) very closely on his outstanding studies of the Merina of Madagascar. The Merina were, in fact, all converts to Protestant Christianity, while their former slaves became oppositional Roman Catholics. In various publications, Bloch provides fascinating analyses of the religious politics of Malagasy conversion, the ironies of missionisation, the strategic Christianity of the Merina royals, and the syncretism of slave Catholicism (e.g. Bloch 1994 [1971], 1986, 1994).

Despite these highly convincing accounts, however, the character of Merina Christianity itself remains very unclear.[19] For Bloch, the most important thing about Merina Protestantism is that it exists as, what he calls, 'an ancestral church' (1994 [1971]) That is, the local political structure based on 'demes' (endogamous land-holding descent groups) survived conversion to the extent that pastors are kin-group appointees, and churches are structured around the 'demes' and their group of Merina ancestors. The logic of Merina descent, in which ancestors are accepted as the source of life, continues unchanged in a nominally Christian polity. The rituals of kinship, such as circumcision, contain and perpetuate the real religious logic of the Merina. For Bloch, the relationship of the Merina towards the content of Protestantism, therefore, becomes a side-issue, and he says very little about it.[20] Yet the Merina did choose conversion, and they do encounter Protestant teachings and the Protestant idea of God, a figure who is placed in some kind of shadowy relationship to the ancestors.[21]

There is surely more to know about this than we presently know from Bloch. This lacuna in the account becomes more important because of the place of the transcendental in Bloch's theory of ritual, in which the transcendental is identified with the production of ideology (false consciousness). As I shall argue, the lack of detail on Merina Christianity makes it hard to tell whether Bloch's view of the transcendental is derived from Merina ancestral descent ideas, the influence of Protestantism on the Merina, or the indirect influence of Christian theology on Bloch himself.

For Marx, the key to mystification under capitalism is the alienation of labour, considered as that which animates the means of production. So much is familiar. For Bloch, the key to mystification outside capitalism's heartlands is the alienation not only of labour, but also of the means of *reproduction*, of human life itself (Bloch 1986: 177). The forms of symbolic oppositions that 'will do for any domination' rest, as we mentioned above, on constructing an antithesis between death and life, in which death is falsely presented in ritual as an image of real and lasting life (the unchanging ancestors and their blessing), and is made to appear superior to earthly life. This is why Bloch distrusts ritual and why he sees in it, always, 'a hatred of life'. 'The image created by descent,' Bloch tells us, 'is a fundamental negation of the experience of life, of movement, and of human creativity, which has no place in a world where everything is and nothing becomes' (1986: 169).[22]

This is a powerful repudiation of ritual's false promises of immortality, but what exactly is involved in it? In an astute article, David Gellner has pointed out that Bloch's theoretical model of (all) ritual seems to centre on the ritual of sacrifice (Gellner 1999). Gellner argues, further, that the model of sacrifice evoked is essentially a Judeo-Christian one, drawn ultimately from the Old Testament episode in which Abraham is told by God to sacrifice Isaac as a sign of his obedience. Gellner goes on to suggest that Bloch's theory applies best to political ritual, in which people around the world 'sacrifice freedom for the sake of order', as Bloch says of the Merina (Bloch 1986: 171), and may not well describe rituals whose purpose is 'soteriological', that is rituals which gloss cosmology or perform work for salvation (such as Buddhist prayer) and which may not contain any obvious violent or sacrificial element.

Although, for various reasons, I myself doubt that Gellner has made a fully convincing case on ritual typologies,[23] I am in agreement in finding it important to pay attention to the central position of sacrificial violence in Bloch's theory. Sacrificial violence, in this sense, buys social order at the price of the rejection, or even literal, physical destruction (as in circumcision) of some part of the human self.

Why is that element of violence necessary? Analytically, for Bloch, the violence is necessary because ritual tells a lie about social relations, a lie that is covered up by the forced and specious conclusiveness that ritual brings. But equally, the analytic origins of violence derive from the absolute difference, or distance, which Bloch sees between representations of a post-mortal, or eternal, life and mortal life. And this distance is really just a cover for the absolute and irreconcilable difference between the life of the body and the death of the body that is, in reality, final. In other words, the place of violence in Bloch's theory of ritual seems to rest on an invocation of an idea of the transcendent, in the sense of a perceived gap between human beings and the forces they address in religious activity, such as Merina ancestors. It is in this imagined gap, for Bloch, that ideology is generated; the self-deception that allows one to expect to be able to access an imagined transcendent power is coterminous with violence.

To say that Bloch's theory of ritual assumes and requires a notion of transcendence is, itself, a statement that may require some explanation, particularly because so many different meanings have been given to that term. What I mean by it here is that Bloch is incorporating a view of religion as a radical split between human and non-human powers that is, itself, a view which developed historically in Judeo-Christianity. We can probably trace this understanding back to Hegel ([1807] 1965) who had an indirect but immense impact on the foundational social sciences as well as philosophy. For Hegel, Christianity enacts a historical shift in sensibility compared to the religions of pagan Greece or Rome, in that the Christian God is understood to have gone 'beyond' humankind in space and time in such a way that man is radically separated from him; whereas in pagan religion, divinities were immanent, that is, were always in some sense present and accessible in the physical world. After Christianity, man suffers from the 'unhappy consciousness' of his distance from God, with whom he can only imagine being rejoined after the death of his own physical body. Thus transcendence becomes intimately associated with an ascetic, anti-physical thinking that elevates the things of the 'spirit' and devalues those of the 'body'.

Judaism is thought of as foreshadowing these shifts in many ways and its logics continue in historical Christianity. For this reason the story of Abraham and Isaac with its jealous father-God, its innocent son and its reluctantly filicidal human patriarch, has been the subject of innumerable commentaries and interpretations in this vein, and is sometimes interpreted as the moment in which God first goes 'beyond' the world of the Israelites. Interestingly, given Bloch's emphasis on political violence, it has also sometimes been seen as a moment that founds the social order and religion in Law and obedience.[24] Transcendence and its ascetic logics, that is, are modelled as intrinsically hierarchical.

For Bloch, however, it appears that transcendence (the source of sacrificial violence) is a feature of all religions, as they may be discussed through his theory of ritual. And here, as suggested above, we are left with a puzzle. Merina descent is the ethnographic origin of Bloch's theory. Apparently the Merina ancestors are a power who can be understood as transcendent, at least in the context of ritual, although this runs counter to the stereotypical contrast in anthropology between 'local religions' and 'world religions', especially the Abrahamic religions. Should we conclude with Bloch that 'transcendence' is a feature of all religious systems? It would be easier to argue for this position if we had the evidence to show conclusively that Merina ideas of descent had *not* been importantly inflected by the historical influence of Protestant notions of God – since the Protestant God is definitely conceived as a transcendent power.

The idea of 'transcendent' ancestors, of course, also runs counter to much respected African ethnography (e.g. Kopytoff 1968) which presents ancestors, rather, as immanent in the world and barely distinguishable from living elders.[25] Bloch has recently developed some of these lines of enquiry in work on the idea of 'deference' in ancestor worship, and he was kind enough to gloss this in a very helpful informal communication, as part of a discussion between us on how one should understand the term 'transcendence'. I quote from his response:

> The normal way of thinking about ancestors is not phenomenologically 'counter intuitive'; not because the nature of ancestors is not 'counter intuitive' (it is), but because the way life works is that we take the truth of what others will testify and seem to accept as normally true. This is 'deference', which I talk about in my paper on ritual. Deference obviates an examination of beliefs and therefore enables us to live on the knowledge of others, something called by some 'distributed cognition', and which is at the core of our nature as human beings and of social life.
>
> Deference is not usually a total, permanent stance and most people I know will have occasion to examine, more or less fully, what they accept as true on the testimony of others, and then, in the case of

> ancestors or God, the 'counter intuitive' element will come to the surface.
>
> There are however other occasions when the 'counter intuitive' must come to the fore, though in a different way, and that is when you want interactive communication with ancestors or God (to be cured, for example). Then you must make the 'counter intuitive' *central*, since the fact that you can't ask something of ancestors in the way that you can of your neighbour becomes painfully obvious.
>
> But since such communication is not just difficult but impossible, you obscure it by using non-discursive means of communication – which in fact makes the 'counter intuitive' all the more prominent, but in an emotional way. *This for me is 'the transcendental' ... a ready tool for ideology.*'[26]

'Transcendence', therefore, is seen as context specific but continues to define ritual's ideological functions.

The central difficulty with this formulation, for me, is that it incorporates and perpetuates what is, in fact, not only an inheritance from Christian theology, but a mistake about the character of that theology or, at the very least, an over-selective interpretation of it. I have said that 'transcendence', as here defined, is associated with a notion of a radical split between the spirit (represented as what may be reunited with God after death) and the body (represented as what must be discarded if a transcendent deity is to be reclaimed). Taken to extremes, this vision produces a radically ascetic version of Christianity, which punishes the body, and this vision of Christianity in fact dominates the popular imagination. Yet, as historians have shown time and time again (e.g. Brown 1981; Brown 1988; Bynum 1995), a totally, and solely, ascetic Christianity, either of doctrine or of practice, is a myth, since asceticism has only ever been one strand within Christianity.

In fact, Christianity, which rests on teachings about physical incarnation and bodily resurrection, can never be entirely anti-physical in character; rather, it turns on a recurring paradox. However, it has often been *misrepresented* as a purely ascetic religion and those misrepresentations have often become embedded in the social sciences (c.f. Cannell 2005, 2006a). In my view, the intentional embedding of a notion of violent transcendence hostile to physical human life at the heart of Bloch's universal theory of ritual reproduces this same misrepresentation.

Of course, the image of religious violence in Bloch's work is not simply derived either from Abrahamic sacrifice or from Merina ethnography. If anything, it is over-determined, being equally derived from a Marxism that is critical of religion as ideology. Yet is a straightforwardly materialist Marxism not an assimilation and inversion of the ascetic Christian paradigm? For doctrinal and orthodox Christianity, eternal life *is* the greater reality; for Marx, it is a tragic illusion. For ascetic Christianity, 'spirit' is what enables and signifies a greater truth about human life, while for Bloch it is the opposite; 'spirit' is an ideology, and 'matter', including the human body, is the great reality and a touchstone of truth. Both retain a dualistic hierarchy in which one term must be sacrificed for the other.

Yet Bloch's version of Marx is not the only possible version and perhaps, like the ascetic stereotype of Christianity, it leaves out something important. It is possible to argue that Bloch's theory adopts a Marx seen too much through Althusser, and therefore excludes some of Marx's own most humane insights. But there are other ways than Althusser's to think of Marx. For the philosopher Theodor W. Adorno, for example, materialism is not identified with perfect disenchantment.[27] In a remarkable and densely thought passage, Adorno asks how one is to enable any metaphysics 'After Auschwitz' which is not simply an act of bad faith. The conclusion he reaches is a surprising one: 'But nothing which does not promise something which transcends even life can be experienced as truly alive; no labour of the concept can escape from this' (2000 [1966]: 17).

This 'something', Adorno continues, both 'is' and 'is not'. Although any attempt to recover what is historically past – the relatively innocent hope for the meaningfulness of life and its culmination in a benevolent hereafter – is bankrupt, its bankruptcy is not an adequate stopping point for philosophy:

> the capacity to distance oneself from, and rise above, what one sees... It is not utterly implausible that the part which behaves in this way might be the immortal part of the self... If death is irrevocable, even the assertion of a meaning dissolved into the lustre of fragmentary but genuine experience is ideological. Hence at one of the central points of his work, Bergotte's death, Proust, against all *Lebensphiosophie* (philosophy of life), but also without sheltering

> beneath the positive religions, helped to give tentative expression to the hope for resurrection. The idea of a plenitude of life, even that promised by socialist conceptions of humanity, is thus not the utopia for which it mistakes itself, since such a plenitude cannot be separated from curiosity, from what *art nouveau* called living life to the full, a longing which has acts of coercion and subjugation written into it. (ibid., p.22)

Marx, after all, was fundamentally interested in human *creativity*, which is what interested him about human labour as the source of value. This interest in creativity itself suggests that Marx cannot be understood as a materialist in a literal, 'biologistic' or mechanistic fashion; indeed the former would be anachronistic for Marx's writings, while the latter would be a saddling of Marx with precisely the trickery which he exposes in capitalism as an ideology. For Marx, humans are creatures who can imagine things not yet in existence, and that is what makes them human. Despite its European ethnocentrism, this is the sense of Marx which Adorno's formulation echoes and carries forward. And this is, I think, an insight worth listening to for anthropologists who have, perhaps unwittingly, duplicated the mistake which Adorno here identifies, that of imagining that it is possible for a 'secular' and materialist social science to escape metaphysics. It is not possible but, perhaps, it is not even desirable. Nothing is truly alive if it does not contain the capacity to imagine something which transcends even life. So to characterise ritual as epitomising a 'hatred of life' is, at any rate, to describe only half the human thought and impulse that is contained there, self-deceiving though ritual may often be.

A final twist on this discussion of Bloch's theory is that – and given the intelligence of his approach this is hardly surprising – Bloch has, himself, at times noticed and commented on the importation of Christian vocabulary into anthropological theory. He quotes approvingly, for instance, de Heusch's critique of Evans-Pritchard's *Nuer religion* on this count (Bloch 1992: 24ff.; de Heusch 1985: 21–33; Evans-Pritchard 1956: chs.8, 9, 10). My own reading of Evans-Pritchard, as it happens, does not support de Heusch's criticisms,[28] but this is by the way. Bloch also comments explicitly on the Abraham and Isaac myth (1992: 28), and I do not wish to imply that his usage of it is naive; indeed, he deliberately combines it with elements of Detienne's (1989) alternate paradigm of

Greek sacrifice as commensality to create a new model. But this new model nevertheless reproduces the essential elements of violence, sacrifice and transcendence that we have discussed above.

In my view, the idea that the 'secular' sciences ever completely separated themselves from the inheritance of Christian theology is a misconception. As John Milbank (1990), among others, has argued, the 'secular' itself is only an imagined category. The more anthropology attempts to purify itself of its complex theological inheritance, the more likely it is to find that the repressed has returned in some form or another.

Of course, to note resemblances and even derivations is not the same as showing that a theory is wrong. Bloch may be right that Abrahamic sacrifice represents one variation on a universal religious theme. But on the other hand, there may be paradigms of sacrifice in the ethnography that are less readily assimilated to this model, because they do not make death central to their logic. Lambek's ethnography of Sakalava sacrifice as the productive labour of women in childbirth (this volume) points in this direction, as may my own ethnography of Bicol religious labour sketched above. My suggestion is not that we should abandon general comparative enquiry, but rather that the tendency in theoretical anthropology to force a choice between 'true' materialism and 'false' metaphysics may replicate aspects of ascetic theology through inversion, and thus lead us into accounts of human life which are less true than an acceptance of the paradoxical aspects of human experience.

RITUAL AND THE 'ZAFIMANIRY QUESTION'.

I began this paper by describing two contrasting ethnographic situations in order to say what American Mormons and Bicolano rural Catholics think matters about ritual. Without being in any way indifferent to ritual's declared objectives, I argued that each group in different ways explicitly claims that what also matters about ritual is the experience of participating in it. For Mormons, the experience of temple ritual is vitally important; indeed it is formative in what makes and keeps them in the LDS church. For Bicolanos, although the experience of ritual is not subject to the same self-conscious anxiety, ritual is still thought of as *made through* the experience of those taking part in it as they are 'sharing' the feelings of Christ, Mary and other religious figures.

In addition, I argued that some American Latter-day Saints are explicit about experiencing the temple as the space of greatest intellectual, spiritual and emotional creativity within a church that, even for its supporters, is recognised as being at times over-bureaucratised. This creativity of thought within the temple is experienced by many people who continue to be believers; but it is also experienced by people who go on to become excommunicates. These excommunicates from the LDS church may continue to retain a strong Mormon faith in exile, or they may become atheists, agnostics or members of other churches. They therefore represent a spectrum of those who (from a standard Marxist-materialist point of view), though in opposition to the church as an institution, continue to inhabit the 'false consciousness' of a religious worldview, to those who, from the same point of view, have liberated themselves or been liberated from it. But in either case, they have done their thinking inside the space of the temple and its rituals. I argued that, in fact, it is the very 'unspeakability' of temple ritual which keeps this space for thinking open despite the extreme formalisation (or what Bloch calls the vagueness and rigidity) of the actual ceremonies there performed. Combined with the strong valuation of individual religious experience in Mormonism, this creates interestingly unpredictable outcomes, rather than the homogenisation that might be expected.

I understand my ethnography to represent indigenous theories of what matters in ritual. The fact that both these theories place a high importance on *experience* as a constitutive aspect of ritual is probably closely connected to the particular histories of Christian thought which they individually represent (although, as we saw, Bicolano notions of interiority are not solely produced by Christianity).

I then set these indigenous theories of experience and ritual alongside one strong tradition in theoretical anthropology, taking as examples the Catholic convert Evans-Pritchard and the atheist Maurice Bloch. I argued that, despite the differences in their personal orientation to religion, these two authors share an understanding that the theory of ritual cannot be based on the experience of those who participate in it, and that this claim itself is probably inherited from a Protestant Enlightenment strand in thought about religion.

Evans-Pritchard had a complex attitude to religious experience. Usually, he tried to keep his personal belief separate from his sociological enquiries; he did, however, observe how the religious experiences of local people may possibly be better conveyed by anthropologists who have some feeling for such experience than by what he called the religiously tone-deaf. As Engelke observes, he sometimes 'wanted to call into question, if only momentarily, the sway of Durkheim's atheism' (Engelke 2002: 6). Other anthropologist-believers, such as Victor Turner (1962) and, more explicitly, Edith Turner (1992), both Catholic converts, have also attempted to create sociological accounts which would leave open a space for the possibility of the reality of religious truth, as they themselves, as well as their informants, might apprehend it.

This piece is not written from the viewpoint of a practising Christian. I do, however, want to express a certain scepticism about the link between anthropology and atheism which, it seems to me, may have unintended consequences in theory, even when, as with Bloch's work, it is at its most brilliant and suggestive. At the least, we might ask what a theory which excludes the relevance of experience to ritual can tell us about places and times where people explicitly express the centrality of experience to ritual? And, if Mormon and Bicolano narratives are the ideological productions of distinct strands of Christian history, we might also ask in what ways, and to what degree, they differ from some of the theoretical paradigms we use to examine them.

ACKNOWLEDGMENTS

Earlier versions of this paper were presented at two very stimulating 'Zafimaniry anthropology' workshops held at the London School of Economics in June 2005 and January 2006. I would like to thank Catherine Allerton, Maurice Bloch, Paola Filippucci, Simon Jarvis, Michael Lambek, Jonathan Parry and Danilyn Rutherford, each of whom has provided valuable comments on the argument of the paper at different stages. The British ESRC funded my U.S. fieldwork.

NOTES

1. Temple recommends are granted only to adult church members after an interview in which the bishop will check that the member is adhering to the church's moral standards and beliefs and is paying his tithes.
2. Conversely, Latter-day Saints' living rooms often carry nuances of the temple.

3. Some hostile critics even suggest that some form of sensational or criminal activity is involved in the ceremony; this is quite false.
4. The Church, under the current President (and, for the Saints, Living Prophet) Gordon B. Hinckley, is supporting a worldwide expansion of temple building. At present, converts in locations where the church is less established (as in much of Africa) may live thousands of miles from the nearest temple and may visit it only once in a lifetime, or never. For those in the States with easy local access, the church encourages visits once a month, or even more often.
5. Including the Old and New Testaments in editions that are variants of the King James Bible, as well as the additional scriptures given by revelation during the lifetime of Joseph Smith: the Book of Mormon, Doctrine and Covenants, and the Pearl of Great Price.
6. Of course, wards vary and some meetings are much more individual than others. Many commentators have linked the current trend to what O. Kendall White has called 'Neo-orthodoxy' in the Church leadership (White 1987) with a general caution, or even fear, among some Church members about saying anything of which the Church hierarchy might disapprove. I recall one of our Sunday School teachers reading us out a note from his instructors' manual on a famous subject in Latter-day Saints folklore (The Three Neophytes) which said simply 'Discourage Speculation'.
7. Although it is difficult to generalise, the University of Utah is itself regarded as more liberal in stance than Brigham Young University in Provo, which is attended by many Latter-day Saints.
8. Guides at the Boston Temple Open House, which I was fortunate enough to attend in 2000, did the same.
9. I am indebted to Maurice Bloch for this summation of the situation.
10. The Quaker view in which ideally a minister should *only* speak 'in the light' (that is, with the direct prompting of the Holy Spirit) seems to be one logical extreme of this configuration as Keane describes it. Cf. Bauman (1983).
11. Looked at another way, all adult Mormons, or at least all men, are members of the priestly elite.
12. This contrast is, at best, a stereotype, and may have arisen only following the Counter-Reformation.
13. Universal, that is, among adults who have received their endowments. I leave aside here the intensely disputed problem of whether or not Mormon women have a right to the priesthood that is equal to and/or similar in kind to that of men.

14. For the sake of brevity, I refer here only to rituals explicitly addressed to the local Catholic Christ; however, the logic of spirit medium-ship and healing in Bicol is intimately linked to this (cf. Cannell 1999: esp. part II).
15. Literally 'Father who is laid out' (i.e. in death). This kind of image of Christ is known in Spain as the *Santo Entierro*; however, European relations to this figure are differently configured.
16. For a sceptical reading of models of sacrifice premised on the forfeit of a life to the gods cf. Ruel (1990). For a highly suggestive alternative reading of a model of sacrifice based on effort such as the work of childbirth (the production of a new life ideally without the loss of she who produces) cf. Lambek (this volume).
17. People did sometimes comment that particular individuals would do well to listen to the moral messages of the *Pasion*, but they were usually speaking of people not actually taking part, such as errant bachelors.
18. Asad's main target here is primarily the American tradition of symbolic anthropology that he identifies with Geertz. His treatment of Bloch (1990: 132) does not do the theory justice, and nor can the claim that symbolic anthropology does not deal with power be rightly levelled at Bloch.
19. Partly because, as he candidly explains, he felt for some years that most other topics were more interesting than Christianity.
20. He has suggested recently that the Old Testament patriarchs stressed by the largely low-church missionaries may have appealed to the Merina taste (personal communication).
21. Compare for instance Green's (2003) account of Pogoro Catholicism, which is highly specific about how the Pogoro assign demarcated roles to the ancestors and the priest. Green was, of course, a student of Bloch.
22. So marked is this distrust of descent ideology, that at times it almost seems that Bloch thinks it is worse than capitalism, e.g. 'The creativity that is devalued and then fetishised in capitalism is only the creativity of labour, whereas among the Merina labour *and* human reproduction are merged. This is a difference between the ideology of capitalist and non-capitalist systems' (1986: 177).
23. Gellner is not alone in having pointed to rituals that do not seem to fit Bloch's model of violence and social order. It is difficult to weigh his views against Bloch's, however, since Bloch's response would be that apparently 'soteriological' rituals are usually simply one element in a longer sequence which contain violent elements elsewhere, or at a delay of time, or latent within them (cf. Bloch 1992: passim). The argument therefore revolves around what is the right unit of analysis. Moreover, both authors appear at times to reduce all aspects of religion to ritual.

24. Lukes (1973) intriguingly suggests that one of the few discernible influences of Durkheim's Jewish background on his social theory is his emphasis on society (and so also religion) as founded in law.
25. A possible confusion here arises in relation to Bloch's support for Kopytoff's (1968) suggestion that African ancestors are *not* thought of as different in kind to living elders. In 'Are religious beliefs counter-intuitive?' (Bloch 2000) Bloch argues against Boyer's account of religious ideas as defined by their 'counter-intuitive' character by showing that Malagasy people also generally think of their ancestors as normal agentive presences. Bloch explains the fact that the actions of dead ancestors among living people may be experienced as normal (although seemingly 'counter-intuitive' by Boyer's criteria) through the workings of 'deference'; understood as a cognitive tendency of human beings to save time by accepting information from trusted and authoritative others unless there seems to be a reason not to do so. Ancestors for Bloch are phenomenologically 'normal' most of the time and are considered as being 'in the world' with the living; thus, we could say, as being immanent. However, within ritual – the arena in which ancestors are called upon to act – this shifts, and what we have been calling the 'transcendent' character ascribed to Malagasy ancestors in Bloch's writing again emerges. When the living call upon dead ancestors, it becomes painfully clear that the dead cannot answer in the same way as the living. As the personal communication quoted from Bloch below shows, for Bloch this means that transcendence is a 'ready tool for ideology' since it is in this context that the living may deny, through ritual, the facts of mortality which otherwise would be staring them in the face.
26. Maurice Bloch, personal communication, 23 September 2004 (punctuation and emphasis are mine).
27. On Adorno's modified agnosticism, cf. Jarvis (1998).
28. Since it seems to me that Evans-Pritchard, although he uses the *terms* 'sin', 'expiation', etc. borrowed from Catholicism as de Heusch claims, does not mislead the reader in the way that de Heusch implies. Rather, Evans-Pritchard's usage is one which explicitly and consciously *contrasts* Nuer meanings with these more familiar terms (cf. for example Evans-Pritchard 1956: 177, 194 and passim). I take this to be part of what Evans-Pritchard meant when he said that the Nuer taught him more than anyone else about (his own faith in) God (Engelke 2002).

REFERENCES

Adorno, T.W. 1996. 'Meditations on metaphysics', *Negative dialektik*, Frankfurt am Main: Suhrkamp. Unpublished translation by Simon Jarvis.

Asad, T. 1993. *Genealogies of religion: discipline and reasons of power in Christianity and Islam*, Baltimore: Johns Hopkins University Press.

Bauman, R. 1983. *Let your words be few; the symbolism of speaking and silence among seventeenth-century Quakers*, Cambridge: Cambridge University Press.

Bloch, M. 1974. 'Symbol, song and dance and features of articulation: or is religion an extreme form of traditional authority?', *Archives Européennes de Sociologie* 15: 55–81.

—— 1982. *Death and the regeneration of life*, M. Bloch and J. Parry (eds), Cambridge: Cambridge University Press.

—— 1986. *From Blessing to violence: history and ideology in the circumcision ritual of the Merina of Madagascar*, Cambridge: Cambridge University Press.

—— 1992. *Prey into hunter; the politics of religious experience*, The Lewis Henry Morgan Lectures (1984), Cambridge: Cambridge University Press.

—— 1994 (1971). *Placing the dead: tombs, ancestral villages and kinship organization in Madagascar*, Prospect Heights, Illinois: Waveland Press.

—— 1994. 'The slaves, the king and Mary in the slums of Antanamarivo', in N. Thomas and C. Humphrey (eds), *Shamanism, history and the state*, Ann Arbor: University of Michigan Press.

—— 2002. 'Are religious beliefs counter-intuitive?', in N. Frankenberry (ed.), *Radical interpretation in religion*, Cambridge and New York: Cambridge University Press.

—— 2005. 'Where did anthropology go? Or the need for human nature', in *Essays on cultural transmission*, Oxford: Berg.

Brown, P. 1981. *The cult of the saints: its rise and function in Latin Christianity*, London: S.C.M. Press.

—— 1988. *The body and society: men, women and sexual renunciation in early Christianity*, New York: Columbia University Press.

Bynum, C.W. 1995. *The resurrection of the body in Western Christianity, 200–1336*, New York: Columbia University Press.

Cameron, A. 1991. *Christianity and the rhetoric of empire; the development of Christian rhetoric*, Berkeley: University of California Press.

Cannell, F. 1999. *Power and intimacy in the Christian Philippines*, Cambridge: Cambridge University Press.

—— 2005a. 'Immaterial culture: "idolatry" in the lowland Philippines', in K.M. George and A.C. Wilford (eds), *Spirited politics: religion and politics in Southeast Asia*, Ithaca, NY: Cornell Southeast Asia Program Publications.

—— 2005b. 'The Christianity of anthropology', *Journal of the Royal Anthropological Institute* 11(2): 28–44.

—— 2006a. 'Introduction', in F. Cannell (ed.), *The Christianity of Anthropology*, Durham, NC: Duke University Press.

—— 2006b. 'Reading as gift and writing as theft', in F. Cannell (ed.), *The Christianity of anthropology*, Durham, NC: Duke University Press.

—— n.d. 'The importance of heresy for anthropology'. Paper presented (in absentia) at the American Anthropological Association, December 2005. Presentation for the panel: 'Christianity and/in anthropological thought: historical questions, contemporary dilemmas and future prospects'. Organisers: K. O' Neill and W. Garriott

Csordas, T. 1995. 'Oxymorons and short-circuits in the re-enchantment of the world; the case of the Catholic charismatic renewal', *Etnofoor* 8: 5–26.

Davies, D.J. 2000. *The Mormon culture of salvation*, Hants: Ashgate.

De Heusch, L. 1985. *Sacrifice in Africa; a structuralist approach*, Bloomington: Indiana University Press.

Detienne, M. and J-P. Vernant, 1989. *The cuisine of sacrifice among the Greeks*, Chicago: University Press. (Translation of *La cuisine de sacrifice en pays Grec*.)

Engelke, M. 2002. 'The problem of belief: Evans-Pritchard and Victor Turner on "the inner life"', *Anthropology Today* 18(6): 33–8.

Evans-Pritchard, E.E. 1960. 'Religion and the anthropologists', The Aquinas Lecture (1959), *Blackfriars*. Reprinted in *Essays in social anthropology* (1962), London: Faber and Faber.

—— 1965. *Essays in primitive religion*, Oxford: University Press.

—— 1970 (1956). *Nuer religion*, Oxford: Clarendon Press.

Frankenberry, N.K. and H.H. Penner. 1999. 'Clifford Geertz's long-lasting moods, motivations and metaphysical conceptions', *Journal of Religion* 79: 617–40.

Geertz, C. 1973 (1966). 'Religion as a cultural system', in *The interpretation of cultures: selected essays*, New York: Basic Books.

Gellner, D. 1999. 'Religion, politics and ritual'. Remarks on Geertz and Bloch, *Social Anthropology* 7(2): 135–53.

Green, M. 2003. *Priests, witches and power; popular Christianity after mission in Southern Tanzania*, Cambridge: Cambridge University Press.

Hegel, G.W.F. 1975 (1807). 'The spirit of Christianity and its fate', in T.M. Knox (trans.), *Early theological writings*, Philadelphia: University of Pennsylvania Press.

Hubert and Mauss 1968 (1899). 'Essai sur la nature et la fonction du sacrifice'. Reprinted in M. Mauss, *Oeuvres* vol. 1 'Les fonctions sociales du sacré', Paris.

Ileto, R.C. 1979. *Pasyon and revolution: popular movements in the Philippines, 1840–1910*, Quezon City: Ateneo de Manila University Press.

Jarvis, S.P. 1998. *Adorno: a critical introduction*, Oxford: Polity Press.
—— 2000. '"Old idolatry"; rethinking ideology and materialism', in M. Rossington and A. Whitehead (eds), *Between the psyche and the polis*, Aldershot: Ashgate.
Keane, W. 2007. *Christian Moderns: Freedom and fetish in the mission encounter*, Berkeley: University of California Press.
Kopytoff, I. 1968. 'Ancestors as elders in Africa', in Grinker and Steiner (eds), *Perspectives on Africa* (1997).
Lukes, S. 1973. *Emile Durkheim, his life and work. A historical and critical study*, London: Allen Lane.
Milbank, J. 1990. *Theology and social theory; beyond secular reason*, Oxford: Basil Blackwell.
Pouillon, J. 1982. 'Essay on the verb "to believe"', in M. Izard and P. Smith (eds), *Between belief and transgression*, Chicago: University of Chicago Press.
Rafael, V.L. 1988. *Contracting colonialism, translation and Christian conversion in Tagalog society under early Spanish rule*, Quezon City: Ateneo de Manila University Press.
Robbins, J. 2003. 'The anthropology of Christianity', *Religion* special issue 33(3).
Ruel, M. 1982. 'Christians as believers', in J. Davis (ed.), *Religious organization and religious experience*, London: Academic Press. Reprinted in M. Lambek (ed.), *A reader in the anthropology of religion*, Oxford: Blackwell (2002).
—— 1990. 'Non-sacrificial ritual killing', *Man* 25(2): 323–35.
Sahlins, M. 1996. 'The sadness of sweetness: the native anthropology of Western cosmology', *Current Anthropology* 37: 395–428.
Toscano, M. and P. 1990. *Strangers in paradox: explorations in Mormon theology*, Salt Lake City: Signature Books.
Turner, E. 1992. *Experiencing ritual: A new interpretation of African healing*, Philadelphia: University of Philadelphia Press.
Turner, V. 1962. *Chihamba, the white spirit*, Manchester: Manchester University Press for the Rhodes-Livingstone Institute.
White, O.K. Jr 1987. *Mormon neo-orthodoxy: a crisis theology*, Utah: Signature Books.
Wilcox, S.M. 1995. *House of glory: finding personal meaning in the temple*, Salt Lake City: Deseret Book.

CHAPTER 6

WHAT MAKES PEOPLE WORK?

Olivia Harris

What makes people work? The straightforward answer is in order to live. Such a pragmatic and materialist response seems transparent in the context of Western social and economic theory; and yet I believe this would not be the answer offered by the Andean peasants whose lives I have studied. At the very least, if it were possible to phrase the question meaningfully in the Aymara language, they would be more likely to respond that they work in order to live well, or that it is in the nature of human beings to work, that God has endowed them with the faculty to work, and that if they did not, they would be less than human; work is an affirmation of human personhood, and of the community to which they belong. My argument in this chapter is that the question of what makes people work is a central feature of the way that human existence is understood within different cultural and historical repertoires and, following Graeber, that a satisfactory understanding of the nature of work requires a broader understanding of value (Graeber 2001).

The question perhaps has particular salience in Western thought which reveals a deep ambivalence in the value accorded to work. From many perspectives work has a negative value. As John Burnett writes of nineteenth-century British working-class people: 'For most, work was taken as given, like life itself, to be endured rather than enjoyed' (1974:15), while the 'leisure class' identified themselves precisely through their ability to live without working. For them, work was an attribute of the poor.[1]

This negative evaluation is clear in ancient Greek ideas. Aristotle for example argues in *The politics*: 'Those who are to be citizens must not be agricultural workers, for they must have leisure to develop their virtue, and for the activities of a citizen' (Aristotle 1992: 1329a, 1). The only way to master necessity was to own slaves, who were not fully human because they were subject to necessity rather than masters of it. Peasants were also servile because they, too, were subject to necessity (Arendt 1958: 83–4), and while craft work was not in itself considered degrading as an activity, it came to be seen as contemptible because of the ties of dependence, which arise when people do not consume what they themselves produce (and therefore depend on others for their livelihood), and also because of the growth of slavery (Mossé 1969: 27–9). In the lapidary statement of Vernant: 'for Plato, work is unconnected to any human value, and from some perspectives work appeared to him as the antithesis of the essential core of what it is to be human'[2] (Vernant 1965 [II]: 12).

According to this philosophical tradition, at the heart of human existence is the quest for freedom and the high value accorded to it. People only work if they have to ('necessity'), and compulsion is often seen as originating outside the individual worker, hence the recurrent imagery of slavery. A similar attitude of disdain towards work was found among the early Church fathers – for example in St Augustine's view that the contemplative life was the highest that a man could aspire to. At the same time, an alternative current within Christian theology understood work as a spiritual value, as a means of expiating humanity's inherent sinfulness (Le Goff 1980) and of avoiding temptation. Thus, the sixth-century rules of the Benedictine monastic order proclaimed that 'idleness is the enemy of the soul'. Here the ethical value of hard work is essentially a negative one, a means of mitigating the sinful nature of humanity. Hard work is not seen as a good in itself.

According to this perspective, work was a means of emancipation not only from sin but also from servitude if it was performed 'freely'. Christian missionaries were committed to preaching the redeeming value of work to those who did not understand it, or for whom nature discouraged the proper habits of industry. In a particularly chilling example concerning the early efforts of the London Missionary Society in Tahiti, a missionary who had formerly been a slave overseer in Jamaica arrived to establish a similar sugar industry on the island of Moorea at the beginning of the nineteenth century, but found that the natives were unwilling. Considering that 'a too bountiful nature on Moorea diminishes men's natural desire to work', he ordered all bread fruit trees to be cut down in order to compel them (Lewis 1988: 4).[3]

Where they encountered powerful civilisations, with subject populations well used to hard work, the response of missionaries and colonial ideologues was more ambivalent. For example, the Inka state, which dominated the central Andean region from what is today northern Ecuador to central Chile, astonished and impressed the first generations of Spanish who encountered it in the sixteenth century. So civilised were its inhabitants, their customs similar to those of the Christians in so many respects, that some believed that Saint Thomas must have evangelised them centuries earlier. Contradictory positions are to be found in the sixteenth-century historical record, in the writings of Spanish priests and administrators. How did the former Inka state come to be so wealthy, so prosperous, if not by enslaving its subject populations? What made the Indians work so hard? How to make them work harder? How to force them to work in the mines while at the same time proclaiming the Christian doctrine of free labour?

In the very different circumstances of late-twentieth-century rural Bolivia, comparable ambiguities were expressed concerning the life of the peasants. On the one hand they were seen as 'poor', 'ignorant', innocent; but on the other as fortunate in the security of their land, and, therefore, as having a duty to share with townspeople who had little or no land. They were admired for their strong communal ethic, but at the same time derided for their lack of entrepreneurship. Above all, the expanding discourse of development classified them as hardworking but poor, as people whose labour was insufficient to satisfy the needs they had, or were supposed to have.

'FIELDWORK'

The work ethic is central to the anthropological enterprise in a particular way, derived from nineteenth-century fieldwork of natural history (Gupta and Ferguson 1997). The practice, and the ethic, of fieldwork has been retained even though, increasingly in the twenty-first century, anthropological research is located not in 'fields' but in city streets or bureaucratic institutions. I first went to 'the field' in the early 1970s, living in a rural community of the Laymi *ayllu* in the Andean highlands of Northern Potosí (Bolivia).[4] When people saw me writing in my notebook, they would ask me what I was doing. The puzzlement on their faces was patent when I responded saying that I was working. The word I used (*tarwajkta*) was a loan from the Spanish *trabajo*, which I often heard used by local Aymara-speakers, and it took me some time to realise that it meant something different.

My question of anthropology focuses on the nature of work, because it touches on a fundamental aspect of what it means to be human, and also because it encapsulates an important aspect of the encounter between anthropologists and those they study. In the rural Andes I was confronted by a variety of expectations and values about work that in different ways I have been trying to understand ever since.

For me 'fieldwork' tends to be 24/7, in spite of Maurice Bloch's sage advice to close the door from time to time and read a Jane Austen novel. Living in a peasant community where people mostly wore clothes they had made from the cloth they had woven from the wool they had shorn from their own flocks, where they lived in houses they had built from the earth bricks (*adobe*) that they had produced, thatched with the straw they had gathered, where they ate the food they had sown and harvested, I experienced the feeling of encountering a place that corresponded to European myths of a pre-modern utopia, and at the same time an undeniable sense of unease at the fact that my student grant permitted me to buy my food, clothes and sleeping bag, and also to own status symbols such as a watch, a tape-recorder and a camera. Hence my need to explain that I was working when I was sitting at home. Informed by the theories that equated intellectual and manual labour, I naively assumed the interchangeability of all forms of 'work'.

As I spent time in the community, I gradually learned more appropriate responses, and also their strategic value as ways of heading off inquisitive questions as to exactly where I was going, and who I was planning to spend the day with, just as everyone else did. On meeting or passing anyone at any time of day a brief formal greeting must be exchanged. If you pause to chat for a moment you ask 'What are you doing?' or 'Where are you going?'

To this enquiry there are a number of ways of responding, the most general in spatial terms: for example, I'm going up the mountainside, to my fields, to the river, staying here, staying at home. This genre of responses, importantly, does not specify an activity, even though there is always some kind of goal in going to or staying in a particular place. It is, among other things, a recognition that many kinds of activity take place throughout the day: working, yes, in the sense of expenditure of energy to produce food or care for the livestock, but also chatting, playing, flirting, singing and so forth.

However, some activities that involve a special commitment of energy, time and concentration are linguistically marked. One of the most important is ploughing, usually with a team of two bulls pulling a simple wooden plough, to open up the ground in March/April before it gets too hard with the winter frosts, so it can be sown in September. The first ploughing for the Laymis is the quintessentially male activity, although women may guide the plough when furrows are prepared for sowing, an altogether less arduous activity. When I would ask women what qualities they admired in a man and what they looked for in a husband, they would almost always respond 'one that goes out to plough'. This may seem obvious. Not only was agriculture the basis of their livelihood, but the analogies between ploughing and copulation are widely recognised, and were reinforced in this case by the fact that when I asked men what quality they looked for and most admired in women, they usually responded by referring to the way a woman would prepare a delicious meal to take out to the man who is ploughing in the fields.

The uniformity with which people responded in this way indicates that these are the quintessential activities of the married couple that forms the basis of the household: the man ploughs and the woman feeds. At the same time this division of labour is an act of seduction, metaphorically if not also literally. It is interesting that the Spanish loan-word *wapu* (*guapo*) is used approvingly of men's as well as women's energy, their capacity for hard work especially in those activities proper to their gender. In Spanish *guapo* means pretty, or sexy. In the Aymara of Northern Potosí the sexual connotations are also there but they are expressed as appreciation of a person's vitality in work.[5] People of either sex who are thought to be lazy (*jayra*) find it hard to find a spouse.

At the same time some work – including ploughing – is tough and hard (*ch'ama*), and endurance is at the heart of personhood and human virtue. The word *ch'ama* refers equally to the toughness and strength of the person, and to the difficulty they encounter. This is particularly clear in the case of the work that makes the earth fruitful, labour that is especially fraught in a high mountain environment. In the rituals associated with the sowing season, young men sometimes impersonate the team of ploughing bulls, harnessed to the heavy wooden plough which is decorated with willow fronds (*molle*) and driven across the fields, and whenever men drink together they roar and cry out that they are the bulls of the hamlet. The imagery of bulls is central to the understanding of male work.

Bulls (a Spanish import) seem to occupy the same semantic space as the feline serpent – *amaru* or *katari* – of Andean mythology, which was closely associated with the torrential rains and swollen rivers of the Andean summer (Zuidema 1985; Harris 1994). Men become bulls in ritual, when they fight and when they plough, in a kind of mimesis of the dangerous but potent mountainous landscape, which is the source of the meteorological forces that make life possible, but that can also destroy it. Bulls and ploughing are the supreme human manifestation of the cosmic energy that both revitalises and threatens, closely linked to the power of the ancestors which causes the crops to grow.

While the direct complement of a man's ploughing is the delicious food prepared by his wife, cooking is not described as *ch'ama*. The context in which I have most frequently heard women use the term is to evoke the toughness of rearing and bearing children. There is, however, no close semantic association between ploughing and childbirth that is found in some European languages (notably through the term *labour*). Childbirth in Andean languages is illness, pain (*usuña*), a disequilibrium in the normal functioning of the body, or it may be seen in terms of metaphors of war (Arnold and Yapita 1999; Platt 2001). Rural women see their increasing numbers of children – what has been described as the process of 'maternalisation' that has resulted from the decline in their productive activities in recent years (for example as more items of clothing are acquired through the global used-clothing trade) – as an increased burden, more *ch'ama* (Arnold and Yapita 1996).

I eventually understood that the generic term for work in Spanish (*trabajo*) in Aymara refers exclusively to ploughing, not surprisingly, given the high value attached to this form of work. The appropriate response to questions about what I was doing which I then learned, when I was sitting in the sun with my notebook on my knees, or perhaps indoors reading or writing with the radio on, was not that I was working, but 'doing papers' (*papil lurkta*).[6] Anthropologists have often noted the absence of generic terms for work, and the same was true in the regional Aymara. This is hardly surprising since work as an abstract category arises in particular kinds of economy. The task, then, is to understand how people in their particular lived worlds experience and value the expenditure of energy in pursuit of a livelihood. Is it always experienced as necessity, or sometimes as voluntary? What do different forms of 'work' mean, and what are their consequences?

One of the fundamental activities classed as 'making' or 'doing' (*luraña*) is weaving. Weaving is not *ch'ama*, but is the prototype act of creation, used as a root metaphor for many other forms of activity. Weaving and sewing enhance peoples' attractiveness. Young people work hard to produce new clothes for the main festivals and show off the latest styles. In so doing they demonstrate that quality of being *wapu*. They also show that the wearer has been able to generate in other people – their spouse, but even more important their cross-sex siblings – the desire to help them dress well, the desire to be *wapu*, to use their energy creatively. However, although weaving and other forms of textile production are highly esteemed, my discussion will centre mainly on the values attached to the kinds of work involved in cultivation that are covered by the term *ch'ama*.

There is an intrinsic link between work, relationship and consumption in Laymi communities. Before work is started on any field, or on preparing raw wool for spinning, it is always known for whom, or for what, the end product will serve. For example, fields may be sown 'for food', in other words for household consumption, or perhaps 'for a fiesta' if the household is sponsoring a saint's festival. Or a young man or woman may cultivate a crop 'for money' in order to buy clothes or adornments. The way that productive activity is intrinsically relational used to be particularly clear in the case of spinning and weaving. Men and women who related to each other as 'siblings' used to weave and make clothing for each other throughout their lives, and those who loved each other made beautiful things to express and consolidate the relationship. In Laymi practice the way produce circulates is intrinsically linked to how, and by whom, it is produced (Harris 1982). Through work, people create themselves through their agency and at the same time create others for whom they work, or with whom they share the fruits of their labours (see Canessa 1998).

This kind of celebration of human energy, creativity and capacity to make and expand relationships through work is not particularly unusual in anthropological literature. However, it is more striking in the rural Andes for two reasons. First, because the peasants form part of an intensely hierarchical social world, and one in which they have been severely exploited at times. Second, because it is not only work performed by people for the strengthening and nurturing of their own networks of social relations that is celebrated as a positive value, but also, and perhaps more importantly, work carried out as, and for, the collectivity of which they form part.[7] These features have received less attention in anthropological debates and raise particular problems of interpretation.

WORK AS VALUE

Much has been written about forms of cooperative labour in the rural Andes. It is, in fact, significant that the extensive discussions of Andean reciprocity focus almost exclusively on forms of labour exchange (e.g. Alberti and Mayer 1974), rather than on the exchange of objects, which is more typical of the broader literature on reciprocity and the gift. For many Andean peasant communities, it is their institutions of cooperative labour that distinguish them from outsiders. Thus it is natural that the new generations of educated indigenous activitists privilege these institutions as they seek to formulate the basis of their difference from – and also their superiority to – other social groups. In Bolivia, one of the earliest organisations that heralded the development of the militant Aymara movement (*Katarismo*) took its name from a form of labour exchange – *mink'a* (Albó 1987). A number of commentators within and outside the movement have argued that Aymara ethics are inherently superior to Western morality in that they prioritise the collective, rather than individual self-interest (Temple 1989).

Some of these forms of labour-exchange are inherently two-way. While they instantiate an ethic of cooperation and valuing of the community above the self, they also have a pragmatic function by distributing labour across households to cover major times of demand (for example in preparing for a religious festival) (Harris 1982). There are also work parties, attended by large numbers of people, which really are parties with a festive atmosphere, even when each person brings their own lunch with them (this type of work is known as *faena*, and all households must send at least one representative).

However, the work parties are often more festive when held by individual households for agriculture or house building. In the maize-producing valleys, when I lived there in the 1970s, most phases of the agricultural cycle were organised in festive work-parties known as *chuqu*.[8] It was unseemly to cultivate the fields alone. One of the most striking ways in which the *chuqu* system in the valleys operated was that only the more prosperous households with two or more adult members would actually organise a work party. The lands of widows or the very old were attended to by those present, after they had completed the work on the lands of the host household, and before they all relaxed with a delicious meal, plenty to drink and music at the end of the day. People dressed up in their best clothes to go out to work together, and decorated the yoke of the plough with willow fronds, as they did in the ritual of ploughing. My own categorisation of agricultural labour as dirt, sweat and toil derived from my reading of European history and literature. According to these values, good clothes in European agricultural communities were reserved precisely for the days on which people did not work and on which they went to church to perform rituals to reproduce their social world and social values: in other words their 'Sunday best'. Here was a case where the sheer difference of what I experienced threw my own assumptions concerning the separation between work and ritual into sharp relief.

As many have described, these work parties really are parties (e.g. Gose 1994), a vivid example of what others have noted as the potential for conviviality through work (Ortíz 1979; Passes 2000).[9] It was on such occasions that I sometimes had Zafimaniry-type conversations. People were well aware that not everyone worked in this way, and I recall being asked once, as we sat gazing out over the mountains chewing coca during a rest-break, whether people worked in this way in *Inkiltira*. Laymi people were in no doubt that the way they worked together was an important aspect of what made them human beings.

In my experience, it was not only the sociability and the sense of occasion that made work parties important to people, but also the work itself. 'We help each other,' people would say. While in many parts of the Andes help in cultivation follows a principle of direct delayed reciprocity, the *chuqu* work parties of Laymi hamlets do not operate in terms of strict calculation of debts and credits. For other Andean regions, too, ethnographers have suggested that peasants emphasise the ethic of mutual help rather than that of two-way exchange (e.g. Gose 1994). By contrast, calculations of reciprocity are made far more strictly in the loan or gifting of objects or things (Harris 1982). The difference lies in the different understandings of ownership. Things are attributes of people, an expression of their own vitality and that of their kin. The vitality of a landholding community, its capacity to make the earth bear fruit, is an expression of the deities that protect and succour life, but may also punish and kill – deities whose worship is articulated through the rituals of the landholding community. Agricultural work is a prime example of the continual flow of energies between deities and humans and, especially in the practice of collective work parties, it is part of this ritual complex.

This commitment to collective and cooperative labour is what most persistently distinguishes 'real people' from the townspeople (known as *q'ara*).[10] While the peasants recognise that townspeople are also Christians, theirs is a different notion of morality and personhood. Time and again ethnographers have reported that the peasants consider that townspeople do not know how to work, or are lazy (Arguedas and Ortíz 1973; Gose 1994). I was surprised, even shocked, at how Laymis would give quantities of their harvested crops to townspeople who would come to visit them in the fields, begging, and offering in exchange only a small gift, such as a box of matches or some oranges. When I suggested to them that it was unfair, and that the better-off, or at least socially superior, townspeople were exploiting them, they sometimes responded that the townspeople did not know how to work, that they felt sorry for them because they had no land, and that was why they wanted to help them. Goudsmit has reported a similar generosity, or naivete, in nearby Toracarí, which is dominated by landowning families. Peasants round Toracarí continue to help and serve the townspeople, both working on their land and running errands for them, when there is no obligation for them to do so (2006).

When I describe the kinds of unforced generosity I witnessed, and of which I was sometimes myself the recipient, I have often been met with bafflement. How is this 'uneconomic' behaviour to be explained, especially given the UN statistics that consistently identify Bolivian peasants as amongst the poorest people in the Western hemisphere? I recall one anthropologist colleague who specialises on development issues exclaiming in tones of disbelief when I presented some of these points at an academic seminar: 'But nobody gives things away for nothing!' Some would suggest that these peasants were under a misapprehension – one might say a false consciousness – about their economic role. Instead of understanding the ways they were exploited by outsiders, they responded to townspeople's demands with pity and generosity. In their own understanding, their explanation would surely be that such acts demonstrated their own superior humanity.

This is not the socialist utopia imagined by some left-wing intellectuals. The high value accorded to collective work institutions is accompanied by intense factionalism and conflict over resources (Albó 1975). Moreover, collective work is often seen as a burden; in fact the Spanish term *cargo* (burden) is often used. But the performance of this obligation is also a virtue, the fulfilling of one's proper role in the universe. When rural dwellers today lament that their neighbours no longer have time to perform collective labour because they have migrated to the city, it is not so much the tasks that have been left undone that they are thinking of, but the way in which they have become less human and the quality of their lives has declined (Calestani forthcoming).[11]

I am not arguing that Andean peasants are culturally programmed to work harder than anybody else. To the contrary, I have witnessed occasions when people have been criticised as selfish for going out to tend their fields when others were celebrating the patron saints with days of drinking and feasting, because they prioritised their private interests over the need to attend to the well-being of the community through ritual. Furthermore, when bonded labour for the benefit of landowners was abolished by the Bolivian Agrarian Reform in 1953, productivity fell dramatically as peasants turned their attention to festive consumption. A common refrain from landlord families to this day across the region is that the peasants need the authority of the landlords to work hard; now that the systems of forced labour have been abolished, peasants have become lazy. Writing of a former Ecuadorian hacienda, Barry Lyons suggests that this view is shared by some of the older peasants too (Lyons 2006). And it would come as a surprise to many development workers to learn that there is a strong work ethic in Andean rural communities, since they more typically perceive an unhealthy commitment to festive consumption that seems to be the very opposite.

My argument here, then, is not so much about the intensity of work, nor the number of hours, but the positive value attributed to it. Nor am I suggesting that Andean peasants do not complain about their lot, or put up lightly with abuse and injustice; rather that their complaints do not focus on work as such, and that through their work they seek to maintain equality within and between communities, and to satisfy the demands of the townspeople. However, it is not enough to propose that different cultural groups invest work with different values. In the Andean case, it can be argued that work is sacralised, seen as an obligation, both because it is part of a continuous mutual nurturance between humans and deities, and because rights to land are articulated through collective work. For example, Gary Urton has shown in his study of Pacariqtambo (southern Peru) that collective work is in an important sense constitutive of the *ayllus* of which the village is composed (1992). In daily life, *ayllu* organisation is not readily apparent. However, when some task must be undertaken for the benefit of the community as a whole – for example, cultivating a field with barley to sell for improvements to the school or repairing a section of the church wall – it is usually divided up between the *ayllus*, into units of work known locally as *chhiutas*. The communal organisation of these tasks ensures that the work is distributed equally both between constituent groups and within each group. Crucially, each community is differentiated, composed of sub-units that compete fiercely with each other and that perform similar tasks in alternation.

Peter Gose's ethnography of Huaquirca (also southern Peru) addresses not the relations between different *ayllus* but between commoners and notables, in other words between social classes. In particular, he stresses the egalitarian ethos of work parties – known locally as *ayni* – which are used for the early stages of cultivation, but not the harvest. His analysis centres on the cyclical seasonal rhythm between the collective egalitarianism of the growing season and the more individualised appropriation of the ripe crops during the dry season. And while commoners elaborate culturally their communalism and their role as workers as part of a broader egalitarian ethic, notables elaborate culturally their role as appropriators and consumers and refuse to join in *ayni* work parties, even though they do perform some agricultural labour (Gose 1994: 237).

As both Urton and Gose suggest, cooperative labour is essential for different kinds of claims to land. Indeed, it may in and of itself constitute a claim, as I witnessed on one occasion on the Laymi border. It concerned a large field, the rights to which were disputed with the neighbouring *ayllu*. The entire community went together to plough it in March and thereby successfully took possession of it for sowing the following September. The separate plots were assigned to households that had insufficient land, in other words not all households that took part in the work party received an allocation.

What, then, of labour performed outside the ambit of the rural community? In some cases it is just a job – working as a porter, migrating to Chile to work in agriculture, or to the Chapare region to work in the cocaine industry – a means to earn extra cash with which to fund expenditure of one kind or another. But in the case of mining, something more like an alternative community is created in the underground galleries and passageways, as the miners chew coca leaves and pour libations to the deity of the mines – the *tiyu* – before they move into their positions in the work team (Nash 1979). Pascale Absi, in particular, has shown how mining labour in Potosí today is a 'total social fact', as much religious and social as it is economic or political (2003). In order to have success, miners must be 'caught' by the underground deities whose worship forms an important part of their working life. Their work serves to ensure that the forces that animate the world are put in motion. Their ritual offerings are a constitutive element of the solidary work groups that extract mineral from the mountain, and that also participate in cooperatives and trade union activities.

Most theories of value concentrate their attention on the things that work produces, what some have called objectified labour. What is striking in the examples I have discussed is the emphasis on work itself as an expression of value. Doubtless this is in part the effect of the mountainous environment: at such high altitudes the results of agricultural labour are unpredictable. However, while environmental factors may help to explain their origins, the values expressed in work in Andean communities cannot be reduced to an effect of the environment, but are embedded in rights to land, the constitution of social groups and also in the reproduction of a subordinate relationship to townspeople. Feeding is a key value in the Andes. Through work parties, social units come together as commensual groups; they feed the earth and through work they in turn are fed. Graeber has made a similar argument with reference to Melanesia (2001: 70).

AN ANDEAN POETICS OF WORK

The ways that collective work embodies social value is illustrated in evidence from the sixteenth-century record. The complex and unfamiliar organisation of work on a grand scale by the Inka state impressed the early chroniclers and Crown officials – even though they were often undecided as to how to evaluate it – as they grappled with the difficulties of integrating the Inka state into the mercantile economy of Castille. The slippages and inconsistencies in their accounts are especially illuminating.

Finley writes of Ancient Greece: 'The Greek language had an astonishing range of vocabulary for slaves, unparalleled in my knowledge' (1973: 98). I would want to make a comparable, if more modest, claim for sixteenth-century Aymara, with reference to the terms describing different aspects of work. Early colonial dictionaries of Andean languages reveal a veritable poetics of work. For example, the Jesuit Bertonio in his Aymara dictionary lists under the Spanish *trabajo* a range of Aymara terms for work:

– to stretch the hands in many directions
– to work in two fields in a single day
– to work in the field without raising one's head
– to work hard, achieving what normally two people could barely do
– to work diligently as a good worker
– to work as a strong man without feeling tired
– to work hard in grinding *quinua*
– to work the whole day
– a very good worker. (Bertonio 1956 [1612][I]: 454; [II]: 221, 296, 393)

It seems likely that Bertonio compiled the dictionary in close collaboration with bilingual informants. We can imagine the Jesuit asking how to say *trabajo* in Aymara, and being intrigued by the wealth of responses he received. It is striking that this is not a list of different *categories* of work, nor of similes, but of different *aspects* of hard work, and that Bertonio did not associate them with a comparable range of terms in Spanish.

The way that the constitution of groups was bound up with their work obligations is clear from what we know of the Inka tribute system. The census was organised on a decimal basis, such that work quotas for the state – for example, work on state lands, spinning and weaving, or servicing the roads – was allocated by the head or ruler of each unit, down to the smallest level of a unit of five households. Here, too, we see a system in which the unit of tribute was not a quantity of maize, tubers or cloth, but workdays (Murra 1980). The Inka state, known as 'the four *suyus*' (*Tawantinsuyu*), was thus conceptualised as a gigantic division of labour, since the term *–suyu*, used to denote provinces, means 'that part of a task that one or more persons takes to work on, for example a church, a field, a building, etc.' (Bertonio 1956 [1612][II]: 331–2). As with Urton's *chhiutas* today, the relationship between subgroups within a larger whole was constituted through work allocations. Importantly, though, this division of labour was one in which tasks of a similar nature were divided up – or at least differences between them were not emphasised – rather than the classic Durkheimian concept of a complementary and organic unity derived from different kinds of labour (Durkheim 1893).

In his description of the Inka census categories, the Andean writer Waman Puma illustrated just how deeply identity was expressed in terms of capacity to work. From the oldest to the youngest, each category was identified in terms of its job. Even eighty-year-olds and the very young were included, the former as allowed to do nothing and to sleep all day, and the latter as 'of no use' if they were one-year old, but as requiring the work of someone else to look after them if they were young babies (Guaman Poma 1987 [1615]: 192–3, 204–7, 212–3, 224–7).

The scholar-soldier Garcilaso de la Vega – son of an Inka princess and a Spanish conquistador – described how the peasants would work for the Inka on his lands:

> Each worker who went to work in the field of a widow or orphan was obliged to take his own food with him since, they argued, the burden of their own wretchedness was all these poor people could bear, and they should not be charged with the care of others... After the fields belonging to the poor, they ploughed their own, always in common, then those of the *curaca* [local ruler] and finally, the last of all, those of the Inka. For this occasion, they wore their festival dress, ornamented with gold and silver, and on their heads, crowns of large bouquets of feathers. They sang praises to the Inka while working, and this labour was thus transformed into a festival. (Garcilaso de la Vega 1943 [1609]: Book V)

When I first attended a *chuqu* work party, I was struck by the similarities to this passage. The gold and silver were missing, as were the songs of praise to the Inka, but Laymi young people sometimes decorated their hats with a 'bouquet of feathers', and the festive atmosphere was certainly recognisable. We do not need to invoke some mystical concept of culture to accept that a core of values and practices may have remained in operation through changing historical circumstances, as Bloch demonstrated for the Merina circumcision ritual (1986). Under the Inkas, festive work was in part a direct prestation to the state; under the colonial regime it became the way that each *ayllu* met its tribute obligations and thereby confirmed its rights to land; in the late twentieth century, it remained as a means of confirming communal rights over the land worked by each household (Harris 2000). Festive dress can be understood as the means by which the collectivity makes visible the articulation of power and celebrates its own prosperity.

Perhaps even more strikingly than Garcilaso's description of agricultural work, a similar emphasis on festive dress to celebrate going to work can be found in the account of a parish priest in the Potosí region writing some twenty years after Garcilaso. Describing how the Indians prepared to travel to the vast silver mines of Potosí to perform their obligatory labour-service (*mit'a*) he noted:

> When a *mita* captain leaves for Potosí, he goes accompanied by his Indians all dressed up for war, with their traditional arms and elegant in their feathers. (Ramírez del Águila 1978 [1639]: 131)[12]

Here the elegant attire signals an unexpected sense of privilege and status. The Indians' willingness to work was clearly puzzling to the Spanish. The same priest, in the midst of a long passage lamenting the terrible fate of Indians who work in the Potosí mines, suddenly comes out with the following phrase: 'Once they get to work, they do it with great enjoyment and humour as though they were at a fiesta.' Then he reverts to the denunciatory tone typical of the clergy against mining work, that the risks are terrible, that *mit'a* Indians are like slaves, and so forth.

We need not suppose that mining labour was pure pleasure to detect, in this ambivalent account, that the standard anti-*mit'a* rhetoric of the Church did not entirely fit the facts and that there was a professional pride and enjoyment in even the most arduous work (Platt,

Bouysse-Cassagne and Harris 2006: 368–73). Another aspect that is emphasised in the sources is how closely work was tied to the value of fulfilling an obligation to the ruler. Thus, the Indians sang praises to the Inka as they worked his fields, and went to serve the king in the mining *mit'a*.

This degree of obedience to their superiors was considered akin to slavery by many Spanish observers. Thus, Juan de Matienzo, a judge in sixteenth-century La Plata (the capital of the colonial Audiencia) and a key figure in the administration of the Potosí region, interpreted as servile the way that the Indians obeyed the commands of their lords, and identified the Inka system as slavery, in that it did not allow Indians private property, nor to use their own free will, and forced them to work for no payment (1967 [1567]). Similarly, Capoche, a mine owner who benefited directly from the *mit'a* system, wrote in the 1580s with evident disdain for those whose labour he profited from:

> One can see how humble and simple-minded the Indians are. After all, even when they have an excuse not to have anything to do with the mines, they offer themselves up as a sacrifice rather than let their master down. (Capoche 1959 [1585])

In the case of mining labour, its close association in early modern Spain with slavery must have fed into the general contempt for those miners in Potosí who obeyed their superiors with 'servility'. In the Andes, the requirement of the His Most Catholic Majesty that his new subjects be turned into free men was combined with the growing need to make them work harder, especially in mining as the boom years of the mid-sixteenth century turned to crisis. It was a conundrum that the Spanish Crown never managed to solve (Cole 1985).

Another aspect of the Indians' work practices that Spanish observers found inexplicable was their preference for working in large groups. Polo Ondegardo in particular emphasises this: 'among these Indians there is a very ancient custom of running their affairs and organizing everything by the whole group' (*regirse por comunidades en todo*). He goes on in tones that mix admiration with exasperation:

> It must be understood that if there is public construction work to be undertaken, for which they are required, say, to contribute 100

> Indians in collective labour, they work with less hardship than for example if later they are asked to send just one Indian, even if he is paid at double the standard rates. In the first case they work according to their customary system, which was never a fixed tax. Anything else is seen as a real burden, insofar as it does not come within the normal system of tribute duties. (1990 [1571]: 150, 178)

We have little idea of the extent to which the subsistence land of the peasant farmers was also worked by the collectivity in the Inka period, but the efficiency and importance of assigning tribute labour to groups, whose leaders then allocated the work to smaller groups or individual households, is clear from the sources. With a wealth of such examples, it is understandable that the right-wing French historian Louis Baudin (1928) described the Incas as the 'first socialist state', comparing it with the Bolsheviks in its centralism, lack of individual liberty or property, and the glorification of hard work.

It is understandable that the Andean 'joy in work' that the sources describe, the apparent indifference to individual freedom and self-interest that were already core values in sixteenth-century Spain, should be compared by Baudin to twentieth century totalitarian regimes.[13] However, we should note minimally the lack of a totalising concept of society in the Inka state, and the likelihood that 'singing praises to the Inka' in fact embodied rights to land and the feeding of the landscape deities.

THE SPECTRE OF COERCION

The contrast between Spanish and Andean commentators concerning the value of the Andean work ethic is striking. While Garcilaso de la Vega writes in celebratory terms, the Spanish writers reveal their disapproval of the Indians who work hard, but in the wrong way. For Matienzo or Capoche, the problem was that Indians were subject to the will of their ruler, and therefore servile and not free. For Polo, it was the irrationality of preferring collective work when there was apparently nothing to be gained from it. In both respects these writers reveal their preference for stripping individuals of their broader social relations when work is at issue. The implication is that men should leave social relations behind when they go to work.[14]

This abstraction from the social context is of course a crucial aspect of political economy. Adam Smith identified productive work as the source of wealth, but productive work in general, not in its social context. This formed the basis for Marx's development of the labour theory of value, the abstract concept of labour power divorced from the human particularity of the individual worker (Arendt 1958: 85). The Communist Manifesto states the position eloquently: '[the bourgeoisie] has left intact no other bond between one man and another than naked self-interest, unfeeling "hard cash"' (Marx and Engels 1998 [1848]: 16, 22).

The Marxist concepts of abstract labour and the labour theory of value were developed with reference to the capitalist mode of production, as a means of explaining the mechanism by which the worker was alienated from the product of his/her labour, and thereby exploited by the owners of the means of production.[15] However, these concepts have been carried over into anthropological discussion more broadly, in contexts where capitalist forms of extraction do not prevail – for example, to establish how far the value of an object is a function of the labour time involved in producing it (e.g. many of the chapters in Wallman 1979). As many have noted, this kind of abstraction – which for Marx typified capitalist relations of production – treats work in isolation from the lived social relations which encompass it, and which it creates and recreates.

Marxist concepts have also inspired studies that chart the nature of exploitation in different social and historical contexts. Thus, for example, some have argued that the function of the ideologies of reciprocity and cooperation widely found throughout the southern Andes may be to mask the existence of inequalities and exploitation (e.g. Sanchez 1982; Painter 1991: 98). Godelier similarly argued that the Inka state drew on an earlier form of reciprocal and communal work in order to organise new relations of production and mask the oppression and domination on which they were based (Godelier 1977: 68). The problem with such approaches is that they assume that values and institutions which had served more egalitarian functions in the past remained operative through some process of inertia, and that the exploited peasants were unable to understand the fundamental change that had taken place.[16]

More broadly, in theories of social evolution priority is often given to notions of exploitation and alienation, such that there is an assumption that social inequalities involve a degree of coercion. Why else would people give up their freedom, and subordinate themselves to another?

Undoubtedly, the coercion is all too real in many cases, for example in cases of conquest and enslavement or where land and other means of production are monopolised by a few. However, even where the idea of coercion is not explicitly invoked, it may hover in the background. Consider for example Sahlins' *Stone Age Economics*, which offers an apparently benign view of the different stages of social evolution (1974). He argues that production increases as social authority increases. Without what he terms 'chiefly power', people do not work hard or generate a surplus. In his idyllic portrayal, foragers and hunter-gatherers were the 'original affluent society', devoted to the pursuit of leisure. Even those whose livelihood is characterised by the 'domestic mode of production', which succeeds foraging in Sahlins' loose evolutionary schema, accord as much importance to 'relaxation and diversion, to rest, ceremony and visiting' as they do to work (1974: 58). In this text, Sahlins is unspecific about how chiefly power operates and how much coercion it may involve, since he claims that 'the indigenous category for exploitation is "reciprocity"'. Nonetheless, when considering the overall structure of the book, it is hard not to read into his argument a narrative of the origins of drudgery and obligation, involving the loss of former agency.

The shift in anthropological attention away from work and production to what is produced and how it circulates, to objects – 'things' in Appadurai's (1986) formulation – and to exchange, was consonant with broader shifts in the global political economy away from the productivism of the socialist bloc to the dominance of neoliberalism, and away from labour to post-Fordism and consumption. However, at the same time, the problems of Marxist abstractions also inspired a more nuanced ethnography of work that privileges the lived experience of workers and the ways they give value and meaning to their activities.

It is safe to assume that manual workers have always had their own counter-cultural evaluations of their own worth – the 'dignity of labour' (see Thompson 1963). Thus, ethnographers have shown how those who work even in the most despised and menial of jobs have their own satisfaction and self-esteem, as well as a reciprocal disdain for those of higher social standing (Searle-Chatterjee 1979; Day 2007). Even in the classic industrial labour process of factories and steel mills, the objective exploitation to which workers are subject may seem a sought-after privilege in comparison with their former lives (Parry 1999; 2005). There can be a ludic element even in situations of intense managerial pressure (Burawoy 1979); and the shop floor can generate gift relationships and deeply personalistic ties (Mollona 2005). Repetition in the labour process, it has been argued, brings its own satisfaction (Ronco and Peattie 1988).

CONCLUSIONS

My argument has outlined a gross contrast between 'Western' and 'Andean' ideas in order to explore the ways that value may be attached to, or dissociated from, manual work. While the comparison may be overdrawn, I find it striking and thought-provoking. As so often, an apparently general, neutral question such as 'what makes people work?' turns into further questions concerning its implicit assumptions, and the recognition that they are part of a long history.

For the Ancient Greeks, work was *ponos* – toil and suffering (Vernant 1965: 16–36). In the biblical tradition, too, the consequence of original sin was unremitting toil. In the Genesis myth, God's words to Adam were: 'cursed is the ground for thy sake; in sorrow shalt thou eat of it all the days of thy life ... in the sweat of thy face shalt thou eat bread til thou return unto the ground', while painful motherhood and subordination to her husband were Eve's punishment (Genesis 3: 16–18). The idea that manual labour is a form of servitude runs deep in Western values, for all the counter-cultures of workers themselves, and for all the proclamations of the value of work by Christian thinkers, and later by the Enlightenment and Romantic movements (Campbell 1989: 9–17).

Today, with the secular decline of manual work, one might expect that this negative value would be disappearing. However, notions of servitude and exploitation attach to a far broader category of work practices. For example, a recent monograph that describes the managerial surveillance, the search for incentives, the ever longer hours of current work regimes in advanced capitalism, claims that modern work is a form of slavery, and the book is strikingly entitled *Blood, Sweat and Tears*, even though the work regimes it discusses do not typically generate blood or sweat (Donkin 2001).[17] Indeed, much recent 'management theory' starts from the premise that people work better if they are free to make decisions about how to do it, in some sense to feel that they do it voluntarily (Murphy 1993; Philippon 2006). This received wisdom reflects the longstanding

European preoccupation with work as a form of bondage and coercion. The same theme is found in the persistent myth, which recurs in many guises and many settings, of a former golden age in which work was less exploitative, less hard, more rewarding, less alienated, less alienating (see Joyce 1987; Pahl 1988: 5).[18] Of course, this is not to suggest that working conditions do not sometimes get worse, but to question the implication that there has been a continuous and relentless downward trend since the Neolithic.

I suggest that the prevalence of slavery in the ancient world has infected Western ideas about work and personhood more profoundly than is recognised. In the case of ancient Greece and Rome the connection is obvious and well-known, but much less so for the biblical tradition. And yet the ancient Hebrews too had suffered slavery, in both Egypt and Babylon, and the historical memory of these experiences and the liberation from bondage is etched deep into the message of the Bible (Yerushalmi 1982). While the origin of the Genesis narratives is unknowable, it is highly likely that they were written down in their present form during or after the return from Babylon, in other words after the experience of enslavement (Dancy 2001: 40).[19] It seems that the opposition between freedom and coercion plays a foundational role in Western ideas about work. Any form of compulsion can be quickly assimilated to a condition of servility, insofar as it represents a partial limitation on freedom and thus on full personhood. In some senses, work is understood as the antithesis of freedom. The concept of alienation, too, suggests that some aspect of the person has been separated off, abstracted from social relations, and that positive value accrues to the products of work, but rarely to work itself.

The paradoxical attitudes of sixteenth-century Spanish commentators to the Andean work practices they observed were surely a product of this opposition between freedom and coercion. The Inka state was not based on slavery; it is arguable that slaves were not found in the Inka world at all. However, many Spanish writers at the time emphasised the lack of freedom of those who laboured, as we have seen, leading a few modern scholars to argue that the Inka system was slave-based (e.g. Choy 1960). The point at issue is whether the forms of 'servility' that the Europeans perceived were experienced and understood as a diminution of their personhood by those who occupied such positions. There is good evidence that they were not (see Murra 2004).

In similar vein, my own difficulties in making sense of the work practices I witnessed in twentieth-century Bolivia derived from a concept of exploitation which took for granted that part of the value of the peasants' work in an intensely stratified society was extracted from them and hence alienated. And yet in many ways work seemed more like a performance of value, a celebration of the power of the community. The Genesis story that people recounted to me in northern Potosí exemplifies the contrast, offering a very different aetiology of the origins of work from that found in the biblical Genesis. In the previous world epoch, I was told, there was no sun, only the moon, and people did not need to work, since everything they needed, including clothes, grew miraculously of its own accord. The rising of God, manifest in the dawning sun, inaugurated the present age, the 'age of the Christians'. The Christian God gave the new people raw materials to work on: the 'three miracles' of food-plants, livestock and metals, and it is as Christians that they identify themselves as hard workers. Work, then, in the Andean Genesis is presented as a form of blessing and well-being.

Anthropology has perhaps too readily reproduced the message of the biblical Genesis in assuming the negative value of work, as the implications of Andean practice in distinct historical periods help to clarify. The examples I have given suggest that the *obligation* to work should not be equated with a notion of *coercion*. Not that Andean peasants today, or in the past, meekly accepted injustice and bad treatment, nor that value is always realised in practice, but that their concept of justice includes working with and for the collectivity of which they form part, often in competition with another collectivity, and often for those in authority over them; and that value lies not only in the product of work, but in its very performance.

ACKNOWLEDGEMENTS

My warm thanks to Jonathan Parry and Rita Astuti for their thoughtful editorial support, to participants in the original Zafimaniry Workshop, and to Harry Lubasz for his comments on earlier drafts.

NOTES

1. Veblen 1924. Bertrand Russell recounts hearing an old Duchess say: 'What do the poor want with holidays? They ought to work' (2004 [1932]: 4).

2. 'comme l'antithèse de ce qui dans l'homme est essentiel'.
3. A similar – if slightly less dismal – narrative is given by the Comaroffs in their extensive study of missionary activities in Southern Africa (1991). In many areas, it is Christian conversion that is seen as inaugurating the work regime. As Melanesian Orokaiva people told Erik Schwimmer: 'The people of olden times did not take up work (*pure*) for it was only Jesus Christ who gave them work (*pure*) to take up' (Schwimmer 1979: 287).
4. The *ayllu* is a landowning group of varying size. My account of peasant life refers mainly to the 1970s up to the mid-1980s. Since then some things have changed with respect to work practices, while others remain as I experienced them. For this reason I have used the present tense in parts of this essay.
5. Harvey notes a similar meaning for the Spanish *vivo* in the Cusco region (personal communication).
6. The term *luraña* refers to a human act of transformation. An obvious parallel to the doing of papers is tending the fields (*yap luraña*), which can refer to any aspect of cultivation.
7. I deliberately leave vague what scale of collectivity is involved. Although this may depend on the context, what is crucial is that it is a unit that has collective rights over land.
8. In other regions these parties are known as *ayni* (southern Peru) or *minga* (northern Ecuador, Colombia). In Northern Potosí, as in much of Bolivia, the terms *ayni* and *minga/mink'a* are less emphasised than in other Andean regions, and refer mainly to two-way exchanges of labour.
9. In my experience, there is a strong sense of 'collective effervescence' in *chuqu* work-parties. Durkheim, who recognised the powerful impact of ritual, undoubtedly underestimated the effect of collective work in his discussion of mechanical solidarity (1893).
10. The term *q'ara* means not properly clothed, lacking the 'social skin' of mutual obligation and assistance that define personhood.
11. It should be noted that in many Andean regions, especially at lower altitudes where conditions of agriculture are easier, institutions of collective labour are not found today, or only in minimal form.
12. While an exploration of the ways in which war and soldiering intersect with ideas about work is beyond the scope of this essay, it is worth noting that war and soldiering are significant in many ways. For example, in this region there was historically a close association – if not direct identification – between mining and warfare (Platt, Bouysse-Cassagne and Harris 2006).
13. The 'joy in work' (*arbeitsfreude*) was a powerful theme in the development of German nationalism, where in the ideas of some ideologues

it represented a total subordination to the greater good of the nation (Campbell 1989).

14. It goes without saying that none of these writers took women's work into detailed consideration.
15. Marx also subscribed to the Enlightenment view that human personhood is realised by the creativity of work, and the human capacity for purposive intention (Marx 1970 [1887]: 178; see Ingold 1983). In the 1844 Economic and Philosophical Manuscripts he argued that capitalist wage labour was responsible for the 'disappearance of all creativity and joy from work' (see Campbell 1989: 20).
16. Godelier's shift some years later to an interest in the semantics of work indicates his own dissatisfaction with his earlier position (Godelier 1980).
17. Some authors have suggested that different aspects of work can be identified through the semantics of the terms 'labour' and 'work' (for example Arendt 1958; Firth 1979). I have avoided any kind of definitional distinctions of this kind because of their universalist pretensions.
18. Sennett's recent account (1998) of the increased demoralisation of a flexibilised workforce invokes a similar contrast between the present and a past in which workers and employees had more self-respect.
19. In this spirit, Maurice Bloch has repeatedly pointed to the importance of slavery in Madagascar for understanding Merina ideas about work, land and the power of the ancestors (see for example 1986; Parry, this volume).

REFERENCES

Absi, P. 2003. *Les ministres du diable. Le travail et ses représentations dans les mines de Potosí, Bolivie*, Paris: Harmattan.

Alberti, G. and Mayer, E. (eds) 1974. *Reciprocidad e intercambio en los Andes peruanos*, Lima: Instituto de Estudios Peruanos.

Albó, X. 1975. *La paradoja aymara: solidaridad y faccionalismo*. Cuadernos de Investigación 8, La Paz: CIPCA.

—— 1987. 'From MNRistas to Kataristas to Katari', in S. Stern (ed.), *Resistance, rebellion and consciousness in the Andean peasant world*, Madison: University of Wisconsin Press.

Appadurai, A. (ed.) 1986. *The social life of things: commodities in cultural perspective*, Cambridge: Cambridge University Press

Arendt, H. 1958. *The human condition*, Chicago: University of Chicago Press.

Arguedas, J.M. and A. Ortíz 1973. 'La posesión de la tierra, los mitos prehispánicos y la visión del universo en la población monolingüe quechua', in J. Ossio (ed.), *Ideología mesiánica del mundo andino*, Lima: Ignacio Prado Pastor.

Aristotle. 1992. *The politics*, London: Penguin Books.

Arnold, D. and J. de D. Yapita 1996. 'Los caminos de género en Qaqachaka: saberes femeninos y discursos textuales alternativos en los Andes', in S. Rivera Cusicanqui (ed.), *Ser mujer indígena, chola o birlocha en la Bolivia postcolonial de los años 90*, La Paz: Ministerio de Desarrollo Humano.

—— 1999. *Vocabulario aymara del parto y de la vida reproductiva de la mujer*, La Paz: Instituto de Lengua y Cultura Aymara/Family Health International.

Baudin, L. 1961 (1928). *Socialist empire: the Incas of Perú*, Princeton: Van Nostrand.

Bertonio, L. 1956 (1612). *Vocabulario de la lengua aymara*, La Paz: Universidad Mayor de San Andrés.

Bloch, M. 1986. *From blessing to violence: history and ideology in the circumcision ritual of the Merina of Madagascar*, Cambridge: Cambridge University Press.

Burawoy, M. 1979. *Manufacturing consent: changes in the labour process under monopoly capitalism*, Chicago: University of Chicago Press.

Burnett, J. 1974. *Useful toil: autobiographies of working people from 1820s to 1920s*, London: Routledge.

Calestani, M. forthcoming. *Creating our own well-being: local perspectives and cultural constructions in the Bolivian Altiplano*, University of London: PhD thesis in Anthropology.

Campbell, J. 1989. *Joy in work, German work. The national debate 1800–1945*, Princeton: Princeton University Press.

Canessa, A. 1998. 'Procreation, personhood and ethnic difference in Highland Bolivia', *Ethnos* 63(2): 227–47.

Capoche, L. 1959 (1585). *Relación de la villa imperial de Potosí*, Madrid: Biblioteca de Autores Españoles CXXII.

Choy, E. 1962. 'Desarrollo del pensamiento especulativo en la sociedad esclavista de los Incas, *Actas y trabajos*, Lima: Segundo congreso nacional de Historia del Perú, II: 87–102.

Cole, J. 1985. *The Potosí mita 1573–1700*, Stanford: Stanford University Press.

Comaroff, J. and J.L. Comaroff. 1991. *Of revelation and revolution* (vol. 1, *Christianity, colonialism, and consciousness in South Africa*), Chicago: University of Chicago Press.

Dancy, J. 2001. *The divine drama. The Old Testament as literature*, Cambridge: The Lutterworth Press.

Day, S. 2007. *On the game: making a living in prostitution*, London: Pluto Press.

Donkin, R. 2001. *Blood, sweat and tears: the evolution of work*, London: Texere.

Durkheim, E. 1893. *De la division du travail social*, Paris: Félix Alcan.

Finley, M. 1973. *The ancient economy*, Berkeley and Los Angeles: University of California Press.

Firth, R. 1979. 'Work and value: reflections on the ideas of Karl Marx', in S. Wallman (ed.), *Social anthropology of work*, London and New York: Academic Press.

Garcilaso de la Vega 1943 (1609). *Comentarios reales de los Incas*, A. Rosenblat (ed.), Buenos Aires: Emecé Editores.

Godelier, M. 1977. 'The concept of social and economic formation: the Inca example', in M. Godelier, *Perspectives in Marxist anthropology*, Cambridge: Cambridge University Press.

—— 1980. 'Work and its representations: a research proposal', *History Workshop Journal* 10: 164–74.

Le Goff, J. 1980. *Time, work and culture in the Middle Ages*, Chicago: University of Chicago Press.

Gose, P. 1994. *Deathly waters, hungry mountains. Agrarian ritual and class formation in an Andean town*, Toronto: University of Toronto Press.

Goudsmit, I. 2006. *So far from God, so near the mountains: peasant deference to the state and landlords in the Bolivian Andes*, University of London: PhD thesis in Anthropology.

Graeber, D. 2001. *Toward an anthropological theory of value. The false coin of our own dreams*, New York: Palgrave.

Guaman Poma de Ayala, F. 1987 (1615). *Nueva corónica y buen gobierno*, J.V. Murra, R. Adorno and J. Urioste (eds), Madrid: Historia 16.

Gupta, A. and Ferguson, J. (eds). 1997. *Anthropological locations: boundaries and grounds of a field science*, Berkeley: University of California Press.

Harrell, S. 1985. 'Why do the Chinese work so hard?', *Modern China* 11(2): 203–26.

Harris, O. 1982. 'Labour and produce in an ethnic economy', in D. Lehmann (ed.), *Ecology and exchange in the Andes*, Cambridge: Cambridge University Press.

—— 1994. 'Condor and bull: the ambiguities of masculinity in Highland Bolivia', in P. Harvey and P. Gow (eds), *Sex and violence. Issues in representation and experience*, London: Routledge.

—— 2000. *To make the earth bear fruit. Ethnographic essays on fertility, work and gender in Highland Bolivia*, London: Institute of Latin American Studies.

Ingold, T. 1983. 'The architect and the bee: reflections on the work of animals and men', *Man* (n.s.) 18(1): 1–20.

Joyce, P. 1987. 'Introduction' in P. Joyce (ed.), *The historical meanings of work*, Cambridge: Cambridge University Press.

Lewis, N. 1988. *The missionaries*, London: Secker and Warburg.

Lyons, B. 2006. *Remembering the hacienda: religion, authority, and social change in Highland Ecuador*, Austin: University of Texas Press.
Marx, K. 1970 (1887). *Capital*, vol.1, London: Lawrence and Wishart.
Marx, K. and F. Engels 1998 (1848). 'The communist manifesto' in M. Cowling (ed.), *The Communist manifesto: new interpretations*, Edinburgh: Edinburgh University Press.
Matienzo, J. 1967 (1567). *Gobierno del Perú*, Paris and Lima: Travaux de l'Institut Français des Études Andines, XI.
Mollona, M. 2005. 'Gifts of labour; steel production and technological imagination in an area of urban depression, Sheffield, UK', *Critique of Anthropology* 25(2): 177–98.
Mossé, C. 1969. *The ancient world at work*, London: Chatto and Windus.
Murra, J.V. 1980. *The economic organization of the Inka state*, Greenwich, Conn.: JAI Press.
—— 2004 (1966). 'Nueva información sobre las poblaciones *yana*' in J.V. Murra *El mundo andino: población, medio ambiente y economía*, Lima: Instituto de Estudios Peruanos.
Murphy, J.B. 1993. *The moral economy of labour. Aristotelian themes in economic theory*, New Haven: Yale University Press.
Nash, J. 1979. *We eat the mines and the mines eat us*, New York: Columbia University Press.
Ortíz, S. 1979. 'The estimation of work: labour and value among Paez farmers', in S. Wallman (ed.), *Social anthropology of work*, ASA Monograph no.19, London and New York: Academic Press.
Pahl, R. (ed.) 1988. *On work: historical, comparative and theoretical approaches*, Oxford: Blackwell.
Painter, M. 1991. 'Re-creating peasant economy in southern Peru', in J. O'Brien and W. Roseberry (eds), *Golden ages, dark ages. Imagining the past in anthropology and history*, Berkeley: University of California Press.
Parry, J. 1999. 'Lords of labour: working and shirking in Bhilai', in J. Parry, J. Breman and K. Kapadia (eds), *The worlds of Indian industrial labour*, New Delhi: Sage Publications.
—— 2005. 'Industrial work', in J. Carrier (ed.), *A handbook of economic anthropology*, Cheltenham: Edward Elgar.
Passes, A. 2000. 'The value of working and speaking together: a facet of Pa'ikwené (Palikur) conviviality', in J. Overing and A. Passes (eds), *The anthropology of love and anger: the aesthetics of conviviality in native Amazonia,* London: Routledge.
Philippon, T. 2006. 'La vraie crise de la valeur travail', *Le Monde*, 1 September.
Platt, T. 2001. 'El feto agresivo. Parto, formación de la persona y mito-historia en los Andes', *Anuario de Estudios Américanos* 58(2): 633–78.

Platt, T, Bouysse-Cassagne, T. and Harris, O. 2006. *Qaraqara-Charka. Mallku, Inka y Rey en la provincia de Charcas, siglos XV-XVII*, La Paz: Plural Editores.
Polo Ondegardo, J. 1990 (1571). *Relación de los fundamentos acerca del notable daño que resulta de no guarder a los indios sus fueros*, L. González and A. Alonso (eds), Crónicas de América 58, Madrid: Historia 16.
Ramírez del Águila, P. 1978 (1639). *Noticias políticas de indias*, J. Urioste (ed.), Sucre: Imprenta Universitaria.
Ronco, W. and Peattie, L. 1988. 'Making work: a perspective from social science', in R. Pahl (ed.), *On work: historical, comparative and theoretical approaches*, Oxford: Blackwell.
Russell, B. 2004 (1932). *In praise of idleness*, London: Routledge Classics.
Sahlins, M. 1974. *Stone age economics*, London: Tavistock Publications.
Sanchez, R. 1982. 'The Andean economic system and capitalism', in D. Lehmann (ed.), *Ecology and exchange in the Andes*, Cambridge: Cambridge University Press.
Schwimmer, E. 1979. 'Self and the product: concepts of work in comparative perspective', in S. Wallman (ed.), *Social anthropology of work*, London and New York: Academic Press.
Searle-Chatterjee, M. 1979. 'The polluted identity of work: a study of Benares sweepers', in S. Wallman (ed.), *Social anthropology of work*, London and New York: Academic Press.
Sennett, R. 1998. *The corrosion of character. The personal consequences of work in the new capitalism*, New York: Norton.
Temple, D. 1989. *Estructura comunitaria y reciprocidad: del quid-pro-quo histórico al economicidio*, La Paz: HISBOL-CHITAKOLLA.
Thompson, E.P. 1963. *The making of the English working class*, London: Victor Gollanz.
Urton, G. 1992. 'Communalism and differentiation in an Andean community', in R. Dover, K. Seibold and J. McDowell (eds), *Andean cosmologies through time: persistence and emergence*, Bloomington, Indiana University Press.
Veblen, T. 1924. *The theory of the leisure class: an economic study of institutions*, London: Allen and Unwin.
Vernant, J.P. 1965. *Mythe et pensée chez les Grecs II*, Paris: Petite Collection Maspéro.
Wallman, S. (ed.) 1979. *Social anthropology of work*, London and New York: Academic Press.
Yerushalmi, Y.H. 1982. *Zakhor: Jewish history and Jewish memory*, Seattle: University of Washington Press.
Zuidema, R.T. 1985. 'The lion in the city. Royal symbols of transition in Cuzco', in G. Urton (ed.), *Animal myths and metaphors in South America*, Salt Lake City: University of Utah Press.

CHAPTER 7

WHAT KIND OF SEX MAKES PEOPLE HAPPY?

Laura Rival

Many commentators have pondered the contemporary Euro-American obsession with erotic pleasure. Some of them have also reflected on the puzzling gap that usually seems to separate erotic fantasies from the actual experience of sexual pleasure. Their conclusions as to the meanings of everyday sexuality have, more often than not, been contradictory. For sexologists, good sex is eminently physical and practical – all it needs is getting the mechanics of stimuli right in order to climax to orgasm. Psychoanalysts, by contrast, focus on the unconscious mind and the socially rebellious way in which humans often organise their sexual drives (Bristow 1997: 61). Freudian thinkers start from the premise that all social bonds are ultimately sexual (Erikson 2005) and human beings fundamentally incestuous (Héritier et al. 2000). Law and morals, reinforced by the fear of castration, universally ensure that unconscious wishes for sexual encounters with parents or siblings are kept at bay (Freud 1983 [1950]).

The celebrated poet and writer Octavio Paz defined love as the discovery of the mysterious unity of life (Paz 1993: 105). Like all animals, humans copulate and reproduce sexually; but unlike any other biological species, the human species alone can transform the sex act into both voluptuous attraction and deep attachment through a wide range of practices, institutions, rites and representations (ibid., p.106). Master deconstructionist Michel Foucault deplored our current obsession with erotic pleasure, adding with dark scepticism that sex 'has become more important than our soul, more important almost than our life' (Foucault 1978: 156, quoted in Bristow 1997: 10). Foucault did not believe that eroticism and love could be universally fused into the 'double flame' celebrated by Paz. Many thinkers today, like Foucault, analyse sexuality as a distinctly modern and historically specific construction, a construction that cannot be readily applied to sexual arrangements found in past and non-Western societies (Weeks 1995). And what about the neo-Darwinian accounts of human sexuality, proposed by evolutionary biologists and psychologists? These focus on the genetic basis of the differing psychosexual behaviour of men and women. Natural and sexual selection are believed to explain, for instance, the fact that men prefer pornographic magazines, while women get more pleasure out of romance novels (Symons 1979: 170–80). Faced with such a bewildering array of positions what, the anthropologist may ask, makes sex erotic? What kind of sex makes people happy?

Indigenous views are often revealed in clashes between differing practices. If I ask myself: 'What kind of sex makes my Huaorani friends happy?', I immediately think of an incident, vividly remembered and recorded in my field notes, which occurred approximately halfway through my first period of fieldwork, and which alerted me to the highly contextual reality of erotic thought and behaviour.

I had followed 'my' family group (*nanicabo*) downriver to an important meeting that Shuar and Quichua organisations had convened with the oil companies. The meeting was followed by a big party to celebrate Elf Aquitaine's donation of a school and a health centre to a Shuar settlement. Oversized loudspeakers blasted trendy tunes of 'tropical music' (*musica tropical*), to which a mixed crowd of indigenous settlers and 'nationals' (*mestizo* colonists), oil workers, soldiers, prostitutes and farmers danced energetically. I saw two prostitutes approach Mengatohue, an old Huaorani shaman. They invited him to an erotic dance. Mengatohue seemed to respond favourably to their advances, smiling back and joking. Apparently willing to be initiated in the art of brothel dancing, he started to imitate the prostitutes' arm and hip movements with gusto. But nothing in his derisive gesturing betrayed any sign of arousal. The dance lasted some time, the old man mocking the two young women, the latter responding with indulgent superiority, until they grew tired at their lack of success and turned their attention to a more receptive man, a Shuar who had worked for years on the oil frontier.

When the party finally ended in the early hours of the morning, the improvised dance hall became increasingly quiet. It had gradually turned into a dormitory for the Huaorani guests, and everyone was now asleep. The following day, the party was commented upon endlessly. Jokes and excitement are normal fare in the aftermath of such occasions. But, this time, my travel companions also assailed me with questions about *cohuori* (non-Huaorani) customs: Do the *cohuori* always pay for sex, as they do to get food in shops and restaurants? Do the women who sleep with men for 'laughing sex' have babies? Is it because they eat the body of Christ and drink his blood (i.e. are Catholic) that *cohuori* behave like this? Their puzzlement at the sexual behaviour encountered on the oil road was caused not only by its contrast with their own ways, but also by its departure from what they had learnt through exposure to evangelical Protestantism and strict Christian ethics. My own puzzlement stemmed from the fact that even though the two, very attractive, prostitutes had – undoubtedly – made Mengatohue laugh, their erotic dance did not turn him on. He was not seduced.

My attempt in this paper is to describe ethnographically what kind of sex makes a Huaorani man or woman happy, and, by comparing their ideas about sex and love with those found in other Amazonian societies as well as in ours, to explain why their way of behaving sexually, as opposed to their way of fantasising about sex, is best described as *diffuse sensuality*. After having outlined the main characteristics of the Huaorani longhouse and the sex practices that take place under its roof, I discuss some of the fantastic representations of human sexuality contained in myths. I then briefly compare Huaorani sexuality with that of two other Amazonian societies, on which two well-known ethnographies of sexuality have been written. I end with a few remarks on the challenges of studying the general and the particular when talking about the human condition.

SENSUALITY, WELL-BEING AND SEXUAL PLEASURE IN THE HUAORANI LONGHOUSE

Living well is the central ambition of the Huaorani women, men and children who so freely shared their daily lives and values with me during fieldwork. The Huaorani justify many of their ways of doing things and many of the decisions they make with a simple phrase: 'because we want to live well' (*manomaï huaponi quehuemonipa*).[1] *Huaponi quehuemonipa*, often shortened to *huaponi*, an expression continuously used in conversations (as a form of acquiescence) or during visits (as a salutation), refers to the pleasure of sharing life together. People who belong to the same longhouse[2] care for each other and attend to each other's bodily needs.

The longhouse (material embodiment of the diffuse mix of intimacy, relaxed sensuality and warm physical contact that characterises *huaponi* relations between co-residents) consists of a vast rectangular roof that extends to the ground, where neither the hard sun nor the cold rain can penetrate; where the warmth of each woman's hearth can be felt; where there is always something to drink or eat; where one can relax in a hammock in total comfort; and where everyone can be at ease. It is the domain of domestic peace, stability and mutual compatibility, erected by 'the true humans' (*huaorani*) against outside threats and hostilities. Sex and age differences are played down, and a great deal of equality and freedom ensues. Because individuals of both sexes show a high degree of self-sufficiency in providing for their own needs, togetherness is not lived in such a way as to generate dependency. Men and women, adults and children freely move in and out of the longhouse to trek in the forest or to visit relatives. Yet they firmly belong to their collective residence, which comes to acquire its own identity, both in the eyes of insiders and outsiders. House-groups come to be 'united in life'. The expression *ayeromonque quehuemoni* ('we live together as one') implies that co-residents are the ones who matter. By continuously feeding each other, eating the same food and sleeping together, co-residents often develop a shared physicality that ends up being more important than that resulting from genealogical bonds. People actually say that, by living together side by side, they gradually become 'of one and the same flesh' (*aroboqui baön anobain*).

The longhouse is built in a joyful atmosphere (*totequehue*, 'living laughing'). While senior men erect the central poles, mature men prepare the wooden frame, and younger men and boys collect the palm leaves that will make the outer roof. Women, led by the oldest woman of the house, clean the forest floor and level it, while looking for potsherds and other signs of previous human occupation. Another group of women and girls go into the forest to collect the special palm leaves used for the inner roof.[3] Each married woman has her own hearth, on which her husband and children may cook. Each couple has its own conjugal hammock, shared by their youngest children. A man married to two or three sisters takes turns sleeping in his various conjugal hammocks. Sex and births occur in the hammock, by a woman's hearth, inside the longhouse. And it is there, as well, that a woman takes pleasure with a lover: she the host, he the visitor.[4] Old couples with adult children tend to sleep side by side, each in a separate, individual hammock. Bachelors sleep apart in the back of the longhouse, or, sometimes, in an adjunct shelter, and so do very old widows and widowers. Not only is the longhouse strongly associated with a founding grandmother figure, but it also – literally – becomes the tomb of a woman too old to go on living (Rival 2005, and in press). In short, the longhouse objectifies important symbolic and organisational aspects of kinship, in particular the identity of women with uninterrupted consanguinity, of men with domesticated affinity, and the idea of co-residency with sensual intimacy.[5]

Each *nanicabo* is known to other house-groups under a collective identity derived from its corporeity and communal existence (Rival 2002). Yet, these corporeal units are composed of highly self-sufficient, autonomous persons, whose unique, individual characteristics are publicly acknowledged and greatly appreciated. *Huaocä*, the individual person, has great value in this society, and her full development is nurtured by all possible means. Like in most highly mobile societies, pregnancies are spaced. Gaps of five to seven years between full siblings are common. Only *wanted* babies survive and are cared for. Breastfeeding is prolonged, and women breastfeed, in addition to their own children, their sisters' children, and, sometimes, their grandchildren as well. When I visited Bebantoque in the summer of 1989, she often had her sister Nemo's one-year-old daughter at one breast, while her own six-month-old son was at the other. On 25 August, I noted in my diary that she was breastfeeding both a baby monkey and Nemo's daughter. Nemo had gone up-river with her husband and older children. The baby monkey had survived a hunt, and Bebantoque was raising it as a pet for her children. When I asked the old Guiketa to tell me his life story, he started by saying that his father had been killed in a raid while his mother was pregnant with him. A few months after he was born, his older brother died of a snakebite, at which point his mother decided not to look after him any longer. 'My mother said: "Why should you live when my dear older son is dead?" From then on, I was cared for by my sister. She saved me; she gave me a happy childhood.'

Infinite care is taken of infants, and great attention given to young children. Although the mother has prime responsibility for childcare, especially in the first year, the father takes an active role as well, as, in fact, do all the longhouse members. Their dedication to their new member is very physical, as one might expect, given the vulnerability and needs of a young life. But there is something more to it. People really enjoy the presence of young children; they are a source of marvel, laughter and happiness. Babies are associated with what is new and beautiful. Men, women and children simply enjoy spending a great deal of time playing and interacting with babies and toddlers. Such playful interactions are exactly what *huaponi quehuemonipa* is all about. Things do not change much when children grow up and develop, or learn to walk and talk. Education is based on an ethos of pleasure and care, and of full respect for bodily needs, including emotional needs. Children are encouraged to grow fast and become autonomous. As they get older, they learn to value independence and self-sufficiency through a non-authoritarian education that respects them as individuals. Like their adult kin, they spend much time in the forest. They hunt small game and gather in bands, the younger learning from the older. Although pan-Amazonian, the ethos of personal autonomy found among the Huaorani, whose historical past is marked by violent conflicts and the constant fear of raiding parties, is particularly developed. Children are taught to survive and look after themselves from a very young age.[6]

In Huaorani land, no one can be coerced in any way. No one can force or order another person to do something. It is also understood that one should not force oneself either. Learning and the execution of acts occur through voluntary (rather than wilful) participation. Coercion brings about illness, danger or evil spirits. To accomplish anything good, one must be in harmony with oneself and with one's surroundings. Personal autonomy, freedom of movement and mobility are closely related, and often expressed through poetic imagery involving flying birds. Cobari sang a beautiful song about *maeñe* (a type of blue parrot) in Quihuaro on 24 January 1990, which ended with the lines: 'When a drinking party is announced, we swiftly run to it, run, run through the forest… When there are conflicts and disagreements, we decamp in no time, like the *maeñe* bird.'

Individuals who made one's autonomy possible are vividly remembered. Yohue, from Zapino, sang a love song in memory of his mother the day I visited him in 1990. In this song, Yohue started by comparing himself, as a baby, with the *chahua mango* fledgling cracking its shell open while in the nest. 'Like this bird,' sang Yohue, 'I was born in a large nested leaf [i.e. hammock].' He then went on to remember all the things his mother did for him:

> She allowed me to grow and develop through her care. She did so many things for me, helpless creature, so I could grow. I could not even get the food to my mouth, but she fed me, she gave me everything, and this is why I will never forget her. When I was a toddler, she kept the ground clean so that I would not harm myself or fall in the mud. Thanks to her, I have grown into a strong youthful man, and I can sing today, with pleasure and delight. Full of joy, health and strength as I am today, I shall never forget her. My memory is sharp, and I am a fantastic singer.

The song was at once very personal and totally generic. Yohue undoubtedly did remember *bara* (mother) as he sang, but he was also fully aware of the fact that he was singing a traditional Huaorani song. Moreover, Yohue did not simply sing the song as he had learnt it; he sang it as his uncle Omayèbè used to sing it. He also added that Omayèbè had learnt the song from Meñèbè. When people remember kin, either dead or absent, they do so in this very concrete, vivid way. What they remember are the individual idiosyncrasies of the person being remembered, for instance, the unique way she walks (or walked), talks (or talked) or sings (or sang). In addition to an infinite number of physiognomic details, what is remembered are the characteristic expressions, tone of voice and demeanour of a particular individual. Individuals are much valued for the diversity they create (Rival 2002: 100–2). Creativity and innovation result from such unique bodily expressions, and there are as many ways of being embodied as there are individuals.

The well-being of individuals does not conflict with the well-being of the collectivity (*nanicabo*), for the one implies the other. Social values do not generally conflict with personal experience.[7] Togetherness is expressed and continuously re-asserted through sharing practices. When a *nanicabo* member is sick, all residents respect the same food prohibitions. It is this shared, collective curing-effort that helps the patient to recover his, or her, good health. Longhouse members share illnesses, parasites, a common dwelling and a common territory. Love and care are social relations that create solidarity through intimate and sensual bodily practices. True individuals are never alone (Rival 2005). *Huaponi*, glossed here as sensual happiness, is inseparable from love, *huaarete pone* ('think the good, the beautiful').

Children are central to this ethos of personal autonomy and communal sharing. They seek sensual pleasure as actively as adults do, for sensuality, which does not require sexual maturity, is an essential part of belonging to the longhouse. Jules Henry's (1941: 19) remark that: 'the basis for man's loyalty to man [among the Kaigáng] has roots in the many warm bodily contacts between them', equally applies to the Huaorani, amongst whom, too, 'children [lie] like cats absorbing the delicious stroking of adults' (Henry 1941: 18). I witnessed much caressing going from adults to children, and children to adults. Caressing is not simply a way of finding human warmth and comfort; it is also a way of learning about a new body and a new person. Looking at someone is not enough; body peculiarities need to be discovered through touch.

The mixture of bodily closeness, physical proximity and sensual intelligence described here is characteristic of daily life, which unfolds in the comfort of proximity and with the intimacy that goes with holding and touching familiar bodies. Such human contact and bonding occur between spouses, cross-sex siblings and male cross-cousins as well. Men who are warming up around the campfire after a day's walk in the forest sit close to each other. They hold hands or crouch against each other, forming a human chain. Young men love to stand around the fire or sleep together, arms around one another, legs slung across bodies, caressing in little knots of three or four. I have not seen young women do so with the same frequency. This mixture of holding and caressing is very different from the overt sexual gestures we have grown accustomed to in our society.[8] To caress allows one to know intimately the shape and the texture of a foreign body, and to begin to understand how it works. What one is curious about is the extent to which another person's body is similar or dissimilar to one's own.

If the longhouse epitomises the sensual nature of physical comforting, then sex, thought of as heterosexual and reproductive, relates to the lovemaking activities of pairs made up of men and women who are not siblings, who belong to the same generation, and who are of approximately the same chronological age. Lovemaking in this sense is hardly differentiated from the state of being married.[9] When a man and a woman marry, they become *nanoongue* ('spouse'). The husband's brothers and classificatory brothers (i.e. parallel cousins) become *nanoongue* to the wife, and the wife's sisters and classificatory sisters become *nanoongue* to the husband. A Huaorani may have sex with any of his *nanoongue*, that is, if a man, with any of his wife's sisters or female parallel cousins, and, if a woman, with any of her husband's brothers and male parallel cousins. Such extramarital liaisons do not cause sexual jealousy or conflict, so long as they are discrete and sporadic. Brother-sister incest is disapproved of, but does occur. Brother-sister incest is morally less upsetting than a sexual affair between affines belonging to different age groups, such as, for instance, an actual or potential son-in-law and his mother-in-law, a man and his father's sister, or a woman and her mother's brother.

I do not have full or first-hand knowledge of Huaorani love and sexual life, but I slept near men and women often enough to know that the lovemaking that goes on in the hammocks when the night sets in is not what we would call erotic passion. Lovemaking is not generally focused on penetration, or on sexual activity centred on ejaculation. As copulation lasts for an unusually long time, it seems that lovers aim to achieve diffuse bodily pleasure. I once visited a distant *nanicabo* with one of my 'brothers', who had awoken the desire of one of the young female residents. Although they had never met before, or heard of each other's existence, they spent the night making love together in her hammock. This, however, did not stop them from continuing to participate in the *nanicabo*'s nocturnal conversations, or from exchanging jokes with other visitors and co-residents. For a woman, 'fun sex' is sex with an unexpected male visitor, especially if he is *huaca* (non-related). Such visits by unrelated Huaorani men often end up with revelry and sexual teasing, as girls and women spray their male guests with manioc drink or other fluids, including breast milk. A one-night stand with a *huaca* lover is called 'copulate with no good reason' (*ononqui niñi niñi imba*). Such sexual encounters are always initiated by the woman; she is the one who proposes, the one who invites, the one who solicits sex.[10] On 19 April 1990, in anticipation of such an adventure, Meñemo sang the following song:

How happy I am, two boys
Came for a visit, the Cononaco[11]
Men are boring,
Come in my hammock to
Chat with me.

The word most commonly used to convey the feelings that exist between spouses, *huarique* ('love'), is not exclusive to the conjugal relation; it equally applies to other intimate relations pertaining to the longhouse. Sexual intercourse is *niye* (for both animals and people) or *nimoi* (only for people). When the male partner ejaculates, said my young friend Cahuitipe, it feels very, very good: *totequehuenga wenguengä* ('ejaculation resulting in a feeling of great joy'). Cahuitipe did not know whether there was an equivalent term for the female partner, nor did he know whether the expression used by women who wish to copulate, which literally means 'let's make another child' (Rival 1998), could be used to mean 'female orgasm' as well.[12]

My general impression is that Huaorani culture does not eroticise sensuality. Genital pleasure is not treated as the most pleasurable of all pleasures, nor is it clearly distinguishable from other bodily pleasures. Straight sex may be fun, but so are many other types of bodily contacts. Bodily pleasures such as the pleasure and contentment felt during sexual intercourse; the pleasure and contentment of a three-year-old caressing the breast of the woman from whom she, or he, is feeding; the merry feeling of someone stroking gently the body of a caressing companion; the gratification caused by the action of delousing someone's head; or the pleasure of being deloused by someone's expert hands, are not differentiated and ranked on a scale. The interest in developing an intimate knowledge of bodies leads to a form of sensuality that merges physical proximity and well-being. Everyone in the longhouse partakes in everyone else's care and well-being. This represents an enormous investment in sustaining life and happiness within a specific group of persons – matched by a parallel and similarly striking disengagement from material possessions.[13] Passionate, exclusive lovemaking might be happening in secret places known only to lovers, but such a possibility was never mentioned to me. I asked many times whether couples would go to the forest to make love. Each time, my question was met with surprise, then puzzlement, and each time the answer was that 'no', this really was not something the Huaorani would do. Another indication that marital sex is akin to the general *nanicabo* sensuality described in the previous section is that men do not have to abstain from sleeping with their wives before hunting or making curare poison.[14]

FANTASY SEX – MYTHS, DREAMS AND WARFARE

Octavio Paz (1993), who defines romantic love in the West[15] as one of our highest civilisatory achievements, links the capacity for love and erotic pleasure with art and poetry. In his recent theory of the evolved mind, Geoffrey Miller (2001) similarly proposes that art is linked to sexual courtship. Going beyond Donald Symons' (1979) focus on our dual-sexed nature, he argues that music, language and culture are largely the by-products of the sex-drive that has pushed male and female humans to communicate and compete with each other over thousands of generations. Although Paz and Miller use radically different arguments and analytical frameworks, they both recognise the central role played by sexual fantasies in human cultures, as well as the inseparability of anatomy and fantasy in human sexuality.

For the Huaorani, imagined sex is very different from lived sexual experiences. Most remarkably, their myths and dreams tend to elaborate one single theme: the lethal sexual attraction between humans and animals. Huaorani sexual obsessions do not concern the nature of sexual desire, or the way in which sexual desire constitutes gendered subjects. Rather, they depict sexual desire and sexual pleasure as something that takes a life of its own in monstrous encounters, as if the sexual organs had detached themselves from the bodies to which they belong,[16] and had become autonomous. Numerous myths tell the stories of Huaorani women who copulate with male animals (anacondas, monkeys, tapirs and so forth). The liaison is usually initiated by the animal partner. However, the sexual attraction is mutual. In some stories, the female human (often already married) continues to live with her human kin, while having an affair with her animal lover. In others, she goes to live with him in his land, sometimes among his people. In all these stories, the women eventually become pregnant and die in due course, their insides devoured by the monstrous foetuses they carry in their wombs. The most popular of these myths involves a young woman who becomes fatally attracted to a giant earthworm (*cuica*).[17]

There are many different versions of this popular myth. Women and girls giggle with delight whenever the myth is told. When the giant worm is inadvertently met in the forest, its sight provokes a similar excitement, in fact, a mild arousal. Measuring about five times the diameter of a human penis, and approximately ten times the length, the *cuica* worm has a peculiar – shall we say suggestive – way of progressing on the forest floor. In most versions of the myth, the worm resides underground beneath his lover's house, next to the hearth. In other versions, the worm lives in the manioc plantation next to the house, underneath a log. In some versions, the human lover is a young, unmarried girl. In others, she already has a husband. In all of the versions I heard, the worm inserts itself in the human body he wishes to seduce *sub rosa*. The girl or woman is sleeping or cooking, for instance. She does not know why, but she suddenly feels unfathomably well, incredibly happy. After several encounters, she realises that it is *cuica* who gives her such awesome pleasure, and she starts participating more actively in the liaison, actually taking the initiative of going to the places where *cuica* hides, and of calling out to him to come out. In some versions, she ends up dying while pregnant. In most versions, a mother or grandmother (if a girl) or a husband (if a married woman) discovers her secret, and kills the worm. The girl or woman falls into a deep melancholy, and, in some versions, ends up dying of sorrow.[18]

On the basis of numerous conversations with informants, as well as ethnographic observations, I have come to understand these myths as expressing the asocial nature of excessive sexual desire and unreasonable attraction. Too much sexual pleasure kills. Pure sexual pleasure is lethal, for it expresses the autonomous desire of the sexual organs themselves. By becoming detached from the bodies to which they belong, they become uncontrollable, and drive their owners to incomparable sensual pleasure, but also to their deaths (that is, unless the conscious realisation of the danger being incurred, or some human intervention, allows the pleasure victims to regain sufficient control to end the voluptuous and deadly encounter). People's erotic dreams involve non-human lovers (animal seducers and cannibalistic spirits [*huine*]) who pretend to be loving humans to better trick their victims. Myths speak of fantastic associations, in which uncontrolled sexual excitement, loss of self and death are irremediably linked. That such myths involve a seduced human and a seducing animal is unsurprising, given the particular importance of animals as significant others in Amazonian societies.[19] The awesome animal sex matches the fetishised human one – this is the thrill; but the animal can overwhelm and destroy its human sexual partner – this is the danger. The myths articulate common Amazonian anxieties about lack of control and self-control, excess and balance. Numerous Amazonian anthropologists, including, of course, Lévi-Strauss, have noted the central importance of self-restraint and self-discipline in Amazonian myths, moral values that must continuously be re-affirmed against forces that weaken human checks on physical appetites. Crocker, among others, beautifully exposes the Amazonian desire to 'master the world of organic form', which, for the Bororo, involves 'the necessity of rules governing the control of organic process, especially that of sexuality' (Crocker 1985: 289). Moderation and the rejection of invading powers as well as of domineering behaviour are central to the Amazonian political project of personal autonomy.

In the Huaorani case, fantasy sex may also be linked to affinity and warfare,[20] although the ritual connection involved here is far more difficult to interpret than that between sex, dream and myth. On 15 April 1990, as I left a distant house in the Yasuní with Inihua, who was going to be my guide for the next six weeks or so, I heard him shout his last au revoir to his kin from the canoe: '*cuñado menqui huati huati bito hermana huati huati menqui*'.[21] The joke was accompanied by the familiar obscene gesture of a right-hand finger sliding to and fro inside the tube formed by the folded-over left hand. As Inihua was leaving his *nanicabo*, he was reminding them (his wife included) that visitors may always be treated as potential affines, and invited to stay. He was also indicating that non-related men (including non-Huaorani men) can always be treated as virtual affines, a relationship potentially or effectively sealed by the sexual union of one man with a sister of the other. In June 1997, I heard the expression *huati huati* in an entirely different context. I was involved in the filming of a mock raid, when a shout made me jump. The film crew had brought a large doll made of rugs to be used in role-play as the victim of a spear-killing attack. As Yehua and his brother thrust their spears into the dummy, they shouted '*huati huati*' with force. The barbed ends of their spears were pushed back and forth through the rugs (the doll's 'entrails') with astonishing force and determination. The extreme rapidity of the slashing movements frightened me. I had never seen these two normally pacific men break loose in such a way.

The contrast between their sudden outburst of fury and their usually gentle, controlled behaviour could not have been greater. Although not a culture of the erect penis, Huaorani culture does contain associations between warfare and sexual violence. Such associations, however, are not of conquering men or victorious warriors abducting and raping the women of the conquered. Huaorani men do not use their phallic power to abuse or humiliate the defeated, and certainly not to violently inseminate unwilling female bodies. Yet, in the *corps-à-corps* encounters of war, men thrust their spears in a way that mystically fertilises their bodies and the bodies they are destroying.[22] But is the action of spear-killing really that of men? As I have argued elsewhere (Rival 2005), killers overwhelmed by rage are not considered to be fully human.

The young men who have worked for the oil companies are aware of the existence of all kinds of sexual behaviours that are morally condemnable. These practices are called generically 'to annoy' (*molestar* in Spanish), 'to do something that irritates' (*buyo aquequi*), or 'to do something that is sinful' (*huihua aquequi*). Such transgressive behaviour does not occur within Huaorani society, and people are generally horrified by the idea of rape (*huihua mahaca*), for instance. In July 2005, a hundred Huaorani women marched on Ecuador's capital city to protest against the alcoholism and the sexual abuse plaguing the villages close to oil fields. The *huihua aquequi* behaviours recognised within Huaorani society are brother-sister incest and adulterous sex, the latter being identified as sinful by those most committed to evangelical Christianity. Brother-sister incest was always disapproved of, but never considered a perversion. The most important rule in the Huaorani ethical code is that sex cannot be used for political domination, which is, according to my informants, what *huihua aquequi* sex strives to achieve. It is therefore not surprising that sexual fantasies do not contain violent images. Of course, *huine* spirits are inherently violent (they are cannibals). However, they do not violate their victims sexually; they devour them.

SEX, CULTURE AND MYTH IN THREE AMAZONIAN SOCIETIES

To what extent are Huaorani views of human sexuality similar to those found in other Amazonian cultures? I summarise here what we know of Amazonian sexual activities (both ordinary and fantasised), focusing more specifically on Gregor's (1985) and Murphy and Murphy's (1974) ethnographies, the only two lowland South American ethnographies dedicated to the study of sexuality. What interests me most particularly in Gregor's and the Murphys' work is their special focus on mythology and ritual, or, as I call it here, 'fantasised sex'. Both the Mehinaku and the Mundurucú share the 'Yurupari complex', with its association of men's houses, myths of archaic female dominance and prohibition on use of the sacred ancestral flutes by women in male initiation rituals. The Yurupari complex, which shows remarkable parallels with the secret men's cults found in Melanesia, has been extensively documented and discussed in the Amazonian anthropology literature.

There are differences between the Mehinaku and Mundurucú kinship systems, marriage rules and rules of exogamy, which I have no room to discuss in detail here. However, when compared to the Huaorani, the Mehinaku and the Mundurucú appear to share numerous sociological characteristics and to depart from Huaorani ways of organising society in broadly similar terms. Like many Amazonian societies depending on bitter manioc, the Mundurucú and the Mehinaku show a relatively well-developed gender division of labour, with women working harder than men. Gender roles are further segregated due to the existence of men's houses. Both cultures stress equally the polluting nature of female genitalia, the need to respect a wide range of sexual prohibitions and the ritual importance of sexual avoidance. Menstruating and birth-giving women are secluded. Women fear pregnancy and worry about having unwanted children. The Mehinaku and the Mundurucú are particularly extreme, and unusual by Amazonian standards, in their ideological assertion of ritual male dominance. In both societies, men traditionally reside in the men's house, which is surrounded by family houses strongly identified with groups of women related through consanguinity (Gregor 1985: 110; Murphy and Murphy 1974: 116, 133). Men proclaim their superiority over women by virtue of possessing erect penes full of semen. Men alone have the fertilising power of procreation. Women do no more than cooking and feeding the foetuses inserted in their wombs. In both societies, however, women normally ignore men's proclamations and in no way see themselves as inferior. The stress on sexual difference and gender antagonism is mainly expressed in the ritual context. It is in myth, rather than in reality, that women are dangerous to men and in which men must control them. Women's exclusion, intimidation and threats of gang rape relate almost exclusively to the rituals surrounding the sacred flutes. Social institutions based on an ideology of patrilineal descent are too weak to secure any real political power to men. It is precisely the lack of hierarchy and of power asymmetry that exacerbates men's ritual aggression towards women and that explains sexual antagonism (Murphy and Murphy 1974).

Although Gregor and the Murphys are far more interested in the representation of sexuality in myth, ritual and dream than in people's actual sexual practices and love experiences, their books contain sufficient ethnographic data on the latter to support the view that the ordinary sex lives of the Mehinaku, Mundurucú and Huaorani have much in common. In the three societies, having sex is characterised by the same relaxed freedom, as well as by the same lack of technical savoir faire or imagination. Gregor (1985: 9, 34) speaks of the lack of variation in positions, and Murphy and Murphy (1974: 152) of 'an active preoccupation with sex, but little of a colourful nature'.[23] The straightforwardness of heterosexual sex, and the horror manifested at positions or actions other than straight vaginal penetration, including foreplay and clitoris stimulation, parallel strong moral views on what constitutes legitimate sexual relations. For example, the Mehinaku, like many other Amazonian people, hold that 'the only proper sexual object is a cross-cousin of the opposite sex' (Gregor 1985: 9). They see proper human sexuality as that which distinguishes humans from animals, and civilised tribes from savage forest-dwelling groups (Gregor 1985: 52).

The three authors equally view child socialisation as reinforcing the absence of any sense of guilt and the lack of sexual repression. Sexual encounters are not considered secret or shameful. They form an integral, and quite public, part of human life. Murphy and Murphy (1974: 151) note that 'the Mundurucú do not have the acute sense of embarrassment about sex that is characteristic of our own society, and they do not insist on total privacy'. Sexual freedom is simply a part of the general freedom from interference that governs egalitarian societies. I would add that in many Amazonian societies, marriage is a gradual affair that starts with a young man visiting his sweetheart at night in her hammock in her communal house. Such visits are subjected to the same gossip that surrounds extramarital affairs, but no action is taken to legalise the union until the birth of the first child.[24]

Gregor and the Murphys also report the muted character of sexual jealousy, both for men and women, but especially for men.[25] As sexual freedom continues pretty much unabated after marriage – as long as it is discrete – extramarital affairs are very common. Gregor (1985: 37) adds that sexual liaisons give way to long-lasting, affectionate relationships. This explains why extramarital affairs, far from being a source of conflict, bring cohesion to village life.

To this, we can add the mention of more institutionalised forms of extramarital sex in some Amazonian societies. The Araweté, for example, practice 'sexual mutuality', as they say, by which two couples spouse-share over a given period of time, and become ritual friends (Viveiros de Castro 1992: 168). That adultery, far from being a source of shame or humiliation, contributes to social solidarity partly explains why sexual banter is not only well developed, but also a source of constant entertainment in Amazonian communities. The muted character of sexual jealousy is also probably related to the right, granted to women, to have lovers and to enjoy sex. Murphy and Murphy (1974: 150) stress that 'women maintain a strong degree of control over their sexuality, despite male ideology'. Gregor (1985: 33) mentions that it is usually Mehinaku women who choose which of the four culturally acceptable positions the couple adopts during a sexual encounter. Finally, it is clear that native theories of procreation, embryology and multiple paternity militate against strong sexual jealousy.[26]

To recapitulate, like many post-colonial Amazonian societies, the Huaorani, Mehunaku and Mundurucú are remarkably egalitarian. Amazonian political institutions and ideologies are not generally conducive to domination, coercion or oppression. Historical change is denied, ignored, or re-articulated in mythic terms referring to a primordial era, a time when animals and humans were not differentiated. Or, when historical change is wholeheartedly embraced, it is not accepted with nostalgic reference to ancestral traditions, but, rather, as the process through which kinship is created anew in each generation. Personal autonomy is not only highly valued, it is also central to the organisation and continuity of social groups (Rivière 1984). Endogamous kindred-based residential groups represent the social ideal of identity, sameness and non-differentiation. The incorporation of 'others', considered necessary for social reproduction and cultural continuity, is a source of both danger and creativity. Reciprocity is difficult to achieve, and exchange a source of ambivalence.

Compared to Mehunaku and Mundurucú society, Huaorani society is more extreme in its endogamous and autarkic tendencies. Warfare and predation are, beyond the units of sharing or reciprocal exchange, essential components of social reproduction (Rival 2002, 2005). Another aspect of Huaorani 'particularism' is the total absence of rape and domestic violence from social relations. The only form of physical violence, which consists in spearing 'enemies' during a killing raid, is most often exercised by men against men. On-going residence, founded on a unique combination of individuality and togetherness, allows persons and communities to unfold in time through the cumulative experience of living side by side, day after day. Such absorption in domesticity may seem dull and boring, but it makes people incredibly happy; the Huaorani are gregarious fun-lovers. Sensual bonding, as diffuse as food sharing, unfolds as one aspect of the pleasure of living in each other's company. Love and care are social relations that create solidarity through bodily practices. These sensual practices constitute, manifest and reproduce love (as a form of collective well-being and happiness) and the value of living as one content body. Sensuality is not centred on genitalia, nor is it the exclusive domain of adult heterosexuality.

When it comes to fantasised sex, the Mehinaku (Gregor 1985: 55, 150), like the Huaorani, find lovemaking with animals 'better than human intercourse'. However, here too, animal sex constitutes 'a threat to normal sexual relationships', expressing a similar anxiety regarding orgasmic pleasure and the loss of self-control it entails. However, the Huaorani would not interpret what Gregor calls (wrongly in my view) 'bestiality' in Freudian terms. Huaorani men are not locked in a continuous struggle 'with the problems of masculine self-definition and separation from women' (Gregor 1985: 10). To them, loss of self-control is not linked with loss of male identity. In fact, mentions of animal sex in Huaorani mythology concern women far more often than men. The myths express more a concern with the monstrous child that may result from the sexual union of a female human and a male animal than they do with orgasm as a source of boundary loss, although the two are closely interrelated.

According to their ethnographers, masculine identity amongst the Mehinaku and the Mundurucú is particularly fragile and vulnerable, certainly more than it appears to be amongst the Huaorani, at least at first sight. Gregor (1985: 9–10) notes that sex brings ambiguity to Mehinaku social life, which, from the male point of view, becomes divided between sentiments of warmth and connectedness with women on the one hand, and a great deal of anxiety, fear, antagonism and insecurity on the other hand. Murphy and Murphy (1974: 226–31) talk of a Mundurucú masculine personality structured by anxiety, chronic sexual frustration and high levels of dissatisfaction, leading to high levels of sexual antagonism. Moreover, the three authors identify fundamental similarities between the battle of the sexes and male psychosexual identity in both Euro-American and Amazonian cultural settings. Euro-American and Amazonian men, they argue, equally view women as alluring, emasculating and arousing primitive fears of dependence and loss of male identity. Following Freud, they explain the presence of identical psychodynamics in the Amazon basin and Euro-America with reference to universal anxieties aroused by the separation from the mother, which similarly structure individual male personalities all around the world. The contribution of social anthropology, therefore, is to show how social arrangements and institutions interact with these psychosexual proclivities. Whereas the ongoing battle of the sexes and the pervasiveness of sexual ideas is blunted in Euro-American societies (divided by class, education, religion, race, vocation and so forth), it is manifest in Amazonian villages, particularly those organised around men's houses, where 'the intensity of the men's house pattern is directly related to the structural features that unify the men in opposition to the women' (Gregor 1985: 209).

This all too brief comparative discussion allows us to see that what is at work here may be less universal than Gregor and the Murphys claim. More than the universality of masculine psychology, it is the contrast between sexuality as lived in ordinary social life and as represented in myth and ritual that their ethnographies make so plain. The masculine vulnerability they find expressed in dream, myth and ritual is also present in Huaorani society, but in a different realm, that of warfare. Huaorani men do not feel threatened by women and sex, but they are subject to fits of homicidal rage, which cause them to lose their humanity temporarily. As I have argued elsewhere (Rival 2005), to retain or regain their humanity, Huaorani men must belong to affinal matrifocal networks. This brief comparative sketch highlights fundamental aspects of Amazonian gender and personhood that require further comparative analysis and further theorising (Rival ms). To accomplish this task adequately, ethnologists need to address the striking contrast found between Amazonian sexual practices and the sexual world painted in myths. Myths, rituals and ideological statements constitute only one source of cultural knowledge about sexuality and human nature. The challenge of understanding human sexual behaviour remains that of reconciling everyday ordinary sex with ritualised sex, animated as it is by the fantastical possibilities of the human imagination.

LOVE, EROTICISM AND THE HUMAN CONDITION

I have so far established that the diffuse sensuality found in the Huaorani longhouse, far from being exceptional, is typical of the free and relaxed attitude to sex found in Amazonia, including in groups characterised as living particularly anxious or tense sexual lives, such as the Mehinaku or the Mundurucú. But to what extent can we say that Amazonian ways of loving and having sex are comparable to ours? This is obviously a very difficult question to answer, given the peculiarly Western objectification of sexuality alluded to earlier. Bloch (2000), who follows Malinowski in his endeavour to explain cultural variability with reference to universal human needs, cautions us to study invariant human nature in a way that describes accurately the modes of symbolic communication found in human societies. The challenge, as always, is to differentiate what in human action is conditioned by our common biological make-up from what is the product of history. The shift in dominant representations of sex that has taken place during the twentieth century, from Victorian hyper-repression to the present-day commodification of erotic desire and normalisation of transgressive behaviour (in the name of individual freedom and choice), could not have been more extreme. Moreover, the multicultural societies that make up contemporary Euro-America exhibit a bewildering range of attitudes, behaviours, values and beliefs. However, there is ground to argue that the sensual activities I have described in this paper are not as distant from our own everyday practices as it may appear.

We, too, long for physical expressions of sex that are not dissimilar to the infantile need for physical contact. As Malinowski (1927: 246–50) contended, such need is not sexual, even if it has often been construed to be so, at least since Freud's Oedipus complex gained credence. Even in our culture, which increasingly represents sexuality as an abstracted domain of transgressive potentialities, erotic behaviour is firmly embedded within mundane sociality (Rival et al. 1998), and gets muted within households. Working couples with children lose libido through sheer physical exhaustion. To enjoy lovemaking in the way envisaged by Octavio Paz, and cultivate it as passionate and exclusive erotic love, requires time and a certain detachment from the constraints of reproduction and the burdens of childrearing. It is terribly hard to imagine Tristan and Iseult, or Dante and Beatrice, as parents. Another important cause for 'the relative hypo-sexuality of the married state' (Symons 1979: 112) has to do with the fact that individuals forming a family unit undergo complex changes of emotions. A child's birth creates new relations of intimacy within the family. Parents intuitively feel that *the same kind* of love should apply to all individuals belonging to the household. Family love, they feel, should be non-exclusive.[27] There is also the common fear in parents, which easily translates into shame and the loss of sexual stamina, that their children might catch them in the act.[28] Of course, these facts are gendered in complex ways, and whether men and women love and desire sex in the same way is hotly debated in Euro-America, as it most likely is in most societies.

As I have tried to show in this paper, there are greater cultural variations between representations and ritualisations of sex than there are between conjugal experiences of sex. We do not find in Amazonian societies Paz's notion of love as the purifying movement from sex (the low and animal), via eroticism (the cultural and refined pleasure of the flesh), to love (the noble and synthesising sentiment), which fuses body, mind and soul into one single and exclusive passion for the beloved. Nor is sex thought of as the necessary hygienic release of biological energy envisaged by Reich. Sade's erotic art of seduction and domination and Bataille's aesthetics of morbid transcendence are equally absent. Eroticism developed historically within courts peopled by divinised humans and anthropomorphic deities who used their sublimate arts to enliven daily routines structured by racial, class and gender divisions (Paz 1993), all of which Amazonian social worlds are entirely devoid. Twenty-first-century Euro-American representations are unique in their utopian definitions of sexuality as sexual desire and the will to identity. By contrast, Amazonian constructions tend to build on the ordinary pleasures of embedded sexuality. The health of bodies and minds is maintained through the nurture and care of individuals longing for physical comforting. Happiness is cultivated as a birthright, and life sustained as peace and contentment. The need for affection, especially in children, whose condition of vulnerability reminds all of the precariousness of human existence, gets gratified on demand. Love and sex consist of a set of practices that are deeply embedded in relational contexts. They are not divorced from mundane domesticity, or from reproduction taken in the broader sense. In short, what seems to be most at variance in human sexuality is not domestic sex within family units and the corollary 'familiarity [that] dulls the edge of lust' (Symons 1979: 110), but rather, mythical, mystical or ritualised sex. Such imagined sexuality, I have argued, involves others who are, more often than not, unequal others.[29]

Symons' (1979: 127) thesis that sexual activity tends to be reduced by marriage and that the emotional attachment of long-married couples changes from the orgasmic to the affectionate calls us to revisit Westermarck's theory of incest avoidance, monogamous marriage and exogamy (Rival ms). No one has done more than sinologist Arthur Wolf (1993, 2005) to show the continuing relevance of Westermarck's understanding of the human aversion to marrying housemates, or to revive anthropological interest in 'the incest taboo.' By looking at the connections between sexuality and parenthood, Wolf and his associates (Wolf and Durham 2005) have established three important facts. Firstly, they have compiled new scientific evidence confirming Westermarck's Darwinian induction that inbreeding is dangerous (Wolf and Durham 2005: 25–7, 134–5). Secondly, and on the basis of detailed empirical research, they have proven that early association inhibits sexual attraction (Wolf 1993). Moreover, they have shown that humans are not alone in avoiding sexual intercourse with consanguineous kin. Incest avoidance is found amongst primates, as well as in a number of other animal species (Wolf and Durham 2005: 62–7, 162–3). Thirdly, by looking at human sexuality in terms of its biological and psychological aspects, they have shed new light on its cultural meanings and social functions. Having rejected both Lévi-Strauss's emphasis on gift exchange and exogamy and Freud's perpetual struggle between selfish sexual drive and repressive social order, they propose a range of non-functionalist explanations of the link between biology (inbreeding avoidance) and social institution ('the incest taboo'). The non-functionalist explanation of the incest taboo proposed by Wolf is based on a new evolutionary understanding of developmental psychology that reconciles Melanie Klein's psychoanalytical tradition with Konrad Lorenz's ethology. For Wolf and his colleagues, sexual bonds must be differentiated from asexual bonds, and sexual imprinting from asexual imprinting:

> [t]he bonds an infant forms with the mother and other care-takers are fundamentally different from those formed between adult sexual partners. Infant/caretaker bonds are inherently contrasexual ... attachment and aversion are two aspects of the bonds formed in infancy and early childhood ... what natural selection selected for is a universal disposition to form contrasexual attachments to those persons by whom and with whom one is reared. (Wolf in Wolf and Durham 2005: 14)

Erickson, a contributor to the volume edited by Wolf and Durham (2005), uses a slightly different terminology. He contrasts two types of bonding that are biologically and psychologically distinct, each 'adaptive within a different social context', 'familial bonding' (also termed the 'familial type of social affiliation') and 'sexual affiliation', adding that 'the propensity for sexual affiliation develops much later than that for familial bonding' (Erickson 2005: 175–7).[30]

The data presented in this chapter certainly supports the thesis that not all human bonding is of a libidinous nature – as affirmed by Freud. Much of what I have described as everyday, lived sexuality among the Huaorani, other Amazonian peoples, and, for that matter, among ourselves, seems to fit Erickson's category of 'familial type of social affiliation'. However, to argue, as Wolf does, that 'attachment is inherently contra-sexual' (Wolf 1993: 167), requires deeper thinking about the meanings of 'sexual' and 'erotic'. As I have tried to argue here, we need to understand much better the nature of sexual arousal on the one hand, and the nature of enduring attachments between spouses on the other. Rather than erecting a tight wall between sexual and familial affiliation, as Erickson does, or contrasting marriages involving association before the age of three and marriages in which the couples are not brought together until later (Wolf 1993: 161), as Wolf does, we need to return to the questions Durkheim (1898) raised in his critique of the Westermarck effect. As Lévi-Strauss (1983) has argued, promiscuity and conjugality do not exclude but imply each other. The institutionalised coexistence of monogamy and promiscuity has given rise to different social arrangements and cultural representations.

The sex that makes people happy in everyday family contexts is quite unlike the fantasised sex that excites and arouses them. For example, the Muria, who represent erotic freedom and marriage as incompatible, have instituted the bachelor's house, where young unmarried men and women are left to learn and experience the arts of sexual pleasure before stepping into conjugal monogamy, economic partnership and parenthood. Unmarried and married lives are based on very different, yet complementary, principles, and social solidarity depends equally on both (Elwin 1947, Gell 1992). Among the Mehinaku and the Mundurucú, the men's house also creates a form of social solidarity different from, and complementary to, that of the extended uxori-matrilocal household. However, the conflicted masculinity that ensues does not allow for the same neat partition in the life cycle between erotic sensuality and family love. In their attempt to escape the institutionalised tensions pervasive in Amazonia between affinity and consanguinity, the Huaorani have created a longhouse where diffuse sensuality leaves very little room for erotic expression, and a society where exogamy cannot be fully realised.

NOTES

1. In conversations that I have had the opportunity to have with them over the years, old Huaorani such as Guiketa, Quimo or Dabo used the same reasoning to justify their decision to follow Dayuma and the SIL missionaries and live in the first mission bases. Their dear relatives had been killed off by the enemy, they felt deeply lonely and abandoned, but 'Nemo [missionary Rachel Saint] loves us, God loves us, and we live well again'. The mission village, with its church, health centre and North American style log cabins, had become the enlarged symbolic equivalent of the longhouse. And the Huaorani who left the SIL Protectorate, fleeing as far as they could from missionary influences, did so for the very same reason of 'living well'. They resented having to live on Guiketa's land and hunt his game, having their marriage alliances overseen by Dayuma, and being forced to abide by strict evangelical rules. They also found Dayuma and the missionaries particularly stingy and unfair in their distributions of outside goods.
2. The longhouse residential group (*nanicabo*, plural form *nanicaboiri*) constitutes the basic social unit of Huaorani society. Huaorani people prefer to marry close. Preferred marriage is between bilateral cross-cousins, giving rise historically to a high degree of endogamy. Marrying close is especially valued by women (Rival, in press). A child may have more than one biological father (Rival 1998). Compared with other Amazonian societies,

the Huaorani have been, and to some extent still are, remarkably mobile, autarkic and endogamous. The Huaorani's fierce egalitarianism, present-oriented ethos and rejection of elaborate gardening have led them to avoid inter-ethnic contact and exchange. Their hunting and gathering economy is matched by a close-knit egalitarian social organisation based on strong ties and shared communal patterns (Rival 2002).

3. Men behave particularly boisterously while building the house frame and preparing the outer roof. Sexual jokes cover a wide range of topics, from adulterous adventures to suggestions of incestuous matches between, for instance, parallel-cousins or men and women separated by a wide age gap. Bachelors, the favoured targets of such jokes, are subjected to the double-entendres of their adult male kin. Women tend to ignore male banter and bawdy laughs. They weave impassively the inner roof, while singing in chorus. A woman may occasionally engage in rapid verbal jousting with a male companion, to everyone's delight.
4. In Chapter XIII of his *History of human marriage*, Westermarck (1921: 455–76) marshals as much ethnographic evidence as was available at the time in support of Darwin's thesis that male sexual desire is stronger than the female one, and that males initiate courtship. The counter-examples he gives (i.e. women initiating courtship) are almost all from South America.
5. Lévi-Strauss (1983: 195) wrote that 'the house is the objectification of a relationship', and Bloch (2005) fruitfully applied this insight to the Zafimaniry context. He showed how the centrality of the monogamous marriage finds material expression in the elaborately carved wooden houses for which the Zafimaniry are so well known. Cf. also Malinowski (1927: 182): 'The hearth and the threshold not only symbolically stand for family life, but are real social factors in the formation of kinship bonds.'
6. Often left behind by hosts gone trekking, I had many opportunities during fieldwork to evaluate the extensive forest knowledge, economic skills and resourcefulness of Huaorani children.
7. Except in the case of orphans, whose survival and welfare depend on the protection they receive from individuals who choose to take them under their wing. A protégé is considered a member of his or her protector's house-group only as long as the latter is able to take on this responsibility.
8. It is misplaced to mistake such behaviour for homosexuality, defined in the *OED* as 'sexual attraction only to persons of the same sex'. Both Catholic and Evangelical missionaries have spread rumours of homosexual behaviour amongst the Huaorani on flimsy evidence. Archbishop Alejandro Labaca, who was speared to death in 1987 by a group of non-contacted Huaorani, wrote in his diary that on several occasions he had to share his blanket with Huaorani men who caressed his genitals (Labaca 1988: 63). The behaviour

in question concerns masturbation, and nothing else. Although I did not discuss this directly with my Huaorani friends, such caressing seems to me of the same nature as the sensuality described in this chapter. It consists of a mixture of great curiosity for new bodily forms, and a response to felt bodily needs for mutual pleasure. Our own experience of sexual attraction (either hetero- or homo-) does involve the same elements of curiosity and pleasure of giving pleasure, but these aspects are, it seems to me, greatly overshadowed by our Western ideological obsession with sexual desire, possession and orgasm.

9. Called 'two making' (*mina pa*), 'it is a good thing that they should sleep together in the same hammock' (*hua ñoô imba*), 'sleep as one', (*arome mö*), or simply 'sleep together' (*mö*), or even 'multiply through copulation' (*niñcopa*).
10. Gregor (1985: 33) mentions the case of a woman who made love with her lover in her own hammock, not far away from where her husband was sleeping. His Mehinaku informant told him: 'A little danger is pepper for sex'.
11. She is referring to the male youth of her local group.
12. I was also unable to establish this fact in discussions with women. Gregor (1985: 33, 86) experienced the same difficulty in establishing the existence of female orgasm.
13. Huaorani material culture is made up of a few basic artefacts perfectly adapted to nomadic life and freedom of movement. Everything can be easily made, packed and replaced.
14. Several men told me that they would not, however, sleep with a one-night-stand lover before hunting or making curare poison. I was also told that before making spears, one had to sleep absolutely alone.
15. A historical synthesis of Arab erotic influences, Tantric ecstatic experiences and Provençal *amour courtois*, as Paz saw it.
16. Elwin (1947: 102) reports similar beliefs among the Muria, who regard the sexual organs, whether male or female, as living things with an independent life of their own.
17. Unidentified species of the genus *Andiorrhinus*. Gregor (1985: 53–4) found a very similar myth among the Mehinaku of Brazil.
18. There is an equivalent myth about male sexual pleasure, but I did not hear it as often. In the two versions I know, a married man goes fishing. He is called by a *bufeo* (Amazon dolphin, *Inia geoffrensis*), who wants to seduce him. Her genitals are very similar to a woman's, only deeper, softer and moister. After making love for the first time with the she-dolphin, the man finds her so desirable that he cannot stop himself from copulating with her over and over again. Never has he experienced such intense pleasure.

He ends up wasting all his semen and blood; he drowns, and dies in his animal lover's dwelling at the bottom of the river. In a third version I heard, the man was having a sexual liaison not with a dolphin, but with a giant otter (*nutria, Pteronura brasiliensis*). However, the story was identical. Mehinaku men fantasise about having voluptuous but lethal embraces with the feared anaconda (Gregor 1985: 183).

19. Patrice Bidou (2001: 32) reminds us that when Claude Lévi-Strauss was asked by Didier Eribon 'What is a myth?' he answered that, for an Amerindian, a myth is a story about the time when humans and animals were not yet distinct (my translation).
20. Lévi-Strauss (1983: 83–4) explains very well the dangers of autarky and closed endogamy, using Tylor's famous rendering of the choice between 'either marrying out or being killed out'. It is quite clear that Lévi-Strauss's first-hand ethnographic experience in Amazonia has influenced his general understanding of marriage strategies.
21. Literally: 'Brother-in-law (in Spanish), brother-in-law (in Huao), I am going to fool around (in Huao) with your sister (in Spanish), fool around (in Huao), my potential affine (in Huao).'
22. The description of the Shuar *tsantsa* (shrunken head) celebrations offered by Michael Harner (1972) lead the reader to interpret them as involving a kind of virtual-sex encounter between the killer and the avenging soul (*muisak*) trapped in the *tsantsa*, as well as between his wife and the *muisak*.
23. Elwin (1947: 97) makes similar remarks about the Muria's 'simple, innocent, and natural attitudes to sex', which is all the more remarkable, given the institution of the village dormitory (*ghotul*), where boys and girls sleep together and are emotionally and erotically involved with a series of partners before marriage (they marry their cross-cousins). Moreover, the choice of sexual partner in the *ghotul* obeys taboos broadly similar to those operating in Amazonia. Although Gell (1992: 190) is critical of what she sees as Elwin's romanticisation of the *ghotul* as a model institutionalisation of adolescent free sexual love, her ethnography is consistent with Elwin's. Both Elwin's and Gell's ethnographies demonstrate that the mixed village dormitory works at creating intimate physical closeness between adolescent boys and girls before marriage. Relational exclusivity and sexual jealousy cannot develop inside the *ghotul*, which reinforces collective harmony, interdependence and autonomy from the adult world. The kind of 'innocent' sexual pleasures the two ethnographers describe recall the ones I have just described among the Huaorani. Here too the give and take of bodily pleasures is not obsessively focused on penetration or ejaculation. As Elwin (1947: 433) notes, '[a] diffused affection does not promote sexual potency'.

24. The Huaorani are a notable exception to this general pattern (Rival 2002, in press).
25. If we are to believe Napoleon Chagnon, this would not be the case in Yanomami society, where sexual jealousy is the prime cause of warfare.
26. I have discussed, for instance, the Huaorani belief that a child cannot form in the mother's womb unless semen accumulates through repeated intercourse, and, in some cases, through intercourse with more than one man (Rival 1998, in press). The same belief is found in many Amazonian societies, where the couvade is often found in association with uxorilocality, if not matrifocality.
27. No wonder that the loving practices of the Londoners studied by Miller (1998) tend to centre on consumer goods, which materialise everyday practices of attachment, identification, care and concern for one's co-residents. These Londoners 'make love' while shopping, an activity that best expresses their long-term commitment to each other.
28. 'Avoiding the primal scene' is the main reason the Muria give to explain why they prefer to send their growing children to the *ghotul* (Elwin 1947: 322–5). Kenyatta (1953: 161) explains that in the bachelor huts of the Gikuyu, where sexual indulgence is governed by rules not unlike those found in the *ghotul*, brothers and sisters avoid the deep embarrassment that witnessing each other's erotic acts would cause by not meeting their sweethearts in the same huts.
29. Cf. Uchiyamada (1999) for a telling description of sexual relations between unequal partners.
30. Erickson further uses the anti-Freudian distinction between sexual and asexual bonds to differentiate incest avoidance as biological adaptation from incest as pathological manifestation.

REFERENCES

Bidou, P. 2001. *Le mythe de tapir chamane. Essai d'anthropologie psychanalitique*, Paris: Odile Jacob.

Bloch, M. 2000. 'A well-disposed social anthropologist's problems with memes', in R. Aunger (ed.), *Darwinizing culture. The status of memetics as a science*, Oxford: Oxford University Press.

—— 2005. 'Questions not to ask of Malagasy carvings', in M. Bloch, *Essays on cultural transmission*, Oxford: Berg.

Bristow, J. 1997. *Sexuality. The new critical idiom*, London: Routledge.

Crocker, J.C. 1985. *Vital souls. Bororo cosmology, natural symbolism and shamanism*, Tucson: The University of Arizona Press.

Durkheim, E. 1898. 'La prohibition de l'inceste et ses origines', *L'Année Sociologique* 1: 1–70.

Elwin, V. 1947. *The Muria and their ghotul*, Oxford: Oxford University Press.

Erikson, M. 2005. 'Evolutionary thought and the current clinical understanding of incest', in A. Wolf and W.H. Durham (eds), *Inbreeding, incest, and the incest taboo. The state of knowledge at the turn of the century*, Stanford: Stanford University Press.

Foucault, M. 1978. *The history of sexuality. Vol. I: an introduction*, New York: Random House.

Freud, S. 1983 (1950). *Totem and taboo*, London: Ark Paperbacks.

Gell, S. 1992. *The ghotul in Muria society*, London: Harwood Academic.

Gregor, T. 1985. *Anxious pleasure. The sexual lives of an Amazonian people*, Chicago: The University of Chicago Press.

Harner, M. 1972. *The Jivaro, people of the sacred waterfalls*, New York: Doubleday Natural History Press.

Henry, J. 1941. *Jungle people. A Kaigang tribe of the highlands of Brazil*, New York: Vintage Books.

Héritier, F., B. Cyrulnick, A. Nouri (eds) 2000. *De l'inceste*, Paris: Odile Jacob.

Kenyatta, J. 1953. *Facing Mount Kenya. The tribal life of the Gikuyu*, London: Secker and Warburg.

Labaca, M.A. 1988. *Cronica Huaorani*, Pompeya: CICAME.

Lévi-Strauss, C. 1983. 'La famille', in C. Lévi-Strauss, *Paroles données*, Paris: Plon.

Malinowski, B. 1927. *Sex and repression in savage society*, London: Routledge and Kegan Paul.

Miller, D. 1998. *A theory of shopping*, Cambridge: Polity Press.

Miller, G. 2001. *The mating mind. How sexual choice shaped the evolution of human nature*, London: Vintage.

Murphy, Y. and R.F. Murphy. 1974. *Women of the forest*, New York: Columbia University Press.

Paz, O. 1993. *La llama doble. Amor y Erotismo*, Barcelona: Editorial Seix Barral.

Rival, L. 1998. 'Androgynous Parents and Guest Children: The Huaorani Couvade', *Journal of the Royal Anthropological Institute* 5(4): 619–42.

—— 2002. *Trekking through history. The Huaorani of Amazonian Ecuador*, New York: Columbia University Press.

—— 2005. 'Soul, Body and Gender among the Huaorani of Amazonian Ecuador', *Ethnos* 70(3): 285–310.

—— In press. 'Proies Meurtrières, Rameaux Bourgeonnants: masculinité et féminité en terre Huaorani (Amazonie équatorienne)', in C.N. Mathieu (ed.),

La notion de personne femme et homme en sociétés matrilinéaires et uxori-matrilocales, Paris: Odile Jacob.

—— Ms. 'Love, eroticism and human nature'. Amazonian musings on Darwin and Westermarck.

Rival, L., D. Slater and D. Miller. 1998. 'Sex and sociality: comparative ethnographies of sexual objectification', *Theory, Culture and Society* 15(3–4): 294–321.

Rivière, P. 1984. *Individual and society in Guiana – a comparative study of Amerindian social organisation*, Cambridge University Press: Cambridge.

Symons, D. 1979. *Evolution of human sexuality*, New York: Oxford University Press.

Uchiyamada, Y. 1999. 'Two beautiful untouchable women: processes of becoming in South India', in Day, S.E. Papataxiarchis and M. Stewart (eds), *Lilies of the field: marginal people who live for the moment*, Boulder, Col.: Westview Press.

Viveiros de Castro, E. 1992. *From the enemy's point of view: Humanity and divinity in an Amazonian society*, Chicago: The University of Chicago Press.

Weeks, J. 1995. *Invented moralities. Sexual values in an age of uncertainty*, Cambridge: Polity Press.

Westermarck, E. 1921. *The history of human marriage*. vol. I, London: Macmillan and Co.

Wolf, A. 1993. 'Westermarck redivivus', *Annual Reviews of Anthropology* 22: 157–75.

Wolf, A. and W.H. Durham (eds) 2005. *Inbreeding, incest, and the incest taboo. The state of knowledge at the turn of the century*, Stanford: Stanford University Press.

CHAPTER 8

HOW DO WOMEN GIVE BIRTH?

Michael Lambek

In the beginning are the container and the contained, the knife and the umbilical cord. All of us are born of women, expelled and cut apart from them, our life achieved at some risk to our mothers, and at some pain. These facts are obvious. But the idea of birth as a kind of positive sacrifice has hardly captured the Western imagination. Western thought opposes birth to death, and attachment to separation, and it genders these processes so that women are the givers of life and the attachers, and men are the takers of life and the separators. Childbirth has generally been seen as passive and its pain understood as a sort of punishment, Eve's destiny.[1] Similarly, if on another register, ethnographers have been relatively silent about the dangers of childbirth and how these figure in the imagination of our subjects.[2]

If, in the Western tradition, women have little positive association to sacrifice and the struggle over social continuity takes place between fathers and sons,[3] this pattern is hardly universal. Consider Ndramarofaly, Lord of Many Taboos, or, as I read his name, Lord of Many Taboo Violations, a Sakalava prince who lived in Madagascar during the late eighteenth century and from whom I take the question of my title. Ndramarofaly was obsessed with the question and is reputed to have cut open the bellies of pregnant women in pursuit of an answer. Yet today this Sadeian anatomist is one of the most popular and socially active royal ancestors in Mahajanga and the vast majority of his numerous spirit mediums are women.

In this chapter I try to make sense of Ndramarofaly and the salience his question has for Sakalava and so the essay is also implicitly an answer to the question: How might an anthropologist discover 'Zafimaniry questions' (see Preface) in myth? The body of my own investigation is constituted by Sakalava mythopraxis – the mix of narrative and performance – as I encountered it in and around the city of Mahajanga during the 1990s. The protagonists are royal ancestors of Boina, a polity founded around 1700, who possess the living in the form of spirit possession (*tromba*). Succession still operates and a hereditary ruler reigns. Gender distinctions are more important conceptually than politically; the present ruler is a man but he was preceded by his mother.[4] In mythopraxis women play a central role. At first sight, ancestral women are portrayed as victims, dying either at the hands of men or in the process of giving birth. However, their vulnerability is also a source of strength. When Sakalava consider the relationship of birth to death, or mothers to sons, what they imagine may be quite different from what is portrayed in traditions where the male voice, exclusively, is hegemonic.

What I call mythopraxis troubles secular divisions between myth and history, past and present, myth and ritual, religion and (bio)politics. Sakalava mythopraxis is comprised of three entangled registers, namely spirit possession, material remains and narrative. In *The weight of the past* (Lambek 2002) I emphasised forms of practice, curation and performance at the expense of narrative per se; this essay is one attempt to rectify that. Nevertheless, I take narrative to be but one register of expression rather than a discrete object in its own right ('myth'). Narrative locates the exploits of royal ancestors genealogically, sequentially and in the past, yet a striking fact of the Sakalava poiesis of history is that it also enables simultaneity. Ancestral characters irrupt in the present through the bodies of spirit mediums, engaging the living and each other. They provide a set of historical voices that offset one other in the manner Kenneth Burke described as dramatic irony (1945). Even the present is ironised by the past, and hence its hold as literal reality is destabilised. One could view this simultaneity as an expression of the paradigmatic dimension of myth, foregrounding the axis of comparison or substitution that Lévi-Strauss (1963) argued is as relevant as the syntagmatic, linear or narrative dimension. Moreover, it reinforces Lévi-Strauss's demonstration that myths are not discrete or singular entities but can only be understood in relationship to one another, as transformations within a larger structure (1969). However, the point of using the word 'mythopraxis' is that the narrative, or mythical, dimension is inextricably connected to the performances and practices of the spirit mediums.

The characters of mythopraxis are formed through events that took place when they were alive and especially around their deaths. Each spirit evokes a particular narrative and these narratives contextualise and interpret each other. In a sense, each character condenses the narrative from which it is constituted. The narratives I abstract and summarise below are rarely recited explicitly or in their entirety. Rather, they form a kind of tacit backdrop, specific details serving as objects of allusion, means of interpreting or validating, when necessary, what is seen or encountered in another register. Ancestors are public figures, but their lives are private; recounting their stories can be a shameful exposure, a means of weakening rather than honouring them. However, the paradoxes of the secret follow; there must be a play between the revealed and the concealed.

The interest in individual rulers does not necessarily correspond to their respective roles in the affairs of state, to history and politics as Westerners ordinarily think about them. Sakalava historicity is not primarily about evoking past glories. Bragging, in any case, degrades its subjects. The focus is more on transgression and violence, through means that are either less direct or much more visceral than an academic essay makes possible.

How do women give birth? Why do birthing mothers sometimes die? What is the secret of life? What are the sources and limits of women's reproductive power? These are profound questions and they don't necessarily have simple or specific answers. One cannot readily attack them in the spirit of empirical investigation, as Ndramarofaly did. Indeed, I have not sat down with specific women and men and asked them these questions. Nor have I overheard them asking them directly for themselves, though I frequently encountered informal theological bridge-building between the Abrahamic religions and Sakalava ancestral tradition. Instead I describe the mythopraxis from whose interpretation such questions emerge or of which such questions may be said to form an interpretation. I follow Lévi-Strauss in that I take myth to be the crystallisation of a set of primary oppositions (life/death, female/male, etc.) rather than a specific argument or moral. Nevertheless, the narrative line can be dramatic and compelling, and myth is not merely the unreflected or unrationalised *product* of thought (or act of thinking, of the mind turning over, as it does in dreams) but a *source* of, or for, thought, contemplation or rationalization, from which listeners and practitioners can draw pleasure, instruction or wisdom in a variety of interpretations, much as we do in watching Shakespeare or reading detective novels (to take only two familiar genres). Indeed, many of our own large questions receive their best treatment in this form and philosophers themselves increasingly draw upon literature or film to find better answers or better questions.

In sum, rather than attempting to reproduce or describe a logical argument, specific model or set of ordinary practices concerning birth and death, I elaborate the texture of the cultural tradition, the corpus of semi-public 'texts', like that of Ndramarofaly, in which these issues take a specific form. Thus, instead of providing answers to the questions, I ask, whence come the Sakalava questions themselves? What has led Ndramarofaly to take such an interest in them? Not surprisingly, my interpretation leads to classic anthropological concerns with descent and succession. It leads also to questions of power and sacrifice, commitment and betrayal, sex and death, as well as of birth itself.

Insofar as I draw not from the ethnography of ordinary life, from descriptions of, or talk about, actual childbirth (whether commoner or royal), the epistemological basis of this chapter is rather different from others in the volume.[5] But mythopraxis is as 'real' as any other institution of social life and does condense a body of cultural knowledge and a local philosophy. If at arm's length from the everyday or commonsensical posing and response to questions, it has the advantage of preserving historical thought. And ordinary Sakalava who wish to ponder such questions might be provoked by engaging their mythopraxis, much as someone might turn to biblical texts or secular literature.[6] Indeed, one could go further and suggest that their very subjectivity, as women and men, is shaped by it (Moore, 2007).

It is instructive that Ndramarofaly was not enquiring about conception or about the role of sexual intercourse in procreation. Perhaps these points are too obvious or perhaps they are simply irrelevant to Sakalava for the larger issues to which birth is linked. Whatever the case, I never heard anyone theorise or portray conception – and I believe it is a telling fact about Sakalava that they focus, rather, on birth. Sakalava assume the male role in conception by means of intercourse but they don't elaborate on paternity; they do return repeatedly to questions of motherhood and birth. This is in keeping with the general valuation of performance over essence or substance (Astuti 1995, cf. 1998, 2000) and with understanding kinship through idioms of containment and decontainment (Gould n.d., cf. Bamford 2004). The incontrovertibility of birth also attracts.[7] There is only one thing more patent – and that is death.

Unlike sexual intercourse, birth is a locus of agency exclusive to women and, hence, also an object of male fantasy about their own beginnings. Insofar as the question of how women give birth concerns the potency of women's bodies and of women's intentions, it is puzzling to men. For different reasons it is problematic for women. Indeed, it forms an intrinsically heteroglossic question, inflected by gender and double-edged: asked by men; asked simultaneously, but differently, by women of themselves. The question has the propensity for being thick in the Ryle or Geertz sense of metapragmatics (Geertz 1973): men imagining women's knowledge, women parodying men's interest, etc. Ndramarofaly's curiosity is a man's, as is his method for satisfying it. Yet in taking on his persona, his female mediums appropriate male curiosity about women and his violence towards them, transforming or revealing it as a form of love. Today Ndramaro, Lord Many, as his name is affectionately shortened, would seem, rather, to care for women than to harm them, and frequently manifests as a healer. At the same time, his very presence evokes the story for which he is known. What is evident here is less ambivalence than polyvalence,[8] constituted through a series of frames; no woman – or man, for that matter – approves of Ndramaro's crimes, yet they continue to recall them and to appreciate the character. This is not entirely unlike our rehearsal of, and interest in, the villains of literature or works of art that portray violence.

The polyvalence, one could say, is overdetermined, stemming from the many characters that comprise the Sakalava corpus, the double-voicing and framing characteristic of spirit possession, the distributive nature of mythical knowledge and the absence of explicit, authoritative versions, and from the different ways women and men, people of different royal factions, distinct social locations or unique personal experience interpret each character and their interrelationships (Lambek 2002). For reasons of space I suppress discussion of alternate versions. However, I hope to demonstrate that imagery of violence directed *at* women, also speaks to, and *for*, women.

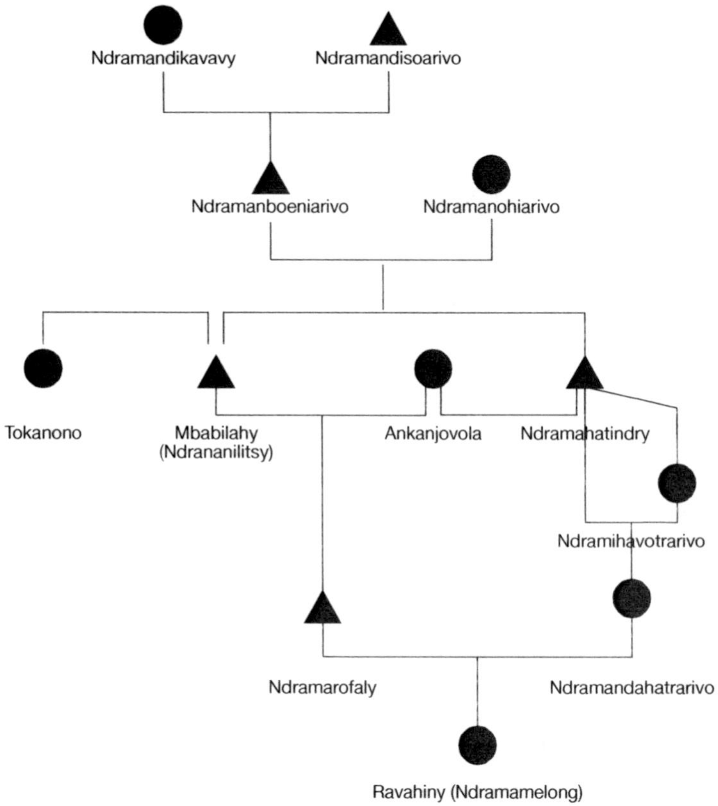

Figure 8.1 Genealogy of Sakalava rulers of Boina

Having contextualised the place of Sakalava narrative, I now proceed to link together some royal figures. I present my account 'backwards', beginning around 1819 and ending five generations earlier, around 1700.

Scene I. Daughter and Father

The culmination of Sakalava power and prosperity was achieved during the lengthy reign of Queen Ravahiny, at the beginning of the nineteenth century. Historical documents describe the lively international trade in Mahajanga and the wealth that flowed into the Queen's coffers. She had a powerful army and huge herds of cattle, and she received tribute from as far as the court of Imerina. Within five years of her death all this was reversed. The Merina army overran the capital in 1824, Ravahiny's successor fled, and the kingdom fragmented into a number of smaller polities. Merina domination was succeeded by French colonialism and, eventually, by incorporation into the Malagasy nation-state with its capital in Imerina.

I do not know whether it is more accurate to say that Ravahiny reigned or ruled (cf. Evans-Pritchard 1964). Whatever the extent of her power and however much she shared it with advisors, she was certainly respected and venerated during her lifetime. Yet her splendour is not represented in contemporary Mahajanga. Ravahiny is hardly mentioned and her *tromba*, known as Ndramamelong, rarely appears. People explained that, as the Queen was very old when she died, the *tromba* can do little but sit.[9] I suspect a stronger reason for the disinterest is that her death was not very striking. Most *tromba* are characterised by their mode of dying, and most did not die of old age. An additional factor to ponder is that despite the rule of queens, female ancestors appear less frequently than males and almost never at public festivities. Female *tromba* are embodied almost exclusively by female hosts; it is explained that they do not wish to enter men or that it would be unacceptably promiscuous for them to do so. The majority of hosts of male ancestors are also women, but there are plenty of male mediums as well.

If Ndramamelong rarely appears, her father, who never reigned, is among the most popular spirits in Mahajanga. He is none other than Ndramaro. Ubiquitous at possession ceremonies of all kinds, Ndramaro wears a bulky red loincloth, ties his hair in a topknot, and brandishes a spear. He sits on a low stool, bouncing vigorously or beating his chest, and drinking copious amounts of rum. Ndramaro, women say, was wild (*maditra*, *sauvage*). Rude and countrified, he is unfamiliar with urban refinement and ignorant of the ways of Europeans who, already during his lifetime, were plying their trade in Mahajanga. Ndramaro spent much of his youth in the forest, accompanied by his hunting dogs, and is even sometimes referred to as a bandit (*fahavalo*). Yet, despite his intimidating appearance, usually in portly women, and his violent past, Ndramaro is rather benevolent.

This uncouth Lord of Many Taboo Violations evokes the pre-colonial epoch but he also serves as a transitional figure. He is more approachable than his own forbidding ancestors. His genitor and his pater (father and father's full younger brother) are understood as founders, respectively, of the Bemazava and Bemihisatra royal factions that vie to reign in Mahajanga.[10] As the son of each, Ndramaro mediates between the factions and between his ascending and descending relatives. Ndramaro's ubiquity also stems from the fact that he unites, in his person, an alliance between two fraternal and sometimes competitive branches of royalty. His mother is Zafinifotsy, the royal clan of White or Silver, whereas his father is Zafinimena, the royal clan of Red or Gold. Red rules in the region of Mahajanga whereas White is dominant in regions further north and east. White has greater seniority in Mahajanga but less authority. Ndramaro appears in gatherings of his Red relatives but he also accompanies his maternal kin, where his red clothing stands out among figures garbed exclusively in white. He epitomises singular unity.

Ndramaro never reigned in Boina, if for no other reason than that he died young. His father's brother, Ndranavia, a noted diviner (*moas*), is said to have killed him by means of medicine (*fanafody*) in order to stop his violent investigations. Ndramaro died alone, deep in the forest; some say people were led to his body, wedged up in a *sakoa* tree, by his loyal hunting dogs, others that his body was never recovered. His tomb, located at his pater's cemetery, is supposedly well guarded by a dog, but there is disagreement over whether he occupies it.

Ndramaro briefly married and his single child, a daughter, eventually ruled. In direct line to succeed on both sides (*ampanjaka mena*), Ndramamelong had impeccable credentials and it may well be that the narratives I present concerning her ancestors were developed during her reign.[11] It is said that her parents were brother and sister, another instance, from today's perspective, of Ndramaro's violation of taboo. But as noted, in Sakalava historicity – as opposed to Sakalava history – Ndramaro plays the more significant role. Moreover, his position as Ndramamelong's father is incidental to his representation. Far more interesting to Sakalava than the question of fathers and daughters is that of mothers and sons.

Scene II. Birthing Mother

Ndramaro's grotesque obsession with the literal source of babies can be linked to the concern of the royal lineage with limiting births in order to minimise potential conflict over succession. But on a more personal level it is surely connected to his unfinished relations with his mother and to the conditions of his own birth.[12]

Ndramaro was raised by his father's youngest brother, Mbabilahy (not the uncle later reputed to have had him killed). Fearing future rivals, Ndramaro's genitor had the habit of putting his infant sons to death. Mbabilahy was saddened by this and so took Ndramaro after he was born. Ndramaro's mother, Ankanjovolamanjaka (Queen Silvershirt) followed her son and began to live with her brother-in-law. Having conceived Mbabilahy's child, Ankanjovola subsequently met her end in the act of childbirth.[13]

People do not like to talk about the subject and most Mahajangans deny any knowledge of her circumstances. It is dangerous and inappropriate to comment on the lives of the royal ancestors and their deaths can only be referred to euphemistically. But mediums in active possession by the Mother of Ndramaro (Maman' Ndramaro), as Ankanjovola is called, sit braced with their legs apart, panting or shuddering heavily, supported by another woman leaning against their back. Moreover, Ankanjovola abhors pregnant women. She will not rise in their bodies or appear in their presence and she does not like her mediums to give birth. Cattle sacrificed on her behalf must not carry any trace of a foetus. All this is in keeping with the rule that *tromba* avoid the things associated with their deaths.

Once a woman is possessed by Ankanjovola, she no longer gives birth, although the Queen will allow a medium to raise children if asked politely. In fact, most of Ankanjovola's mediums are childless or have lost babies. Sometimes they swell in false pregnancy. It could be said that they identify with her, or make sense of their circumstances, by means of possession by her. However, it is equally the case that the mediums' lives serve to interpret the character of the ancestor. One woman described how when her sister-in-law, a medium of Ankanjovola, appeared pregnant, her relatives assumed it was false. To their surprise, she did give birth; however, she has had only the one child. Ankanjovola is described as reserved (*miavong*) and harsh (*mashiaka*) but also as very clean (*madio*) and abhorrent of dirt, traits characteristic of the sister-in-law as well. Of course, not all childless (or obsessively clean) women are possessed by Ankanjovola, and it is important to note that she signifies not infertility, but the danger of childbirth and the unpredictability of the outcome of pregnancy. Her mediums are usually host to her husband, Mbabilahy, as well.

Ankanjovola appears infrequently. When she rises, the medium's body struggles with the contractions of birth. This is a powerful performance, all the more so for the fact that, like ordinary Sakalava women giving birth (Feeley-Harnik 2000), she does not cry out in pain and the birthing itself is never spoken of. The performance has great poignancy because it is childbirth that never achieves culmination; it is the act of struggling to give birth, not the positive resolution, that is performed; it is a woman suffering in childbirth and it signifies her imminent demise. Here is a brief description of Ankanjovola rising in a woman who was still undergoing initiation into full mediumship (September 1995):

> Ankanjovola's son, Ndramaro, her husband, Mbabilahy, and her brother, Ndramandenta, are present, in possession of their respective mediums, as the client dons a matching silk shirt and headscarf.[14] Ankanjovola enters very powerfully, but gradually, slowly intensifying her shuddering until she is fully present. A woman sits directly behind, her legs to either side of Ankanjovola's hips and with a pillow covered in a cloth placed at her back. The client's husband sits behind this woman, his back to her, to brace her as Ankanjovola strains and pushes back hard. Mbabilahy holds his white cloth over his wife, whispering soothingly, then remains hovering over her with affection and concern. Someone wields a rattle, another plays a stringed *valiha*, and others sing as each person, including her brother, inclines in turn towards the Queen. Ndramaro sits briefly on her lap, adding to the weight, before moving down to her feet. The other *tromba* urge the client's husband forward. He inclines his head to Ankanjovola and offers her some money, but it is rejected. Shortly after, Ankanjovola leaves the body of the client and enters that of the presiding medium who has donned a blouse of pale yellow silk with silver threads. The performance is repeated and Ankanjovola acknowledges the respect she receives by dabbing her perfumed handkerchief onto the heads of all who incline to her. Women massage her thighs and Ankanjovola accepts some money, speaking in a very high voice.

Ankanjovola signifies, for women, the disappointments and dangers inherent in childbirth. Her male offspring are killed and another infant dies at birth and is the cause of her own death, leaving only her son Ndramaro. As queen, she is a kind of sacrificial figure, limiting her reproduction and offering her life for the avoidance of sibling rivalry and the good of the polity. But for all women, to be pregnant is to risk personal safety and autonomy for a greater good. Conversely, to give up on ones reproductive capacity can be acknowledged by being possessed by Ankanjovola and contributing to reproducing her ancestral legacy. In the course of active possession, she is shown homage, respect and sympathy by her husband, brother and other kin, by the medium's own menfolk, and by other women. People seek her blessing.

Scene III. Single Breast, Single Offspring

Ndramaro was raised by Mbabilahy, henceforth referred to as his father (Baban' Ndramaro), who himself produced no other offspring.[15] Ndramaro and his mother were caught between competing brothers. The older brother, Ndramahatindry, was legitimate successor to his father and ruler of Boina, but a ruthless man who killed his infant sons. The younger brother, Mbabilahy, moved away and was invited to settle in the domain of a woman with whom he established relations of (fictive) siblingship.

This woman had only one breast and so was named Tokanono (One-Breast). Her only child, a daughter, died unmarried and childless.[16] Tokanono was a seer (*moas*) whose insight led her to give domain over her land to Mbabilahy. In return, he promised to ensure continued observance of her rites and care of her tomb. Mbabilahy established a tomb village for himself and his descendants at no great distance from hers. Each year a ceremony is held by Mbabilahy's followers at Tokanono's tomb before the service at the royal cemetery of Betsioko. The peculiarity of Tokanono's service is that the cow sacrificed on her behalf must contain a foetus in its womb.

Leaving no descendants, One-Breast signifies the limit of singular birth and nurturance. Mbabilahy has no direct descendants either, but gains them through the son of his wife and his brother, much as he gains dominion from his fictive sister. Tokanono is clearly opposed to Ankanjovola; the meat from Tokanono's sacrifice cannot be eaten precisely by anyone who is a medium of Ankanjovola, whose own sacrifice must be a beast that is not pregnant. If Tokanono is literally only 'half' a mother and continuously seeking to consume fertility, Ankanjovola is a kind of 'double' mother (of one son to two fathers) who subsequently avoids fertility. Ankanjovola's fate is determined by maternity, Tokanono's by its absence (no descendants). But in both cases, as mediated by the bovine sacrifice, the imagery concerns the relationship of mother-with-foetus.

In one respect Ndramaro is the product of affinity. His mother is Zafinifotsy, her husband Zafinimena. An alliance is set up; her son partakes of both lines. The frequent presence of Ankanjovola's brother in performances of possession emphasises the point. But Ankanjovola's story has equally to do with consolidating a single line. The fact that the brothers share a wife and son produces singular descent at the most intimate level and limits the line of succession. Ndramaro is the son of two brothers who compete for rule and whose later descendants continue to do so. In his own generation he has no competitors because on one side his genitor has killed his brothers and on the other side his pater's child dies. The death of Ankanjovola effectively terminates further procreation in this line. Ndramaro's subsequent investigation of women's wombs can be seen not only as a kind of retrieval of the lost mother but also as a search for missing siblings – or even as a technique, in the legacy of his genitor, to exclude their appearance. Ndramaro's solitary treks in the forest indicate the loneliness and puzzlement of singularity – of having no full siblings and fathering no siblings.

Singularity is also a factor in marriage. Ndramaro married his sister, a daughter of Ndramahatindry through a different mother. In fact, according to one tradition, Ndramahatindry married his own daughter, Ndramihavotrarivo. It was the daughter of this union – simultaneously Ndramaro's half-sister and his niece – Ndramandahatrarivo, whom Ndramahatindry married off to Ndramaro.

The story of this marriage does not circulate widely in Mahajanga. I heard it only once, from an elderly medium. She recalled that when Ndramaro was born, Mbabilahy took the baby.

> Mbabilahy and his wife went far off into the countryside [*añala*] to raise him. When Ndramaro was grown, Mbabilahy took him to meet the king. They beat drums and danced the *rebiky* [a dance of royal celebration that – significantly – signifies the competition between two fraternal lines] to respectfully greet [*mikwezi*] the king. The king, Ndramahatindry, recognised his son, but did not reveal this. He said to his younger brother [*zandry*]: 'You have just one child, let us marry him to my daughter.' The younger brother could not decline, fearing

> that if he rejected the offer Ndramahatindry would kill Ndramaro. So he was agreeable [*tsy manahy*]. The couple were married, but Ndramaro left very quickly, a few days after the wedding and before he knew his wife was pregnant.
>
> So Ndramaro's sister [and wife] had only one child, Ndramamelong. Ndramaro is an only child and gives birth to only one child. [*Ndramaro lalahy toka, miteraka toka.*] Ndramahatindry had said to his brother: 'Since you give birth to single offspring [*miteraka toka*], let us marry them.'

The emphasis here is on the singularity of succession, but there is something more. The story provides a deeper explanation for Ankanjovola's death in childbirth. In forcing a marriage between the siblings, Ndramahatindry was exacting revenge for the theft of his child and the refusal to acknowledge his paternity. In this version, Mbabilahy and Ankanjovola had fled to the bush where Ankanjovola pretended to give birth to Ndramaro. The narrator added, specifically, that it was Ndramahatindry's anger (*heloko*) that produced the uterine illness (*marary kibo*) that subsequently killed Ankanjovola. The logic of her mediums who swell in false pregnancy is now clear.

For women today, neither Ankanjovola's role as wife to competing brothers, nor her role as daughter and sister to the Zafinifotsy, proves her main significance. The story of Ankanjovola, and especially her performance in spirit possession, is not directly about her relationships with men. Nor is it directly about motherhood, about the potential and rewards of pregnancy or childbirth. Most critical is something of which the literature on pre-colonial societies is surprisingly silent – namely the danger of pregnancy and childbirth.

From this experience men are excluded. Certainly, Ankanjovola's son was excluded – and we know what he did subsequently.

Scene IV. Brothers

That Ndramaro's two fathers, themselves full brothers, are opposed to one another has its roots in their respective relations with their own mother. Once, when their father, Ndramboeniarivo, returned from a military expedition he heard a rumour that his wife, the boys' mother (and Ndramboeniarivo's own FaSiDa), had been unfaithful during his absence. He questioned each of his sons closely. The youngest son,

Ndrananilitsy, protested: 'I cannot know, Father, my back was turned.' Since then, he has been known by his supporters as Mbabilahy, a name which appears to mean Man-who-turns-his-back but sounds like Man-who-carries-on-his back. The allusion is to the common manner in which women carry their infants, strapped to their backs, but also to the way in which attendants bear the ancestral relics in procession (Lambek 2002). 'Bearing' in this sense refers to the caring aspect of kinship and kingship. In his response to his father and in averting his vision by turning his back, Mbabilahy showed care for his mother, anticipating also the way he would care for her descendants, including Ndramaro. By contrast, the older son, Ndramahatindry, affirmed their mother's infidelity and even named the interloper.

It is evident that the competition between the brothers transcends the politics of succession and has deeper, Oedipal roots. One brother served as witness, possibly false witness, to his mother's adultery. The other, 'turned his back'. The younger son doesn't see, or refuses to see; the older son not only betrays his mother but also appears to have observed her, and thus, insofar as sight is knowledge, to have been party to the sexual act. Both sons loved their mother. One identifies with her, becoming a maternal, or nurturing, figure in his own right; the other rejects her in fear of his own incestuous desire. The latter subsequently kills his infant sons, no doubt out of sexual, no less than political, rivalry and possibly suspecting them of having been conceived in adultery. Put another way, for denying his obligation to his mother he loses his own sons.

Scene V. Husband and Wife

In accusing his mother, Ndramahatindry exhibits jealousy and callousness, but his subsequent violence towards his own sons has a precedent in the act of his father. On learning of their mother's ostensible infidelity, the boys' father, Ndramboeniarivo, flew into a rage and murdered his wife. He disfigured her, cutting off her nose and ears. The terror and brutality of his act has reverberated down the centuries and still exerts a powerful effect. The suffering continues to be born by the couple's respective mediums, whose paths may never cross, and before whom the events may not be alluded to without causing them much anguish. This is as true for Ndramboeniarivo, a powerful and not entirely uncommon figure in the city of Mahajanga, as it is for the single medium of his wife Ndramanohiarivo, who lives in isolation by her grave in the countryside.

Her name can never be pronounced at the shrine in Mahajanga, nor does she appear in the city. An elderly medium recalled seeing her once, long ago. She held her cloth over her nose. Ndramboeniarivo rose, calling longingly for his wife ('*Vadiko, Vadiko*') but she left at once. She is angry and rises infrequently in her medium.

Another medium noted that when Ndramanohiarivo rises in the bush she keeps her face covered by a white cloth – even when she is walking – and she sways back and forth. Ndramboeniarivo's medium would die should he visit her home. Should they happen to appear together at the cemetery of their son (at Betsioko), the woman would leave immediately. In contrast to other royal couples they cannot be hosted by the same medium.

Scene VI. Mother and Son

In sum, here is the bloody tale so far. The brutal murder of a wife by her husband provokes their son in turn to kill his male offspring. One child escapes with his mother, who dies in childbirth, and he subsequently kills pregnant women until he is put to death himself. Three generations of violent men, three generations of female victims.

Ndramboeniarivo's act cannot be attributed to simple jealousy. Adultery is not unheard of in Mahajanga and does not usually produce violence. Women's mobility and sexual agency are relatively unrestricted. Ndramboeni was a favoured person, the single offspring of the union of his parents, the sole ruler. He inherited the kingdom his father had founded, the land and people his father had conquered. He was the father of several legitimate children. He had every benefit and privilege. His name, originally pronounced Ndramboniarivo, means, Lord Who is Above Thousands or Lord of the People a Thousandfold. Why was he so ready to listen to gossip (*resaka*); why was his retribution so quick and so terrifying? Why such ruthless violence?

It can only be explained – insofar as violence of this order *can* be explained – through Ndramboeni's relationship with his mother. She is Ndramandikavavy, Lady Who Surpasses All Women, the most powerful woman in the Sakalava ancestral regime, and, indeed, the single most respected ancestor.

Adultery on the part of his wife not only cheats Ndramboeni (or challenges his paternity), it also raises the spectre of the violation of a promise made to his mother by his father. It had been promised Ndramandikavavy that only her descendants would rule in Boina. Ndramboeni was the single joint offspring and his reign was the first instantiation of that promise. Any infraction by his wife risked abrogating the promise immediately in the next generation; were she to become pregnant by another man, the continuity of descent from Ndramandikavavy could be lost. In this triangle, Ndramboeni's loyalties are clear. Grief at the loss of his mother, compounded by anger and humiliation, turns to rage against his wife.

Note that the question of paternity is relevant here because it disrupts the line of descent originating from a woman. Conception becomes salient only insofar as it threatens to displace the priority of birth.

Why are Ndramboeni and his mother so close? Why was the promise made to Ndramandikavavy in the first place? And why, when it is threatened, must the son respond so savagely? Why, indeed, is the promise to Ndramandikavavy still honoured today? We have arrived at the first mother and the beginning of the cycle in this Sakalava equivalent of the chronicle of the ill-fated house of Thebes. This chronicle, though, is about the flourishing of the polity of Boina.

Scene VII. Boina, c. 1700

Like Abraham from Ur, or Moses out of Egypt (though they did not know the analogy at the time), the Sakalava Zafinimena, the Clan of Red or Gold, comprising men and women with their children and their herds, have marched north, some 1000 kilometres from Menabe, Great Red, where their leader's older brother succeeded to the throne. The leader wonders how to establish legitimate rule over the new countryside. 'If you want to reign successfully here,' said the oracle, 'if you and your descendants are to flourish, you must give up what is dearest to you, what you cannot bear to part with [*raha tsifoinao*].' The King pondered this. He offered the strongest and most beautiful cattle from his herd, but they were not acceptable. He proposed his gold, his coins and jewellery. He offered precious Chinese porcelain. The King was stumped and grew despondent. Finally his wife heard of his dilemma.

The Queen understood at once. 'I am what is most precious to you,' said his lovely, forthright and proud wife. 'The oracle refers to me.' And so she offered herself. Some say she cut her own throat or that she bravely presented her neck to the knife. Others say she was buried alive, urging people to have courage and finish the job. No matter how it happened, her blood came into contact with the earth, sanctifying and potentiating it (*mankamasing tany*) and thereby establishing her husband's attachment to Boina, but also – and not incidentally – rooting the rights of her own descendants, and thus of herself, in perpetuity.

It is as if the willing death of a woman is transformed into a birth.

UNDER THE SIGN OF THE MOTHER

I must forgo a full portrait of Ndramandikavavy and only summarise a few key points. The Queen willingly sacrificed herself on condition that her son and his descendants would have exclusive right to rule. But more than this, it is implicit that her sacrifice was conducted in his stead. She died so that he might live. Furthermore, by taking such courageous action, she pre-empted and, in effect, emasculated her husband. He continued to rule, but the authority was hers. This is evident in performances of spirit possession. The Queen is very affectionate with her son but rudely dismisses her husband and chases him away. The Queen is a harsh and decisive interlocutor, whereas the King complacently confirms what people want to hear.

As in the Greek narrative, the triangle is simultaneously personal (Oedipal) and political. Yet in Sakalava mythopraxis fathers and sons mostly do not confront one another directly; father-son violence is mediated by the actions of the mother. Ndramboeni succeeds and replaces his father, but the act that makes this possible is carried out by his mother. Moreover, while never consummating their relationship, mother and son remain objects of each other's desire.

The Queen also ensures her son's singularity. The interpretation made earlier of Ankanjovola's death here finds its confirmation – Ndramandikavavy gives her son the privilege of having no full siblings. Death prevents her from giving birth to additional children who could compete either for his mother's affections or for the throne. And as part of her contract with her husband, she specifically excludes any of his offspring from other wives – Ndramboeni's half-siblings – from succession. By the time they arrive from Menabe it is 'too late' and all that is left for them is to rule over the cemeteries. Sakalava royalty were obsessed with reducing the number of competitors in each generation. They even produced a 'medicine of fewness' known as *vy lava tsy roy*, the 'long iron that is not two' (Feeley-Harnik 1991), a sacred staff that is a kind of materialisation of the contraceptive effects of Ndramandikavavy's sacrifice and that may have been directly linked to it (Poirier 1939: 66). Since members of the royal family of both sexes were notorious for taking lovers, succession is specified within a specific marital union and it is primarily within this union that the 'medicine of fewness' should operate.

Hence the key players in royal succession in Boina have been mothers and sons. The ideal ruler is a man born of a royal mother. The system is neither patriarchal nor matrilineal; ideally both spouses are members of the royal clan and successors to the throne are, thus, like Ndramamelong, royal on both sides. Sometimes succession is through royal fathers, but every ruler traces descent back to the Son and thence to both his parents (referred to respectively as Grandmother and Grandfather [*Dady* and *Dadylahy*; note that the male form is secondary, literally 'male' *dady*]) at the head of the genealogy. The founder is not a single man, nor a single woman, but a couple.

The Son's generation was the ideal – a ruler through both his mother and father, and having no full siblings. The Son's singularity is underscored by the older half-siblings on either side who cannot rule. The family triangle is thus a perfect exemplification of fully bilateral ancestry.[17]

The Son (Ndramboeni) responded to intimations of his wife's unfaithfulness in a fashion totally uncharacteristic of Sakalava. But the unprecedented brutality of his act is understandable in terms of what he owes his mother and his closeness to her. His wife's adultery risks rendering his mother's death for naught. Moreover, the extent of the wife's violation becomes evident once it is realised that her lover is none other than Ndramboeni's paternal half-brother, the head of the very line that the promise extracted by Ndramandikavavy had been designed specifically to exclude. Ndramboeni's wife, herself, is also a member of his father's lineage but not his mother's.

LINES OF ANALYSIS

We have moved back five generations, from Queen Ndramamelong to Queen Ndramandikavavy, from Ndramaro who cut open women in order to find the source of life to his great-grandmother who killed herself in order to provide the kingdom with life. Is there a single, or conclusive, message in all this violence? If the Sakalava produce single rulers, their mythopraxis, like all strong stories, leaves itself open to multiple forms and layers of interpretation.

The simplest interpretation, the Malinowskian one, is that Ndramandikavavy provides the charter for the monarchy of Boina, both for the legitimacy of its ruling line and for the means of ascertaining succession. Rule must stay within Ndramboeni's line of descent and legitimate royal offspring must be few, to minimise segmentation. Indeed, the concern with limiting the number of royal siblings is quite explicit. This may mark a kind of political revolution designed to shift away from the segmentary polity that led to the dispersal of the lineage and the move to Boina in the first place. Rendering the royal ancestors so violent, and so ready to overlook the morality of ordinary folk, also reinforces, in the tradition of sacred kingship (De Heusch 1985), their extra-human quality and hence both their symbolic potency and their actual power.

The framing of possession and the composition of relatively discrete generational episodes invite a supplementary interpretation of the narrative line, or 'syntagmatic' dimension, paying particular attention to what Lévi-Strauss (1963) calls the 'paradigmatic' dimension, in which the episodes can be understood as transformations of one another. Along the paradigmatic dimension the chain of motivation between acts is irrelevant; rather, each act can be seen – and used – as a kind of interpretation of each of the others. One could say that Sakalava mythopraxis surveys the various 'tragic ways of killing a woman' (Loraux 1987), each repeating the argument that the mother's death is the surest way to restrict the number of her offspring. However, a pure structuralist analysis is a kind of anti-interpretation, merely attending to the play of signifiers (like Tokanono's cow, who must carry a foetus, as opposed to Ankanjovola's, who must not) in generating an array of alternatives. The resulting display of sex and violence may be thrilling to its audience but contain no moral.[18]

While compelling, a structuralist analysis is insufficient in this case for two main reasons. First, the paradigmatic dimension is complemented by the syntagmatic one with its strong narrative line of unfolding events and consequences. The episodes are not, simply, a set of mathematical transformations but are anchored in the story of successive generations of a family. The acts of each generation are shaped by those of the preceding one, such that each episode makes sense in relation to what preceded it. Furthermore, the generational sequence not only repeats, elaborates and reinforces the political messages but it also transcends the merely political; it invites an interpretation in terms of human motivation and it evokes the great passions – ambition, rage, jealousy and so forth. Although I do not have the space to describe them here, performances of the characters, by means of spirit possession, offer an acute and subtle rendering of the underlying psychological forces at play, and this is reinforced by the comments of my interlocutors.

Second, what we have is not a rarified realm of pure myth but a grounded, embodied practice. Insofar as the characters are incarnated by contemporary Sakalava, they cannot help but be psychologically realised or interpreted. The ways in which ordinary Sakalava are seized by particular ancestors and forced, thereby, to reinterpret their personal lives; the means by which spirit mediums are able to give effective and convincing performances; and the dialogical spaces opened up by performances, both between the various characters and between the characters and their audiences – all suggest a psychological and political salience that a purely structuralist analysis avoids. As the characters and events are realised in human lives, their interpretation is intrinsic and ongoing.

Where the subjects are pregnancy, birth, siblingship and violence against women, one can assume that there is a salience to ordinary experience and to relations between the sexes. I emphasise that the mythopraxis is at arm's length from everyday life and does not directly represent the experience of ordinary women and men in their relations with one another. Nevertheless, like art and literary forms with which we are more familiar, the mythopraxis cannot but draw relevance from these experiences and relations and, thus, offer a resource through which they can be thought. I offer a few suggestions of the issues that may be at stake for various (not all) participants.

On the one hand these stories emphasise singularity and attempts to avoid producing siblings. This is the ideal of reproduction in the royal family, but certainly not among most other Sakalava. Singularity of offspring implies a singular relationship between the child and his, or her, parents. The mythopraxis encourages reflection on mother-son attachment and the dangers of excessive love. Unfulfilled in his marriage to a sister, Ndramaro seeks his deceased mother in other women; his mother steals her son away from his father and dies in childbirth as a result. Her two husbands – who are full brothers – exhibit contrasting, but equally strong, attachments to their mother who, in turn, is victim of her husband's rage precisely because of his attachment to his own mother. This mother not only dies for her son but continues to display her intimacy with him through generations of mediumship.

The flip side of this love is violence against women. Ndramandikavavy is the victim of her husband's weakness, Ndramanohiarivo of her husband's jealousy, Ankanjovola of male rivalry and the dangers of childbirth. Yet the women are agents as well as subjects, and the violence is neither condoned nor directly gynophobic. In volunteering for sacrifice Ndramandikavavy steps into history, ensuring not only the future of the polity but, also, her own central and enduring presence within it. In generation II the son kills his wife to avenge his mother. In generation III the mother rescues her son from the violent father; in performance she is treated with care and respect. And in generation IV, where the son seeks his origins in women, rehearsing the death of his own mother, his random violence proves intolerable and his father's brother decisively puts an end to it by killing the wayward son. The latter's daughter comes to the throne and rules for many years during the height of Sakalava prosperity. In generation V the monarchy comes of age and equilibrium; Ndramandikavavy's contract is fulfilled in Ndramamelong.

While it might be tempting to interpret the mythopraxis functionally as reinforcement of, or resistance against, patriarchy, this is clearly inadequate because what is being elaborated is not a patriarchal system. The founding ancestors are a male/female couple and bilateral descent is critical. The power of women is not belittled or denied, and although less often than men, women too have succeeded to the office of monarch. Moreover, the kinship-gender system of ordinary Sakalava is also characterised by a relative equality between the sexes and gender divisions that are not especially sharp; women are mobile, dissolution of marriage relatively easy and domestic abuse infrequent.

One way to read the mythopraxis is as a message concerning the continuous vigilance necessary to maintain women's rights against a backdrop of potential male dominance. The mythopraxis does not provide an ideal portrait of women or a sexually egalitarian society; rather, it locates women as actively demanding recognition of their worth as social and political actors. Women affirm their power and courage as birthing mothers and acknowledge the sexual tension between women and men. Bilaterality is effected to counteract an ostensible patrilineal norm in which the king's son by his first wife might well have been the successor. Hence it obviates polygyny and the competition among co-wives and half-siblings. Bilaterality equally demonstrates the determination of mothers to exercise rights in, and through, their children and hence their rights to becoming ancestors. Sexual adventure both enlivens personal experience and challenges orderly succession. Mythopraxis describes less a model of gender relations than a mode of gender politics.

Ndramandikavavy's sacrifice was hardly conducted without self-interest. If it was performed on her husband's behalf, she turned it to her own ends, effectively transforming his opportunity into hers. She watches jealously over her rights and intends to see that the bargain is kept in perpetuity.[19] It is both for and through her resoluteness that she is remembered (Lambek 2007). Ndramandikavavy does not mince words and her message to women is to be assertive, not to suffer in silence.[20] Her female descendants identify with her; they refuse polygyny and are said to have difficulty remaining in a marriage.

The message evoked by Ndramanohiarivo is not that women will be punished for being unfaithful, but rather that male violence against women is a terrible thing. Her husband remains guilty and susceptible to punishment to this day. Moreover, insofar as she is pictured as being at fault – and I have never heard her directly so accused – her failing was less that of a wife than of due respect for Ndramandikavavy. She failed to live up to the moral order constituted by her mother-in-law, not that of patriliny or patriarchy.

For Sakalava, what one suffers in silence, and honourably, is not what is inflicted illegitimately by others, but what one bears in carrying out one's legitimate role. Women's silence in childbirth is a silence of ownership and self-respect, not of intimidation (Feeley-Harnik 2000).[21] Death, too, is something of which one should not speak. Ndramandikavavy's death is both widely known and carefully silenced. To reveal it is simultaneously to honour and to shame her, to acknowledge her power and to weaken it. It must be represented indirectly; the name should evoke the story rather than introduce the retelling. To speak about it is also dangerous – to inadvertently raise her attention and anger. But honour trumps shame; Ndramandikavavy is not a passive victim and she sets her terms. She initiates the action; her sacrifice establishes her as not just a wife, but as a queen, a mother and an ancestor, indeed, as a *founding* ancestor and even as *the* founding ancestor. It gives her rights over her husband and she is not shy about asserting them. Her husband offers no resistance.

For men the mythopraxis argues neither that they must fear women nor repress them. It acknowledges their attraction to women and especially their indebtedness and attachment to their mothers. Men must recognise their mothers for the pain and danger endured in bearing them. And so they must give up, sometimes, what is dearest to them, as the first king gave up his beautiful wife, as Ndramboeni destroyed his wife, as Ndramahatindry pushed his wife away, or as Ndramaro renounced his wife for life in the forest. But all this merely reinforces the power and significance of women, both as mothers and as wives, as agentive subjects and as objects of desire. Women can rely on the fact that men will continue to pursue them, just as men can rely on the fact – but not take for granted – that women will continue to give birth to their children and successors.

CHILDBIRTH AND SACRIFICE

Feeley-Harnik (2000) begins her strong essay on Sakalava childbirth with a story in which God gives the rights in children to fathers because, when tested, a man said he would willingly give up his life for that of his child whereas a woman said she would renounce the child's life before her own. Feeley-Harnik notes the discordance between this story and the heroism attributed locally to women in childbirth. Childbirth is described as a spear battle; mothers triumph over their pain and assert their claims to offspring by remaining silent during labour. She tentatively (and correctly, in my view) attributes the story to Muslim influence. If so, is there a Sakalava alternative? I suggest that I have presented it. Ndramandikavavy explicitly gives up her life so that her son can live, in much the way that Ankanjovola later dies in childbirth and that – according to statistics cited by Feeley-Harnik – so do 2.4 mothers in 1000 live births.[22] Perhaps these women (their fate subject to silence in so many societies, as in much ethnography) are the indirect referents of the victims of Ndramaro's predations.

The story Feeley-Harnik heard is, of course, a complete reversal of the facts. In the Abrahamic tradition fathers *are* willing to sacrifice their sons, and in Greek myth fathers *do* sacrifice daughters. In Sakalava tradition mothers *are* evidently willing to sacrifice themselves for their children.

Sakalava mythopraxis both inverts the generational relationship of the Abrahamic myth and changes the role of women from passive to active. In each episode the mother dies and is replaced by a son, yet her identity as mother remains salient. Ndramboeni values loyalty to his mother above that to his wife. Among Ndramboeni's sons it is the one who is loyal to his mother who proves the hero and inherits his brother's wife and son and, in effect, the kingdom. By contrast, the role of daughters is negligible. Ndramandikavavy and the king have no daughter together; Ndramboeni has no sister. Mother-daughter relationships are ignored or, as in the case of Tokanono, portrayed as leading nowhere. Ndramanarakadreny, Lady Who Follows her Mother, is the common genealogical epithet for figures who drop out of historical memory without providing descendants and who are buried alongside their mothers. Nevertheless, Tokanono also demonstrates agency. Offering dominion to her fictive brother in return for her commemoration as an ancestor parallels Ndramandikavavy's contract.

Ndramandikavavy's motherhood is not simply biological and private, an instance of *labour* (Arendt 1999), but also a public and political *act*. She has dramatically ensured her significance across time and also the political significance of her female descendants. It is my contention that Ndramandikavavy's act also raises childbirth itself out of the mundane and into the heroic. Her sacrifice is likened to the act of giving birth in that the life of the child is placed in competition with that of the mother. The Queen's wager is comparable to the dangers women face in childbirth, as epitomised by Ankanjovola. Just as Ndramandikavavy's sacrifice is a form of birth (birth of the polity), so do Sakalava liken giving birth to sacrifice, the dangerous, valued act from which the social world begins and from which men and women flourish.[23]

CONCLUSION

Most interpretations of myth are offered from a male perspective – and indeed there is much in the content of Western myths to make them plausible. But the Sakalava corpus is different and it speaks as much from, and to, women as it does from, and to, men. It speaks to women's experience – especially to death in childbirth (and implicitly to lack of contraception) and to vulnerability to male violence. But it transcends, rather than dwells, on women's subjection. Bloch (1986) has noted that

Malagasy ritual production proceeds by means of symbolic violence against women, albeit in the service of both men and women. From the perspective of Sakalava mythopraxis, this is not to be equated with their conquest.

In the end, the mythopraxis is not about 'women' or 'gender' per se, but about death and birth and ensuring unitary social continuity. The issue isn't infertility, miscarriage or multiple births (twins), but the problem of limiting *successive* births. The death of the mother is one solution but this, in turn, raises the more general point about the danger to women of giving birth.

I do not wish to reduce Ndramandikavavy's historical character to motherhood, but she does lay down her life for her son and both her husband and son must honour her for it. That such sacrifice is not simply a single heroic deed but risked at every birth is reinforced by Ankanjovola's performance. Through the mediation of Ankanjovola, every woman can identify with Ndramandikavavy, putting herself at risk for the purpose of having or saving her child, asserting agency and assisting in social reproduction. Like Ndramandikavavy, women must subject themselves to pain and danger without complaint, must freely and courageously accept childbirth or mediumship. And so, all Sakalava women deserve to be honoured.

Towards the end of his book *Beginnings*, Edward Said takes up the thought of Vico, for whom human history begins with the effort taken to bury and set the dead in order. Said concludes, after Vico, that there must be an: 'intentional beginning act of will to have a history and a continuity of genealogy' (1975: 371). It is presumably no accident that it is the mother whose death signifies the intentional beginning of the Sakalava polity and who comes to signify determination. Giving birth itself is construed as an 'intentional beginning act of will'. It is the risk of dying in giving birth, of death on behalf of life, which informs this intentional act.

Answering Ndramaro's question of how women give birth – or not – has led to questions about men, male violence towards women, and the love between mothers and sons. But ultimately Sakalava answer that birth is achieved through the courage and determination of women. It is this resoluteness, manifest in the bellies of pregnant women, which Ndramarofaly is after.

ACKNOWLEDGEMENTS

I offer this chapter with great affection and admiration to Maurice Bloch, an inspiring leader in the field of Zafimaniry studies. The latter can be taken both as a metonym for Malagasy ethnography and in the sense intended by Rita Astuti, Johnny Parry and Charles Stafford for whose invitation and collective editorial diligence I am much indebted. Maurice himself offered a characteristically bracing critique of an earlier draft. Gwyn Campbell, Sarah Gould, Eric Jennings and Andrew Walsh supported my initial provocations, and all the members of the workshop that gave rise to this volume, especially Christina Toren, offered insightful responses. The Social Sciences and Humanities Research Council of Canada has generously supported fieldwork in Mahajanga, conducted in six trips, of four to six weeks each, between 1993 and 2001. My Malagasy sources mostly prefer to remain anonymous. They are diverse and, except where specifically noted, in general agreement with one another, though providing different details. Further acknowledgments can be found in Lambek 2002.

NOTES

1. On passivity, cf., for example, Martin 1992. For a long time I myself persisted in calling this essay 'How Are Babies Born?'
2. But cf., amongst others, Allerton (this volume); Hershatter (in press); and also the extraordinary thesis in progress on pregnancy and its dangers in northern Pakistan (Emma Varley, University of Toronto).
3. I am thinking primarily of Abraham and Oedipus and the various transformations of their respective stories.
4. Unless otherwise specified, I refer to the Bemihisatra faction of the Sakalava polity.
5. Feeley-Harnik (2000) provides a vivid ethnography of birth among Sakalava of Analalava.
6. Many Sakalava are Christian or Muslim and so might turn, as well, to their respective texts and traditions.
7. Paternity becomes incontrovertible only when illness or blockage is attributed to ignoring or denying it (cf. Feeley-Harnik 2000).
8. I owe this phrase to Emmanuel Tehindrazanarivelo (personal communication).
9. I have not encountered Ndramamelong directly. Her elderly medium described her as walking with a cane (*tongozo*).

10. The two factions have quarrelled for many decades. The shrine currently active at Mahajanga belongs to the Bemihisatra faction. The stories I recount are taken mainly from members of this faction.
11. The stories certainly validate her right to rule, placing her in the most direct line from the founders. Ndramamelong herself married a Muslim outsider (*Arabo*), thus changing the nature of royal alliance and diluting the purity of subsequent rulers. She may have been the first Muslim ruler of the dynasty.
12. I say 'surely', but such interpretations were, mostly, not stated explicitly by Sakalava consultants.
13. The baby appears to have died as well. Gender is unstated, likewise whether it was a miscarriage, stillbirth, breech delivery, etc., or even a false pregnancy. Ankanjovola owes her name to the fact that at her marriage she was adorned with so much jewellery it appeared as though she were dressed in silver.
14. The shiny silk (*dalahany*) is an Arab import worn by all the pre-colonial queens.
15. In another version, Mbabilahy is genitor and Ndramaro the product of his mother's adultery with her husband's brother.
16. Some people mention two offspring, both childless. On women with one breast, cf. Obeyesekere (1984).
17. Another version links the story to polygyny. Ndramandikavavy's sacrifice asserted she was best-loved among her co-wives (Hébert and Vérin 1970), even though she was a junior wife and had given the king but a single offspring. Here, if wives are the source of dispersion and disunity, so Ndramandikavavy forges unity and a single line of descent.
18. I thank Maurice Bloch (personal communication) for this point.
19. But while the story told by women says that Ndramandikavavy demanded her son's right to rule as the price for her sacrifice, the deeper point is the converse: the price for her son alone to rule was her sacrifice.
20. She is also jealous of women whom she suspects of having designs on her husband and is not shy of telling them off.
21. Feeley-Harnik suggests that a woman who cries out in childbirth might be suspected of having committed incest. In Mayotte, when a senior man cried while pinned under a fallen granary, this was seen not as a sign of prior incest but as incest itself (Lambek 1993). That is to say, 'incest' (*mañan antambo*) is the illegitimate reversal of ordinary role relationships and not restricted to sex per se.
22. She is citing the maternal mortality rate for Madagascar as a whole for 1980–7 as computed by the Population Reference Bureau, Washington, DC 1990 (Feeley-Harnik 2000: 143).

23. That sacrifice is a form of beginning, hence of birth, is argued in Lambek 2007. Like birthing mothers, sacrificial cattle must indicate free intention by uttering no complaint (Lambek 2002).

REFERENCES

Arendt, H. 1999. *The human condition*, 2nd ed., Chicago: University of Chicago Press.

Astuti, R. 1995. *People of the sea*, Cambridge: Cambridge University Press.

—— 1998. '"It's a boy," "It's a girl"! Reflections on sex and gender in Madagascar and beyond', in M. Lambek and A. Strathern (eds), *Bodies and persons*, Cambridge: Cambridge University Press.

—— 2000. 'Food for pregnancy: procreation, marriage and images of gender among the Vezo of western Madagascar', *Taloha* 13: 173–92.

Bamford, S. 2004. 'Conceiving relatedness: non-substantial relations among the Kamea of Papua New Guinea', *JRAI* 10: 287–306.

Bloch, M. 1986. *From blessing to violence*, Cambridge: Cambridge University Press.

Burke, K. 1945. 'Four master tropes'. Appendix to *A Grammar of Motives*, New York: Prentice Hall.

De Heusch, L. 1985. *Sacrifice in Africa: a structuralist approach*, Manchester: Manchester University Press.

Evans-Pritchard. E.E. 1964. 'The divine kingdom of the Shilluk', in *Social anthropology and other essays*, New York: The Free Press.

Feeley-Harnik, G. 1991. *A green estate*, Washington DC: Smithsonian.

—— 2000. 'Childbirth and the affiliation of children in northwestern Madagascar', *Taloha* 13: 135–72.

Geertz, C. 1973. 'Thick description: toward an interpretive theory of culture', in Geertz, *The interpretation of cultures*, New York: Basic Books.

Gould, S. N.d. 'The children of ancestors: child circulation and kinship in Marambitsy, Madagascar' (provisional title, PhD dissertation in progress, University of Toronto).

Hébert, J.-C. and P. Vérin. 1970. 'Le doany de Bezavo', *Bulletin de Madagascar* 287: 373–6.

Hershatter, G. In press. 'Birthing stories: rural midwives in 1950s China', in J. Brown and P. Pickowicz (eds), *Dilemmas of victory: the early years of the PRC*, Cambridge: Harvard University Press.

Lambek, M. 1993. *Knowledge and practice in Mayotte*, Toronto: University of Toronto Press.

—— 2002. *The weight of the past*, New York: Palgrave-Macmillan.

—— 2007. 'Sacrifice and the problem of beginning: meditations on Sakalava mythopraxis', *JRAI* 13(1): 19–38.

Lévi-Strauss, C. 1963. *The structural study of myth. Structural anthropology I*, New York.

—— 1969. *The raw and the cooked: introduction to a science of mythology. Vol. I*, London.

Loraux, N. 1987. *Tragic ways of killing a woman*, Cambridge MA: Harvard University Press.

Martin, E. 1992. *The woman in the body*, Boston: Beacon.

Moore, H. 2007. *The subject of anthropology: gender, symbolism, and psychoanalysis*, Cambridge: Polity Press.

Obeyesekere, G. 1984. *The cult of the goddess Pattini*, Chicago: UP.

Poirier, C. 1939. 'Les royaumes Sakalava Bemihisatra de la cote nord-ouest de Madagascar', *Mémoire de l'Académie Malgache* XXVIII: 41–101.

Said, E. 1975. *Beginnings*, Baltimore: Johns Hopkins University Press.

Varley, E. N.d. 'Kalashnikovs and *Kala jhadu* (black magic): Sectarianism, sorcery, and insurgent reproduction in Pakistan northern areas' (provisional title. PhD dissertation in progress, University of Toronto).

CHAPTER 9

WHAT HAPPENS AFTER DEATH?

Rita Astuti

Anthropologists, starting with Hertz, have claimed death as their object of study. They have been able to do so by transforming death from a purely biological into a pre-eminently social phenomenon. As Byron Good (1994: 2) has noted in the context of a discussion of illness and disease that equally applies to death, this transformation was deeply counter-intuitive and required a strong act of consciousness because, like death, illness and disease appeared so evidently and uncompromisingly biological.

With the possible exception of the Hadza and other immediate-return hunter and gatherer groups (Woodburn 1982), ordinary people all around the world appear to be capable of this same strong act of consciousness. They, too, transcend the reality of biological death by routinely transforming lifeless, stiff, cold corpses into sentient ancestors, wilful ghosts, possessing spirits, pure souls or their equivalents, all of whom defy the biological constraints that impinge on human social life and on human creativity.

In his comprehensive analysis of the processes through which humans transcend the discontinuity of their finite existence, Bloch (1982, 1986, 1992) has given us an account of how this transformation is accomplished in ritual. In this paper, I want to ask how it is enacted in people's minds. Ann-Christine Taylor (1993) has brilliantly described the hard mental work that the Jivaro are expected to undertake when someone dies. In order for the dead to be transformed into spirits, the living must forget their faces. And so, people work at painstakingly dis-remembering the dead, as they chant graphic descriptions of the decomposition process in an attempt to erase the familiar faces from their minds.

Although the Jivaro may be unique[1] in their explicit emphasis on the *mental* work that is required to give the dead a new existence, we can assume that everywhere the transformation of corpse into ancestor, ghost, spirit or whatever, will have to take place as much in people's minds as it does on the burning pyre, underground, in the sky and so on. Quite simply, for the dead to survive, people must keep them alive *in their minds*. The research I have undertaken amongst the Vezo of Madagascar is an attempt to look closely at how this is done.

Arguably, most people around the world will have cause to reflect on what might happen after death, as they will also have cause to reflect on the other existential questions that are addressed in this volume. As anthropologists, we may gain access to such reflections by witnessing moments in which our informants explicitly engage in philosophical speculations of the sort described by Bloch (2001) for the Zafimaniry; or we might choose to infer our informants' existential conundrums and their attempted solutions from their mythopraxis (e.g. Lambek, this volume); from their life histories (e.g. Carsten, this volume); from their committed efforts to understand how the world works (e.g. Keller, this volume); and so on.

The strategy I shall adopt in this paper is markedly different, though complementary, to those adopted by the other contributors. While I shall start with two ethnographically based accounts of what Vezo adults say about the continuing existence of a person's spirit after death and what they say about the brutal finality of death as they handle the corpse of a close relative, the core of my investigation is based on the results of a simple experimental design that records the judgements that Vezo people make when they are asked very specific hypothetical questions about what happens after death to a person's heart, eyes, ears, memory, vision, sensation, knowledge, emotion and so on. This methodology is intended to reveal the way people apply their knowledge about the consequences of death to make novel inferences (for example, now that such-and-such a person is dead, do his eyes work? Does he hear when people talk? Does he remember the location of his house?), rather than to elicit previously articulated beliefs in the afterlife that people would offer in answer to more open-ended questions such as: 'What happens after death?'

The choice of this methodology is motivated by the long-standing realisation in anthropology that what finds its way into language provides only limited cues to people's thought and knowledge (e.g. Firth 1985: 37), and by previous research in Madagascar on people's understanding of the process of biological inheritance that found a significant discrepancy between what Vezo adults say and the knowledge they deploy when they are invited to make novel predictions about the resemblance between parents and their offspring (Astuti 2001; Astuti, in press; Astuti et al. 2004). As we shall see, the significance of this methodological approach in the present case is that it affords a detailed and nuanced picture of how exactly, in which contexts and how frequently the dead find a place to survive in the minds of their living descendants.

THE FIRST ETHNOGRAPHIC ACCOUNT: THE SURVIVAL OF THE *ANGATSE*

During a sombre conversation with my adoptive Vezo father near the end of my last visit, he told me that when he dies – which he anticipated would happen soon – I will not need to listen into my mobile phone or to look at my computer to receive the news of his death. Instead, he will visit me in a dream. This will be the sign that he is dead. He clearly liked the idea that he would be able to travel from Betania, where he lived and would be buried, all the way to the other side of the world to convey the news to me. Smiling, he observed that we were having a 'real' conversation on precisely the topic I had come to ask all those questions about. Having studied so hard, I surely knew what he was talking about, didn't I?

I did. He was drawing on the idea that when a person dies, his 'spirit' – known as *fanahy* up to the moment of death – permanently departs from the body. In such a disembodied, ghostly form, the spirit of a dead person – now known as *angatse* – can travel where his body could not, even as far as London. However, without a body, the *angatse* is invisible (*tsy hita maso*), and moves around like wind (*tsioky*). To be seen by living people, it must enter their dreams, where it appears together with its original body, just as it was when the person was alive.

In a sense, it is somewhat misleading to say that the spirit of the dead enters the dream of the living, since these dreams are more like encounters between fellow spirits. During sleep, the *fanahy* of living people temporarily detaches itself from the body and wanders until waking time.[2] If one's *fanahy* travels to market, one dreams about the market; if it travels to sea, one dreams about the sea; if it is approached by the *angatse* of a dead relative, one dreams of that relative. Most of one's *fanahy*'s nocturnal activities reflect one's preoccupations during the day and especially one's thoughts just before falling into deep sleep. However, the encounters with *angatse* of dead people are different because they are originated by the will of the dead, rather than by the thoughts of the living. In this sense, *angatse* can indeed be said to force their way into the dreams of the living, in a way that is perhaps not so dissimilar from the more dramatic and complex forms of spiritual intrusion that go under the name of spirit possession.

Adults report that they only dream about the *angatse* of their dead relatives, although I have come across a few instances in which the visitation was made by close friends who had recently died. All dreams that involve dead people are bad and frightening because they bring the dead too close to the living. But since one is only accountable to one's dead relatives, only dreams that involve *them* are actually dangerous.

Dreams about one's dead relatives must be promptly recounted to members of one's immediate family and to the senior person who has the authority to call upon the particular individual who appeared in the dream.[3] The meaning of some of these dreams is plain and straightforward: the dead person complains that she is hungry because her (living) son cannot be bothered to buy food for her, or she says that she feels cold because her house (i.e. the tomb) is falling apart; she might herself offer food to the dreamer or put her cold hand on the dreamer's forehead. All of these are bad, dangerous dreams, which have immediate effect on the dreamer (a fever, an ear-ache, some swelling), and which require immediate action (an offering of rice or even the slaughtering of a head of cattle) to appease the offended spirit and prevent further illness or death. Other dreams are less obvious. For example, one night I had a short dream in which I saw the face of a dead woman I had met fifteen years earlier during my first period of fieldwork. At the time of my most recent visit, her daughter – one of my sisters-in-law – was very ill. As she wasted away, most people agreed that the most likely reason for her illness was that her mother was angered by the fact that after so many years her children had yet to honour her by giving her a cement cross (cf. Astuti 1994, 1995). On my part, fearing that my sister-in-law might have TB, I convinced her to visit a clinic, where, unfortunately, my fears were confirmed. The night after committing myself to pay for the taxi fare to get her daily to the dispensary to take the necessary medications,

I dreamt the face of her dead mother. Her piercing eyes just stared at me, until I woke up, startled. First thing in the morning, I told my sister-in-law and her husband about my dream. Her interpretation was that this was not a bad dream, and that her mother was probably thanking me for taking care of her.[4] Her husband agreed and said that I should not fear because, according to his thinking, mine was not a bad dream (notably, they never claimed that it was a *good* dream). We decided that no action was needed.

Many dreams become known only after they have caused illness or death. This is typically the case of children's dreams. Adults are adamant that their children do not understand anything about what happens to people after death. This is considered a good thing, because it means that children are spared dangerous thoughts that are too difficult for them and that could render them vulnerable to the visitations of their dead relatives. Their ignorance, however, does not give them full protection, and so children routinely fall ill following a dream initiated by an angry *angaste*. Given their lack of wisdom and understanding, children are not expected to recognise the significance of these dreams, nor are they expected to remember or to recount them – indeed, they may be so young that they do not even know how to speak. But if children get ill and their illness persists and defies treatment with Western medicines, parents will approach a diviner and will ask him to look into the cause of their child's illness. It will then be revealed that the child is sick because of a dream in which the *angatse* of a certain dead relative touched her forehead or gave her food; an explanation will also be offered as to why the dead relative is angry and what actions must be taken to appease the *angatse* and restore the child's health.[5]

Either directly or through the mediation of a diviner, dreams are, thus, the channel through which the dead communicate with the living: in dreams, the dead can be seen with their original body form, they can talk and be heard, they can move and be seen, they can touch and be felt.[6] On their part, when the living wish (or are forced) to communicate with the dead – for example, to ask them to protect one child who is going on a school trip and another one who is sitting his exams; to neutralise the difficult words spoken by a father to his son and to lift the anger from their hearts so that they can successfully complete the construction of their new canoe; to inform them that the new canoe is being launched; to respond to a dream in which complaints were made and food was requested; to inform them that my son and I had arrived or were about to leave – they gather at an appropriate time and location, they talk to invisible listeners and they make offerings to invisible consumers.

THE SECOND ETHNOGRAPHIC ACCOUNT: WHEN ONE'S DEAD, ONE'S DEAD

On the afternoon of Saturday 22 May 2004, after only three days of illness, *tompokovavy*[7] died. She was thirty-seven years old and a mother of two. She lived in Lovobe, the next Vezo village south of where I lived with her older sister Korsia. Although I was not as close to the deceased as I am to Korsia, my closeness to Korsia meant that I was involved in the funeral in a way that I had never experienced before – a way that I am not sure I would have voluntarily chosen for myself.

Tompokovavy died in the town of Morondava, where she had been taken on Thursday to be looked after by a private doctor she trusted (despite the fact that he had failed to save the life of her newborn baby, who had died only five months earlier). The doctor administered several different injections, and prescribed several bottles of intravenous drips and a concoction of pills and syrups (which were later buried alongside the coffin). On Friday she seemed to get better, but by Saturday morning she was vomiting, she was shivering, she was speaking nonsense, and then she died. Her death was announced on the local radio, so the family back in Lovobe knew almost immediately what had happened. By late afternoon the body, wrapped up in a blanket and laid out on an improvised stretcher, had made its first river crossing from Morondava to the beach of Betania. Escorted by a large crowd of villagers, it was taken south to the second river crossing. On the other side, a fire had been lit where Lovobe villagers were waiting for the arrival of the corpse.

The Lovobe river is vast and that night it was very rough. The stretcher was precariously put on board the small canoe that shuttles people back and forth during the day. I was invited to be the first one to cross, together with my son. We were asked to hold on tight to the stretcher to prevent the body from falling off. Propelled by a dinky sail and by the paddling of two strong men, we eventually got to the other side. We were soaked, as was the corpse. The stretcher was offloaded onto the beach amidst a dramatic surge of wailing by the women who were waiting for us. The attention soon turned to me and to my son.

We were told to go near the fire to get warm and dry ourselves while we waited for the rest of the crowd to cross over. I told the women that *tompokovavy* was also wet, that a corner of her blanket had dipped into the water, and I suggested that, perhaps, we should move her, too, close to the fire. One of the women looked at me with a mixture of incredulity and sympathy and she told me not to worry myself, that my sister could no longer feel cold or hot, and that it no longer made any difference to her whether she was wet or dry. A bit reproachfully, the woman told me to worry about my son instead, as he was playing with the fire and was set to burn himself.

After entering her mother's sister's house that night, *tompokovavy* was taken off the stretcher and was laid onto the planks of the bed. She was, however, left wrapped up in her wet blanket, because her family has a taboo against washing corpses after sunset. Thus, we washed and dressed her first thing the next morning. Before we started, the mother, who had spent the night in the house with her dead daughter, was asked to leave, for it was decided that witnessing the procedure would be too much for her. After forcing her out of the house, the doors were shut, leaving inside three senior women, Korsia and myself. We unwrapped and undressed the body. Using a perfumed soap and water from a bucket, we soaped and rinsed it, first one side and then the other. The water was cold, and in the chill of an early winter morning, our hands soon got icy. While Korsia rinsed off the last traces of soap, with an obsessiveness that held her pain at bay, I stepped back from the bed and I rubbed my hands vigorously. The old woman who was standing next to me offered the matter-of-fact comment that we could have heated up the water but that, stiff as she was, *tompokovavy* would not have felt the difference.

Once she was dressed in her best skirt and silky blouse – which, after much pulling and stretching, we had to cut along the back – we undid her elaborately patterned braids and combed her hair. Since the comb has to be disposed of with the corpse, we were given a half-broken comb of really poor quality. To get it through *tompokovavy*'s thick mane, the hair had to be yanked. The woman who held the head against the pull remarked that for this one time it did not matter if Korsia – who was doing the yanking – had a heavy hand,[8] since her sister could no longer feel any pain.

After arranging her hair into two simple braids, which helped to keep the collar of the blouse in position, we were ready to lay out the two embroidered sheets that Korsia keeps at the bottom of her trunk, ready for this use. As we moved the body to slip the bottom sheet under it, we realised that we had forgotten to put on *tompokovavy*'s favourite bra. Korsia was upset, because her sister never left the village without a bra. But the effort of re-negotiating the blouse, the braids and the collar was judged too much by the older women. They told Korsia that it would be just fine to put the bra alongside the body, together with the other items of clothing (a few sarongs, a blanket, a Benetton jumper) we were going to pack inside the coffin. One of the women added that, in any case, *tompokovavy* would not exactly need a bra where she was going, for, although she had big breasts, she would have no chance to swing them around. This observation cut the discussion short.

I was not entirely surprised by the comments that were uttered around the body of *tompokovavy*, because I had heard similar statements towards the end of other funerals I had attended. Typically, when the time comes to remove the body from the house to take it to the cemetery, the people most closely related to the deceased – the mother, the husband, the children – are likely to protest, to ask for more time, to cling to the body. It is the job of older, wiser people to remind them that the deceased no longer feels or hears anything, and that it does not make any sense to keep the body in the village since it will not come back to life but will, rather, just go on to stink (Astuti 1995: 114–5). The gist of these more ritualised exhortations is clearly the same as that of the comments about *tompokovavy* – as the old, wise people say: 'when one's dead, one's dead'. And yet the remarks about *tompokovavy* had a different depth to them, as they captured the personal, practical and emotional struggle involved in handling a lifeless, stiff, cold body. These remarks were a quiet and poignant commentary on the reality of biological death.

Each of these two ethnographic accounts provides a compelling answer to the question of what happens after death. The answers, however, are notably and predictably different: one account delivers the answer that the deceased will continue to want, to feel cold and hungry, and to judge the conduct of living relatives; the other account delivers the answer that after death the person ceases to be a sentient being. In other words, the two accounts manifestly contradict each other.

The lack of consistency and systematic rigour in people's beliefs has been reported in a variety of ethnographic contexts (e.g. Leinhardt 1961 on Dinka religion; Leach 1967 on Australian Aborigines' and Trobrianders' procreation beliefs; Parry 1982 on Hindu understandings of death and regeneration; Luhrmann 1989 on magic and witchcraft in London; Stringer 1996 on Christians in Manchester; Bennett 1999 on Manchester elderly women's competing rationalist and supernatural narratives about the afterlife; Saler 2005 on Wayú religion), perhaps most emphatically in the case of Melanesian cosmologies. In that context, the claim was made that anthropologists have tended to over-systematise their informants' religious beliefs and to disregard the fact that, far too often, people have only a fragmentary understanding of the nature of the supernatural entities they address in ritual, or of the cosmological principles that give meaning to the symbols they use (Brunton 1980). The lively debate that ensued (Juillerat et al. 1980; Jorgense and Johnson 1981; Morris 1982; Juillerat 1992; cf. also Barth 1987) focused on whether anthropologists can legitimately go beyond the limited (and often secretly guarded) exegesis provided by their informants to produce their own analytical models of indigenous cosmologies. As noted by Whitehouse (2000: 81–8) in his critical assessment of this debate, there is an important distinction to be drawn here between analytical models that occupy the minds of the anthropologists (such as Gell's 1975 sociological interpretation of the Umeda fertility ritual) and the representations that are distributed in the minds of their informants; anthropologists run into problems when they assume a priori that their analytical models have psychological reality for their informants.

One possible strategy to avoid such problems is to engage systematically in the study of the mental representations that are held by one's informants and, whenever they are found to be contradictory (as seems to be the case with Vezo representations of what happens after death), to give a detailed account of how exactly they are held simultaneously in people's minds and of how (if at all) they get articulated with one another. This is what I aim to do in what remains of this paper.

The ethnographic evidence I have presented above suggests two (non-mutually exclusive) ways in which the two contradictory accounts of what happens after death might get articulated in people's minds: on the one hand, the two accounts could be articulated through the ontological distinction between two separate components of the person, one that perishes – the body – and one that survives – the *angatse*; on the other hand, they could get articulated through a contextualisation, such that each account is relevant to different contexts of action.

The experimental study I am about to describe aimed to explore both of these dimensions by inviting Vezo adults to reason about the consequences of death in response to different narrative contexts. The protocol I used was originally designed by developmental psychologists Paul Harris and Marta Giménez (2005) to investigate Spanish children's understanding of death and the afterlife. I adapted it and used it, in the first instance, to interview twenty-three men and women, aged between nineteen and sixty-two years (mean = thirty-three years).

I first asked them to listen to a short narrative about a fictional character called Rampy. They were told that Rampy was a very hard-working man, who one day fell ill with a high fever and was taken to the hospital by his wife and children. The doctor gave him four injections, but after three days he died. Participants were then asked a set of fourteen questions, half of which were about the continued functioning of some of Rampy's body parts and bodily processes (e.g. now that Rampy is dead, do his eyes work? Does his heart beat?), and the other half were about the continued viability of some of his sensory (e.g. now that Rampy is dead does he hear when people talk? Does he feel hungry?), emotional (e.g. does he miss his children?) and cognitive functions (e.g. does he know his wife's name? Does he remember where his house is?). For ease of exposition, in what follows I shall refer to the properties that target body parts and bodily processes as 'bodily properties', and the properties that target sensory, emotional and cognitive functions as 'mental properties'.[9]

There are three points that are worth making before proceeding with the analysis of participants' responses. The first one is that, inevitably, the discrimination between 'bodily' and 'mental' that is afforded by the English language captures only imperfectly the discrimination between 'what pertains to the body' (*mikasky ny vatanteňa*) and 'what pertains to the mind/spirit' (*mikasky ny sainteňa; mikasky ny fanahinteňa*) that is afforded by the Vezo language. Such are the limits of translation. Nonetheless, the point of this particular exercise is not to accurately translate words from one language into another, but to map conceptual discriminations that may, or may not, be drawn by Vezo adults (for a discussion of the problems involved in concept diagnosis, cf. Astuti et al. 2004: 16–18). Ultimately, whether a conceptual discrimination between what pertains to the body and what pertains to the mind/spirit is made by Vezo adults can only be decided by inviting them to reason inferentially about such properties. The protocol I used was designed with this aim in mind.

The second point is a simple matter of clarification. In what follows I shall refer to participants' *negative* answers (e.g. Rampy's eyes do *not* work or Rampy does *not* hear when people talk) as *discontinuity judgements*: judgements that state that life and death are *discontinuous*, that what works in life no longer works in death, that what was felt in life is no longer felt in death and so on. By contrast, I shall refer to participants' affirmative answers (e.g. Rampy's ears work or Rampy knows his wife's name) as *continuity judgements*: judgements that state that life and death are *continuous*, that what works in life continues to work in death, that what was felt in life continues to be felt in death and so on.

The third and final point is that, given the nature of this publication, I shall not present the statistical analyses that back up the claims I shall be making about the significance of certain discriminations made by my Vezo informants. Interested readers should refer to Astuti and Harris (submitted) where such analyses are presented in full.

The first, and most striking, result is that participants gave an overwhelming majority of discontinuity judgements (80 per cent overall). This underscores the saliency of the ethnographic account that says 'when one's dead one's dead' in guiding people's reasoning about what happens after death. However, in line with the other ethnographic account I presented above (that says that the body rots but the spirit survives), participants were on average significantly more likely to give discontinuity judgements for the 7 bodily processes (mean number = 6.6) than for the 7 mental processes (mean number = 4.7). In other words, they differentiated between bodily processes that cease at death and sensory, emotional and cognitive processes that continue after death.

Nonetheless, an equally striking finding was that just under half of the participants (43 per cent) gave discontinuity judgements for *all* the mental processes they were questioned about. They reasoned, in other words, that death entirely extinguishes the person and they left no space in their minds for the survival of the *angatse*. To justify their stand, they typically invoked the deadness of the corpse: the fact that Rampy's body will rot, that he will be buried under the ground, that he has no means of seeing, hearing or thinking because his head will soon be full of worms, and so on and so forth.

The fact that so many people in this study did not seem to embrace the idea that the deceased preserves at least some mental capacities is somewhat surprising, since participation in rituals that address the surviving spirits of the dead is nearly universal. This observation raises the following empirical question: could a manipulation in the way the task is designed – specifically, a change of the narrative context in which the continuity/discontinuity questions are asked – decrease the number of discontinuity judgements and curb participants' annihilating stance? The reason this question is worth asking is that if we were to find a way of shifting people's judgements from discontinuity (all properties cease to function) to continuity (some properties remain viable) we would come closer to understanding the mechanism that keeps the dead alive in people's minds.

To pursue this question, I asked a new group of twenty-three adults aged between nineteen and seventy-one years (mean = thirty-five years) to listen to a different narrative about a different fictional character, called Rapeto. He had lots of children and grandchildren who, on the day he died, were with him inside his house. Now that he is dead, his children and grandchildren often dream about him. Rapeto's family has built the cement cross for him – the major ritual that Vezo undertake to remember and honour the dead (Astuti 1994, 1995) – and they are happy because the work was well accomplished. The questions about Rapeto were identical to those about Rampy, but instead of being introduced by: 'Now that Rampy is dead…' they were introduced by: 'Now that Rapeto is over there at the tombs…' From now on, I shall refer to the first narrative about Rampy as the Deceased narrative and to the second narrative about Rapeto as the Tomb narrative.

Before discussing the results produced by this contextual manipulation, I should explain why I recruited a new group of participants to respond to the Tomb narrative rather than approaching the same participants who had responded to the Deceased narrative (in other words, why I opted for a comparison across rather than within subjects). The reason was pragmatic. Consider that I had to approach wise and respected elders and ask them, with a straight face, whether they thought that once Rampy is dead his legs move or his heart beats. As I had already experienced when conducting another study (Astuti et al. 2004: 30), the main challenge consists in overcoming people's suspicion that, by asking far too obvious questions to which she already knows the answer, the experimenter is wasting their time and denying them their due respect. My long-standing relationship with the villagers meant that I could pre-empt their concern and reassure them that my questions were not intended to fool them, but were, rather, a genuine attempt on my part to learn what people think about a topic as difficult as death. My interlocutors typically responded by reassuring me that they would never doubt my good intentions. Having established that I trusted them as good teachers and that they trusted my genuine desire to learn, the death interview could proceed, and did so smoothly. I felt nonetheless that it would have been difficult to motivate a second interview. For the contextual manipulation to yield meaningful results, it could not be explained to participants, and this would have meant approaching them again with seemingly identical questions for no apparently good reason. I therefore decided to settle for a design that did not allow a, perhaps more desirable, within-subject comparison, but which did, however, safeguard the trust of my informants.

Let me now present the results. Just like the participants who heard the Deceased narrative, those who heard the Tomb narrative overwhelmingly gave discontinuity judgements (73 per cent overall), and they also differentiated between bodily (mean number = 6.2) and mental processes (mean number = 4). However, participants in the Tomb condition were different in one respect, in that they were significantly less likely to give discontinuity judgements for mental properties than their counterparts in the Deceased condition. The overall shift in the distribution of judgements is captured in Figure 9.1, which shows the percentage of participants that gave each of the possible numbers of discontinuity judgements (from 0 to 7) for mental properties in either the Deceased or the Tomb condition. To be noted is the definite shift away from the skewed distribution in the direction of discontinuity judgements for mental properties in the Deceased condition to a much flatter distribution in the Tomb condition (the percentage of participants who judged that all mental faculties cease at death went down from 43 to 13).

There are two possible interpretations for this result. The interesting one, which I shall pursue, is that the effect was produced by context. The uninteresting one is that the difference was driven by a cohort effect – that is, the participants recruited in the two tasks were taken from two different populations (for example, younger people in one study, older people in the other). Given the many variables that could affect the way people reason in the task (including, perhaps, how recently they lost a close relative or have had a vivid dream about a dead relation), it is clearly difficult to control for everything. However, in recruiting participants, I did my best to control for age, gender, education and church attendance,

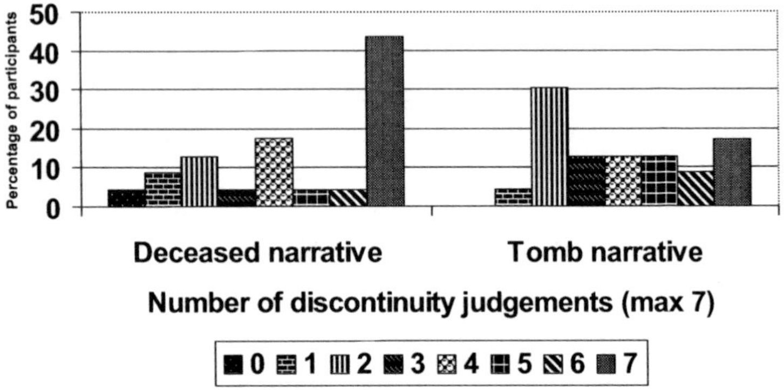

Figure 9.1 Distribution of discontinuity judgements for mental properties by narrative

making sure that the profile of the two groups was, as far as possible, homogenous. Therefore, although I am aware that it is impossible to entirely rule out the possibility of a cohort effect and that therefore one has to proceed with some caution, I shall proceed nonetheless and suggest that it was the different priming I gave participants in the two experimental conditions (Deceased *versus* Tomb narrative) that caused them to give different responses to my questions. In other words, my interpretation is that the brief evocation of the contexts in which the living work for the dead to honour and appease them was enough to reduce the likelihood that participants would reason that the deceased is mentally inert and totally extinguished.

This finding reminds me of a comment made by Evans-Pritchard about the fact that his Azande informants used to casually hang their baskets on the ancestral shrines, and that it was only during religious ceremonies that the shrines became more than convenient pegs. He concluded – against Lévi-Bruhl who, in this context, was his polemical target – that 'mystical thought is a function of a particular situation' (Evans-Pritchard 1934: 27, quoted in Lukes 1982: 269). In other words, that context affects thought.

Now, Evans-Pritchard was interested in using context to rescue practical thought from the claim that primitive people are trapped in mystical 'never land'. My emphasis is slightly different, as I intend to use the effect of context that I have captured with my data to expose *both* the fragility of people's 'mystical' representations of life after death *and* the strength of the contexts that manage to sustain them.

The first part of the argument goes like this: if it is true that a simple manipulation of narrative context manages to shift people into a different frame of mind, as shown by the different inferences they make, it might also be the case that the frame of mind they have shifted into is easily lost, if the context changes. I want to illustrate this point with a piece of ethnographic evidence.

When the head of my adoptive family addresses the dead, he always ends his whispered monologues by stating loud and clearly: 'It's over, and there is *not* going to be a reply!' Every time, the people around him laugh at the joke as they get up to stretch their legs and drink what is left of the rum. But what exactly is the joke? The humour, I suppose, lies in imagining what would happen if one were to expect a reply from dead people, as one does when one talks with living interlocutors: one would wait, and wait, and wait! In other words, people laugh because, as the ritual setting draws to a close, they shift out of the frame of mind that has sustained the one-way conversation with the dead and they come to recognise the slight absurdity of what they are doing. Indeed, my father's joke is probably intended to encourage and mark that shift, as he brackets off the always potentially dangerous one-way conversation with his dead forebears from ordinary two-way conversations with his living friends and relatives. The point I wish to stress is that it takes just a simple joke to break the spell and to call up one's knowledge that the dead can't hear or see or feel cold or, indeed, give a reply.

The experimental and ethnographic evidence I have just presented suggests that people's representations of the continuing mental life of the deceased are highly dependent on context. I recognise that this sensitivity to context probably means that people's tendency to attribute enduring properties to the deceased could be boosted by manipulating the narrative context of the death interview even further. For example, if instead of being about a stranger, such as Rapeto, the narrative could have been about a deceased person close to the participants – a deceased husband or a daughter who had recently passed away – perhaps respondents would have given more continuity judgements than they did in the Tomb condition. Nonetheless, what I wish to emphasise here is the converse point, namely that there are times and places when the dead are *not* kept alive in people's minds, as shown by the pattern of responses to the Deceased narrative. This, I submit, reveals a certain fragility in people's representations of the afterlife – to go back to Byron Good, a fragility in the 'act of consciousness' with which the Vezo de-naturalise death.

Arguably, the source of this fragility is the fact that death – as Lambek (this volume) puts it – is even more patent than birth. This is probably why, in the course of development, Vezo children come to understand that death is the end of sentient life much earlier than they understand how the spirit of the dead might manage to live on. This is not the place to present the studies I did with children (cf. Astuti and Harris, submitted), but I shall just mention that by age seven Vezo children demonstrate a pretty solid biological understanding of both animal and human death which, as we have seen, is not discarded in adult life. It takes children a further ten years to slowly build up a representation of what happens after death, which entails the survival of the spirit and the attribution of appropriate properties to it. Developmentally, the representation of the continuing mental life of the dead is a slow construction which emerges from the realistic appreciation that – in the words of a nine-year-old boy – when one is dead 'the body goes bad, the skin is all decomposing and inside the tummy is full of worms'. This ontogenetic perspective might explain why the early understanding of death as the end of all sentient life continues to act as a default, a default that can only successfully be challenged and overcome in certain limited contexts.

Interestingly, I found evidence that during the course of development children come up with exciting, sometimes frightening, and highly idiosyncratic understandings of what kind of entities *angatse* are, of why adults offer food to the dead, of why they ask for their blessing, and so on (cf. Astuti, in preparation). And this takes me to the second part of my argument about the strength of the contexts that sustain the existence of the dead in people's minds.

One striking aspect of the distribution of judgements across both versions of the task (Deceased and Tomb condition) is that, as shown in Figure 9.1, the number of discontinuity judgements given by those participants who judged that the deceased would retain at least some mental properties ranged all the way between 0 (all properties remain viable) and 6 (only one property remains viable). This means that there was remarkably little agreement about the exact functions that the deceased would retain – for some it was hearing, for others it was knowing one's wife's name and remembering the location of one's house, for others still it was all of the above plus feeling hungry and so on. In other words, there was great variation in the way people represented to themselves the details of what happens after death.

Although not entirely surprising – Vezo adults pointed out that, being themselves still alive, they cannot fully understand how *angatse* do things and what their mode of existence actually is – this variation is worth commenting on. Let me give an example. In the open-ended discussions that followed the more structured death interviews, several adults puzzled over the question of how exactly the *angatse* of dead people manage to eat, drink or smoke what is offered to them. Some speculated that *angatse* feed by inhaling the smell and extracting the flavour from the food. Evidence for this, they claim, is that the meat that is distributed after slaughtering a cow that is being offered to dead people does not taste the same as the meat that one buys at the market for family consumption; the first type of meat is reportedly tasteless because all its flavour has been consumed by feasting *angaste*. Others were more tentative and rather unsure, wondering how *angatse* could possibly eat – since they don't have a body, surely they don't have a mouth! Maybe all that happens is that they see the living throwing the morsels of food (which are likely to be eaten by passer-by animals) and that is all they care about – to be remembered and to be shown respect. The most radical position was that offering food or drinks or cigarettes to dead people makes no sense at all: has anybody ever tried to stuff food in the mouth of a dead person, or to get a corpse to puff a cigarette? The only reason people bother to cook meat and rice and to light the tobacco is that for a long, long time this has been the Malagasy way of doing things. In truth, what really happens is that the food is eaten by the living and the tobacco just goes to waste. As for the dead, well, the dead are just dead.[10]

Note, however, that this endemic difference of opinion does not stop people – children included, who have a whole different set of ideas about how the *angatse* feed (cf. Astuti, in preparation) – from coming together and actually offering food, rum and tobacco to the dead. When this has to happen, the focus is on performing the correct actions, on using the correct utensils, on saying the correct words on the right day and at the right time. The fact that different participants bring very different personal interpretations of what they are doing does not interfere with the smooth orchestration of the offering.

This is a remarkable achievement, based on what Bloch (2005) calls 'deference'. As people gather to get things done, they are likely to stop speculating how the dead are going to eat the rice or smoke the tobacco or listen to the invocation or, even, whether they are going to reply. Instead, they defer to whomever it was that, a very long time ago, originated this way of doing things and they just align themselves with it.

And so long as *this* happens, the dead will continue to find a space to live on in the minds of their living descendants.

ACKNOWLEDGEMENTS

The research on which this chapter is based was funded by the Economic and Social Research Council, UK (Research Fellowship R000271254, 2002–5). I wish to thank Maurice Bloch, Larry Epstein, Charles Stafford, Johnny Parry and the participants in the workshop Anthropology and Other 'Zafimaniry Questions' for comments on earlier drafts of this chapter. I am indebted to Paul Harris for his collaboration on this project, to Nicola Knight for his assistance in data analysis, to Sean Epstein for his help in the collection of data in Madagascar, and to the villagers of Betania, Madagascar, for participating in this project. I dedicate this article to the memory of Larry Epstein.

NOTES

1. The claim here is that the Jivaro may be unique in this respect among non-professionals. It is evident that the mental work of mourning is crucial to professional psychoanalysts and psychotherapists.
2. Because one's spirit is detached from the body, being asleep is like being dead. Several adult informants told me that if a person's face is smeared with *tabake* (a yellow paste derived from medicinal woods) while she is asleep, the spirit will be unable to recognise the body it belongs to and will fail to reconnect with it, causing that person to die.
3. Dreams about a friend are recounted to the friend's relatives in case they wish to interpret the dream as a warning to them.
4. They were not troubled by what, to me, seemed a contradiction, namely that the mother was making her daughter ill and at the same time she was thanking me for providing medical care for her.
5. In their diagnostic practice, diviners often reach into the dreams of adults as well as into those of children. Even if adults remember and recount their

dreams, they may fail to give the correct interpretation. For example, they may decide that a particular encounter was not a bad dream and that no action was needed. For several months, nothing happens, but when the person suddenly falls ill and no effective cure is found, the diviner will see the forgotten dream, the patient will remember it and the appropriate action will be taken.

6. This is important because touch is one of the most direct ways in which dead people can inflict pain and illness on their living descendants.
7. The term *tompokovavy*, literally 'my female master', is used to refer to the deceased in order to avoid mentioning her name as a sign of respect.
8. Literally, 'hot' hand (*tana mafana*). Whether one is slaughtering an animal, combing hair, giving a massage, a cool hand is good and a hot hand is bad (e.g. a cool hand causes the animal to die straight away, a hot hand causes the animal to struggle).
9. The complete list of properties was as follows: BODILY: Do his eyes work? Do his ears work? Does his stomach need food? Does his heart beat? Do his legs move? Does a cut on his hand heal? Does he age? MENTAL: Does he see things around? Does he hear when people talk? Does he feel hungry? Does he know his wife's name? Does he remember where his house is? Does he feel cold? Does he miss his children? Participants were asked each set of seven questions in one of two random orders. Half the participants received the bodily questions followed by the mental questions and half received the reverse order.
10. Keller (2005: 171 ff.) notes that in their radical rejection of ancestral customs, Seventh-day Adventists in Madagascar emphasise the absurdity of believing that a pile of rotting bones might actually eat or drink what is offered to them in sacrifice. They, too, invoke the refrain: 'dead is dead'.

REFERENCES

Astuti, R. 1994. 'Invisible objects: funerary rituals among the Vezo of western Madagascar', *Res. Anthropology and Aesthetics*, 25: 111–22.

—— 1995. *People of the sea: identity and descent among the Vezo of Madagascar*, Cambridge: Cambridge University Press.

—— 2001. 'Are we all natural dualists? A cognitive developmental approach', The Malinowski Memorial Lecture 2000, *Journal of the Royal Anthropological Institute* 7: 429–47.

—— In press. 'Revealing and obscuring Rivers' natural pedigrees: biological inheritance and kinship in Madagascar', in J. Leach and S. Bamford (eds), *Genealogy beyond kinship: sequence, transmission and essence in ethnography and social theory*, Oxford and New York: Berghahn.

—— In preparation. 'Death, ancestors and the return from the dead: cognitive development and cultural transmission in Madagascar'.

Astuti, R. and Harris, P. Submitted. 'Understanding mortality and the life of the ancestors in rural Madagascar', to appear in *Cognitive Science.*

Astuti, R., Solomon, G.E.A. and Carey, S. 2004. *Constraints on conceptual development: a case study of the acquisition of folkbiological and folksociological knowledge in Madagascar*, Monographs of the Society for Research in Child Development 277(69): 3.

Barth, F. 1987. *Cosmologies in the making: a generative approach to cultural variation in inner New Guinea*, Cambridge: Cambridge University Press.

Bennett, G. 1999. *Alas, poor ghost: traditions of belief in story and discourse*, Logan: Utah State University Press.

Bloch, M. 1982. 'Death, women and power', in M. Bloch and J. Parry (eds), *Death and the regeneration of life*, Cambridge: Cambridge University Press.

—— 1986. *From blessing to violence: history and ideology in the circumcision ritual of the Merina of Madagascar*, Cambridge: Cambridge University Press.

—— 1992. *Prey into hunter: the politics of religious experience*, Cambridge: Cambridge University Press.

—— 2001. 'Postmodernism: the nature/culture debate in just another guise?', *Irish Journal of Anthropology* 5: 111–15.

—— 2005. 'Ritual and deference', in M. Bloch *Essays on cultural transmission*, London School of Economics Monographs on Social Anthropology 75, Oxford: Berg.

Brunton, R. 1980. 'Misconstrued order in Melanesian religion', *Man* (n.s.) 15(1): 112–28.

Evans-Pritchard, E.E. 1934. 'Lévi-Bruhl's theory of primitive mentality', *Bulletin of the Faculty of Arts*, (Faud I University, Cairo), II, 1, extract deposited in Tylor Library, Institute of Social Anthropology, Oxford, p.9.

Firth, R. 1985. 'Degrees of intelligibility', in *Reason and morality* (ed.) J. Overing, London and New York: Tavistock Publications.

Gell, A. 1975. *Metamorphosis of the cassowaries: Umeda society, language and ritual*, LSE Monographs on Social Anthropology 51, London: Athlone Press.

Good, B. 1994. *Medicine, rationality and experience: an anthropological perspective*, Cambridge: Cambridge University Press.

Harris, P.L. and Giménez, M. 2005. 'Children's acceptance of conflicting testimony: the case of death', *Journal of Cognition and Culture* 5(1–2): 143–64.

Jorgensen, D., Johnson, R. 1981. 'Order or disorder in Melanesian religion?', Correspondence, *Man* 16(3): 470–5.

Juillerat, B. (ed.) 1992. *Shooting the sun: ritual and meaning in West Sepik*, Washington and London: Smithsonian Institution Press.

Juillerat, B., Strathern, A., Brunton, R., Gell, A. 1980. 'Order or disorder in Melanesian religion?', Correspondence, *Man* 15(4): 732–7.

Keller, E. 2005. *The road to clarity: Seventh-day Adventism in Madagascar*, New York: Palgrave Macmillan.

Leach, E. 1967. 'Virgin birth', *Proceedings of the Royal Anthropological Institute* 1966: 9–50.

Leinhardt, 1961. *Divinity and experience: the religion of the Dinka*, Oxford: Oxford University Press.

Luhrmann, T. 1989. *Persuasions of the witch's craft: ritual magic in contemporary England*, Cambridge, Mass.: Harvard University Press.

Lukes, S. 1982. 'Relativism in its place', in M. Hollis and S. Lukes (eds), *Rationality and relativism*, Oxford: Basil Blackwell.

Morris, B. 1982. 'Order or disorder in Melanesian religion?' Correspondence, *Man* 17(2): 350.

Parry, J. 1982. 'Sacrificial death and the necrophagous ascetic', in M. Bloch and J. Parry (eds), *Death and the regeneration of life*, Cambridge: Cambridge University Press.

Saler, B. 2005. 'Finding Wayú religion', *Historical Reflections/Reflexions Historiques* 3(2): 1–16.

Stringer, M.D. 1996. 'Towards a situational theory of belief', *JASO* 27(3): 217–34.

Taylor, A.-C. 1993. 'Remembering to forget: identity, mourning and memory among the Jivaro', *Man* 28: 653–78.

Whitehouse, H. 2000. *Arguments and icons: divergent modes of religiosity*, Oxford: Oxford University Press.

Woodburn, J. 1982. 'Social dimension of death in four African hunting and gathering societies', in M. Bloch and J. Parry (eds), *Death and the regeneration of life*, Cambridge: Cambridge University Press.

CHAPTER 10

HOW DOES GENOCIDE HAPPEN?

Michael Stewart

Surveying the mass crimes of the twentieth century, beginning with the Turkish killings of the Armenians in 1915 and proceeding through (to take just a few examples) the mass slaughter of ethnic and other minorities in the Second World War, the massacre of around one million persons in Bali in 1965, the thirty-six-year-long campaign against the Mayans in Guatemala, the assault on the Bosnian Muslims and the Rwandan Tutsis in the 1990s, up to the horrors of Darfur today, we can discern a clear enough pattern, at least in one respect.

At the moment they take place, the status of such killings as 'genocide' appears to outsiders to be ambiguous and inherently implausible. The world turned the other way during the Second World War, preferring not to believe. After Cambodia a new political generation had, supposedly, learnt for itself that such things can, and do, still happen. But it allowed the criminally incompetent to represent it in Bosnia in the form of a UN envoy whose hand-wringing and procrastination allowed the ethnic cleansers to turn his presence into one of their primary devices for pursuing mass crimes. It claimed not to have had time to notice in the Rwandan case and, as I write, it is shame-facedly looking at its collective feet, denying that the slaughter in Darfur is, properly speaking, genocide and hoping that no one will force it to take action against the criminal regime in Khartoum. It is only after the event that genocides appear with certainty, and without ambiguity, to have taken place. It is only in their aftermath that world leaders and the peoples of the world behind them vow that genocide must never happen again.[1] It may well be that a desire to disbelieve is built into the individual psyche. It has certainly been a cornerstone of the present world order, in which the rights of sovereign states to do as they wish with their citizens are paramount.

Naturally, the intellectual foundations of a non-interventionist stance in international affairs lie mostly in realpolitik considerations. But in this paper I wish to examine whether a restrictive definition of genocide and a misleading model of how this particular crime occurs also ties the hands of agencies that might otherwise feel compelled to act. I am, here, following a fellow anthropologist who prophetically pointed out that the recognition of the genocidal strategy pursued by Franjo Tudjman and Slobodan Milošević in the former Yugoslavia against the Bosnian Muslim population was hampered by a 'holocaust' model. At a conference held in December 1993 Cornelia Sorabji talked of the 'franchise organisation' that seemed to have been adopted by Serbian and Croat leaders in their attempt to destroy the Bosnian Muslim population. She pointed out that the Serbian and Croat campaigns looked so different from the holocaust model – slaughter on an industrial scale, pursued with bureaucratic regularity – that commentators were unable to see its true, genocidal, nature (Sorabji 1995). Eighteen months later Dutch, British and French troops stood by as Serbian forces massacred 7000 Muslim men in the environs of Srebrenica.

I want to take Sorabji's argument a stage further to explore the ways in which state policy can be radicalised towards genocidal murder without the kind of pressing ideological fanaticism and bureaucratic central coordination found in the case of the Jewish holocaust.

THE CATEGORY OF 'GENOCIDE'

I treat 'genocide', here, as a modern and not a universal phenomenon: the very term 'genocide', as I am using it, is a neologism coined by a Czech legal scholar, Rafael Lemkin, in 1943, in order to provide a workable, legal definition of the atrocities being committed in Europe at that time. Lemkin articulated a particularly modern horror at the crime of destroying a *community of fate* – a 'people as such', in the sense of a national or ethnic group formed not by its own wishes and choices (like a political party or football club) but by ascription, whether through birth or the judgement of others. As the full extent of the criminality of the Nazi regime was revealed for the first time in 1945, it was only natural that the scale and resolution of the execution of the Jewish holocaust ensured that this became *the* genocide, *the* mass crime that must never be forgotten and never be allowed to happen again. It was in this spirit that the founding documents of the post-war international order, the Universal Declaration of Human Rights and the Convention on the Prevention and Punishment of the Crime of Genocide, were drawn up (the latter with Lemkin's advice).

In very recent years, thanks in large part to the creation of the International Criminal Tribunals for former Yugoslavia and Rwanda, legal theorists and practitioners have begun to re-examine the foundations of the Genocide convention. Case law, such as that arising from the prosecution of General Krstić for his part in the massacre of male Muslims in and around the town of Srebrenica in 1995, has deepened and broadened understanding of both folk concepts and key notions in international law. 'Complicity in' and 'aiding and abetting' genocide, as well as definitions of the extent of killing necessary for murder to count as genocide, have been at the heart of litigation and legal argument.[2] What I wish to question in this paper is the broader matter of what constitutes the crime of genocide and the way in which we imagine genocidal practices to come into being. In legal terms this issue is dealt with by the requirement that, for an act of mass murder to count as genocide, a 'special intent' must be established on the part of the perpetrator/s. As the legal scholar Alexander Greenawalt has shown, the exact meaning of 'special intent' is highly ambiguous and subject to numerous, contrary, interpretations (1999).[3] Put in plain, sociological language, the problem arises in the common implication of the notion of intent when applied to the bureaucratic machinery that carries through the destruction of a population: that there be some 'general programme' or 'plan' for an extermination policy. As Lemkin himself put it, genocide signifies 'a coordinated plan of different actions aiming at the destruction of essential foundations of the life of national groups'.[4] It is my contention that the notion of 'intent' is ill-framed for a crime that is always a collective endeavour requiring an elaborate division of labour. The coordination of different institutions that is necessary for genocide may arise under conditions quite other than those representing a 'coordinated plan'. This essay thus joins forces with Greenawalt's powerful critique (taken from a legal-theoretical standpoint), with an empirical consideration of how state policy becomes radicalised to the point at which genocidal measures are initiated.[5]

Although, in a restricted sense, I address a quasi-legal issue, it should also be obvious that a problem of 'Zafimaniry anthropology' (see Preface) lies not far from my attention. Questions as to how and why genocide happens, as well as how individuals become caught up in it, recur amongst victims of this act, as the history of Maurice Bloch's own family bears witness. On the forty-sixth anniversary of the day when Pierre Bloch, Maurice's father, was transported from a holding camp in Compiègne to Auschwitz, Maurice's mother, Claudette Kennedy (née Rafaël), began to write a memoir setting out in stark, uncompromising prose her own passage through the years of Nazi occupation and the concentration camps to which she was deported. Like other writers of such memoirs, Maurice's mother does not so much attempt to explain as to chronicle. But the presentation of the events poses its own Zafimaniry question about the way genocide takes place. With hindsight, it is easy to wonder how a highly educated and informed scientist could be so apparently naive as to present herself at the German Kommandatur in Paris demanding information on her disappeared husband. What was it that prevented her from seeing the nature of the powers she was dealing with? This essay, by attempting to analyse the process of bureaucratic radicalisation that enables genocide, may supply some of the materials for an explanation of the all too common experience by which people manage to miss and ignore the signs that genocide is emerging.

WHO IS RESPONSIBLE FOR GENOCIDE?

The murder of millions of Jews can be described, at one analytic level, as the playing out of the obsessions of a single man and his clique, aided by leading activists of a blindly loyal party. From the outset of his political career Hitler had been a notorious anti-Semite, one who developed a particular form of 'redemptive anti-Semitism' (Friedlander 1997). For Hitler, the struggle against the Jews was 'the immutable basis and obsessional core of his understanding of history, politics and action'.[6] By solving 'the Jewish question', the Nazis would redeem the German nation from its tragic past and would recover the greatness of the German people.

For the Jews, there is a clear chronology of policy and legal writ which provides the framework of the persecution, starting with one of the earliest significant pieces of legislation Hitler's government put through, the Law for the Restoration of the Professional Civil Service, which drove Jews out of public service.[7] At least until the secret, extra-judicial decisions of the war years, the framework of laws provided the mantle of legitimacy for Nazi policies leading to total excommunication.[8]

Rafael Lemkin's pre-Convention discussion of the nature of genocide (1944) retains a sense of the complexity of social process as state employees and others try to destroy 'the essential foundations of the life of national groups'. But thanks in part to the sheer thoroughness and systematic nature of the persecution of the Jews in the latter years of the war, from 1941 to 1945, a model of 'genocide' as the execution of '*an overall plan*', whether written or not, for the extermination of a people has come to dominate almost all thinking on the issue.[9] Until very recently, historians of this period have, consequently, been engaged in an almost mystical quest for a *Führerbefehl*, an order from the Führer that would provide the basis for, and the ultimate explanation of, the Final Solution.

However odd this approach may seem to social scientists with our predilection for seeking structural causes, such a quest may seem less irrational if one recalls one of the crucial distinguishing features of German fascism as a system of rule: the organisation of governance around the cult of the Führer. After 1933, the whole of public life was reorganised around the so-called *Führerprinzip*, the absolute personal loyalty of subordinates to superiors all the way up to the office of the Reich's Chancellor. A few lines in *Mein Kampf* discussing a tiny group of children born to German mothers of black American soldiers quartered in the Rhineland during the Allied occupation led almost immediately after the takeover to an entire anthropological programme being set up to determine the racial worth of the children. Loyal doctors were then found who secretly and illegally whipped the several hundred victims off the streets and sterilised them.

Even more dramatically, a single petition, written to Hitler by the parents of a blind and partially paralysed child, is credited with launching the wave of 'euthanasia' killings that, by the time they were slowed down in 1941, had put to death nearly 200,000 mentally ill or physically disabled people, including at least 6000 children. Despite the ideological predisposition among doctors and other professionals to accept radical, interventionist population measures, when asked to start killing, as opposed to preventing reproduction, their leaders refused – at least until so ordered by the Führer. The whole programme could not have been conceived without an ideology of population 'hygiene', but without Hitler it is not clear that this drastic mode of implementation would have been taken.[10]

The fact, then, that in all the 700 pages of *Mein Kampf* there is not a single mention of the Gypsies is highly significant. It is true that in contrast to the defenceless Rhineland children, who provided a cost-free opportunity for a fateful experiment, going after much larger social groups like the Gypsies would have required more resources and coordination. But it was not just the scale of the problem that differed. The absence of interest by Hitler in the Gypsies remains a central feature of the Gypsy story.

Moreover, whatever Hitler's personal predilections, the struggle against what had traditionally been called the 'Gypsy nuisance' could hardly be cast – as that against the Jews was constantly – as a battle for national salvation. There were no Gypsy owners of banks, nor had they played a leading role in the spread of capitalism in Germany. And though they were likened to Jews for their restless wandering and rootlessness, they could not be presented as representatives of an anti-German, cosmopolitan world conspiracy. No street names had to be changed to remove their Gypsy associations. The Gypsies were, in brief, in a totally different position to that of the Jews in the Europe of 1933.

And yet, they did not escape internment, 'preventive custody', sterilisation, a wave of early killings and later mass deportations to concentration camps. During the war, in every country that fell under Nazi rule, in every city, in every village, in every concentration camp, Gypsies, like Jews, were persecuted because of their birth. By the end of the war, two thirds of Germany's Gypsies, a greater proportion of Czech and Croatian Gypsies and scores of thousands elsewhere were dead. Of those who remained in Germany many had been sterilised; others had been crippled through slave labour. In some regions, like the Ostmark (Austria), nearly 90 per cent of the Gypsies died. In this case, legal texts, official commentaries, secret decrees and the paper trail of their implementation form only one part of the story, and they do not take us to its dark heart. It is in the initiatives of town hall *genocidaires* and racists in various positions of authority that we have to turn if we want to grasp the dynamic of the segregation, exclusion, persecution and, ultimately, genocide of the Gypsies.

In the absence of any central legal or political resolution, between 1933 and 1938 a profound change occurred in the way Gypsies were dealt with, day to day, by the state administration. Pre-Nazi policy rested on a systematic distinction between 'domestic' and 'foreign' Gypsies – drawing from a much older approach to poor law and welfare payments based on the idea that only the 'local' poor had to be supported by the state administration (Geremek 1994; Fricke 1996). Any Gypsies not slated for expulsion/deportation should be sedentarised and put to work. As late as June 1936, this essentially reformist programme, that put faith in the educational power of 'work' and 'home', was still the officially articulated policy of the Interior Ministry and the security apparatus. By December 1938 the ground had shifted. The *Reichsführer* SS and Chief of the German Police, Heinrich Himmler, now declared that in the treating of Gypsy issues 'the racial aspect' of the question was always to be kept in the foreground. All initiatives should aim at the racial 'isolation' (*Absonderung*) of these aliens.[11] Having achieved effective segregation, the authorities would then work to prevent any further racial mixing with comrades of the people's community. How did this shift occur?

The general point I wish to make can be put thus: in the broader context of the Nazi social revolution you did not need a central plan and specifically targeted ideological programme in order to arrive at the wholesale redefinition of a social problem in racialist terms. A body like the police arrived at the point where it worked, in Lemkin's words, towards the 'disintegration of the political and social institutions, of culture, … and the economic existence' (1944: 79) of a problematic minority without being led or directed to that goal by some central intention. All that was required was a broad definition of social policy as proceeding from the inborn characteristics of racial groups and then a series of what I will call 'instances', cases or clusters of problems around which a number of diverse conjunctures brought together state organs and produced the coordination and radicalising of their activities. This paper deals with one such instance, one that occurred at a crucial early stage in the move towards the genocide of the Gypsies. The initial shift – a new definition of the category '*Zigeuner*' that eliminated the enlightened notion of educable 'Gypsies'– was accomplished through nothing more menacing than the resolution of conflicts between the Frankfurt police and other parts of the state administration over how to treat different Gypsy defendants in a series of trials that began in 1936.

What follows, then, is an ethnographic reconstruction of how a small group of police officers turned an affray in a pub, one Saturday afternoon, into something resembling a series of show trials. Janosch Korpatsch had once been reputed to be the richest Gypsy in the German Reich and his arrest led to prosecutions involving himself, his broader family and scores of other unrelated Gypsies. Recalling these events after the war, one of the defence lawyers involved described a police 'battle against the Gypsies'.

THE KING OF THE GYPSIES

After the event, Janosch Korpatsch must have marvelled at the miserable alliance of mishap, envy-fed vengeance and malign persecution that left him, in the new year of 1936, as chief trophy of the Frankfurt police. The Nazi press were past masters at the staged and manipulated scandal and in Korpatsch they had been given their first exemplary Gypsy, a hate figure who, like countless Jews before and after him, could serve as a warning to all around, Gypsy and non-Gypsy alike. The Frankfurt police were quick to advertise their capture of 'the Gypsy Chief', instigating a press campaign that mocked him as 'a despot who rules over a clan with one hundred and ten wagons'. In other newspapers he was pilloried as a 'traitor to the people's economy'. According to stories that appeared across the country, Korpatsch's clan represented a double burden on the hard-working, tax-paying burghers of every town they visited. As professional criminals who lived from the proceeds of smuggled foreign currency, gold and other precious metals, they were leaching wealth from the state. At the same time, they were stealing from the honest German worker by sending their women and children, decked out as the very image of neglect, to claim welfare support. On the morning of Saturday 11 January 1936 the possibility that he was about to fall into a trap from which he would never emerge cannot have crossed his mind.

The spring of the trap was nothing more unusual than a pub brawl in the wake of a dispute over a failed horse deal. Korpatsch's old business rival Stephan Rosenberg, also known by the nickname Matscho, had sold a horse to a German delivery man. Flush with success Matscho invited everyone on the Gypsy camp around to the local bar to celebrate his luck. Korpatsch had, since Christmas, been suffering something of a liquidity crisis and hoped to benefit from Matscho's trade by persuading the German to swap his new horse for another one that Korpatsch owned. He asked for a small supplementary payment to compensate him for the lower value, in his eyes, of Matscho's horse. As the investigating officer later put it: 'it is common that in trades like this almost the whole kinsfolk becomes involved and expresses an opinion on the value of a horse. For the most part on such occasions a considerable amount of alcohol is shared. And so it was at this horse trade.'[12] The German at first expressed interest, but on the point of concluding the deal and paying Korpatsch he changed his mind. At once 'the Korpatsch gang laid the blame on the Rosenbergs', though Korpatsch himself blustered and bragged. What did the Rosenbergs mean when they said he was desperate to do business? He had money for fifty horses: 'what is it you want, you poor devils, we have more dollars than you can imagine! I have your weight in dollars! I could buy the whole inn with my dollars while you rot in your endless chatter.'[13]

Both parties had good reason to be irritated by what they saw as the other's un-Romany behaviour, but when Matscho's wife, Maria Rosenberg, made disparaging remarks about Korpatsch's horse, the insult became insufferable.[14] Glasses were thrown, then smashed and used as weapons. Chairs and stools were raised and brought down on each other. One of Korpatsch's sons, Oskar, was heard to shout out cheerfully, as he barred the door, that the only way out this afternoon would be through the windows, and another German latecomer to the action noted how a great number of Gypsy women were laying into the 'very respectable Gypsy Jungo Rosenberg. Amongst other things, I heard, "You Jew, you should be hung up and done to death."'[15] Just as everyone had been driven out of the bar by the publican, who kept a rubber cosh for such occasions, the municipal Public Order Police (*Schutzpolizei*) arrived.

For Korpatsch, these were unfortunate developments. Most of the argument in the bar between the two families had taken place in Romany so that the German bystanders had little idea as to its content, but during the increasingly furious exchanges the Rosenbergs appeared to call him a *Devisenschieber*, a black market trader in currency.[16] The Exchange Control Regulations of February 1935 forbade private citizens to hold any foreign currency. How far, or consistently, these regulations were enforced varied widely from place to place.[17] The Frankfurt police saw themselves as the vanguard of the struggle against the Gypsies, leading earnest discussions with the town administration over the best way to control 'the Gypsy menace'. They were, thus, likely to act ruthlessly against Korpatsch.

The timing, too, of his arrest was unlucky. Ever since the Nazi takeover there had been talk of reforming the administration of the radically decentralised police forces. In recent months, Wilhelm Frick, as Interior Minister, and Heinrich Himmler, as head of the Gestapo, had both been manoeuvring to position themselves ahead of the forthcoming unification and centralisation of all police departments (Browder 1996: 86–7). Amongst officers interested in the so-called *Zigeunerfrage,* these developments loomed large, as such a reorganisation would inevitably lead to a relocation and enlargement of the work of the national Gypsy Centre, then based in Munich. The two detectives most involved in the Korpatsch investigations were determined to establish Frankfurt as an alternative site.[18] An accusation of 'foreign currency' dealing against a man who was already known to the police as 'Chief of the Hungarian Gypsies' was just the thing they needed. Within weeks they were putting out stories that no fewer than 600 officials had been working, full time, to lay bare the full dastardy of the man who was now, entirely misleadingly, named as the 'King of the Gypsies'.[19]

And, with Korpatsch, they had struck lucky. A first search of Korpatsch's camp site on the Saturday evening produced a substantial find of foreign gold and currency, with a total value estimated at 6,406 RM – a considerable sum at a time when a professional salary was in the region of 800 RM a month.[20] The Korpatsches insisted that these were wedding jewels but the police were having none of it. This was, after all, a case designed to make waves, and by accusing Korpatsch under the currency regulations they would be able to add the political crime of 'treason against the folk economy' to his charge sheet.[21]

With the help of the media, *Kripo* headquarters now worked the case along the lines of a well-rehearsed and familiar scenario, mobilising the local population in a small-scale version of the national 'manhunt days' (*Fahndungstag).* A story was prepared for the Monday edition of the local Nazi paper, the *Frankfurter Volksblatt*. By exaggerating tenfold (to 1200 gold dollars) the sums involved and claiming that 'hundreds of thousands of marks in foreign currency have been hidden away', the newspaper could pretend that the police had stumbled on a major criminal racket. Legal papers from a murder case that had been found during a second search of the caravans were no longer 'received from a lawyer', as the police notes stated, but 'presumed stolen from a judge'.[22]

More importantly, the article made clear that the Korpatsch 'affair' was not just about the pursuit of an individual Gypsy family. In an implicit reference to the ongoing centralisation of police activities, the article reassured members of the folk community that they had some reason to hope that the reign of Gypsy 'insolence' and 'shameless lies' might soon be brought to an end.

A STATE WITHIN THE STATE

In fact, just a few hours after the *Frankfurter Volksblatt* hit the news-stands, two days after Korpatsch's arrest, the police investigation was already beginning to fall apart. Despite the arrest of many members of Korpatsch's extended family there was still no sign of the vast funds that had been announced in the press. Then, on the Monday morning, three of the key Rosenberg witnesses against Korpatsch came into the police station and explained that they had been drunk on Saturday and enraged by the various insults flung at them in the course of the argument. They wanted to withdraw all their allegations.

By the end of that week, if the police were to have assessed objectively all the evidence in their hands they would have been disappointed. A fight that resulted in a mere 50 RM of damage was a trivial incident. Moreover, all the gold that had been found in the Korpatsch caravans had been accounted for with an official reckoning from a previous tax investigation in Altona in 1927.[23] However, for the reasons of departmental politics just examined, Chief Inspector Nussbaum and his boss, Police President Beckerle, were determined to pursue the case as a high-profile trial. Nussbaum declared that further investigations into the foreign currency dealings of the Korpatsches were, for the time being, closed. But none of the arrested would be released. In order to disrupt the 'good functioning of the Gypsy news service' all of them would be kept under arrest, in solitary confinement, with no visitors.[24]

It is worth pausing to assess where the police thought they were at this stage of their enquiries, for we can see here how little they were progressing according to a well-marked road map. In a report for his Police President, Nussbaum explained that the Gypsies had been able to frustrate his officers' best efforts because of their 'complete disregard for honest behaviour'.[25] Janosch Korpatsch was refusing to help the police at all, 'not because he wants to protect the others but simply because he deliberately works against anything and everything the police do'.[26] This idea of the old Gypsy deliberately setting himself against the system per se caught the Chief Inspector's imagination. In this light, the case no longer involved an ordinary, self-interested petty criminal but, rather, the type of person Nazi criminology identified as a social wrecker and menace to society.

This marked a significant politicisation of the case. In other respects, however, Nussbaum couched his argument in very traditional terms. The problem with Korpatsch, he believed, was that he was a 'foreign Gypsy' (though he was born in Arnsberg his ancestry was Hungarian) and so was 'self-consciously internationally oriented'. All the foreign Gypsies, he explained, lie 'without restraint and work according to their own clan laws against those of the law-enforcement agencies'. By contrast, 'the German Gypsies have lived for years with the might of the state and have come to terms with that and, knowing that otherwise they draw the short straw, have adjusted themselves to the surrounding conditions'.[27]

The National Socialist task was to bring these foreign Gypsies into line and make them behave like the German ones. This line of argument was, as I have said, represented throughout the state administration right up to the office of Himmler himself.[28] But between the end of January, when Nussbaum wrote the report just quoted, and the beginning of March this stance lost its foothold within the Frankfurt police. This happened as a direct consequence of an unexpected development in the Korpatsch case.

On the third day of his investigation Nussbaum received a telegram from a man called Fritz Stabani, who appeared to be a Lübeck police officer offering special insight into the background of the Gypsies now in custody. On further investigation Stabani turned out to be an 'Aryan' civilian who had lived for many years amongst Gypsy families on a camp near Lübeck. He styled himself as a writer, and legal advisor to the local Gypsies, though Nussbaum quickly wrote him off as a crank.[29] Nonetheless, he found a role for himself in the Korpatsch scenario. In the course of a telephone conversation that followed his telegram, Stabani reminded Nussbaum of a notice in the Police Circular published just a few weeks earlier detailing accusations of 'tribute collection' by Gypsies in the Saar. Stabani explained that it was those same families from the earlier circular who were involved in the new case. Nussbaum immediately ordered up the original files, realising their potential to widen the investigation beyond the currency allegations, the only evidence for which was evaporating before his eyes.[30] But the files contained a surprise that would enable him to break Korpatsch's steadfast refusal to cooperate and expand the whole scope of the case.

When the Rosenbergs had come into the police station and retracted their accusations against Korpatsch, Nussbaum assumed that the two Gypsy families had decided to put their fight in the bar behind them and renew cooperation. But a careful reading of the new Saarbrucken files revealed that the January brawl was no accidental flare-up. The Rosenbergs and Korpatsches were, Nussbaum learnt, originally from two quite distinct groups of Gypsies. The Rosenbergs belonged to the so-called German Gypsies (Sinte as we know them now) who had lived in German-speaking lands for several centuries, while the Korpatsches and their relatives (many of whom now bore German-sounding names) were considered to be 'Hungarian Gypsies', members of kin groups that had migrated from the east, mostly from the Austro-Hapsburg empire in the nineteenth century. The two populations had also occupied very different economic niches. The Rosenbergs were renowned musicians and had, in the past, enjoyed a far higher status than the 'foreigners', who were concentrated in the less respectable horse and fur-clothes trades. But in post-war years the tables had been turned as the taste for nineteenth-century 'Gypsy music' declined. The 'old' German families fell into poverty and now had to compete with the 'upstart' Korpatsches – 'so called better Gypsies' as the Rosenbergs sardonically referred to them. Korpatsch, who had once been a firm ally of the Rosenbergs, having helped one of them escape a murder charge in 1921, had since totally fallen out with his old friends.

The lesson for the police was clear: with care, Nussbaum could play one family off against the other. During the Saar investigations the Rosenbergs had come (mistakenly) to believe that Korpatsch was the source of accusations that they were extorting a kind of head tax from other Gypsies pursuing a trade in the Saar, 'on the land of the Rosenbergs'. The original police investigation had collapsed for lack of evidence but the bad feeling and desire for mutual revenge remained.

Now, using the Rosenbergs' fear that Korpatsch wanted to put them behind bars, and Korpatsch's certain knowledge that he was in prison because of Rosenberg denunciations during and after the pub fight, Nussbaum set about undermining Korpatsch's confident refusal to seek revenge on the Rosenbergs. Having persuaded some of the Rosenbergs to denounce Korpatsch for tribute collection, he took the signed allegations to Korpatsch. After six weeks of solitary confinement, and confronted with the new 'outrageous accusations' of Jungo and Matscho Rosenberg, on 27 February Korpatsch gave in and told Nussbaum what he wanted to hear: that he had on occasion paid tribute to the German Gypsies.[31] Nussbaum now had the families where he wanted them: each accusing the other of the same crime and each likely to produce more and more extravagant claims in response to the other's denunciations.[32]

From the point of view of the broader development of anti-Gypsy policy, it is not so much the details of Nussbaum's trickery that mattered but the way the content of these mutual allegations pushed Nussbaum into uncharted territory in terms of police policy. In contrast to his earlier assumptions about 'Hungarian' criminals and 'law abiding' German Gypsies, in the conflict in the Saar it was the Germans who had been demanding illegal tribute payments from the foreigners. At the outset of his enquiries, Nussbaum believed that Korpatsch, as 'King of the Gypsies' was the extortionist-in-chief. It was only at the beginning of March, with Korpatsch's evidence, that he was able to build a picture of a system of mutual tribute-taking in which all the various Gypsy families were involved. By the end of the month Nussbaum went so far as to admit that the victims of the extortionists were 'almost exclusively foreign Gypsies', but by then he had found a new theoretical schema to explain his evidence.

In reading through the files compiled by his detectives, Nussbaum was particularly taken by, and carefully underlined, those sections of the transcribed interviews where it emerged that the Gypsies had adopted language taken over from the German state administration to describe their 'tributary system'. Some of the Hungarian Gypsies claimed to have heard a relative of the Rosenbergs, Reinhold Lorier, talking of himself as the 'Chief Constable' (*Hauptwachtmeister*) of the Saar,[33] and on another occasion, at the St Wendel market, one of Korpatsch's in-laws sardonically referred to one of the 'German Gypsies' as 'Baron'.[34] Even more striking, a Johann Rosenberg (who, confusingly, was in fact a 'Hungarian' but who had adopted a respectable German Sinto name to buy himself some peace from the non-Gypsy authorities) told his interrogators that he had paid the 'true' Rosenbergs their tribute without making a fuss because he 'supposed they had legal authority (*Herrschaft*) over the territory'.[35] For their part, the Rosenbergs referred to Korpatsch's own dependents as his 'subjects' (*Untertan*)'.[36] These were, of course, circumstantial, perhaps trivial, pieces of evidence. Still they would help Nussbaum prop up his novel case that, under the lenient eyes of the rural gendarmerie, the Gypsies were running a 'state within the state', with parallel political structures and a tax system to support them.

Moreover, they were doing so in some style. On 16 March, Nussbaum complained that 'the extortionists live extremely well from their unadulterated idleness', managing to 'blow away huge sums in drinking parties'.[37] And here the gradual politicisation of the police and their alignment with Nazi ideology and policy comes to bear on the development of the case. *Kripo* officers prided themselves on their professionalism in contrast to the amateurish theatrics of the Gestapo, who had recruited intensively from within the Party and worked under direct Nazi domination. But the *Kripo*'s stance of 'aloofness from the "corruption" of partisan politics was a form of naiveté. In conjunction with their staunch nationalism it left them vulnerable' to all kinds of political pressures (Browder 1990: 91). Under the guise of 'doing what was necessary to protect society' themes from the Nazi world view were absorbed uncritically into the *Kripo* subculture. So, while in the past inter-Gypsy tribute payments were tolerated as a matter that only concerned the Gypsies, Nussbaum now argued that they represented proof of the damage Gypsies were doing to the people's economy. This secret state had to be funded from somewhere and, as unproductive 'parasites', the Gypsies could only raise funds by begging, swindling or stealing them from 'German folk comrades'.[38]

In order to stand these ideas up, when Korpatsch was condemned to seven months for the 'affray' in Schweizer's inn on 4 April, Nussbaum turned his full attention to a series of 'economic cases'. Foremost was the currency trial (the political implications of which made it the most ideologically salient) but Nussbaum also revived a whole series of 'swindling' charges against Korpatsch that had been abandoned several years earlier for lack of evidence.[39] Nussbaum's goal was not so much to highlight the individual deceits as the pattern of repeated criminality that he wanted to argue characterised a whole milieu. Although the sums involved were piffling, the victims could be profitably presented in the guise of that old German figure, much used by the Nazis, *Deutsche Michel*, the poor guileless German victim of alien cunning.[40]

SHIFTING THE TERMS OF REFERENCE

The issues at stake in these months are well illustrated by an application made by Dr Max Levi, counsel to Jungo Rosenberg, one of the 'German Gypsies', on 22 May 1936. Addressing himself to the public prosecutor, Levi requested that his client, as a man of previous good character, be released on bail. He had a wife and two small children. He had served and been wounded during the battle of the Somme – documentary proof from the Central Office for Certification was presented. He had worked as a musician and always paid his taxes – five tax receipts were enclosed – and the police had always considered him a reliable man. He could not, Levi argued, be counted amongst 'those Gypsies who without any real basis obtain a migrant travelling license'. It was true that he possessed such a licence, but he had been permanently resident in Hamburg for years already and so was genuinely eligible.[41] There were, Levi suggested, no grounds for further remand.

In essence, Levi was saying that his client should be considered on the merits of his individual case. The fact that he was of Gypsy descent should not be a decisive factor in the interpretation of the law. Levi knew, however, that to present his brief this bluntly was a hopeless endeavour.[42] Even the democratic police had been inclined to treat all 'Gypsies' as more suspicious than other citizens. And now the police were being formally enjoined to think in terms of biological-criminal communities. Habitual criminality was a mark of inferior, foreign blood and vice versa: all Gypsies were, thus, suspicious. In an attempt to get his client around such calloused reasoning, Levi turned to a version of the old strategy, drawing a distinction between what one might call 'the good' and 'the bad' Gypsy; between the kind of Gypsy who obtained papers under false pretexts and his honest client, who, Levi implied, was not really a Gypsy at all in the usual sense of the term. Jungo Rosenberg was a member of the German Sinte, many of whom lived lives superficially indistinguishable from other lower-middle-class Germans.

Presumably, the June 1936 Himmler decree (which still made the distinction between foreign and domestic Gypsies) gave Levi reason to believe that his client might be treated in much the same way as in the pre-Nazi period. In fact, the prosecutor rejected Levi's application out of hand. Not only did he not give it a moment's consideration, Jungo Rosenberg found himself still sitting in jail a year and a half later, lost in the entrails of the legal system, without so much as pre-trial hearings on the horizon. In December 1937, Rosenberg himself penned a pitiable plea for something to be done in his case: 'after nearly two years I can bear the solitary confinement no longer and I have no idea any more what to tell my wife who is now suffering from heart disease, let alone my two small children'.[43]

Rosenberg was the victim of a radicalisation at the heart of the local state that was never articulated in public and which was then, and is still, therefore, doubly hard to read. This radicalisation was driven in part by the momentum of the Korpatsch cases as they proceeded through the usual channels but also in part by the search for an institutional footing from which to claim leadership in the 'struggle against the Gypsies'. A further source of dynamism was the chance contribution of figures like the 'writer and legal advisor' Fritz Stabani who sent a number of letters to Nussbaum after his initial telegram and phone call of 13 January.

It was puzzling, Stabani thought, that while the Jews were being persecuted for living 'according to their own laws' nothing was being done about 'the Gypsies who live in Germany and appear to have exactly the same laws as the Jews. The only difference is that the Jewish laws are put down on paper and the Gypsy law is preserved right up to the present day by oral transmission. And yet it retains all its force. The Gypsy law is an institutional manual,' he continued, 'for effecting crimes against the non-Gypsies. Crime raised to the level of law.'[44] Stabani had offered to come down in person to Frankfurt to confront these renegades, if the *Kripo* there would cover his costs. Nussbaum rightly judged that the 'writer' was on his uppers and seeking a new source of income, but this did not stop him from adopting Stabani's theoretical conclusions as his own when called upon to produce a synthetic paper for a conference of public administrators.

It was the institutional conjuncture of the bureaucracy that next pushed Nussbaum forward. There had long been discussions about the creation of a new Reich Gypsy Law in which the Frankfurt city administration had taken a public stance, and a meeting of regional department chiefs of the state administration had fortuitously been called for 16 March in order to discuss new approaches to 'the Gypsy question' in this context.[45] Thanks to his role in the Korpatsch enquiries Nussbaum was now asked to articulate his new position at this meeting. Unable to quite make the break yet from the traditional terms of reference, he began his presentation with the old cliché of the 'alarming picture of criminality among the foreign Gypsies'. But then he changed tack. '*All Gypsies* are work-shy and overwhelmingly dishonest, both those who have lived long in Germany, but also those who have immigrated in the past few decades from the east. They are self-consciously internationalist and are to be seen as anti-state elements. They live by their own moral law which cannot be harmonised with the customs and laws of the Germans.' In order to explain and justify this shift from traditional police understandings, Nussbaum turned to Nazi racial theory: 'ever since the [1935] Nuremberg laws the Gypsies, like the Negro bastards in the one-time occupied Rhineland, do not count as part of the Aryan race'.[46]

Nussbaum acknowledged that the formal behaviour of the German Gypsies differed from that of the foreigners but he now saw this as a matter of display and pretence. For while it was true that the '"German" Gypsy is anxious to pass', the same person had no difficulties bringing his 'aberrations' – such as cheating or avoidance of military duty – in line with his conscience. They all displayed what he dubbed: 'Jewish trickiness'. Having lived through weeks of frustrating conflicts with Gypsies who used public officials' ignorance of their nature to ease their passage through the criminal system, he concluded that: 'a code of criminal procedure designed to deal with German people is cut to the German measure. For the Gypsies it provides a fine protection against the force of the German state.'[47]

Here Nussbaum was stepping well outside conventional wisdom. The suggestion that special legal provision be made for an ethnic group is the clearest evidence of this. Likewise, several years before such ideas came onto the national agenda, Nussbaum proposed incarcerating all Gypsies in internment or labour camps so as to crush their dishonourable morals and practices. And here he coined a new trope: the Gypsies constitute an 'organisation of illegal secret societies' (*Geheimbündelei*), which, as everyone knew, were forbidden in the new Germany. 'And yet the Gypsies in Germany continue to speak their own language and live with their own laws.' His own work in the few weeks just past, as well as reports from the gendarmerie, had revealed what every serving officer knew: hundred of moronic and criminal Gypsies still make their 'pilgrimage around Germany'.[48] Only by dealing decisively with their whole way of life could radical progress be made.

AD HOC BUT NOT CHAOTIC RADICALISATION

For the time being, proposals like these were destined to remain the stuff of municipal committee rooms. On this occasion, the regional officials could agree nothing more radical than the forced settlement of all Gypsies in Frankfurt, with the aim of expelling them at the earliest opportunity. Nussbaum found a similar reticence in the face of radical demands when his cases were dealt with by some of the judiciary. Registrar Heiland was a keen advocate of fierce measures in the currency cases and personally got the chance to give Korpatsch twelve months' imprisonment, with subsequent loss of civil rights, for one of the 'swindling' cases, but his was not the only stance. The twelve-month sentence was slashed at appeal by a judge markedly less influenced by political considerations. Likewise, neither of the two most substantial of the 'tribute' accusations produced satisfactory outcomes for Nussbaum. In one, the judge found that the German Rosenbergs' demand for 'compensation' from some Hungarian Rom who had borrowed their name[49] was not a matter of 'obtaining an unlawful pecuniary advantage'. The judge, who otherwise displayed no fond feelings towards the Gypsies, observed that they could indeed reasonably claim that their reputation had been harmed by the unauthorised adoption of the name Rosenberg by the 'Hungarians'. In his view, they had perfectly legitimate grounds for a 'claim for damages'. And in the case of the two elderly Rosenberg brothers who were finally brought to court in 1938, while Nussbaum had been determined to prove that the raising of tribute was done collaboratively and systematically (in other words that it was part of a sustained criminal activity), the judges were not impressed by the evidence and passed short, sixteen-month sentences, which they declared already served in light of the two years the Gypsies had spent on remand.

'Uneven development' within the state administration is not the same as no development. Nussbaum's investigations had stretched the length and breadth of the Reich and had involved the Berlin *Kripo* as well as the Munich Gypsy centre. The overlap of personnel between the Frankfurt and the Saar cases had, at a personal career level, allowed Nussbaum and his superiors to make a smart political move, extending their jurisdiction outside their own region.[50] This marked them out as detectives willing to work in the spirit of a reformed and centralised police force. Hundreds of caravans had been searched and as many persons interrogated across the country, many of them repeatedly, first in the currency cases and then while investigating the 'tribute system'.[51] In this way *Kripo* offices and their staff around the country had been brought to understand that they, too, could take a new role in combating the Gypsy 'plague'.

Moreover, as the correspondence in the files indicates, it was not just 'cranks' like Stabani who felt called upon to write in with advice, but also police officers from other regions trying to formulate their thinking in a more systematic fashion. A Sergeant Jebens of Melsdorf, who introduced himself as an officer with a 'special personal interest' in the Gypsy question, railed against tolerance of interracial unions but even less intimate communication upset him too: 'on the horse market I have observed how German blooded horse dealers transact with the Gypsies, these very Gypsies named here, the families of Korpatsch, Kaikoni, Mirosch, and host drinking parties for them'.[52]

Later, on the occasion of the two mass deportations of Gypsies to the General Government in 1940 and 1943, it was these same police offices who were delegated to decide who went and who stayed. They were then under orders to work with a new distinction between 'racially pure' and 'mixed' Gypsies, but no more than in 1936 is there reason to think that the ideology promulgated by Berlin was decisive.[53] Here too, at the moment of 'selection', it was local practice which determined who would live and who would die – and this local practice had been formed in cases like the one discussed here.[54]

THE SPECIFICITY OF THE GYPSY GENOCIDE

One of the peculiarities of the persecution of the Gypsies is that, in most localities, when the Nazis came to power they found people already in place who, like Sergeant Jebens, had 'a well founded interest in the Gypsy question' and were ready and willing to take the opportunities on offer to implement more radical and effective measures.[55] In Berlin, few of their suggestions were given serious consideration in the years after the takeover. But many of the officials who wrote letters in vain to various ministries were more successful in transforming local treatment of Sinti and Roma – to what extent depended on a host of factors including the balance of political forces and the intensity with which the 'Gypsy question' was felt locally.

It was at the interface of central inertia and local mobilisation of new state resources that Gypsy policy developed. Since this argument has focused, so far, exclusively on a single case, it may be worthwhile briefly demonstrating that this was the location of radicalisation more generally. If we take the early development of the Gypsy camps, we see that what began as slightly stricter versions of municipal camps for travellers metamorphosed gradually towards ethnic internment lager. In fact the appearance of continuity is deeply misleading for the *Zigeunerlager* can only really be understood in the broader context of the entire 'camp system' that the Nazis were in the process of constructing.[56] Like the scores of mini Concentration and Labour Camps that sprung up in 1933, the municipal Gypsy camps had a characteristically ad-hoc and local nature.[57] Above all, they had no legal basis whatsoever – not even executive decree. In creating them, each city council operated more or less as it saw fit, using whatever Circular Instructions were in operation at the time. In Berlin, an instruction to establish a 'manhunt day' to track down Gypsy criminals provided the pretext.[58] In Hamburg, a year later, the Mayor turned to the decree of 14 December on the Preventive Struggle against Crime, the provisions of which allowed closed camps for 'improvement', through labour, or, helpfully, for 'sundry other purposes'.[59] Just as the legal basis of the camps was determined by unchecked local power, so, in the absence of any overarching regulation, each camp developed its own system of regulations.

If the evolution of the camp order was not planned at the outset, this does not mean it was determined entirely by chance. While a camp like Marzahn was set up in order to make Berlin *zigeunerfrei* for the foreign 'guests' at the Berlin Olympics, almost no thought was given to how order would be maintained. Once in existence, by an almost ineluctable logic, regulations were introduced which governed an increasing number of the inmates' activities. Within a short period a camp superintendent and a police watch had been appointed: what was the point of forcing all the Gypsies to live in one place if not to control their activities and to reduce the threat they posed to the surrounding population? The coming and going of residents could be restricted to departure for work (eight to ten hours) or for shopping (a much more limited time allowed for those without work). To ensure the Gypsies obeyed these rules, a register could be kept of all departures and arrivals. To enforce registration, punishment would be introduced for failure to present oneself. And what was the point of controlling the movement of the Gypsies if outsiders were allowed free entry?[60] As this ever sharper residential and physical segregation of the Gypsies was implemented, so blatant discriminatory measures were also introduced, followed by gradual exclusion from the last remaining bastion where Gypsies had a place in German society, the school system. And little of this required decrees, laws or written orders.

CONCLUSION

Despite the scale of the attack on the Gypsy peoples, there has been little true accounting with this past in any of the countries where Gypsies were targeted – with the exception of Germany since 1985. Neither in practical nor in ceremonial terms were any of these Gypsy victims, or their surviving relatives, treated with anything like the respect they are due.[61] After the war Romany victims of the Nazis campaigned, some of them to the end of their lives, for proper acknowledgement of what they had been through, as well as for some sort of monetary compensation for everything they had lost. In many cases this was a fruitless endeavour. Between 1956 and 1985, the German state refused to acknowledge that the Gypsies had suffered alongside the Jews. Countless Sinti and Roma survivors were refused compensation payments until the day they died.

Apart from prejudice, at the heart of this unwillingness to acknowledge the Gypsies as equal victims of Nazi policy lay the perhaps unavoidable, but fundamentally misleading, parallel of the Gypsy and Jewish persecutions. This model led to a moral hierarchy of victims that was inadvertently built into the institutional structure of the German Federal Republic. The compensation offices, for instance, used Nazi anti-Semitic ideology and practice as their point of reference for defining 'political' persecution. It is essential to understand that the pernicious influence of this misapplied model had little or nothing to do with the personal histories or the political stance of the individuals involved. This much became clear in the 1980s when a new generation of lawyers, prosecutors and judges came to office. Many were ashamed of the failure to identify individual perpetrators or to hold anyone accountable for the persecution and genocide of the Gypsies, and were determined to try and set the historical and judicial record straight.

But the great majority of the cases they opened never made it to court. In a typical instance, the prosecutor published a statement explaining why he had abandoned a case against an Anthropological Laboratory assistant: 'as regards the Gypsies a clear and traceable chain of orders, analogous to the order for the "Final Solution of the Jewish Question" is missing'.[62] A more or less mythologised version of the Holocaust as the outcome of an order from the Führer thus misled the legal professionals. Indeed, the whole approach which considers Nazi policy as something that was always formulated at the top of the political system (as an expression of a clearly formulated ideology or of an order from Hitler, a *Führerbefehl*), and that was then filtered down the state and party hierarchy, is fundamentally misleading, at least when it comes to groups like the Gypsies.

To understand the dynamic of this persecution we have to turn to the way individual 'solutions' to the Gypsy problem were found. All over Germany, and Austria after 1938, Nazi rule offered the chance to thousands of people, civil servants and party men in particular (but plenty of ordinary citizens as well), to turn their private agenda against the Gypsies into state policy. Public order, social reform, a return to a 'healthy community' of productive workers, the re-evaluation of the rural idyll of the farmer and his family in their *hof*, 'a folk community without criminals'; these were the ideological building blocks of these people's world view. Wherever local officials in housing, welfare, labour and police departments identified a 'Gypsy problem', then dealing with those persons could become an inherent and popular part of the Nazi social revolution. In the bright light of the Nazi dawn, these town hall *genocidaires* discovered that social problems, whose resolution had thwarted generations of their predecessors, suddenly appeared in a wholly new, and more manageable, light.

The reformed criminal police increasingly adopted Himmler's dogma that crime, asociality and heredity form a causal triangle, and came to treat 'Gypsy cases' differently from those of other German citizens. The university departments of Anthropology and Genetics in Berlin, and elsewhere, hunted for the gene of 'asocial behaviour', feeding both the police's appetites for new models and those of the 'hereditary health' clinics run across the Reich by doctors hunting for candidates for sterilisation.[63] The City Health Offices vetted those who would marry in order to weed out interracial unions. The wardens of the *Zigeunerlager* (often drawn from SS personnel) operated the selections when deportations to the east began for a short while in 1940 and when they were restarted again in 1943 – and all these various people came together in local meetings like that organised in Frankfurt in March 1936.

If we try and read all these local initiatives and approaches as the unfolding of some central plan, or the inevitable consequence of structural features of Nazi rule, we will never make sense of what happened. Indeed, one of the striking features of the microhistory of this persecution is that, time and again, the fate of individual Gypsies, Gypsy families and whole communities could rest on the arbitrary interpretation and use to which loosely and generally phrased legislation was put. In one case, a Sinti woman might escape sterilisation thanks to the exact application of the law by a Hereditary Health Court. In another, a Gypsy woman who obeyed an order to cease living with a German man found herself arrested and carried off to a concentration camp for then 'leaving her place of residence' without permission. As often as not, it is through tracing the fate of such individuals as they pass through these institutions – often several of them, one after another – that we can see how the Nazi social revolution doomed the Gypsy peoples.

I believe, then, that this account of bureaucratic momentum towards genocide might be taken as the historical norm. What one might call the 'Wannsee-Auschwitz model' would then be the exception. Predictable outcomes may arise from a persecution that has plenty of regional variations, a variety of different routes to killing, and even divergent ideological justifications for the crime. Pattern, here, is not the result of the application of a single and well thought through genocidal intent. Let me be clear. I am not arguing that the Holocaust was 'unique'. The careful planning and hierarchical organisation of the Rwandan massacres is strongly reminiscent of Nazi practice (cf., for example, Lemarchand 2004). But in other, equally exemplary, cases, like that of the Guatemalan assault on the Mayans from 1981 to 1983 or the earlier destruction of the Paraguayan Aché, the formal intent of the authorities was presented as counter-insurgency in one case and modernisation in the other. There was no organised plan to destroy these peoples and the perpetrators of these massacres did not believe that they targeted the Mayan population as Mayans, or the Aché as Aché – they were pursuing government policies, in the way of which Mayans and Aché constituted an obstacle.[64] Nonetheless, the result was genocide.

In fact, as a younger generation of German historians has demonstrated, a similar argument can be applied to the crucial period when the Holocaust developed between 1939 and 1941. This period, of fifteen months' duration or so, can be seen as a transitional phase between systematic persecution and methodical slaughter. Focusing on the period before the Wannsee conference, Ulrich Herbert, Dieter Pohl and others have shown that the practical preparations and, to some extent, even the schema of an industrially organised Final Solution lay less in plans conceived in Berlin than in the improvisations of commanders on the ground on the eastern Front and in the former Polish territory of the General Government.[65] Of course, these perpetrators of the early 'actions' were men steeped in Nazi social ideology and racial thinking, men already utterly brutalised to the consequences of their 'tough but necessary' measures. And their solutions were also greeted with unrestrained enthusiasm in Berlin before being put on a rational, bureaucratic basis at the Wannsee conference. Nevertheless, in the crucial, transitional phase, their murderous acts were less the consequence of a 'general plan' and a clearly expressed 'intent' than solutions to problems that arose in the course of war. The fate of the Gypsies was, in this sense, not so different than that of the Jews in the period after the onset of the war and before the meeting on the Berlin lake. As long as we cling to the Lemkin model of genocide, formed, it should be remembered, long before we had any real documentary evidence as to how the Nazi genocides were prepared, we are bound both to ignore the signs of genocide emerging, as it is sure to do again, and, in its aftermath, to misrepresent the suffering of its victims.

ACKNOWLEDGEMENTS

Some of the arguments here result from a note given to me by my generous colleague, Henriette Asseo of EHESS, at an AHRC funded international seminar in Paris organised by Paloma Gay y Blasco and Catarina Pasqualino. Martin Luchterhandt was extraordinarily generous in giving me photocopies of his archive collection as well as of his handwritten notes when I was beginning my investigation of the Korpatsch materials. Elisabeth Tauber also made very helpful observations on an early version of this paper. I thank the editors, too, for their helpful comments.

NOTES

1. Cf. Prunier 2005.
2. Cf. Appeals Chamber, the Prosecutor v. Radislav Krstic, Case No. IT-98-33-A, Judgment, 19 April 2004, ICTY Judicial Supplement, NO. 49, May 2004, www.un.org/icty/Supplement/supp49-e/krstic.htm.
3. According to the standard interpretation of the Convention, and the majority of the judges in recent cases have sided with this view, it is not only necessary that actors have 'knowledge' of the consequences of their actions but also that they specifically intend that those consequences should result. For a dissenting view see the partially dissenting opinion of Judge Shahabuddeen, in General Krstić's successful appeal against conviction for genocide at www.un.org/icty/cases-e/index-e.htm, pp. 89–117. For the debate among legal scholars, cf. Greenawalt 1999; Jørgensen 2001; Arnold 2003.
4. 'Generally speaking, genocide does not necessarily mean the immediate destruction of a nation, except when accomplished by mass killings of all members of a nation. It is intended rather to signify a coordinated plan of different actions aiming at the destruction of essential foundations of the life of national groups, with the aim of annihilating the groups themselves. The objectives of such a plan would be disintegration of the political and social institutions, of culture, language, national feelings, religion, and the economic existence of national groups, and the destruction of the personal security, liberty, health, dignity, and even the lives of the individuals belonging to such groups.' (Lemkin: 79–95. Also found at: www.preventgenocide.org/lemkin/AxisRule1944–1.htm.)
5. Cf. Greenawalt 1999.
6. Friedlander 1997: 102.
7. Legal moves against judges, lawyers, doctors and then the Law against Overcrowding of German Schools and Universities – used to remove Jews from the centres of learning – followed. In September 1933, the Sacred Earth Law forbade Jews from owning farms or working in agriculture – protecting the sacred birth place of the folk community from contamination. Five years later came the rush of laws and decrees that Aryanised the economy, expropriating Jewish property and finally excluding Jews from all areas of public life. Cf. Friedlander 1997.
8. The Nazis also relied upon a degree of street terror against the Jews – a terrible campaign of public intimidation in the summer of 1935, for instance – and were also engaged in dismantling the very constitutional structures their laws were supposedly grounded in.
9. A crucial consideration is the extent of exceptions: the holocaust model suggesting that very few and only trivial 'exceptions' should evade

destruction – though the convention (and subsequent jurisdiction) talks of destruction 'in whole or in part'.

10. Cf. Burleigh 2002 (1994): 97–100; 2000: 383.
11. Cf. Ministerialblatt des Reichs-und Preuss. Minsteriums des Innern 1938, Nr. 51, pp. 2105–9. Cf. also the implementing instructions, circulated in the Deutsche Kriminalpolizeiblatt, 20 March 1939.
12. Detmold D20 B Zg. 72 189, Beiakte zu Nr 265 (Strauss). Band II, 15 January 1936.
13. Detmold D20 B Zg. 72 189, Beiakte zu Nr 265 (Strauss). Band I, 80R.
14. The Rosenbergs had no doubt been offended that Korpatsch was trying to value his own mare over the one they had just sold, and Korpatsch's people, for their part, were outraged that the Rosenbergs should have broken one of the basic understandings that Sinte and Roma should not get in each other's way when trading with the Germans. Maria was also breaching the rule that women should not speak out in the horse dealings of their male kin.
15. Detmold D20 B Zg. 72 189, Beiakte zu Nr 265 (Strauss). Band I, 107.
16. Detmold Band I, 12.
17. Cf., for example, Sgt Storm's comments at Wiesbaden, Band VI, p.188, dated 18 June 1937.
18. Cf., for example, 1 March 1936 *Hamburger Fremdenblatt* article Sunday edition, p.9 under the title *Die Umtrieb der ausländischer Zigeuner* (Machinations of the foreign Gypsies). Copy in Wiesbaden, 461.16335, Band I, p.58.
19. *Wiesbadener Tageblatt,* 28 February 1936. Copy in Wiesbaden, 461.16335, Band I, p.61.
20. From the dramatic report he submitted on his search of the site it is clear that officer Borkert had been told to make the most of his little action. Cf. Detmold, D20 B, Zg. 72/89, Band II, 14 January 1936, pp.8–9.
21. ML 144, 15/1.
22. *Frankfurter Volksblatt*, 13 January 1936, Nr 12, p.5: *Zigeuner schlagen sich – der lachende Dritte die Polizei* (Gypsies beat each other up – the laughing third party is the police).
23. By then the Kiel police had supplied Frankfurt with a schedule of the currency and gold that Korpatsch had owned in 1927. Comparison of that with the tally in January 1936 suggested that in the intervening period the family had increased its total holdings by some twenty pieces of gold, but had also had to part with a few smaller items. Above all, it showed that the vast majority of pieces were identical to those listed nine years earlier. Detmold, ML 87.
24. He added a simple invention to the file to justify this move. He claimed that a reward 'amounting to 5,000 dollars [sic!] has been offered for the

withdrawal of statements'. Detmold I 145. Nussbaum Bericht, 15 January 1936.

25. Wiesbaden, 461.16335, Band V, p.55.
26. Note written 25 January. Wiesbaden, 461.16335 Band V, p.27.
27. Wiesbaden, 461.16335, Band V, p.55. See also DKPBl 2355/15. Likewise, the *Hamburger Fremdenblatt* article dealing with this case had also talked in identical terms of *foreign* Gypsies who 'set all rules and orders at nought and, in accordance with Gypsy morals, treat all tricks against the population and the state as a noble and good deed'. 1 March 1936 cited above note 18.
28. The June 1936 decree marked some changes in the status quo ante. The Gypsies were described for the first time in such a decree as 'a people alien to the German folk [*Volkstum*]'. And the decree halted the further issuing of permits for travelling tradesmen, the *Wandergewerbschein*, as well as calling for a much stricter control of markets, especially horse markets.
29. In denazifaction documents Stabani presents himself as a circus showman, married to a Gypsy. The British authorities were alerted by someone and refused him a performer's licence and permission to recommence his former occupation. Former Berlin Documentation Centre, now *Bundesarchiv, Entnazifizierung* materials, *ReichsKulturkammer* (RK) Certificates 2703, D0094 , Stabanaki.
30. For this chain of events cf. Detmold, D 20 B Zg 72/89, Band I, pp.218–25.
31. At this stage he still denied ever having paid anything to his old friends Jungo or Matscho.
32. Cf., especially, Wiesbaden, 461.16335, Band V, pp.84–6 for the Korpatsch statement and that whole file for these accusations.
33. Wiesbaden, 461.16335, Band II, p.7.
34. 16335, Band V, p.134r. Report by St Wendel *Hauptwachsmeister* 17 March 1936.
35. 16335, Band V, p.29R. 24 January 1936.
36. See 16335, Band V, pp.167–9R.
37. Wiesbaden, 461.16335, Band II, pp.29–32.
38. 16335 Vol I, p.79, 27 March 1936 Nussbaum to *Oberstaatsanwalt*. Cf. also Brunsch, 2 May 1936, Band V, p.170.
39. It would be wrong to read too much into the fact that such cases existed. Such cases accompany the horse dealer as they do the second-hand car salesman.
40. 461. 16328 WStA, p.14.
41. 16335, Band I, p.115, 22 May 1936. It had been illegal since before the First World War to issue such a licence to anyone without a permanent abode.

42. According to Richard Grunberger, Nazi jurists were fond of citing Nietzsche's dictum that 'Penal law consists of war measures to rid oneself of the enemy' and nowhere was this more true than in relation to 'alien types' (*artfremd*) (Grunberger 1971: 159).
43. Wiesbaden, 461.16335, Band VII, p.292 and 292R.
44. Detmold, D 20 B Zg 72/890, Band II, pp.249–50.
45. On the law, cf., for example, Dr Zindel's letter to State Secretary Pfundner of 4 March 1936 and his 'Thoughts on the design of a Reich Law for the Gypsies' which promised rapid, new and specific proposals. There is no trace of any such in later ministerial papers. Cf. Berlin R18, R1501 5644, pp.215–27. The conference also discussed the problem of how to sedentarise all the Gypsies in new municipal camps. Cf. Sandner 1998: 62–72.
46. Emphasis in the original. Wiesbaden, 461.16335, Band II, pp.29–30.
47. 16335, Band II, p.30.
48. 16335, Band II, p.30–1.
49. When the 'Hungarians' had refused to pay, the German Rosenbergs had published a series of defamatory adverts in local newspapers claiming that the Berlin Gypsies were swindlers and cheats, selling goods which they bought from 'Berlin Jews' at a grotesquely inflated mark-up. The result had been that the fur-coat business collapsed.
50. The procedure involved considerable bureaucratic trouble, since it involved people who were not residents of his police district, but he insisted that the Frankfurt Prosecutor seek Saarbrucken's permission to take over the case. Privately, he believed that the Saar authorities lacked the determination to pursue the Gypsies – as they had demonstrated only a few days earlier when interviewing Eichelmann Rosenberg, son of Jungo. Having failed to break the man's 'obdurately dishonest denials' of involvement in tribute collection, they simply declared it 'pointless pursuing the matter' and, to Nussbaum's outrage, had released him. Cf. Detmold, D 20 B Zg 72/89, Band II, pp.154–5.
51. Cf., for example, the facsimile of a Köln *Landeskriminalpolizeistelle* report on a manhunt day organised there on 18 January 1936, in Fings and Sparing 2006: 110.
52. Jebens to FaM, 25 March 1936, 16335, Band II, p.21–5, here 23.
53. Himmler had become fascinated by the possibility of keeping a few racially pure Gypsies on a reservation in the Slavic slave lands that were to be created after the war.
54. Cf., for example, the personal files of individual Sinti and Roma at Landesarchiv, A Pr. Br. Rep. 30 Berlin C, where the sheer arbitrariness of police procedure can be wondered at.

55. In 1934, the District Mayor of Mosbach, in south-western Germany, had proposed 'setting up a general camp' and two years later the Mayor of Neustadt, near Marburg in central Germany, had come up with the idea of 'a general committal to a closed camp'. In February 1937, a police chief near Detmold in northern Germany bluntly suggested 'putting them into a concentration camp', and in the same year the anthropologist Otto Finger, working out of the Institute for Hereditary and Racial Health, in Giessen, suggested that the entire population be placed in 'security custody' outside the boundary of the cities in some sort of camp. In Thuringia, inspired by the persecution of the 'hereditarily defective', the regional authorities in July 1936 suggested the delivery of all Gypsies into mental institutions for the 'asocial'. And so on.
56. Cf. Jud Newborn, *'Work makes free': the hidden cultural meanings of the Holocaust*, PhD thesis in Department of Anthropology, University of Chicago, especially Volume III.
57. Cf. Burleigh 2000: 198–205.
58. In Frankfurt the same decree was used to justify the 'sedentarisation' of 'domestic' Gypsies.
59. *Grundlegender Erlass über die Vorbeugende Verbrechensbekämpfung durch die Polizei*. Confidential, unpublished decree, circulated in the *Erlasssammlung* Nr. 15. Available at the *Institut fur Zeitgeschichte*, Munich.
60. For Marzahn, cf. Sparing 1997.
61. Cf. Margalit 2002.
62. The Hamburg prosecutor's words from a 1989 decision, in ZSL Ludwigsburg, 414 AR 540/83, Bd. 4, p.233 (799). Cited by Lewy, 223.
63. Gypsies could be sterilised under provisions to prevent the 'hereditarily feeble minded' reproducing. Cf., for example, Daum 1991.
64. Cf. Arens 1976, and Grandin 2003.
65. Cf. essays in Herbert (ed.) 2000.

REFERENCES

Arens, R. (ed.) 1976. *Genocide in Paraguay*, Philadelphia: Temple University Press.

Arnold, R. 2003. 'The mens rea of genocide under the Statute of the International Criminal Court', *Criminal Law Forum* 14(2): 127–51.

Browder, G.C. 1990. *Foundations of the Nazi police state: the formation of the Sipo and SD*, Lexington: University of Kentucky Press.

—— 1996. *Hitler's enforcers: the Gestapo and the SS Security Service in the Nazi revolution*, Oxford: Oxford University Press.

Burleigh, M. 1994. *Death and deliverance: euthanasia in Germany 1900–1945*, Cambridge: Cambridge University Press.

—— 2000. *The Third Reich: a new history*, London: Macmillan.

Daum, M. and H-U. Deppe. 1991. *Zwangssterilisation in Frankfurt am Main 1933–1945*, Frankfurt am Main: Campus Verlag.

Fings, K. and F. Sparing. 2006. *Rassismus, Lager, Völkermord: Die national-sozialistische Zigeunerverfolgung in Köln*, Köln: Emons Verlag.

Fricke, T. 1996. *Zigeuner im Zeitalter des Absolutismus: Bilanz einer einseitigen Überlieferung*, Pfaffenweiler: Centaurus-Verlagsgesellschaft.

Friedlander, S. 1997. *Nazi Germany and the Jews. Volume one. The years of persecution, 1933–1939*, London: Phoenix Giant.

Grandin, G. 2003. 'History, motive, law, intent: combining historical and legal methods in understanding Guatemala's 1981–1983 genocide', in R. Gellately and B. Kiernan (eds), *The specter of genocide: mass murder in historical perspective*, Cambridge: Cambridge University Press.

Geremek, B. 1994. *Poverty, a history*, Oxford: Blackwell.

Greenawalt, A.K.A. 1999. 'Rethinking genocidal intent: The case of a knowledge-based interpretation', *Columbia Law Review* 99(8): 2259–94.

Grunberger, R. 1971. *A social history of the Third Reich, 1933–1945*, London: Weidenfield and Nicolson.

Herbert, U. 2000. *National socialist extermination policies: contemporary German perspectives and controversies*, Oxford: Berghahn Books.

Jørgensen, N.H.B. 2001. 'The definition of genocide: joining the dots in the light of recent practice', *International Criminal Law Review* 1: 285–313.

Lemarchand, R. 2004. 'The Rwanda genocide. Eyewitness accounts', in S. Totten, W.S. Parsons and I.W. Charny (eds), *Century of genocide: critical essays and eyewitness accounts*, London: Routledge.

Lemkin, R. 1944. *Axis rule in occupied Europe: laws of occupation – analysis of government – proposals for redress*, Washington, DC: Carnegie Endowment for International Peace.

Lewy, G. 1999. *The Nazi persecution of the Gypsies*, Oxford: Oxford University Press.

Margalit, G. 2002. *Germany and its Gypsies: a post-Auschwitz ordeal*, Madison, Wisc.: University of Wisconsin Press.

Newborn, J. 1994. *Work makes free: the hidden cultural meaning of the Holocaust*. Unpublished PhD thesis in four volumes, University of Chicago, Illinois.

Prunier, G. 2005. *Darfur: the ambiguous genocide*, Cornell University Press.

Sandner, P. 1998. *Frankfurt, Auschwitz. Die nationalsozialistische Verfolgung der Sinti und Roma in Frankfurt am Main*, Frankfurt am Main: Brandes and Apsel Verlag.

Sorabji, C. 1995. 'A very modern war: terror and territory in Bosnia-Hercegovina', in R. Hinde and H. Watson (eds), *War, a cruel necessity?: the bases of institutionalized violence*, London: I.B. Tauris.

Sparing, F. 1997. 'The Gypsy camps', in K. Fings, H. Heuss and F. Sparing (eds), *From 'race science' to the camps: the Gypsies during the Second World War*, Hatfield: University of Hertfordshire Press.

ARCHIVAL SOURCES

HSTA Wiesbaden
IFZ Munich
LHA Potsdam
STA Detmold
STA Frankfurt
Zentrale Stelle Ludwigsburg

CHAPTER 11

WHY ARE SOME PEOPLE POWERFUL?

Luke Freeman

AN ANTHROPOLOGIST AND A PRESIDENT

In early 2004 I spent two months researching the lives and journeys of young Antandroy cattle drovers who trade cattle across the wild western plains of Madagascar. On the very day I returned to Antananarivo from my first journey, covered in red dust and smelling of straw, I received a telephone call from the Presidency: 'Dr Freeman, the President wants to see you. You must be here in forty minutes.' This was not as unexpected as it might seem, for I had known Marc Ravalomanana many years before when we were both leading different lives. I had written to him to tell him of my arrival in Madagascar.

I hurriedly borrowed a suit from my Malagasy brother, Solo, which turned out to be rather short in the leg. His smart shoes pinched unbearably, so we took a taxi to a shoe shop to buy some new ones. Leaving my sandals there to be collected on the way home, we raced up to the palace, stopping only to buy a tie from a street vendor.

At the palace gates a guard in a red beret directed us to the security room. On a row of plastic chairs people were waiting patiently to be issued with passes. I explained the purpose of my visit to one of three staff behind a long desk. Looking up from his word-search puzzle, he made a phone call, filled out a form in leaking biro and issued us with security badges. A colleague waved a metal detector at us and we stepped through the airport-style security gate. An attentive young man led us across a courtyard in front of the palace, up some steps and into an anteroom. The room was glazed along the southern side, looking out over the suburbs of the capital. From half a mile below us, floating up on the breeze from the shores of Lac Anosy, came the shouts and angry slogans of a public protest against rising fuel prices. The armed soldier sitting in the corner of the room was oblivious to this as he was listening through twittering headphones to a personal stereo. Solo and I sat nervously until the attentive young man returned and led us past a saluting and lavishly brocaded aide-de-camp (does one salute back? I wondered) into the office of the President. He rose from behind a huge leather-covered desk: 'So, Luke, how are you?'

I had not seen Ravalomanana for fifteen years, when, as Madagascar's most dynamic young businessman, he had employed me as his English teacher. He had barely changed: he still looked young – even boyish – and handsome, with dark eyes that seemed to look deep into you. I told him I was now an anthropologist and had just spent a month with cattle drovers. He looked puzzled for a moment, then grinned and thumped his palm on the desk. 'That is what I need! I need to know my own people. You can help me! I must make a speech tomorrow. You will write it for me.' He phrased it in a way that was impossible to refuse.

It was the closing address, to be delivered in English the next day at the World Wildlife Fund international conference. I wrote it that evening on Solo's kitchen table, sprinkling it with proverbs and pleas for the conservationists to respect local knowledge and practice. At eight o'clock the next morning I found myself back at the palace, rehearsing the speech with the President. I coached him in body language and intonation, and that afternoon he delivered it with panache to a standing ovation. He had previously been criticised for his inability to speak in public, a deficiency that only highlighted his political inexperience. Now he had found someone who could fix that for him. He was delighted. Within a week President Ravalomanana had appointed me his special advisor and chief speech writer.

PRESIDENT MARC RAVALOMANANA

This enquiry into individual political power was provoked by the time I spent as a member of the President's staff. However, this is not a personal up-close portrait of Ravalomanana – those insights cannot be published here – nor is it an anthropology of elite politicians and the world they inhabit. Arguing from a conventional anthropological perspective, that the locus of power lies as much in the perceptions and projections of the subjects as it does in the figure and actions of their leader, this study and its conclusions are based as much on my knowledge and observation of ordinary Malagasy people over several years as on my short-term privileged access to the President. Nearly all the ethnographic evidence presented here would have been available to me from a position outside the presidential entourage. But what my association with Ravalomanana did do was to force me to spend time around him, and this is what raised the question that forms the title of this paper. Indeed, it was the personal presentation of power, rather than governmental processes or party politics, which most intrigued my Malagasy friends and family whenever I returned home from the palace. They wanted to know what their president was like up-close, in what way he was different from them, and how that enabled him to rule over them. As well as asking why he was powerful, they were asking why they were not.

Ravalomanana came into politics from a business background, having created a hugely profitable dairy company called Tiko. After only a few years as Mayor of Antananarivo, he stood for president. A long and acrimonious stand-off with the long-term leader Didier Ratsiraka threw the country into chaos and brought it to the verge of civil war. Ratsiraka eventually left the island in defeat in 2002 and Ravalomanana came to power on a wave of public support. He was a new charismatic leader in the Weberian sense, his popular devotion 'born of distress and enthusiasm' (Weber 1948: 249). I was initially happy to work for him as I had known him before he went into politics and I felt that, despite his lack of experience, he represented hope and stability for the country after many years of misrule and severe political upheaval. Advising the President was a chance for me to put my knowledge of Malagasy culture and society to the service of the country and its people. Initially, he did seem incredibly out of touch with his people, how they thought, how they behaved and what they believed – and I don't think presidents should be. So, on the one hand, I saw my work as a kind of advocacy: communicating to those in power the world view and priorities of the ordinary people I had come to know and love. But, on the other hand, I was using my ethnographic and anthropological knowledge to present Ravalomanana's persona in the most culturally persuasive way. So was I serving the President's people or the President's career? Was I people's advocate or presidential spin doctor? Anthropologists rarely have such influence, and it did not always sit comfortably with me. But my natural curiosity got the better of me.

The material basis of Ravalomanana's political prominence lies in the marriage of his personal business career with the wider economic agenda of Western capitalism. Firmly believing in the potential of the free market to transform the Malagasy economy, Ravalomanana's policies are all geared towards enabling private enterprise to flourish. Major international institutions such as the World Bank have been instrumental in supporting Ravalomanana and his agenda of economic liberalism, enacted through the abolition of import tariffs on foreign goods and the promotion of public-private business partnerships along with massive incentives for foreign investment. The European Union recently funded a large road-building project in the north, and the World Bank supports numerous smaller projects. Much of Ravalomanana's political success lies in his ability to attract such finance and negotiate its terms, which are often linked to personally pursuing the fight against corruption in government. In comparison to Ratsiraka, the majority of whose foreign aid and contacts came from France, Ravalomanana has developed productive relationships with a wider spectrum of donors, notably in the English-speaking world. As the largest captain of enterprise in Madagascar, Ravalomanana's own business interests (road-building, distribution, media and agro-industry) stand to gain enormously from these policies. Neither the international backers nor the President himself seem to perceive a conflict of interest here: for both parties it is a marriage of convenience.

As I worked for Ravalomanana I soon learned – to my growing discomfort – how this overlapping of personal business interests with public office is repeated in other realms of the President's life. His political party is called *Tiako i Madagasikara* (I love Madagascar). The first word is very similar to the name of his dairy company, Tiko. The colours of the company and the party are the same: blue and green. Tiko advertisements adorned the stadium for the Independence Day parade. A major electioneering point, and still a central policy enormously popular in this country of feeble infrastructure, is the building of new roads. The graphic which he used for election posters of people building new roads now features on Madagascar's largest banknote.

His political control also embraces the religious domain. The motto that he used throughout the campaign in 2002 was a quotation from Jesus taken from St Mark's Gospel: 'Don't be afraid, just believe.' He still uses it in political speeches today. But the way his speeches phrase it suggests that it is not God we should believe in, but Ravalomanana himself. 'Trust me – Marc Ravalomanana,' he is saying. 'Don't be afraid, just believe in me.' He also uses the motto on signs for his *Fanazavana* (clarity) radio station and in promoting his Tiko products. You see it on banners outside grocery shops: '*Aza matahotra fa minoa fotsiny ihany*,' followed by the chapter and verse (Mark: 5:11). So the name of the gospel maker is confounded with his own, as he uses Mark the Evangelist to evangelise on behalf of Marc the President. There is something (consciously?) messianic about the way he tours the country preaching to the people, much in the way Mark depicts Jesus preaching in Galilee. He has become vice-president of the Protestant Church, historically the church of the Merina political and social elite, of which he is not a member by birth. Business, religion and politics have all become condensed into one banner, one slogan, one man.

This lack of boundaries between Ravalomanana's various roles is often pointed out by his political opponents. But in the long run he will be judged on the country's economic performance. For the moment Ravalomanana has combined the three major dimensions of social stratification: political control, wealth and prestige. These all reinforce each other. His political control rests in his executive presidential powers; his wealth lies in his business empire; his prestige resides in his central position in, and control over, the institutional loci of charisma, namely presidential and ecclesiastical office (Weber 1964). To a population which is 80 per cent rural, which does not have a notable business elite and which is one of the poorest in the world, Ravalomanana's achievement is almost fantastical.

ETHNOGRAPHIC AND THEORETICAL ORIENTATION

While the role of such structural factors in creating powerful figures is undeniable, it is not my main interest here. This chapter focuses principally on which attributes and achievements of powerful figures are particularly convincing; how an image of power is created and sustained; and how it is reflected and refracted between the leader and the people. As befits a speech writer, this paper is more about the projection and perception of power than it is about the material basis of it, though of course these are very closely connected. From this perspective, power is about gathering followers by communicating an aura of unusual efficacy as a person and of natural authority as a ruler. It is about seeking and gaining recognition as a social person who has power (Leach 1954: 10). Western governments and institutions may be supporting Ravalomanana in office, but it was the Malagasy people themselves who put him there and who will remove him if he does not deliver. It is the symbolic communicative power of those foreign connections, rather than their economic effects, which I focus on here. It is to Ravalomanana's advantage, as I show later, that in Madagascar one of the expectations of leaders is that they should accumulate and embody powerful foreign essence.

Here I present Ravalomanana in the context of anthropological studies of people recognised as powerful figureheads. Sahlins' (1963) comparison of Melanesian big men and Polynesian chiefs provides a useful framework for considering the relationship of leaders to followers. He contrasts the work which Melanesian big men have to do to accumulate their following with the rank which Polynesian chiefs inherit that guarantees them theirs. In essence, it is a contrast between achieved and acquired status. Malagasy democracy – perhaps all democracy – combines elements of Melanesian and Polynesian ethnographic types: the need to gather support in order to achieve office, and the support that office provides once achieved. In addition, I draw on Weber's (1964) discussion of three types of authority: legal-rational authority, which operates through generalised rules of jurisdiction imposed by a legitimate agency; traditional authority, which is based on an order deemed to be long established and sanctified by traditionally transmitted rules; and, finally, charismatic authority, which is contrary to the previous two forms in that it is usually held by an innovating leader who is in opposition to aspects of the established society (Weber 1964: 324–406). Weber's distinction set up these types of authority as analytically pure and distinct, but of course they are mixed and overlapping in practice, particularly as a leader moves from being the new hope 'born of distress' to being the safely ensconced incumbent in power. This is where we find Ravalomanana now, straddling the three types: he promises a new economic direction for the country and an end to the corruption of the old regimes; his state duties place him atop the hierarchy of the traditional Malagasy ritual economy; and he exercises his political will through its legal-rational framework. From a structural perspective, Ravalomanana's charismatic authority is becoming 'routinised' into the established order. From another more actor-oriented one, he is skilfully realising the potential of all types of authority, although I doubt that he has ever read Weber. This chapter, then, is about how different, opposing ethnographic and theoretical models of power and authority converge in the figure of a democratically elected president.

'BIG MEN' AND 'EARTH SHAKERS'

According to Sahlins (1963: 289–92), a Melanesian big man achieves his status by means of particular actions and skills, which elevate him above the hoi polloi. He is a social and economic entrepreneur who gathers and mobilises factions to produce crops or livestock. These he accumulates and then redistributes in shows of competitive munificence, which benefit both his faction and himself. He thus combines altruistic exploitation with self-interested generosity. The essential test of Melanesian power is the proven ability to gather goods and followers. And those who gather these attract even more: magnates are magnets. Ravalomanana's incremental success – first with Tiko, then as mayor and now as president – corresponds well with this model of power.

Big men's power, then, lies in their actions, not their status. This kind of power is central to the politics of leadership amongst the people of Sahafatra, small-scale wet-rice cultivators in south-east Madagascar (Woolley 2002). It is remarkably different from the descent-based hierarchies of the highly irrigated highlands. Power in Sahafatra is held by men known as 'earth shakers', who are chosen not by descent, but for their proven ability to access and channel to their people the elemental power of the land. The people of Sahafatra subject the 'earth shakers' to stringent tests to make sure they are up to the job. To them, this creative relationship with the raw power of creation is more important than access to ancestral blessings. As leaders, they marshal the force of the people to harness the autochthonous elemental power vital for life.

It is a similar ability to generate prosperity from the land and people of Madagascar that makes Ravalomanana exceptional. His dairy company Tiko is a rare example of a successful indigenous Malagasy business. It started as a cottage industry employing five people to make and deliver yoghurt. Benefiting from World Bank loans to import modern machinery, Ravalomanana developed Tiko into a huge business now employing five thousand staff. Its products range from yoghurt to Camembert, to ice cream, soft drinks and cooking oil. Tiko products are found in every small town in Madagascar and in many villages, where they are marketed under the slogan, '*Tiko: vita Malagasy!*' – 'Tiko: made in Madagascar!'

So Tiko, then, can be taken as evidence of Madagascar's innate potential, realised by Ravalomanana's 'big man' entrepreneurship. Ravalomanana's wealth is evidence of Madagascar's wealth. It is made from the land and paid for by the earning power of all those Malagasy customers whose money buys his products. The products and the profits are a realisation of the potential of the Malagasy land and its people. It was Ravalomanana's ability to coalesce this native potential, where most other indigenous enterprises have failed, that qualify him, in Weber's terms, as a 'natural' leader, someone with 'specific gifts of the body and spirit, ... supernatural, not accessible to everybody' (Weber 1948: 245). It is this that led many voters to believe that he could do the same for his country as he did for his company.

The material process by which Ravalomanana gathers and absorbs the potential of the Malagasy land and people, and thereby comes to embody it, is mirrored in the democratic process that has made him leader. In material terms, Ravalomanana, as a wealthy entrepreneur, is made up of the physical and human elements that transform grass into yoghurt into profit. In a democratic sense, he is constituted by the political will of the people, which they have transformed into the votes that made him president. His ability to coalesce material elemental power has led to his success in coalescing democratic political power. Both can be seen as kinds of tribute, paid in small amounts by people to a leader who responds through the promise of prosperity. One of his first gestures as leader was to provide every schoolchild in the country with a satchel bearing the slogan: 'We are learning' (*Mianatra izahay*). In the remotest villages, children learned his name and associated it with this gift. He was offering the most precious commodity of all – knowledge – to the people that most represent the potential of the land – Madagascar's millions of children. This act of calculated generosity was excellent political communication. It was the gesture of a 'big man'.

PRESTIGE AND PRIVILEGE

In contrast to 'big men' and 'earth shakers', whose power is a result of their actions, the power of the Polynesian chiefs resides in their office.

Genealogical links to divinity imbue the chief with the prestige of rank, which outlives and is independent of any individual leader. With this prestige comes a set of organisational powers, which extend the personal capacity of the leader: religious roles, military support, administrative structures and special advisors (Sahlins 1963: 295). Bolstered by these privileges, chiefs do not have to go out to collect followers as 'big men' do – instead, followers come to them. And followers stick close to the fund of power because it is in their interests to do so. As I once heard a Malagasy deputy declare at a rally: 'Those who are near the cooking pot get given the rice.'

Of course, unlike Polynesian chiefs, Malagasy deputies and presidents are elected officials. But just like Polynesian chiefdoms, democratic systems bestow on office holders established privileges, which are enormously useful to their hold on that power. One minor example is the right of presidents to appoint wandering anthropologists as special advisors. Foremost of these privileges, though, is what Sahlins (1963: 295) calls the 'organized acquiescence' of the people, that is to say the natural disposition of the public to revere and follow holders of high office because of the material benefits they offer and the aura of potency the office emanates.

When Ravalomanana became president, he inherited the established privileges of power that the democratic state provides. Suddenly he walked on red carpets. He had armed guards. He became the centrepiece of state occasions. From being a politician whom some supported, he became the president at whom everyone gazed. His very presence became an event, what the Malagasy call, using the French word, a *spectacle*. I have seen crowds wait for hours just to get a good view of a presidential motorcade. That is the power of the *spectacle* – it can pull a crowd just through its promise of the extraordinary. Recent anthropological work has rather neglected spectacles of state, concentrating instead on such mundane technologies of power as surveillance, bureaucracy and inspection. Here I am interested not so much in how the state infiltrates people's lives, as how it dazzles their eyes. And I am interested less in the administrative structures of power, atop which may or may not sit a single powerful figure, than in how that figure projects an aura of power that is convincing to the people.

The occasion on which the Malagasy state clamours most loudly and sparkles most brightly is on 26 June, Independence Day. I joined the presidential party at the national stadium and witnessed a three-hour parade of military and civilian pageantry. The parade streamed past to the thumping of the military bands: platoons of army, navy and air force, all marching in step with rifles shouldered and eyes rigidly left; then cadets from each service, precise and serious and shiny; then prison officers; an agricultural brigade shouldering long-handled spades; police; gendarmes; cycling gendarmes riding in formation; riot gendarmes piled in a truck wielding shields and wearing visored helmets. Then came customs officers with sniffer dogs in a trailer; coastguards towing a boat; more gendarmes (towed in an inflatable dinghy and wearing orange life jackets); tanks and armoured cars; a steamroller on a truck; a soldier riding a rotavator; fire engines and firemen (one sweating it out in a kind of silver spaceman's suit); and, finally, a lone frogman in a dinghy.

This was the physical apparatus of the state in full, and as it passed the presidential box every single person on parade – including the frogman – saluted the head of state. The link between all this splendid state hardware and the President was underlined throughout: by the fanfare that greeted him, by his tour of the stadium to the strains of the national anthem. All this focused the event around Ravalomanana. The display sent two concurrent signals to the crowd: on the one hand, it was evidence of the glorious and protective state, the sovereignty and unification of Madagascar; on the other hand, it represented the latent, but clearly terrible, force that the President controlled and could unleash even against his own people. Simultaneously, then, the President emanated both protection and danger, both sunshine and lightning.

Of course, although such regalia and ceremony cover the president in reflected glory, they do not necessarily reflect his actual character. The president may or may not be a wonderfully charismatic leader, but in this instance he doesn't need to be. In fact, the point of such ceremonials is to accentuate non-personal symbolic qualities and thereby mark the leader's difference from ordinary people (Frankfort 1948: 36). The glorious regalia of state create a stunning figure so that the president himself does not need to be one. What is more, the trappings of state power can reinforce the confidence of the leader in their own charismatic potential. This is certainly true of Ravalomanana, who has become more assured of his mission, and more bold in his presentation, as he has settled into power. And the watching public does not necessarily distinguish between the effects created by non-personal symbolic qualities and individual charisma: they may all appear as one dazzling package.

ORDINARY AND EXTRAORDINARY

While Ravalomanana's achievements, office and privileges of power may make him appear extraordinary, there is a risk that he will appear disconnected and aloof. So he also has to present himself as someone who understands the people and possesses the common touch. In public, his image refracts between two poles, as he appears simultaneously to be both of, and not of, the people.

One of the reasons Ravalomanana used me as an advisor was that he recognised the need to appear closer to the Malagasy people, and he guessed that my knowledge of rice farmers and cattle drovers could help him. In the Independence Day speech I wrote for him, which was broadcast on television and radio, I invoked the unity in diversity of the Malagasy people and intimated that the President was listening to their problems and sharing in them. Words are powerful, but when such appeals to closeness are also made through actions, the effect can be even stronger. To record the broadcast, Ravalomanana had been placed at a lectern, but this made his speech very stilted. Taking him aside, I suggested that he deliver the speech seated at his desk in his office instead. The aim was to create a more intimate, less stentorian atmosphere. 'Invite the people into your office,' I said, 'they will feel close to you.' He smiled broadly and turned to the television crew and the aides. 'I have had a new idea,' he crowed, 'we are doing it at the desk in my office. Move everything now!' We did the speech in one take, with the President relaxed and convivial, appearing on people's television sets as if seated in their homes.

Although this change was orchestrated by me, Ravalomanana agreed because he was already aware of the need to appear on the same level as the people. In that sense the idea he claimed as his was his. It just had not occurred to him how it could be adapted to television. But in other contexts he needed no prompting. Immediately after the filming he ordered that a motorcade be made ready for him to take a *tour de ville*. It was Friday, rush hour, the eve of a national holiday. The motorcade sped off hectically through the dusk, taking a wrong turn at Lac Anosy and losing the Mayor of Antananarivo. We dashed through the crowded streets, the walkie-talkies crackling. Suddenly we veered off onto a football field where a pop concert was taking place. The guards jumped out, toting their guns to make a passageway for the President to climb up onto the floodlit stage. He saluted the crowd with his trademark both-hands-in-the-air wave, standing smiling over them in his leather jacket, his wife beside him, while the pop group jauntily played the national anthem. I stood just behind him, looking across the sea of smiling, waving, cheering fans, their faces full of wonder. Then suddenly, as quickly as we had arrived, we left, sweeping through the cobbled streets past Chinese lanterns and firecrackers and the smell of sewage from the open drains.

Other open-air meetings I witnessed were more planned, such as the mayoral inauguration ceremony at Betafo, in the heart of the fertile vegetable-producing area of the highlands. Many in the huge crowd had walked a long way to be at the spectacle. They all gazed up as they heard the approaching thud of the presidential helicopter. Then it emerged from the clouds and landed in a nearby school playground, creating a huge swirling dust storm. A blacked-out four-by-four whisked the President to the field where the crowd were waiting behind a rope cordon manned by gendarmes. To huge applause and cheers he waved and shook hands before mounting the podium, where he enthroned himself in a vast armchair under a beribboned arch. I sat behind him with my fellow speech writer, frantically scribbling the speech Ravalomanana was about to deliver. We were still writing when he started to speak and had to hand it to him page by page via the aide-de-camp.

Before beginning his speech, though, he addressed the cordon of gendarmes, ordering them to allow the people closer to the stage. '*Mandroso*,' he called to the crowd, in the manner of a host inviting guests into his house. The crowd then surged forward like an ocean swell, engulfing the gendarmes in a moment of dangerous mayhem. I saw Ravalomanana operate this ploy on several occasions, and he was clearly aware of the effect it had on the public. The apparently simple gesture is actually a complex piece of theatre. It acts as a snub to the head of security and more generally it is a deliberate undermining of state officialdom. As such, Ravalomanana declares to the people that he is on their side against the faceless conventions of the state. He has no time, he insinuates, for the old order of things. But at the same time, of course, he retains the security the state forces offer. In this one charismatic gesture,

Ravalomanana offers his hand to the people and sticks two fingers up at the establishment.

Although Ravalomanana may be acting the common man, the excitement he generates by doing this is due to the very fact that he is not common at all. The effervescent crowd surges and screams, pushes to get nearer somebody who seems, to them, a kind of Nietzchean Übermensch. For the public, shaking the President's hand is to make a connection with his power and protection. It is like touching an icon. I felt it myself in the early days of working with him. He would be really pleased with my work, but then ignore me for days. When he called on me for advice again, it was like walking from shade into sunshine. Imagine this feeling multiplied in the experience of all those whose hand he shakes, whom he invites to approach the podium.

By collapsing the spatial exclusivity that normally separates him from his people, Ravalomanana is employing a technique of power far more potent than political persuasion. He is generating a physical feeling far more memorable than words. He is offering a physical connection to his source of power.

It should be noted that most of the audience would never have seen Ravalomanana, or any other president, in person, even on television, let alone touched one. Descending in a suit and tie from a helicopter, surrounded by soldiers and regalia, Ravalomanana must have appeared as something very odd and otherworldly. Yet ironically, it is that otherworldliness that made him somehow familiar. Rural Malagasy do not expect presidents to be like them, dressed in rags and carrying spades. Even though they had not seen a president before, the Betafo crowd nevertheless recognised him because he reflected their expectation of extraordinarily powerful entities. Charisma is the expectation of the extraordinary (Feuchtwang and Mingming 2001: 172). Ravalomanana's sheer otherworldliness was proof of his power.

THE PROMISE OF PLENTY

The image that Ravalomanana presented refracted continually, alternating between that of a super-wealthy foreigner and a hand-shaking Malagasy. By approaching the crowd and then withdrawing to the podium, by bringing them closer but retaining a guarded distance, he played on the tension between his accessibility and his inaccessibility, his similarity and his difference, his humanity and his super-humanity. The crowd felt awe, but also connection. Like a divine king – an envoy between two worlds – Ravalomanana stood both within the society and outside it (Evans-Pritchard 1948). It was from this ambiguous position that Ravalomanana played his trump card: he offered to share his extraordinary foreign wealth with the crowd. Departing from his script, he promised to build a tomato-canning plant so that they, the people of Betafo, would have access to wider markets. Then, his speech over, his promises made, he left the podium. His helicopter raised another dust storm and away he flew, like a magician vanishing in a puff of smoke.

To offer a factory is to reinforce the transient physical connection of the spectacle with the promise of more durable benefit. The factory itself will become a symbol which embodies and perpetuates the collective moment (Durkheim 2001 [1915]: 176). On a political level, Ravalomanana is a global corporatist, which is a rare thing in Madagascar. He knows how world markets work and he wants to bring the people of Madagascar into them, which is why the World Bank supports him. Very few country people could exploit the workings of such systems, yet they recognise from his wealth that Ravalomanana clearly can. No other politician can offer anything like this. Ravalomanana is offering the people access to a world far beyond their reach and largely beyond their ken, a world of apparently fruitful labour and profitable harvests. What better way to convince followers that they are backing the right leader?

At one level, Ravalomanana is just offering the people goods, which the cynical might consider bribes. I think he certainly recognises both the political and the economic advantage in such offers. But what he perhaps doesn't recognise is that he is also operating on a symbolic level, tapping into the locals' mystical notion of what an extraordinarily powerful person might bring them. Without being aware that he is exploiting their expectations of the numinous, he is nevertheless meeting them.

Power in Madagascar is often created and maintained through alliances with strangers (Beaujard 1983; Raison-Jourde 1983). In Africa, and indeed the rest of the world, rulers and powerful things frequently originate in foreign places (e.g. Lan 1985). In Madagascar, Europe is known as 'the other side' (*an-dafy*) and is thought of as particularly potent and inaccessible to the ordinary person. It is a place of unimaginable wealth: Betsileo farmers, who earn about fifty pence a day, marvel at the cost (£800) of the air tickets of their compatriots who manage to go abroad to study. These emigrants return with powerful European knowledge and fantastic European spending power. The knowledge creates bewildering technology such as helicopters, which were a favourite topic for scientific speculation in my highland village. On one helicopter trip with Ravalomanana, an isolated hilltop lavatory stop drew from nowhere an instant marvelling crowd. Those with access to this big money are expected to share it with their families, and, if they are politicians, with their constituents. One former Betsileo deputy even campaigned under the pseudonym of Pierre Vazaha (*vazaha* means 'white foreigner'). One of the expectations of leaders is that they will mediate and trade with foreign powers in order to channel their extraordinary riches back to the ordinary people. This is exactly what Ravalomanana was doing in offering a tomato factory. He was calling on the symbolic value and communicative power of his World Bank support.

In any crowd there are sceptics. Not everyone will believe the promises. Although most in the crowd cheered at Ravalomanana's promised munificence, the thrall was not total. Leaving the event, I heard one man mutter: 'He promised us a factory at the election [two years previously] and we still haven't seen it.' There are many Malagasy who oppose him. So Ravalomanana is taking a gamble: he might or might not provide the cannery. My point here, though, is that the promise of such a fabulous gift can only be made by a really powerful person. That, in itself, in the heat of the moment, signals his power. In the long run, though, he will have to deliver.

GIFTS AND HIERARCHY

As gifts create social bonds, and power is largely about the management of social bonds, there is always a logic of power to a gift economy. In Madagascar most gifts are small, and flow from junior to senior people. They mark this difference in status and can be seen as a kind of tribute. Senior people do give gifts to their juniors, but in order to show that this is not tribute, the gift has to be a really big one (Woolley 2002: 136). For the head of a northern Betsileo tomb group this might be a bull for sacrifice. For a president, this might be a factory. Tribute flows upwards, munificence flows downwards. The best-known example of this management of power through exchange is the *hasina* system, which characterised the Merina monarchy. The Merina king

Andrianampoinimerina travelled round his kingdom performing rituals, often at sacred sites won from conquered rivals. Subjects offered pieces of silver to the monarch as a sign of their submission and as a form of taxation. In exchange they received blessings, protection and ultimately prosperity. Both tribute and blessings were known by the same word: *hasina*. By receiving the tribute and bestowing the blessing, the king effectively short-circuited the flow of *hasina* and usurped the role of the ancestors as the givers of blessing (Bloch 1986).

It is hard to know the degree of intentionality involved in such innovation, but that does not mean the action did not have the effect described. Touring the island with Ravalomanana to invest newly elected mayors, I observed that he too was performing actions that could carry ritual messages neither intended nor manipulated by him and of which he was perhaps not aware. Large crowds gathered for the ceremony in which the President bestowed 'honour' (*voninahitra*) on the mayors in the form of sashes, gave a speech, and a bull was killed. The last action is typical of tomb rituals, where it is the sponsors who provide the cattle who play the role of channelling the blessings from the ancestors to the people. The Merina monarch Andrianampoinimerina appropriated the circumcision ritual for this very purpose (Bloch 1986). Ravalomanana did not participate in the slaughter of the bull but the fact of his being effectively its sponsor would have associated him with its usual ritual meanings. He concentrated instead on making a speech and giving out sashes. The bestowing of *voninahitra* is comparable to that of *hasina*, since both are the act of elders and superiors. Similarly, both infer a social and political hierarchy in which the recipient accepts submission to the donor. Just as Andrianampoinimerina appropriated the ritual sites of his conquered rivals, so Ravalomanana performed many inaugurations in those marginal constituencies where he most needed to impress his political dominance.

By giving *voninahitra*, *hasina* or bulls Ravalomanana was acting within a hierarchical framework, which has long been the basis of traditional authority in Madagascar. As Bloch argues, traditional authority is convincing because it binds everybody into this hierarchy, implying, as it does, 'a total order of which both superior and inferior are a part though in different degree' (Bloch 1986: 169). In carrying out his presidential duties, Ravalomanana was using an official ritual framework inherited from his predecessors, although he was not necessarily aware of its symbolic impact. Indeed, much of the ritual potential (such as the slaughter of the bull) would have appeared – to the mind of a cynical spin doctor – as under-exploited. But in inheriting the framework of traditional Malagasy authority, Ravalomanana was able to communicate the fact of his power, without even consciously having to manipulate it. What he brought to it, in the seductive context of a spectacle, is the charismatic presence of an extraordinary person offering marginal peasants a new vision of technologically enabled market opportunities.

So much for the generous aspect of power. However, as mentioned earlier, power can threaten as well as bless. Royal ancestors in particular bless and curse in equal measure (Middleton 1999: 23). The same monarch, while revered as an ancestor, might also be remembered for his brutality (Lambek, this volume). Similarly, while commoner ancestors bestow blessings and prosperity on the living, they also have a dangerous and unpredictable side (Cole 1999; Graeber 1995), rather like the capricious God of the Old Testament. And while the Malagasy see Europeans as fantastic sources of wealth, their narratives of French rule (Cole 2001; Tronchon 1974) remember the brutality and repression of the encounter. This brutality seems inherent in the nature of power. It is as if power could have no force for good if it did not also contain danger.

BRUTAL THEATRE

The brutality of powerful figures is often ostentatious and theatrical, using humiliation to underline hierarchy. As a political tactic, humiliation is not just about the exertion of power, it is also a display of power: 'It is far better to be feared than loved,' says Machiavelli (2003 [1531]: 54). Even though the act of humiliation may be personally motivated, powerful figures are aware that such acts will naturally have wider political implications. The case of the expelled bodyguard illustrates this on a national scale.

As well as a large retinue of security personnel, Ravalomanana employed two non-Malagasy private bodyguards. One was a former martial arts world champion, Jean Marc Koumba. With his laid-back charm, good looks and commitment to the Malagasy people (he organised two hugely successful martial arts festivals), and his frequent appearance on television in the company of the President, Koumba became something of a celebrity in Madagascar. In fact, it was widely – though rather fancifully – suggested that many young women voted for Ravalomanana in 2001 on the basis of his association with the charismatic bodyguard. But the relationship came to a very sudden end in March 2005, when, due to a minor motorcycle accident, Koumba was unable to show up for work. Ravalomanana fired him on the spot, giving him twenty-four hours to leave the country and organising a platoon of soldiers to escort him to the airport. Koumba left behind a deal of back pay and a pregnant fiancée. It was an ignominious exit for the man described by the Malagasy press as having 'a fist of iron and a heart of gold'.

Now, Ravalomanana's reasons for expelling Koumba could have been personal or political – or both. It is possible that Ravalomanana felt sidelined by Koumba's popular charm. Whatever the motives, the expulsion itself was clearly orchestrated for public effect. The use of a military escort both demonstrated the martial forces at the President's disposal and compounded the humiliation, since the escort was made up of Koumba's former colleagues and subordinates. The use of armed guards was also a macabre inversion of the normal airport-departure scenario, in which the departing person is accompanied by a posse of family and friends. The deportation was a dramatic demonstration of the President's unpredictable and immediate power. Koumba was just a character in the drama, like Admiral Byng, punished '*pour encourager les autres*' (Voltaire 1958 [1759]: 85).

Such a theatre of humiliation was enacted on a much more physically brutal scale by Radama I in April 1822 when he was faced by thousands of women protesting against his cutting his hair in the European fashion. When the protestors claimed, invoking tradition, that short hair was not the custom of kings, Radama in effect answered that it was in the tradition of kings to do as they pleased. He then shaved the heads of the ringleaders, executed them and left their bodies to the dogs (Larson 2000: 250, 252). His power was most evident when tested, most strident when under dispute. Naturally, such brutal symbolic cultural politics carries the risk of inciting popular disgust and uprising, as indeed it eventually did later on in Radama's reign.

Impetuous as Ravalomanana's expulsion of Koumba may have been, he appears to have displayed his dominance without suffering significant popular backlash. In fact, he turned the threat of Koumba's growing popularity into a chance to show who was really the boss. The irony is that what initially might seem a cavalier disregard for public opinion actually turns out to be an astute (though often instantaneous and perhaps instinctive) calculation of it. The more brutal the theatre and the greater the infringement of taboo, the more risky the calculation. But shrewdly calculating such risks may, in fact, be an important characteristic of powerful figures.

In a sense, brutality and humiliation are social taboos, for they transgress the limits of normal relationships. Powerful leaders in Madagascar are characterised by their willingness to break taboos that ordinary people would never dare break. At the time of the royal bath in 1817, Radama deliberately ordered his staff to undertake a minor building project at a time in the ritual calendar that forbade all projects of productive labour (Larson 1999: 58). Similarly, one new ruler of the Bemazava monarchy recently turned the royal palace into a disco hall, and blatantly neglected to complete his father's tomb (Sharp 1999). Such deliberate ritual transgressions are not so much a prerogative as a duty. They should be understood as statements boasting of extraordinary power. The perpetrators thereby suggest that they are powerful enough not to worry about transgressing taboos because in effect they have an alliance with the ultimate, unanswerable sources of authority – gods or ancestors – that is, those who made the rules in the first place.

So far I have described how Ravalomanana's actions accord with patterns of behaviour characteristic of powerful figures, and how his persona consequently meets public expectations of powerful entities. That Ravalomanana often achieves this unwittingly does not mean it is not occurring. Now, however, I turn briefly to some of Ravalomanana's particular characteristics and some of the historical contingencies that might have assisted in his ascent.

CHARACTER AND CHANCE

Madagascar, famously rich in unique flora and fauna, is home to more chameleons than any other country (Glaw and Vences 1994). Ravalomanana is one of them. He has an ability to change continually the way he presents himself, according to the context or the audience. In his negotiations with foreign donors, he is the rational advocate of liberal capitalism. In interviews with the world press, he is the fearless scourge of political corruption. In his attendance at church, he is the fervent preacher of Christian morality. In an address to the nation, he is the wise purveyor of ancestral proverbs. Descending from his helicopter, he is the vector of foreign wealth. Dropping in on a pop concert, he is a man of the people. Exiling his bodyguard, he is an authoritarian showman.

Ravalomanana also has an astute ability to balance the different aspects of his public persona against one another. While at times he presents the image of an ordinary Malagasy, he also cultivates a strikingly individualistic persona. While he plunges into the crowd, he also keeps his distance. Apparently high-handed and hot-headed on some occasions, he can be mild and charming on others. Alternately dangerous and protective, foreign and Malagasy, sociable and individualistic, the unpredictability of the persona is partly what gives it its enigmatic and charismatic force (Lindholm 1990: 133). And it makes it hard for his political opponents to know how to read him. It also makes it hard for his advisors to work with him, which is one reason I no longer do.

In the course of human interaction, we all play different roles to different audiences. For someone in power, though, those roles tend to be much more caricatured. This is because the messages they convey are far more public. Moreover, they are much more laden with meaning because they largely embody the interests of their followers (Sahlins 2000: 323). So in the political game of self-presentation, the stakes are high. If Ravalomanana gets it wrong, the political consequences can be huge. But he is a gambler and an opportunist. Expelling his hugely popular bodyguard was a risk, but he got away with it. From our first meeting, he recognised my use to him long before I did. He shrewdly recognised and realised the possibilities afforded by having an anthropologist at his disposal. He fed off my ideas, intuitively moulding the new knowledge he was gaining to the demands of his office.

My role as an anthropologist, who, in Ravalomanana's words, knew his people better than he did, made me unique among his advisors. I contained elements of both *vazaha* (European) and Malagasy. In a televised speech, not written by me, but delivered extempore in the northern Betsileo town of Ambositra, he boasted of how he had engaged a *vazaha* to come and work with him to help the country, a *vazaha* who knew the northern Betsileo area, the language, the mentality and the customs of the people. It was a subtle political statement, simultaneously proclaiming his own connections with the power of 'the other side' whilst invoking a resonant notion of indigenous Malagasy tradition. It is a strategy characteristic of past Malagasy monarchs (Raison-Jourde 1983, 1991).

Ravalomanana's instant appointment of me as a special advisor was typical of his ability to make snap decisions and act on them. It is one reason for his success in business. It appeals to the electorate, too, who often praise him for his ability to 'get things done' *(mahavita raha).* Implied in this praise is a criticism of the rather slow-moving consensual politics which people consider to be typically Malagasy and which they often blame for the country's lack of development. In speech and action, Ravalomanana presents himself as progressive, decisive and direct. It is an idiom known as the 'new way' (*lalana vaovao*), which is particularly associated with the school and educated people (Keenan 1975: 101). The 'new way' is, of course, the European way.

The snap decisions he makes seem impetuous to both opponents and supporters alike. But I think in fact they are intuitive. Perhaps one of the gifts of the powerful is daring to make a decision without knowing why. Ravalomanana operates less on strategy than on opportunism and instinct. Uninvolved in politics until he stood for mayor in Antananarivo, within five years he had ridden a wave of popular support to achieve the presidency. Then he had to learn as he went along. A gift for intuition and opportunistic risk-taking compensated for his political inexperience. And he had the good fortune to come to prominence just as Ratsiraka's power was waning.

The question of historical contingency is slippery. To account for present success by past events risks the error of teleology. Yet some events clearly matter more than others. Sahlins (2000) tells the story of a chief, who, on visiting a neighbouring kingdom, spotted a pig wandering through the village. He claimed it as his by right. This sparked an argument, which, in the existing climate of bad relations, led to all-out war. The pig was the historical contingency that triggered the war, but it was not the cause: 'The war was generations old before it began' (Sahlins 2000: 320).

In Ravalomanana's case, political circumstances favoured his rise: the fall of Ratsiraka; the decline of Soviet influence in the western Indian Ocean; the corresponding rise of commercial and diplomatic ties with Europe and the United States; the growing global dominance of English as the language of business. But while these political factors may have contributed to his success, they do not fully explain it. Nor does the idiosyncratic combination of personal circumstances: the early Lutheran connections that took him to study in Norway; the fortuitous choice of yoghurt as a business venture; the poor command of French. In any ascent to power, luck plays a part. For example, in 1933 Hitler was able to cement his tenuous early hold on power when the Reichstag fire, started by a lone fanatic, gave him the excuse to declare a state of emergency that dramatically increased his powers (Kershaw 1991: 67). In becoming powerful, luck matters. But opportunism – the ability to seize on luck – matters more.

Fifteen years ago, long before becoming president, Ravalomanana seized on a young Englishman living next door to teach him English. Now he has mastered it enough to prefer it to French in his international dealings. This preference carries a huge political message about his calculated reorientation of a Francophone country towards the Anglophone world. The World Bank has found a man with whom it can both do business and talk business. In a fanciful moment one could even speculate that, in some small way, the young English teacher, later to return as an anthropologist, was the pig that happened to wander across the village.

MODELS OF POWER

In this essay I have been interested in the dialectical relationship between public expectations of powerful figures and the creation of Ravalomanana's political person. His actions portray symbolic meanings and are modified accordingly. As I have said, I don't think Ravalomanana is always aware – at least not in the same way that anthropologists are taught to be aware – of the symbolic impact of his actions. When he offers a tomato cannery to a crowd of peasants he sees it more as a politico-economic strategy than the expected fulfilment of a mystical relationship based on a numinous notion of otherworldly power. Nevertheless, the offer's social impact is partly due to the existence of that notion. Ravalomanana repeats the strategy wherever he goes because, without precisely knowing why, he sees that it creates the right reaction. Unlike anthropologists, he doesn't think too hard about it. He trusts his intuition. He takes risks. He learns as he goes along. He consolidates his position of power.

Of course, his power is neither uncontested nor unbreakable. Many Malagasy are fervently opposed to Ravalomanana, but for the moment they have nobody else to put forward who comes anywhere near to challenging him. No other candidate has accumulated and promised wealth as he has. And now, having come to power on that basis, he controls the political domain and has become central to the traditional institutions of state and religious charisma. In democratic systems, the established apparatus and privileges of state favour the incumbent, which is why it took so long to replace Ratsiraka. For the same reason, it may take a long time to replace Ravalomanana. He has become something of an elected monarch.

Leach (1954: 197) claims that in their practical application even monarchy and republicanism may sometimes look very much alike. His point is that the difference between political systems is merely theoretical. He famously illustrates this through the example of the two theoretically contrasting types of Kachin political organisation – one egalitarian and democratic, the other feudal and hierarchical – that are, in fact, constantly in the process of changing into one another. Moreover, individuals are pragmatic in invoking whichever system favours them: at one moment appealing to egalitarianism to avoid paying feudal dues, and at another calling on chiefly connections to promote their prestige (Leach 1954).

The position of power that Ravalomanana is now consolidating is a mixture of types. Having worked a commercial miracle with his Malagasy yoghurt, he passes the test of a Sahafatran 'earth shaker'; having taken office, he now manages the economy of blessing associated with the descent-based systems of the highlands. Like a Melanesian 'big man', he has accumulated wealth and followers; like a Polynesian chief, the aura of his office presents his power as timeless and inevitable. He encompasses the charismatic authority of a self-proclaimed renovator, the traditional authority of the ritual hierarchy and the legal-rational authority of the state.

Leach's point was that theoretical categories are too rigid and that different models of power could operate simultaneously in the same place. This is clearly what is happening in Madagascar under Ravalomanana. It is no doubt also the case in the Pacific: the inherited authority of Polynesian chiefdom is surely not uncontested; and it seems likely that Melanesian 'big men' benefit from the existing ritual trappings of their hard-won status. Similarly, Weber's distinction between different types of authority gets blurred in practice because they are 'ideal types', not empirical reality. Ravalomanana provides a great example of this, getting the best of all Weberian worlds as he stands beneath the Malagasy flag handing out *voninahitra* while at the same time presenting himself as herald of 'the new way', a World Bank corporatist who will bring home the wealth of 'the other side'. The system of republican democracy, which calls for continuous and regular renewal within an existing framework, could be said to be ideally suited to chameleon leaders like Ravalomanana.

This brings us to the interaction of authority and power. While the former operates at the cultural level of prestige, the latter is manifest in the execution of political intent (Ortner 1996: 143). Cultural prestige and political power are not necessarily commensurate, as the case of high-caste but low-power Brahmins illustrates (Dumont 1966). Conversely, it is possible to have power but lack prestige. But in the case of Ravalomanana, and no doubt other democratically elected presidents, power and prestige feed off each other. Ravalomanana mobilised his financial power to back his presidential campaign, and through his media outlets convinced people that a successful entrepreneur would make an effective president. Through the office of president he has acquired both the persuasive prestige of institutional charisma and the mandate to execute his economic and social policies. His presidential power has made him attractive to the Merina aristocracy, who have installed him as vice-president of their church, the FJKM. Something of an arriviste in their midst, he has achieved an elevation in both social status and religious authority. Intent on accruing legitimacy with both the Malagasy people and foreign financiers, he employed me to write speeches that wooed both audiences. With their support he has the mandate and the means to exercise his political will over the country's economic destiny, which is inextricably linked to his own business interests. Here, power and authority work hand in hand, his power being all the greater for this.

Ravalomanana is one of a new kind of leader, a business tycoon with media interests and political ambition, in the mould of Silvio Berlusconi and Thaksin Shinawatra, former prime ministers of Italy and Thailand respectively. It may well be that in the years to come such corporate statesmen will become increasingly common, particularly in poorer countries. They will undoubtedly get there without the assistance of anthropologists. On reflection, that is how it should be.

ACKNOWLEDGMENTS

I am indebted to the editors and other contributors to this volume for their guidance. I also thank Stephan Feuchtwang for his wise insights.

REFERENCES

Beaujard, P. 1983. *Princes et paysans: les Tanala de l'Inkongo*, Paris: Harmattan.

Bloch, M. 1986. *From blessing to violence: history and ideology in the circumcision ritual of the Merina of Madagascar*, Cambridge: Cambridge University Press.

Cole, J. 1999. 'Sacrifice, narratives and experience in East Madagascar', in K. Middleton (ed.), *Ancestors, power and history in Madagascar*, Leiden: Brill.

—— 2001. *Forget Colonialism? Sacrifice and the art of memory in Madagascar*, Berkeley: University of California Press.

Durkheim, E. 2001 (1915). *The elementary forms of religious life* (trans. C. Cosman), Oxford: Oxford University Press.

Dumont, L. 1966. *Homo hierarchicus*, Paris: Gallimard.

Evans-Pritchard, E. 1948. *The divine kingship of the Shilluk of the Nilotic Sudan*, Cambridge: Cambridge University Press.

Feuchtwang, S. and W. Mingming. 2001. *Grassroots charisma*, London: Routledge.

Frankfort, H. 1948. *Kingship and the gods*, Chicago: University of Chicago Press.

Glaw, F. and M. Vences. 1994. *A fieldguide to the reptiles and amphibians of Madagascar*, Lanesboro: Serpent's Tale.

Graeber, D. 1995. 'Dancing with corpses reconsidered: an interpretation of famadihana (in Arivonimamo, Madagascar)', *American Ethnologist* 22(2): 258–78.

Keenan, E. 1975. 'A sliding scale of obligatoriness', in M. Bloch (ed.), *Political language and oratory in traditional society*, London: Academic Press.

Kershaw, I. 1991. *Hitler*, Harlow: Longman.

Lan, D. 1985. *Guns and rain*, London: James Currey.

Larson, M. 1999. 'A cultural politics of bedchamber construction and progressive dining in Antananarivo: ritual inversions during the *fandroana* of 1817', in K. Middleton (ed.), *Ancestors, power and history in Madagascar*, Leiden: Brill.

—— 2000. *History and memory in the age of enslavement*, Oxford: James Currey.

Leach, E. 1954. *Political systems of highland Burma*, London: Athlone.

Lindholm, C. 1990. *Charisma*, Oxford: Blackwell.

Machiavelli, N. 2003 (1531). *The prince* (trans. G. Bull), London: Penguin.

Middleton, K. 1999. 'Introduction', in K. Middleton (ed.), *Ancestors, power and history in Madagascar*, Leiden: Brill.

Ortner, S. 1996. *Making gender: the politics and erotics of culture*, Boston: Beacon Books.

Raison-Jourde, F. (ed.) 1983. *Les souverains de Madagascar: l'histoire royale et ses résurgences contemporaines*, Paris: Karthala.

—— 1991. *Bible et pouvoir à Madagascar au XIXème siècle*, Paris: Karthala.

Sahlins, M. 1963. 'Poor man, rich man, big man, chief: political types in Melanesia and Polynesia', *Comparative Studies in Society and History* 5(3): 285–303.

—— 2000. *Culture in practice*, New York: Zone Books.

Sharp, L. 1999. 'Royal difficulties: the anxieties of succession in an urbanised Sakalava kingdom', in K. Middleton (ed.), *Ancestors, power and history in Madagascar*, Leiden: Brill.

Tronchon, J. 1974. *L'insurrection Malgache de 1947*, Fianarantsoa: Ambozantany.

Voltaire, F. de. 1958 (1759). *Candide*, London: University of London Press.

Weber, M. 1948. *From Max Weber* (trans. and ed. H. Gerth and C. Wright Mills), London: RKP.

—— 1964. *The theory of social and economic organization* (trans. A. M. Henderson and T. Parsons), New York: Free Press.

Woolley, O. 2002. *The earth shakers of Madagascar*, London: Continuum.

CHAPTER 12

HOW DO WE KNOW WHAT IS TRUE?

Christina Toren

I begin with a conversation I had with some young Fijian people, a conversation that took place circa 1982, as we were walking along the road that connects the villages that lie on the coast of the island of Gau, where I did fieldwork. We were passing a place where, someone present remarked, there was 'something' (*e dua na ka*). 'What?' I asked. '*Tevoro*' (devil[s]), came the reply, sotto voce. I said nothing, but my scepticism must have been clear on my face because they began to protest that the land we were passing through belonged to a *vu* (ancestor) who was known to appear to those unwary people who walked alone on that part of the road. I said that I often walked alone, but that I'd never seen a *vu* and that I was really interested to do so – why didn't they appear to me? Everyone laughed: the idea was ridiculous. But why didn't they? Why not? More laughter, and then a comment from one of the young men who said, in tones that suggested amused contempt for my inability to understand: '*Era na sega ni basika mai vei kemuni*' (They're not going to appear here to *you*). 'But why not?' I insisted. '*Baleta ni ko sega ni rerevaka*!' (Because you're not *frightened* of them!)

This snippet of conversation is sufficient to convey an idea that still prevails among my Fijian informants: that it is self-evidently the case that ancestors (devils being the term used for ancestors in their malign guise) inhabit the places that are theirs. The conversation also makes clear that, so far as I am concerned, it is self-evidently the case that they do not. This clash of ideas is the common lot of anthropologists in the field and it can take many, many years before we are able (if ever) truly to credit what our informants tell us to be so. Thus we may characterise as *belief* what our informants *know* and, in so doing, misrepresent them. If I am to correctly represent my Fijian informants, for example, I should say that they *know* the ancestors inhabit the places that were theirs.

Which leads me to the following observation. If I were asked to state as pithily as possible what anthropology has contributed to the human sciences, my answer would be that the corpus of ethnography of different peoples at different times and places demonstrates two things: firstly, that people everywhere take their fundamental ideas of themselves and the environing world to be self-evidently true; and secondly, that the marvellous thing is that the peopled world everywhere confirms all our various understandings of it. What people hold to be self-evidently the case is not usually subject to hypothesis-testing in the broadly scientific mould in which one states a hypothesis and then attempts to disprove it. By and large people reason inductively and make rationalisations after the fact. So, for example, I wanted to subject the beyond-death appearance of an ancestor to what amounted to empirical scrutiny, and my informants were amused precisely because they *knew* that what I wanted was irrelevant to the ancestors' own desires.

I remarked above that this clash of understanding is an anthropological commonplace. What, however, is less often acknowledged is that the profound incommensurability we may encounter between our own ideas and those of the people whose lives we analyse, may prevent us from recognising that often enough we find ourselves in a similar position with respect to those nearest us: our spouses, children, siblings, friends, etc. Our awareness that this is so tends to emerge only when we are in dispute with one another, though it is clear enough, too, in the differences that emerge in, say, rival accounts of what is really happening in the economy. The problem for us as anthropologists is a particularly powerful case of the problem we have in our daily lives: that is, if we are *really* to credit other people's understandings of the world we have to recognise not only that the environing world provides for all the meanings that humans can make, but also that our own understandings are no less amenable to historical analysis – i.e. no less explicable by social analysis – than the next person's. It follows that the explanatory power of our ethnographies must be made to reside in rendering our informants' categories analytical.[1] This is what I am trying to do here.

The focus of this paper is a long extract from a conversation (from 2005) with a middle-aged Fijian couple, Mikaele and his wife

Makereta (to preserve their privacy, their real names are not given).[2] Our conversation bears on the question of how we know what is true, and is predicated on our various ideas about what people *are* – ideas whose difference resides in their similarity to one another. Each of us holds the person to be a locus of relationship – I because I am an anthropologist for whom inter-subjectivity is the primary condition of human being, and Mikaele and Makereta because they live their lives as Fijian villagers in terms of the idea that human sociality evinces itself in mutual obligation, *veiqaravi*, attendance on one another (literally 'facing each other'). And Mikaele, Makereta and I each have well-established (not to say fixed) ideas about what is true and how we know what is true.

The Fijian word that denotes whether or not something is true or real is *dina*; the term also denotes what is proper or genuine, and what is honest or sincere. *Vakadinata* is a transitive form of the base term that denotes believing or crediting something, considering a thing to be true. *Ivakadinadina* may be translated as proof or evidence, also confirmation, also witness.[3] In the Fijian Methodist hymn book, however, the Apostles' Creed is *Na vakabauta*, loosely 'the belief/confirmation': thus the prayer 'believes/confirms God, our Father in heaven' (*vakabauta na Kalou, na Tamada vakalomalagi*) 'believes/confirms Jesus his son' (*vakabauta na Luve ni Kalou*) and 'believes/confirms the Bible' (*vakabauta na Yalo Tabu*), which 'proves to us that we are the children of God' (*vakadinadinataka mai ki na yaloda ni da sa luve ni Kalou*). In respect of the Christian God and the origin gods, belief, in the sense of considering something to be true in face of the possibility that it might be false, is not a concern for the Fijian villagers with whom I worked.[4] They *know* that gods exist – this is not up for debate. What matters then is whether one can be seen *to attend on* a god.

The Fijian categories for belief and truth show why, from an anthropological perspective, the meaning of a category cannot properly be taken for granted, why it requires, always, an ethnographic investigation to establish how it is used and what its implications may be. It follows that this is the case for 'truth', as used by ourselves as well as by others. We have, at least, to acknowledge that the ethnographic investigation should (if only in principle) bear on ourselves as well as on others because meaning-making is a historical process and because the world provides for all the meanings that we make.

Different ideas of knowledge and belief are associated with different ideas of truth, and this is surely important because it provides an instance of a more general problem: that we are, all of us, everywhere in the world, certain that by and large the world conforms to our understandings of it. My interest in this phenomenon is prompted by an experience that is common among anthropologists, the experience of coming to realise, with ever more force as the years go by, that my own ideas of the world and what it is to be human are no more sound, defensible or well grounded – no more valid, than other people's. This realisation is the outcome of fieldwork and of twenty years of ethnographic analysis of Fijian ideas and practice during which I have had constantly to revise my theoretical perspective. And it is more or less impossible to hold on to as *real* precisely because, however aware one is that knowledge is transformed in the selfsame process through which it is maintained (that is, the process of making meaning over time), one cannot ever give up one's own current certainties about the peopled world. This is especially the case, perhaps, if one thinks of oneself, as I do, as someone engaged in a scientific endeavour to understand how we humans become who we are.

My general concern as an anthropologist is to explain something of the biologically microhistorical process of auto-poiesis (self-making) that evinces itself uniquely in every one of us. My explanation rests in the idea of inter-subjectivity as the fundamental condition of human being. Inter-subjectivity entails that we make meaning out of meanings that others have made and are making. So, like any other human being, I am enmeshed in manifold relations with others who have their own understandings of social relations and the way the world is. In any encounter with any other I assimilate the other's understandings to my own and, in so doing, accommodate – more or less – to both the other's ideas of the world and to the other's idea of our relationship. Each one of us is born into a world in the making that is already rendered meaningful in all its material aspects and, over time, we make these meanings anew. Elsewhere I have shown why it follows that meaning is always emergent, never quite fixed, and how, in the ontogenetic process of making meaning over time, knowledge is transformed even while it is maintained.[5] This microhistorical process of genetic epistemology renders each person's ideas unique, even while, from birth onwards, each one of us willy-nilly co-opts the other's in making our own sense of the world.[6] And the process is inevitably felt and lived precisely because 'making sense' always has everything to do with the others, as becomes apparent in any ethnographic investigation of children's ideas of the peopled world and how they arrive at them.

It should be apparent that I am not asserting the simple-minded idea that 'it's all relative', neither do I mean to suggest that a scientific account is no different from any other description of the world. What I am pointing to here is that the peopled world provides for all our historically constituted descriptions of it, such that these always and inevitably partial descriptions are rendered objective in different ways. So, for example, for all they differ significantly from our own, Ambonwari people's ideas about temporality enable linear judgements of time derived from comparing any two processes in terms of their simultaneity, duration and succession. That they consider *pisinim* (meaning span of time, limited duration, period, season) to be intrinsic to a person and his or her practices does not obviate this linearity. They do not, however, insist on making a distinction (as we try to do) between linear and qualitative temporal perspectives. Even so, our understanding of time can be rendered explicable to them, just as their understanding can be rendered explicable to us.[7] This is possible not because certain concepts of time are universal, but because all of us have to come to terms with certain relatively invariant processes instantiated in the peopled world – for example, those that make unavoidable an apprehension of linear temporality.

It may be difficult to credit that other people's ideas are as objectively warranted by the world as one's own, but it is only to the extent that one does so that, as an anthropologist, one recognises the necessity for a theory of human being that is able to explain how this comes to be so. Because this endeavour to explain addresses the historicity of human being in the world – and thus implicates its own historical nature – it may ultimately be impossible. Even so, it seems important to me to attempt an anthropologically valid explanation. My conversation here with Mikaele and Makereta provides a case for analysis – each of us holds to what we know to be true and, indeed, demonstrable.

THE EVIDENCE OF OUR OWN EYES

Mikaele begins his demonstration of how we know what is true with a straightforward instance: we can establish whether Jone, his teenage son, was weeding the garden through the evidence of our own eyes. What is done, rather than merely said to be done, has an effect in the world – one that we can see. He agrees, however, that there are things we know that we don't actually see directly, and gives God as an example.

Text 1

> God exists, but we don't see him. But it is possible for us to say it is true [*vakadinadinataka*] because we [can] prove [*vakadinadinataka*] that there is a God. … I say it is true there is a God. There are many things I can show you – one is the blowing of the wind. We ask: where does the wind come from? Another, the sun, who created the sun? The moon, who created the moon? The stars, who created the stars? This tree, who created it? The animals, who created them? The grass… The falling rain, … the growing trees… The many fish in the sea… [S]ome wise people nowadays say there is no God. But let them say there is no God, how do trees grow? Who made the trees? Who made the sun? Who made the tides? Who made the tide ebb?… Who made the many fish? … We just know there is a God [*Kalou*] who created all and everything there is.

We cannot see the Christian God, but we can know Him through the wonders of his creation, which are everywhere evident to us, and which themselves proclaim God's truth. Mikaele had brought God into the discussion, which prompted me to ask him about the origin gods.

Text 2

> The origin gods [*kalou vu*] still exist. … [They] are gods only of the world [*kalou ga ni vuravura*]… [They] are just the same as people. They're our ancient source from that time, they're as gods from that time. … they're our … grandfathers from generations ago. … At the time when you are attending on him then he will appear… As when you're serving God [*na Kalou*]. Because you want to serve God, God will then give you what you want. It's the same with the origin gods, if you attend on them. … [they] will then give you what you want. But this is just a worldly thing. … They're still effective [*mana*]. … If you attend on them. Still effective [*mana*]. Yes, but as I said before, just something of this world. God … the great God [*Kalou levu*] …

> the true God [*Kalou dina*] … is at odds [*veicalati*] with them. … The great God holds sway over them. … judges them. He is very, very much more powerful than all of them … there is no God in heaven and earth that can equal him. … As it says in the Bible: the great God is a jealous God. … He also doesn't want you to attend on another God in this world. … He wants you to worship him only. If you are attending on an origin god it means that you are at odds [*veicalati*] with his [God's] command. As I say therefore to you, or to us both, the power of the origin gods comes from this world.

Our conversation then turned to whether or not people nowadays are attending on origin gods and how he knows this is so. The origin gods, by contrast to the Christian God, are to be known through the inevitable (if somewhat delayed) misfortune they bring to those who serve them. In this way you can know that someone *has served* an origin god (*kalou vu*) by the evils that befall that person and his (or her) family.

Text 3

> How do we know? When you see how he/she looks, the particulars of his/her life and household. … When you try to know well then you look at his/her household and the children, those who are at school will not achieve well. They will meet many difficulties, his/her children will meet many difficulties. And everything about their family life will not be good. … Some, when, when they are accused of attending on devils, origin gods, some as I said already, it is made evident in their children, their children don't marry, if they marry they don't have children. If they do have children, they have only one. … Some of those who worship an origin god, when they are attending on him, afterwards they know that it is evil – I just hear this – they again return [to the right path], they apologise [*vakasuka*].

So we may know such people too by their own reported confession.[8] I did not ask Mikaele whether it is possible, in his view, to disprove a particular accusation of attending on *kalou vu*, but I think he would begin by saying yes, it could be disproved, and then, given that witches can disguise themselves as concerned and kind-hearted church-goers and that misfortune can come upon us all, give up that position.

In the Fijian view misfortunes that happen to oneself are very likely to be caused by the ill wishes of others who are practising witchcraft (*vakadraunikau*, literally the way of leaves), which is, itself, an instance of attendance on devils (*qaravi tevoro*) or attendance on origin gods (*qaravi kalou vu*). Misfortunes that happen to others, however, are just as likely to be the result of their selfish attendance on an origin god and this is Mikaele's perspective in our conversation; he is not thinking about the possible case of misfortune afflicting himself. In a Western psychological framework, this kind of reasoning comes under the heading of 'attribution theory': observers will call a man who trips over clumsy, where he himself blames the stone in his way. But this tells us little except that humans are likely to blame external forces or events or other people for what observers are likely to say is (in one way or another) their own fault. What is interesting in this Fijian case is rather to see how the practice of attending on an origin god (*qaravi kalou vu* or *qaravi tevoro*) is a perverse instance of *veiqaravi*, attendance on each other.

ATTENDANCE ON ONE ANOTHER

In its narrowest adult interpretation *na veiqaravi vakavanua* (attending on one another in the manner of the land) is reserved for ceremonies such as *sevusevu* or *reguregu* – where, in the case of the first, one presents *yaqona* to chiefs to request they acknowledge one's presence in a place, or, in the case of the second, one presents a whale's tooth in acknowledgement of death. The term *na veiqaravi vakavanua* is synonymous – so far as my adult informants are concerned – with *na cakacaka vakavanua* (literally working, acting, doing in the manner of the land), which may also be used when talking generally of the practice of working together on some communal endeavour. *Veiqaravi* also refers to attendance on chiefs in *yaqona*-drinking and to worship when the reference is to the Christian God. Its literal meaning is 'facing each other', a spatial arrangement that is reiterated over and over again in the arrangement of houses in the village, in the positioning of people vis-à-vis one another in any given ceremony and in the conduct of day-to-day village life.[9]

Veiqaravi is about mutual obligations across houses, clans, *yavusa*, to attend on one another in everyday life-cycle rituals and celebrations (such as those at Christmas and New Year) and activities such as house-building, laying electricity lines for the village, etc. – all of which require that people gather to drink *yaqona* together.[10] Whatever the ostensible reason for its presentation, *yaqona* is always an offering to chiefs and, implicitly, to the origin gods who 'stand at the back' of any installed chief. The preparation, serving, acceptance and drinking of a bowl of *yaqona* is always 'in the manner of the land' and one should not leave a group that is drinking until the large central bowl is dry (*maca*). *Yaqona* is the drink of chiefs; they receive the root as tribute and redistribute it as drink that must be accepted, this being acknowledged whether any chief is present or not.[11] The space in which the drinking takes place (indoors or out) is valued such that chiefs sit above (*i cake*) the large central bowl of *yaqona* facing down the space towards those who sit below (*i ra*) the *yaqona* (facing up towards the chiefs). Mutuality is at once evinced and *constituted* in, and through, the everyday ritualised use of space – i.e. mutuality and *veiqaravi* as given in the ritualised use of space are mutually constituting or, more radically, aspects of one another.[12]

The benign and malign aspects of origin gods (*kalou vu*) are rendered effective (*mana*) through the proper and perverse forms of *veiqaravi*, respectively. In Fiji, one who envies his/her kin and wishes to do them harm, or one who selfishly desires riches or power, drinks *yaqona* on his/her own (or, like as not, in the company of his/her spouse), pouring libations in the name of an ancestor god, and giving the name of a close kinsperson as proposed victim-cum-offering to the god.[13]

Text 4

> Some – the story that we hear about it – some just attend on them inside the house. Some know each other, some have mutual knowledge about it as spouses – the man knows and so does the woman. . . . When someone says 'he/she is in the way of devils', then someone else also says 'but he/she doesn't know on his/her own'. . . . His/her spouse also knows.

My understanding of twenty years ago was that the offering of a kinsperson's name was invariably successful – i.e. that the origin god, empowered by the service being done to him, struck down the named person in a death inexplicable by any other means. According, however, to what Mikaele told me, many a death or other misfortune is attributable to the origin god's turning on his own servant. Whatever the case, you can know one who is attending on an origin god through the manner of his or her *yaqona*-drinking.

Text 5

> his/her *yaqona*-drinking ... is not like that of [ordinary] people, the *yaqona*-drinking goes on every day, drinking *yaqona*, drinking *yaqona*. Together with ... together with his/her spouse they are drinking *yaqona* the both of them in their house. [By contrast] if we are drinking *yaqona* we are telling stories to one another, many of us [together].

Mikaele's emphasis on spouses, together, being responsible points out how even while the house is the foundation (*yavu*) of all social life, *veiqaravi* entails relations across houses. A married couple who selfishly desire to augment the success of their own household through attending on an origin god are bound to harm other households and, ultimately, their own. In serving the god in lonely *yaqona*-drinking sessions held behind closed doors, the spouses are at odds (*veicalati*) not only with the Christian God but also, implicitly, with the chiefs and the origin gods in their benign aspect, who stand at the backs of installed chiefs. *Yaqona*-drinking is central to all Fijian ceremonies and as such it comes under the aegis of chiefs, origin gods and the Christian God.[14] Acknowledgement of the origin gods is occasionally made explicit in ceremonial speeches but is otherwise always implicit in the honorific titles of chiefs which are used in such speeches and which refer to the *yavu tabu* – forbidden house foundations – whose owners (and only occupants) are founding ancestors. The Christian God is called upon in the prayer that accompanies ceremonial speeches. The married couple's exclusive attendance on an origin god suggests that the single household can produce its own prosperity without reliance on other households, chiefs or the Christian God – in short, without reference to *veiqaravi*. But future misfortune is immanent in this denial.

WHY MISFORTUNE COMES FROM SERVING AN ORIGIN GOD

In central and eastern Fiji, among ethnic Fijians, social relations in general, and chiefship in particular, are a function of complementary and opposing concepts of competitive equality (as evinced, for example, in reciprocal balanced exchange over time across houses and clans) and hierarchy (as evinced, for example, in tribute to chiefs). Indeed, one can argue that here instituted hierarchy and competitive equality are fused aspects of a single idea of antithetical duality where each kind of social relations depends for its very continuity on the other.[15] This radical opposition pervades Fijian daily life and informs, for example, sexual relations, kinship, chief-ship and ideas of the person. In the village, the fused opposition between hierarchy and competitive equality is expressed in one's position relative to others in time and space.

One's status in the community at large, as derived from an interaction between rank (chief or commoner), seniority (older or younger) and gender (wife or sister in relation to a given man), marks out one's place above (*i cake*) or below (*i ra*) others in any gathering in house, village hall or church. This above/below axis is applied both to a single horizontal plane (for example one end of the floor space of the village hall, the church or any house is above while the other is below), and to the vertical (for example, it is polite when moving among others to adopt the respectful stooping posture called *lolou*). In Gau, all meetings, gatherings, meals, worship, etc. take place in the ritualised space of the house, village hall and church, and all villagers over the age of five or so are well aware which area of the space is above and which below. People's relative status is evident in their arrangement vis-à-vis one another on this above/below axis.

The above/below axis is constituted out of a transformation in ritual of *veiqaravi* (literally 'facing each other', also 'attendance on one another') which describes the arrangement of houses in the space of the village and suggests mutual ritual obligations across clans. Also, any given house is usually orientated such that its 'land door' faces onto the 'sea door' of the house beside it, thus evoking relations between landspeople and sea-people. *Veiqaravi* may here refer to the balanced reciprocity in exchange over time across houses, clans and *yavusa*. The term also, however, denotes 'attendance on chiefs' when the reference is to a chiefly ceremony, and 'worship' when the reference is to a church service.[16]

Thus the very term *veiqaravi* contains the tension between competitive equality and instituted hierarchy that allows reciprocal exchanges across houses to be transformed in *yaqona* ritual into tribute to chiefs.[17] The fused antithesis of hierarchy and competitive equality here references that between non-marriageable kin (where the paradigmatic reference is to the hierarchical house and clan) and marriageable kin (who as cross-cousins are equals across houses and clans).[18]

The married couple bring misfortune on themselves *because* they deny the principle of sociality that is *veiqaravi* that informs the way according to kinship, according to chiefs, according to the land, according to the church. Considered as a principle of sociality, *veiqaravi* provides for all possibilities, for all the shifting subtleties of relationships that are evinced in people's behaviour towards one another. But when one becomes the servant of an origin god, then that is *all* one can be – his servant. Fijians hold explicitly that the power of a chief, the origin god and the Christian God resides in people's attendance on them, in their willingness to listen (*vakarogoca*) to them and do as they say – this renders their word effective (*mana*) and therefore true (*dina*). You have undertaken to attend on the god and because his *mana* depends on you, his desire for your attendance is insatiable. And even though you abjure all other obligations, you cannot fulfil the promises you made to the god. As Mikaele says:

Text 6

> it just comes to an end, to its full extent, it just reaches its conclusion … The time will come when the origin god will turn into your enemy, and then bite you again. Like that. It's not possible to serve endlessly, to let the drink just go on flowing, to just go on and on and on. The time will come when you two are enemies again. … The origin god is again your enemy. … As I said before: that time of your contract, your contract with him holds for all time [it is accepted as a sacrifice]. It holds, it holds. From the moment that you don't fulfil your contract, from that moment on he will bite you again because of it.

What I am trying to demonstrate here is that from Mikaele's perspective the truth of what he has to say is self-evident, because it is an inevitable outcome of an inexorable logic that is given in *veiqaravi* and that he lives day to day, moment to moment.

BUT HOW DO YOU KNOW?

Earlier in our conversation, I had been pressing him to tell me his view of a particular case.

Text 7

Chris.: But do you believe the story about those two?

Mika.: There are a lot of stories like that that I hear but I can't prove because we don't see anything; ... Perhaps some see ... and they accuse the two of them because of it, but as for me ... I can't prove it because I didn't see with my own eyes anything they [two] did. ... [As for me and you], we [two] are new here, we [two] don't see anything, we [two] can't say whether it's true or false. ... Some, some explanations of this thing, those who are attending on an origin god, the explanation of it that I hear of them is that they're kind persons, they're persons who are concerned for others. In order to cover up their behaviour so that we don't know that they are attending on an origin god, they are usually concerned for us.

Chris.: That means that it's very, very difficult...

Mika.: Difficult. Except if you see him/her when he/she is serving [a god] if you actually see with your eyes while he/she is drinking a bowl of *yaqona*, [while] he/she is speaking.

Chris.: You've seen it?

Mika.: No, I'm just saying.

Chris.: Oh.

Mika.: You can then know that it's him/her. They say of it, those who talk of it, that the people we see, those we accuse of attending on the origin gods, some of them have that kind of behaviour – always concerned, always kind, in order thus to cover their... [Some are] church-going. ... Some who are accused, they are lay preachers in order to cover up their behaviour.

Chris.: That means that it's not possible...

Mika.: ... to know.

Chris.: Yes, it can't be done.

Mika.: Except if you see, if you see him in a place.

...

Mika.: Some, some say – I haven't yet seen it myself – some of them say that they dance in honour of the moon. ... They dance like this [moving his hands in a fast *meke*] like this. Some have told of it. That's their character. Yes, some catch them, they catch people who are dancing for the moon [*meke vula*].

Chris.: It's true?

Mika.: Yes. Some tell of it.

Chris.: In the village, inside the village?

Mika.: In the village and in the other villages in Fiji. This thing, Christina, is in all the villages, in all the Fijian villages there are some people who stand accused of witchcraft. All the villages in Fiji.

Chris.: Is that so … here too?

Mika.: Here too there are some.

Chris.: Yes but the difficult thing, so far as I am concerned, is…

Mika.: Yes.

Chris.: … how … do … you … know?

Mika.: … how … do … you … know?

Mikaele knows what I am going to say; over the years he's heard me ask this question many times. He knows what my question is and is able to reiterate it with me. He is amused too by my persistent scepticism because he *knows* that some people are attending on origin gods. Our conversation continues:

Text 8

Chris.: Yes, but you do believe/confirm [*vakabauta*] it Mikaele, you told me that there are some here. How do you know that there are some?

Mika.: Just the story that we hear. Just the stories like this, like this, that we hear.

When I raise the matter of gossip, Mikaele accepts the truth of this, telling me that of course, 'Some of those who tell stories want to do harm to [others], e? [then in English] *Spoil? Spoil each other?*' And he takes in his stride both the fact that it may be impossible to obtain conclusive proof of witchcraft, and that the former Methodist minister, now dead, had told me he did not believe the stories he was told – for example that the fish someone had given him was the gift of a witch and likely to do him harm.

Text 9

Chris.: The Reverend told his wife, 'Take the fish, say thank you for it, cook it. It will taste good.' He didn't believe these kinds of stories.

Mika.: Mmm. It's Fijian belief [*na vakabauta vaka Viti*].

Makereta.: [wakes up, breaks in] It's not possible for it to disappear as far as we Fijians are concerned. ...

Mika.: He can't accuse a person. He's a minister. He will accept everything that's brought to him. It's not possible even once for him to accuse a person [and] he can't say that thing, that thing, that thing [i.e. he can't choose to accept some dishes, for example, and reject others]. No. He will just take it and say thank you. ... That's their way – all the ministers of the church, the lay preachers, that's their behaviour – all of them. Here it's not possible to discriminate between people, everything that is given from here or there, they accept. ... The belief according to the Bible, according to the Christian Church is: don't accuse anyone of your kin. Take everything that is given to you by your kin.

Throughout our conversation Mikaele, a devout Methodist (like his wife), has recourse to Christian teaching to back up what he says, but these ideas are assimilated to the Fijian idea of the person as a locus of relationship: you distinguish yourself by demonstrating who you are as a function of what you are given to be in relations with others. In so far as ministers do what ministers are given to do, they cannot be harmed. Moreover, the origin gods, in their malign aspect, become manifest in relation to the person whose selfishness is evinced in their very attendance on a god. By the same token the origin gods themselves provide the potential for witchcraft. Indeed, they invented it because, as Makereta says, they want to be attended on. Only thus can they show themselves to be *mana* (effective).

Text 10

Makereta: ...this thing was just created by our ancestors. They just created it so that they might be worshipped as gods, origin gods. ... Some others of us Christians won't hear of it – that there are still some people who believe/confirm different gods, origin gods.

> [But] they will attend on them, it doesn't matter if the church enters in, they just attend on them because their gods are just our ancestors.

MANA AS A MATERIAL FORCE IN THE WORLD

The effectiveness of origin gods, like the effectiveness of chiefs, resides in people's willing attendance upon them. And because it is people who make gods and chiefs powerful, Fijians have ample evidence for their idea of *mana* as an efficacy that is true because it is entirely material. The power of the Christian God is evinced in the attendance upon him of many millions of people all over the world, and is manifestly greater than the power of the Fijian origin gods. Likewise, whether a chief's word is or is not *mana* is there for all to see in people's willing attendance on him and the prosperity of the country that is his.[19] The ritual formula that punctuates ceremonial speeches *mana … e dina* translates as 'it is effective, it is true' but, since it always refers to the speech that preceded it, might more properly be translated as 'it effects, it is true'.[20] Consider the following example where, at the mourning ceremonies for a dead chief, a man of chiefly status offers a whale's tooth to the people whose task it is to attend on the chiefly dead:

Text 11

> I am touching, sirs, the string of the whale's tooth [*tabua*], that our chiefs may be healthy, that our country be one of peace and plenty [*sautu*], a country of mutual love [*veilomani*] [literally that the *sau* – the command or prohibition of a chief – be established in our country, that it may be a place of caring for one another]. The word is already heard. It is effective, it is true [*Mana … e dina.*]

If a chief cannot put his word into effect, what he says is not true. An installed high chief is a living instantiation of the immanent power of the ancestors, which in its legitimate guise today comes under the aegis of the Christian God. The *sau* – the command or prohibition of an installed chief – inevitably and properly harms any one of his people who refuses to listen to him. That is to say his word '*mana*', his word '*effects*': by virtue of their pronunciation the chief's words bring into being the condition they proclaim.[21] But if a paramount fails in his duties towards the people, if he holds onto goods and valuables that are given him in tribute and is not seen to redistribute them, then his country can no longer be seen to prosper, his word is evidently no longer *mana*, and the people have nothing to fear if they, in turn, withhold their allegiance (*nodra vakarorogo vua*, literally their listening to him).[22] In other words, Fijians *know* that it is they who, by virtue of their service and willing tribute, empower their chiefs, who in turn make land and people prosper. This idea extends both to the ancestor gods and to the Christian God. The malign power of the ancestor gods may be unleashed through witchcraft – the attendance on an ancestor by a single person acting alone or with his or her spouse. By the same token, the ancestor gods are *in general* no longer effective because, in general, 'no one attends on them anymore', and the power of the Christian God is plainly evinced in his many millions of worshippers. The true source of a given person's fortune, however, irrespective of whether it be good or bad, *always* remains to be found out – was it effected by the Christian God, by the ancestors acting under his aegis, or by the ancestors in their malign guise?

Truth is, thus, not necessarily given in the nature of things and cannot always be dependent on hypothesis-testing. It is, rather, an effect that can be known and that may take time to become evident.[23] The Fijian idea is that speech or, more generally the word (*vosa*) as it is spoken or written, may be *mana* (effective), and thus what is true (*dina*) may be an outcome rather than already given in the nature of things.[24]

Here it becomes interesting to consider the moral force of language. In a recent paper I drew on my fieldwork in Fiji to argue that a specific moral force always inheres in specific forms of language use. The paper used a given public instance of collective significance to show how truth may be regarded not as an absolute, but as a function of a specific moral force which is itself embedded in, and constituted through, the everyday social relations that we may analyse in terms of sexual relations, kinship, chiefship and ideas of the person. The reader is no doubt well aware that, of course, Fijian villagers have the same ability as any one else to test hypotheses and to differentiate between an assertion that is empirically warranted and one that is not. In certain instances, however, especially those concerning complex social situations, what is seen to be true may even so be understood to be the outcome of a struggle between different speakers, each of whom is intent on establishing his or her own truth as definitive for other people.[25] Thus what fascinates the Fijians I know are social relations, the obligations inherent in *veiqaravi* – attendance on one another – their fulfilment or avoidance, and how they at once manifest and constitute the way according to kinship, the chiefly way, the Fijian way.

Now, given that I am right that a specific moral force always inheres in specific forms of language use, how do we arrive at our sense of what it is? The details of the Fijian material suggest that it is ritualised aspects of language-use that structure the way speakers constitute, over time, their ideas about what language is good for and what its moral force may be.[26] And I would argue that this is the case for people everywhere because, for all of us, the paralinguistic aspects of language-use are inevitably more or less ritualised – that is, say, held explicitly to be more or less rule-governed and at the same time redolent with meaning. All of which suggests, to me, the necessity for studying the ontogenetic process through which children constitute over time their ideas about what speech does, and the conditions that render it good and right – their ideas of the moral force that is given in ritualised aspects of language-use.

In my previous work, I have shown how children's experience of embodying a ritual behaviour or series of behaviours is crucial for the developmental process through which, over time, they ascribe meaning to that behaviour, such that its performance becomes symbolic of that meaning and, as such, obligatory.[27] In other words, the power of ritual to communicate is not given in ritual itself precisely because, in direct contrast to what is spoken, ritual cannot declare its own meaning. Rather, the communicative power of ritual is the outcome of a learning process through which, over time, a person renders certain ritualised behaviours meaningful. It follows that, as an adult, I am coerced by those rituals and ritualised behaviours that I rendered meaningful because, long before I asked myself what they might mean, I had already embodied an indelible knowledge of the 'what' and 'how' of these particular ritual practices. I argue that the same goes for much paralinguistic practice and, if this is indeed so, it follows that understanding any given utterance entails understanding its moral force, that they are aspects of one and the same process – an observation that throws into question any taken-for-granted distinction between the propositional and illocutionary force of an utterance. Propositional force and illocutionary force are perhaps best considered not as separate kinds of meaning, but as aspects of one another – that is to say, the propositional force of an utterance and its performative impact are at once inextricable and embedded in an idea of what language is good for.[28]

In learning to use language we are learning about language itself, what it does and how, and we are also learning how to be in relation to others. We are constituting an idea of ourselves as subjects as a function of intersubjectivity – a process of continuing differentiation in which we go on and on becoming ourselves. Thus a systematic participant observer study of, for example, upper-middle-class French children from, say, four to twelve years old, at school, at home and elsewhere, could reveal the ontogeny of the idea that language is to be valued as an analytical tool, as a means of explaining the nature of the world and the human condition.[29] Indeed, in the course of this same study, we might likewise find out the ontogeny of the complementary and opposing idea that discourse itself is constitutive of what persons are, and can be. For all that they seem to be antithetical these ideas are, likewise, aspects of one another, each manifesting an independence that is only apparent, like the two sides of the continuous surface that is a Moebius strip. And an understanding of the ontogeny of this opposition would allow us to render the ideas genuinely analytical for those whose lives they may indeed inform.[30]

Through my relations with my Fijian informants, I have come to see that it can only be by virtue of making sense, over time, of paralinguistic practice that we arrive at our knowledge of the moral force of what is said or written, our idea of how we know what is true. It follows that an understanding of the moral force of language is bound to be constituted in the very process of coming to be a native speaker of that language and, in so doing, arriving at an understanding of the conditions that make a statement true. And, as we have seen, these ideas, in their turn, entail particular ideas of human being and particular modes of rendering these ideas as objectively given aspects of the world. *Mana … e dina.* It is effective … it is true.

NOTES

1. I tried to make this point in 'Anthropology as the whole science of what it is to be human' (Toren 2002). I failed to notice, however, that somewhere in the copy-editing process the last words of the penultimate paragraph 'rendered analytical' were changed to 'rendered analysable', and thus the whole point of my paper was lost.

2. What is included here are edited extracts from a long conversation entailing interruptions, sceptical murmurs, clarifications and laughter on both our parts. Mikaele was at first perhaps concerned that I might be trying to catch him out but once I made it clear that this wasn't so, he proceeded with interest to discuss the issues raised by each of us. At points he was forthcoming, at points reticent and at points I pushed him to say more, and perhaps the process of transcribing, editing and translating makes what is reported here appear too spontaneous. Even so, I think I have remained true to the spirit of what was said.
3. For the thoroughness of these English glosses for *dina* and its derivatives I am indebted to George Milner (personal communication), who is the author of *Fijian Grammar*.
4. Fieldwork in Fiji occupied twenty months from 1981–83, four months in 1990, two months in 1993 and two months in 2005. In 2005, Gau island had a population of about 4000. The economy is mixed subsistence (gardening, small numbers of pigs, cows and poultry) and cash-cropping, *yaqona* (kava) being the most lucrative crop. Fiji Indians make up almost half the population of Fiji, but on smaller islands like Gau, the population is often almost entirely Fijian.
5. Cf. Toren 1999a: 1–21 and 2002. Note that this idea has little to do with the 'aesthetics of emergence' as discussed by Miyazaki (2004: 133–40), but rather concerns the nature of genetic epistemology as a microhistorical process – one which entails the Piagetian view that our certainties are the outcome of that process. Piaget's driving interest was to understand how the necessity that seems to be given in our categories of space, time, number and so on, could be the outcome of a process of cognitive construction, rather than an innate function of mind as Kant had argued. So, Piaget notes that '[cognitive] structures – *in being constructed* – give rise to that necessity which a priorist theories have always thought it necessary to posit at the outset. Necessity, instead of being the prior *condition* for learning, is its *outcome*.' Cf. Piaget, 1971 (1968): 62 (italics in original).
6. Piaget's idea of genetic epistemology is here modified by the recognition that humans are social in their nature and that *everything* about us, from our bodies to our ideas of the peopled world and the processes in which these ideas are constituted over time, is, thus, informed by our relations with one another.
7. '*Pisinim* … denotes a temporal span between the beginning and end of a process which is essentially characterised by the continuation of sameness of a definite kind. This distinctiveness of the process defines the span. *Pisinim*, whatever its contents, does not represent simply an external dimension of people's lives which then influences a person or is internalised, but is,

rather, already merged with a person and his or her practices' (Telban 1998: 44). Part of the strength of Telban's exploration of Ambonwari *kay* (habit, way, manner) is that he shows how to understand *kay*, we have to grasp the temporal perspective that it entails.

8. One of my informants – a man aged thirty-one, a member of the British army, who has travelled widely and lived outside Fiji – recently told me that as a child he could not understand how *kalou vu*, whom he understood to be protective and a source of good, could also be responsible for witchcraft deaths. He was twelve years old when a number of people in his village, all of whom were related to one another, were possessed by *tevoro* (the *kalou vu* or origin gods in malign guise), and he heard his own grandmother (FFZ) confess to having wanted to see him dead because she was angry with his father who had not done as she asked. I have still to find out what conclusion he – a devout Christian – came to.
9. For a convincing account of the aesthetics of *veiqaravi*, cf. Miyazaki 2000.
10. Hocart 1952: 51–2.
11. All chiefly rituals entail an initial offering of *yaqona* root as tribute (*i sevusevu*, a ceremony that requests, as it were, chiefly acknowledgement of one's presence) and the subsequent redistribution of *yaqona* as drink to all those who are present. *Yaqona*-drinking is at once the most everyday and the most sacred of Fijian rituals. It is by virtue of drinking the cup offered by the chief of the installing clan that a man is made paramount. Fijian chief-ship is constituted, on a day-to-day basis, in a struggle to transform in ritual (paradigmatically in *yaqona*-drinking) balanced reciprocity and equality between cross-cousins into tribute and hierarchy between people and chiefs. That this struggle is in principle unending is a product of the fact that all dynamic, fertile and affective processes are founded in the relation between cross-cousins (cf. Sahlins 1976: 24–46; Toren 1990: 50–118, 1999a: 163–81).
12. Ditto for the fused antithesis between hierarchy and equality that produces the leadership of chiefs (*turaga*) in the *vanua* and of married men (*turaga*) in every household via a transformation of balanced reciprocal exchange into tribute (cf. Hocart 1913; Toren 1999a: 129–45, 163–81).
13. Cf. Turner 1986, who did fieldwork in Matailobau in the interior of Viti Levu: 'In Fiji the *mana* of *kava* can be used to contact the spirit world for evil or good. Another term for sorcery (*drau ni kau*) is *sova yaqona*; that is, "to pour *yaqona*". Fijians never drink *yaqona* in solitude, not even when sorcery is being practised. In that case it is drunk by two people; one prepares the beverage and the other utters the curse while pouring out the *yaqona*. What informants stressed when describing sorcery was the efficacy of *yaqona* itself.'

14. Katz 1999 is an extended description of the uses of *yaqona* with its primary focus on *yaqona* as a medium for contacting the *vu*, ancestors. The book's perspective is that of the healer who uses *yaqona* in his work and includes interesting material on healing, witchcraft, dreams and their significance, and the relation between the Christian God and the origin gods in their benign and malign guises.
15. Cf. Toren 1999: 163–81.
16. A *yavusa* is composed of clans related by descent or marriage and owing ritual obligations to one another (cf. Sayes 1982: 87).
17. Cf. Toren 1990: 74–89 and 1999: 67–82.
18. In Gau, where I do fieldwork, kinship terms are used in reference and address to everyone one knows within and across villages and chiefdoms and routinely extended to take in previously unknown people using a classificatory principle; the terminology is Dravidian. Toren 1999b analyses the ontogeny of the idea that cross-cousinship is the crucial relationship for the extension outwards, so that it may take in all ethnic Fijians, of the mutual compassion (*veilomani*) that defines kinship.
19. Cf. Hocart 1914; also Firth 1967 (1940) who notes that '[m]ost of the translations proposed for *mana* fail to give the reality of the native attitude, because of their abstract nature... "Supernatural power" for instance does represent one aspect of the concept but it leaves out of account the essentially material evidence of such power, and directs attention to the means rather than to the end-product.'
20. Tomlinson 2006 argues convincingly that missionaries produced the nominalisation of *mana*, transforming it from verb to noun. I cannot agree with him, however, that 'the threatening spectre of its diminution or loss' is a recent phenomenon. Rather it seems likely to me that Fijians have always held that their current chiefs could not *mana* (effect) or were not so *mana* (effective) as the remarkable chiefs of 'the olden times' (*na gauna makawa*). Tomlinson's paper includes an able discussion of the extensive literature on meanings of *mana*.
21. Cf. Hooper's Lakeban informant who, talking of the paramount chief, 'suggested that *mana* is an innate characteristic to do with descent ... whereas *sau* is connected with the act of installation, that before this the Paramount Chief possessed it but it was dormant...' He then went on to describe *sau* as others described *mana*, if the people don't do what the chief wants they will suffer because of his *sau* (Hooper 1982: 173). Cf. Quain (1948: 200) who glosses *mana* as 'chiefly power' and *sau* as 'impersonal supernatural power'; cf. also Hocart 1914.
22. Martha Kaplan's fascinating exploration of how Fijian history is imagined by colonisers and by indigenous Fijians, centres on the man who came to

be called Navosavakadua. 'He would speak once, then the command would be fulfilled' (1995: 8). As Tomlinson 2006 points out, 'although the term *mana* was not part of his prophetic name, the concept underpins it'. For analysis of a contemporary instance of the effectiveness of chiefly speech, cf. Toren 2005.

23. I am not suggesting that Fijian villagers are incapable of hypothesis-testing or that they do not consider it possible, but only that there are cases where hypothesis-testing is inappropriate because it cannot tell you what you want to know.
24. Cf. Miyazaki 2004: 85 who argues from his knowledge of a particular Fijian case that the outcome of any given '[i]nteraction is radically indeterminate ... because one side's response depends on the other's manner of attendance'.
25. Cf. Toren 2005.
26. Robbins 2001 contains an interesting discussion of aspects of language-use and ritual.
27. Cf. Toren 1990, 1999a: 83–124 and 2006.
28. Cf. Austin 1962 and Bloch 1974.
29. It is our idea of language as an analytical tool that gives rise to those technological innovations that most powerfully persuade us that we are the ones whose ideas are objectively true, and that other people's are manifestly a function of a so-called culturally relative subjectivity, to which, by reason of our technological superiority, we are immune.
30. I would argue that this holds, too, for the pervasive distinction between cognition and ideology, the logical and the symbolic, and practical knowledge and ritual knowledge; cf., for example, Bloch 1985 and 1986.

REFERENCES

Austin, J.L. 1962. *How to do things with words*, Oxford: Clarendon Press.

Bloch, M. 1974. 'Symbols, song, dance and features of articulation: is religion an extreme form of traditional authority?', *Archives Européenes de Sociologie* 15: 55–81.

—— 1985. 'From cognition to ideology', in R. Fardon (ed.), *Power and knowledge: anthropological and sociological approaches*, Edinburgh: Scottish Academic Press.

—— 1986. *From blessing to violence,* Cambridge: Cambridge University Press.

Firth, R. 1967 (1940) 'The analysis of mana: an empirical approach', in *Tikopia ritual and belief*, London: George Allen and Unwin.

Hocart, A.M. 1913. 'On the meaning of the Fijian word turanga [sic]', *Man* 13: 140–3.

—— 1914. 'Mana', *Man* 14: 97–101.

—— 1952. *The northern states of Fiji*, Occasional Publication No. 11, London: Royal Anthropological Institute.

Hooper, S.P. 1982. 'A Study of valuables in the chiefdom of Lau, Fiji', unpublished Ph.D. thesis, University of Cambridge.

Kaplan, M. 1995. *Neither cargo nor cult. Ritual politics and the colonial imagination in Fiji*, Durham: Duke University Press.

Katz, R. 1999. *The straight path of the spirit*, Rochester: Park Street Press.

Milner, G. 1972. *Fijian grammar*, Suva: Government Press.

Miyazaki, H. 2000. 'Faith and its fulfilment: agency, exchange and the Fijian aesthetics of competition', *American Ethnologist* 27(1): 31–51.

—— 2004. *The method of hope: anthropology, philosophy and Fijian knowledge*, Stanford: Stanford University Press.

Piaget, J. 1971 (1968). *Structuralism*, London: Routledge and Kegan Paul.

Quain, B. 1948. *Fijian village*, Chicago: University of Chicago Press.

Robbins, J. 2001. 'Ritual communication and linguistic ideology: a reading and partial reformulation of Rappaport's theory of ritual', *Current Anthropology*, 42: 591–614.

Sahlins, M. 1976. *Culture and practical reason*, Chicago: Chicago University Press.

Sayes, S.A. 1982. *Cakaudrove: ideology and reality in a Fijian confederation*, Ph.D Thesis, Canberra: Australian National University.

Telban, B. 1998. *Dancing through time. A sepik cosmology*, Oxford: Clarendon Press.

Tomlinson, M. 2006. 'Retheorizing mana', *Oceania*: 76 (2).

Toren, Christina. 1990. *Making sense of hierarchy. Cognition as social process in Fiji*, London School of Economics, Monographs in Social Anthropology, 61, London: The Athlone Press.

—— 1999a. *Mind, materiality and history: explorations in Fijian ethnography*, London: Routledge.

—— 1999b. 'Compassion for one another: constituting kinship as intentionality in Fiji', 1996 Malinowski Lecture, *Journal of the Royal Anthropological Institute*, 5: 265–80.

—— 2002. 'Anthropology as the whole science of what it is to be human', in R. Fox and B. King (eds), *Anthropology beyond culture*, London: Berg.

—— 2005. 'Laughter and truth in Fiji: What we may learn from a joke', *Oceania* 75(3): 268–83.

—— 2006. 'The effectiveness of ritual', in F. Cannell (ed.), *The anthropology of Christianity*, Duke University Press.

Turner, J.W. 1986. 'The water of life: kava ritual and the logic of sacrifice', *Ethnology* 25: 203–14.

APPENDIX

Text 1

E dua tiko na Kalou ia da sega ni raica. Ia, e rawa ni da vakadinadinataka tiko ni da vakadinadinataka ni dua na Kalou. ... Au vakadinadinataka ni dua na Kalou. E levu na ka au na vakaraitaka yani oqo vei iko – e dua na liwa ni cagi. Eda taroga: e lako maivei na cagi? Dua, na matani siga, o cei bulia na matanisiga. Na vula, o cei bulia na vula? Na kalokalo, o cei bulia na kalokalo? Na vunikau oqo, o cei e bulia? Na manumanu, o cei e bulia? Na co, o cei e bulia? Na tau ni uca, na ... tubu ni ... nodra tubu na vunikau, era tubu vakacava? ... Na ika lelevu mai wai. ... da kila ... E so, e so na tamata vuku ena gauna oqo era tukuna ni sega na Kalou. Ia me ra tukuna ni sega na Kalou, e tubu vakacava na vuanikau? O cei e bulia na vunikau? O cei e bulia na matanisiga? O cei e cakava na ua? O cei e cakava na di ni mati? ... O cei e bulia na ika lelevu? ... Keimami sa kila ga ni dua tiko na Kalou o koya e bulia kece na ka kece tu oqo.

Text 2

Kalou vu sa tiko tiko ga. ... kalou ga ni vuravura – na kalou vu. Na kalou vu ... oqo e tautauvata, o ira oqo me tamata ga. O ira noda vu makawa mai na gauna ya, koya vata ko ira me kalou mai na gauna sara ya. ... O ira na kalou vu, o ira ga na ... tukada vakavica sara. ... E na gauna ni ko qaravi koya kina na qai basika mai o koya ... Mevaka nomu qarava na Kalou. Ni ko vinakata mo qarava na Kalou, na Kalou sa na qai solia vei iko na ka o vinakata. Tautauvata na kalou vu, ke ko qarava. Ke ko qarava na kalou vu e na solia mai na kalou vu na ka o vinakata. Ia, ka ga ni vuravura oqo. Sa mana tiko. ... Ke ko qarava. Sa mana. Io, kau sa tukuna oti, ka ga ni vuravura oqo. Kalou ... kalou levu ... kalou dina ... sa veicalati. Na kalou levu o koya e lewai ira. ... O koya kaukauwa cake sara mai vei ira kece. Ia, o koya, tukuna e na i vola tabu, sa ... sa sega tale ni dua na kalou e lomalagi e vuravura me tautautvata kei koya. ... Me tukuna va oqo e na ivola tabu ni Kalou levu, koya Kalou dau vuvu. ... Sega ni vinakata tale o koya mo qarava tale e dua tale na kalou e vuravura oqo. ... E vinakata ga o koya mo qaravi koya ga. Io. Ke ko qaravi tiko e dua na kalou vu kena ibalebale sa veicalati vata kei na nona lewa. Kevaka ... au tukuna gona vei iko, se vei kedaru, na kalou vu na nodra kaukauwa yaco ga na vuravura oqo.

Text 3

Da kila vakacava? Ni o raica na kena irairai, na kena ituvaki na nona bula vata ga kei na nona matavuvale. … Ni ko via kila vakavinaka ni ko raica na nona matavuvale kei iratou na gone, o ratou na vuli o ratou sega ni yacova na vuli vinaka. Levu na ka dredre eratou na sotava, levu na ka dredre eratou na sotava eratou na luvena. Raica tale ga nodratou bula ni vuvale e sega ni vinaka. … E so, ni dau ra beitaka ni qaravi tevoro, kalou vu, e so kau sa kaya oti ya e vakaraitaka vei ira na luvena, na luvena e sega ni vakawati, ke ira vakawati era sega ni vakaluveni. Kevaka era vakaluveni, e na dua ga na luvedra. Ia, e so … [an aside here, a brief conversation with a child who comes with a message] *e so e dau qarava tiko na kalou vu, dau qarava tiko, oti ya era sa kila ni kena sa ca – au dau rogoca ga – era dau vakasuka tale, e ra dau vakasuka.*

Text 4

E so – kena i talanoa eda rogoca – e so ra qarava ga na nodra e loma ni vale. E so era veikilai, era veikilaitaki vakaveiwatini – kila na turaga, kila na marama. … Ni dua sa tukuna va oqo, <koya vakatevoro>, qai tukuna talega e so, <ia oqori sega ni kila duadua>. … Kila talega na watina.

Text 5

na nona gunu yaqona sa sega ni vaka na gunu yaqona na tamata, sa lako tu e veisiga: gunu yaqona, gunu yaqona. Koya vata kei … koya vata kei na watina erau sa gunu yaqona tiko e nodrau vale erau ruarua. Ke da … ni da gunu yaqona eda veitalanoa, lelevu.

Text 6

Kau sa kaya oti ya, io … e vaka i cavacava ga na i vakaiyalayala ga, vakaiyalayala ga. … E dua na gauna sa na qai vuki tale mai na kalou vu me kemu meca, qai kati iko tale. Va ya. Sega ni rawa ni qarava tiko me tawa mudu me sa lako tu ga, lako tu ga, lako tu ga. E na yaco na gauna ni drau veimecaki tale. … Kemu meca tale na kalou vu. … Ko i au sa tukuna oti e na gauna ya na nomu veiyalati, na nomu veiyalati vataki koya me donu tu ga e na veigauna. Me donu me donu. Mai na gauna ni ko sega ni cakava tiko na nomu veiyalati, gauna sara ga e na kati iko tale kina o koya.

Text 7

Chris.: *Ia ko vakabauta na talanoa me baleti rau?*

Mika.: *O iau, levu na i talanoa va oqori au dau rogoca au sega ni dau vakadinadinataka baleta eda sega ni raica e dua na ka me da raici koya me da raica sara e matada qai da beitaka. E so beka raica, e so beka raica era sa beitaki rau kina, ko i au mada ga … au sega ni vakadinadinataka baleta au sega ni raica e mataqu e dua na ka erau cakava. Ia o ira beka, o ira beka na tu makawa ena koro oqo, kedaru na lako mai, kedaru na lako vou mai, kedaru sega ni raica e dua na ka, kedaru sega ni tukuna rawa e dina se lasu. … E so, e so na vakamacala ni ka oqo ni ko ira ka qarava tiko na kalou vu na kena i vakamacala kau sa dau rogoca vei ira ni ra oqo na tamata dau loloma, era dau tamata dau veikauwaitaki. Me ra ubia tiko kina na nodra itovo me da kakua ni kila tiko ni ra qarava tiko na kalou vu e ra dau kauwaitaki keda.*

Chris.: *Ia kena ibalebale sa dredre sara…*

Mika.: *Dredre. Vakavo ke iko raici koya ni qarava tiko ke ko sa raica sara e matamu ni gunuva tiko e dua na i talo ni yaqona, vosavosa tiko.*

Chris.: *Ko sa raica?*

Mika.: *Sega au kaya mada.*

Chris.: *Ah.*

Mika.: *O sa qai rawa ni kila ni o koya. E ra tukuna o ira na dau tukuna ni na tamata ni da sa raica ni da sa beitaki koya ni qarava tiko na kalou vu e so na nona i tovo 'ya – dau veikauwaitaki, dau loloma, baleta me ubia tiko kina o koya na nodra … dau lailotu, e so … era beitaka, e so era dau beitaki, era dau vunau baleta me ra ubia tiko kina na nodra itovo.*

…

Chris.: *Kena i balebale ni sa sega ni rawa…*

Mika.: *… mo kila.*

Chris.: *Ia, sega ni rawa*

Mika.: *Vakavo ke sa raica, mo sa raici koya e na dua na vanua. … E so, e so dau tukuna – au sa bera ni raica mada – e so era dau tukuna ni ra dau meketa na vula. Na vula? E dau meke tiko, va oqo,* [moving his hands in a fast *meke*] *va oqo. E so era tukuna. Aya nodra i vakarau. Io. E so era dau toboka, era sa dau toboka na tamata ko ira meke vula tiko.*

Chris.: *Sa dina?*

Mika.: *Io. E so era tukuna.*

Chris.: *E na koro, e loma ni koro?*

Mika.: *E loma ni koro kei na veikoro tale e so e Viti. Ena ka oqo, Christina, e tu kece ga na koro kece vaka Viti e tu e so na tamata era dau beitaki tu ni ra dau vakadraunikau. Veikoro kece e Viti.*

Chris.: *Sa dina … eke talega e na vanua oqo?*

Mika.: *Eke talega e tu e so.*

Chris.: *Ia na ka dredre vei au…*

Mika.: *Io.*

Chris.: *… ko kila … vakacava?*

Mika.: *… ko kila … vakacava?*

Text 8

Chris.: *Ia, ko vakabauta Mikaele, ko sa tukuna vei au ni sa tiko eke e so. Ko kila vakacava ni sa tiko eso?*

Mika.: *Na i talanoa ga da rogoca. Na veitalanoa ga va oqo, va oqo, da rogoca.*

Chris.: *Ia, raica – oqo … na talanoa oqo, ko kila vinaka ni sa levu na – na cava na vosa? – na kakase.*

Mika.: *Io. Na kakase. Io. Dina oqori. Dina oqori. Kakase*

Chris.: *Levu.*

Mika.: *Kakase. Koya eda rogoca, koya na i talanoa me va oqo, talanoa me va oqo. E so era talanoa era via vakacacani, e? Spoil? Spoil each other? … E sega ni raica rawa e dua kena i vakadinadina.*

Text 9

Chris.: *Ia Italatala sa tukuna vei au ni sa dau tukuna vua <kua ni rere>.<Taura na ika, vakavinavinaka, vakasaqa. E na kana vinaka.> Sa sega ni vakabauta o koya na italanoa vaka oqo.*

Mika.: *Mmm. Ya na … ya na vakabauta vaka Viti.*

Makereta.: [wakes up, breaks in] *E sega ni rawa ni yali na ka ya vei keimami na kai Viti.*

...

Mika.: *O koya e sega ni rawa ni beitaka e dua na tamata. I talatala. O koya na ka kece sa kau mai, o koya na ciqoma. Sega ni rawa vakadua ni beitaka na tamata sega ni tukuna o koya <ka oqori, ka oqori, ka oqori>. Sega. O koya e na taura ga, e na vakavinavinaka. Oyo na nodra itovo kece na i talatala. Nodra itovo kece ga na italatala ni lotu, na ivakatawa, nodra i tovo kece ya. Era sega ni rawa ni vakaduiduitaka na tamata, ka kece e solia mai eke solia mai eke, era ciqoma. ... Ciqoma. Ciqoma. Ciqoma ka vakavinavinaka. ... Na vakabauta vaka ivola tabu, vaka lotu Karisito: kakua ni beitaka e dua na wekamu. Taura kece ga na ka e sa solia mai vei iko na wekamu.*

Text 10

Makereta.*... na ka ya era bula ga mai kina na neimami qase. Ra bula ga mai me ra vakalou kina kalou vu. ... E sega ni rogoca o ira tale eso vei keimami na lotu e na tiko ga e so na tamata era vakabauta tiko na kalou tani, kalou vu. Era na qarava, veitalia kevaka e curu tiko na vale ni lotu era qarava ga baleta oya a nodra kalou ga na neimami qase.*

Text 11

Au tara saka tu mada ga na wa ni tabua, ni bula vinaka na turaga e nodatou vanua, sautu tiko noda vanua me vanua veilomani, a rogoci tu mada ga na vosa. Mana e i dina (cobo).

AFTERWORD

QUESTIONS OF ('ZAFIMANIRY') ANTHROPOLOGY

Jonathan Parry

The preceding chapters have raised some very big issues. As explained in the Preface, it is Maurice Bloch's work that has inspired us to pose them; and it is therefore appropriate that our collection should close with an attempt to take stock of his view on the questions our discipline should address. And there can be no better place to begin than by asking: 'What is anthropology?' 'I know what it is', says Bloch (2000) in a characteristically forthright comment on postmodernist approaches to the discipline:

> I came across it, for example, while doing fieldwork in a Zafimaniry house between the Betsileo and Tanala areas southeast of Ambositra, Madagascar. On one fairly typical evening we were talking about the differences in vocabulary of different dialect groups and different funeral customs of, for example, Indians and Malagasy. But then we moved on to more general theoretical issues: whether we were descended from the same ancestors and if we were, how could it have come about that we had such different languages and customs? We discussed whether children of Malagasy who lived in France are true Malagasy and whether they would want their bodies to be brought back to their tombs; whether it is natural for men to want to have several wives or is that simply the product of custom; and whether all humans love their kinsmen equally, and so on. What we were talking about was, of course, anthropology.

With that kind of enquiry – 'Zafimaniry anthropology' for short – many of our most eminent disciplinary forebears, as well as a great many gurus not thought of as anthropologists, and indeed probably most people who have ever lived, have engaged. Not, though, the large proportion of post-anthropologists who occupy university positions in the subject. They often seem more interested in discussing Derrida and Lacan than in addressing such issues, about which Bloch wonders whether they 'have anything to say'.

The onslaught is renewed, and the front is widened, in a subsequent and more sustained piece with the provocative title, 'Where did anthropology go? Or the need for human nature' (Bloch 2005: ch.1). The discipline has succumbed to 'incoherent fragmentation' and become 'an assemblage of anecdotes' because it lost sight of the core questions that originally inspired it. What went wrong was that the investigation of human nature ceased to be at its centre. The reason for that was the (in an expanded sense) 'diffusionist' critique that blew the evolutionary certainties of the founders of the discipline away.

'Anthropology', as its *Encyclopaedia Britannica* entry by one of these founders began by explaining, is 'the science which … has as its object the study of man as a unit in the animal kingdom' (Tylor 1910). Despite the remarkable physiological resemblances between humans and their nearest primate relatives, they differ 'immeasurably in their endowments and capabilities'. Humans share a common nature; the differences between 'savage' and 'civilised' were ones only of degree. All that was required to explain them was their differential rate of 'progress' along the single-track line of evolution, for it is 'certain that there has been an inherent tendency in man … to develop culture by the same stages and in the same way' (ibid., p.119). On that premise, the pre-history of 'advanced nations' might be recovered through the study of contemporary 'primitive' peoples.

The 'diffusionist' challenge was based on the seemingly self-evident fact that if animals are largely governed by nature, humans are largely the product of culture, which is learned through a cumulative process of inter- and intra- generational transmission within the group, and by borrowing from other groups. Culture, as a consequence, is continually changing and highly variable. Two corollaries were drawn. As a result of the random and unpredictable nature of the myriad interactions from which people might learn, it no longer seemed plausible to postulate a single evolutionary path along which all must tread. It equally seemed clear that human nature could explain little about the enormous variety of social and cultural forms that actually exist – beyond, that is, the truism that they must all in some way be compatible with it. As a result, the investigation of human beings in general dropped off the anthropological agenda. Other disciplines moved in to fill the theoretical vacuum; and anthropology was left 'without the only centre it could have' (Bloch 2005: 9). But though the 'diffusionist' critique was substantially correct, the way in which it has been surreptitiously and unreflectingly extended into a view of culture as somehow floating free of nature (and especially of human nature) is both misleading and debilitating. If anthropology is to be anything at all, Bloch claims, it must return to the fundamental questions that originally motivated it, and must form a 'grand alliance' with cognate disciplines that also study them. Of these, he sees cognitive science and psychology as its most promising partners.

Though an aspiration rather than an accomplishment, for Bloch we are 'in the end ... a natural science' in search of universalistic explanations (Houtman 1988). An anthropological analysis must always be, at least implicitly, comparative; and Bloch has led from the front. In several publications (e.g. 1975a; 1980), the comparison is of a carefully controlled kind, between the two Malagasy groups amongst whom he has done intensive fieldwork: the Merina, irrigated rice cultivators who during the course of the nineteenth century developed a powerful state that dominated much of the island; and the Zafimaniry, a much smaller-scale and less stratified forest-dwelling society of swidden farmers. In all likelihood, we are told (1980: 118), modern Merina society grew out of a social formation that had once been very like that of the Zafimaniry today. Elsewhere, the comparative sweep is wider, contrasting – to pick a couple of examples at random – the social implications of literacy in Japan and Madagascar (1998: ch.10); and ideas about history and personhood, and about the way in which the past intrudes into the present, amongst an elite group of traditional literati in the Yemen with the ideas of poor Bicolanos in the central Philippines, the Merina providing an intermediate case (ibid., ch.5). Most ambitious of all, however, is the general model of ritual elaborated in *Prey into hunter* (1992) which explores the relationship between ritual, violence and political domination, calling on ethnography from several parts of the globe. Bloch consistently goes for the big issues: 'How can people imagine an alternative social order, and act to change the one they have, if (as most sociological theories of knowledge suppose) all their conceptual categories are products of the latter?' 'Why do some societies have more ritual than others?' (1989a: chs.1 and 5). 'Why do people the world over think that sacrificing domestic animals cures sickness?' (1992).

For many anthropologists – take Geertz (1975; 1980) or Dumont (1970) – the real interest lies in difference. Early in his career, Geertz was deeply influenced by Weber; while Dumont claims inspiration from Mauss, in particular for his stress on the difference between 'modern' and 'traditional' societies (Dumont 1986: 4). Bloch's preoccupation, by contrast, is with similarity, and he is distinctly uneasy with this kind of sharp divide and downright hostile to the Weberian emphasis on 'the uniqueness of the West'. In this respect at least, he owes more to the posthumous influence of Malinowski, one of the founders of the LSE anthropology department in which he was originally trained, than he owes to either Mauss (his senior kinsman as it happens) or to Marx (his adopted intellectual ancestor). While Malinowski was concerned to stress what the 'savage' and 'civilised' share, both Mauss and Marx succumbed to the temptation to turn 'primitive' man into the antithesis of the modern.[1]

Consistent with this general preoccupation with similarities, the central problem to which Bloch repeatedly returns in his most recent collection of essays (2005) is that of accounting for 'partial recurrences' or 'incomplete regularities'. This refers to the fact that extremely similar sets of symbolic associations, representations and ritualised behaviours recur in societies that are widely separated in space and time and that have had little or no contact with each other. The details, however, differ so that we cannot speak of identical phenomena. Such is the case, for example, with the widespread association between ideas of commensality and poisoning (ibid., ch.4); and with the 'privileged aggression' which a sister's son is expected to display towards his mother's brother in many patrilineal systems (ibid., ch.9). Most contemporary anthropologists have given up on the challenge of trying to explain such recurrences. Bloch seeks to show (and there are perhaps shades here of Lévi-Strauss) that what accounts for them is some more or less universal existential problem that is, almost everywhere, likely to force itself on human attention. Thus, the association between commensality and poisoning is a surface manifestation of the tension between the necessity of incorporating outsiders and the dangers of doing so. 'Ritual snatching' by the sister's son from the sacrifice performed by his mother's brother indexes the contradiction between a rule of patrilineal descent and the universal propensity of human beings to recognise the bilaterality of kin relations. It is because of such propensities that representations and practices of this sort are *likely* to catch on and get stabilised – though there is no mechanical necessity for them to do so. Whether or not they 'take' is contingent on the different histories of different groups, which is also what explains why the details of each case are seldom the same. Broadly, then, similarities are the product of conundrums and dilemmas that human beings, everywhere, face; differences are down to history and to specific politico-economic conditions. I come back to this split in analytical strategy below.

Anthropology, then, is part of a collective endeavour with other social science disciplines. There is no great divide between 'modern' and 'traditional' societies, large-scale and small-scale ones, or those with history and those without. What makes anthropology distinctive, however, is that its historical roots and empirical focus have forced it to be less irredeemably Eurocentric than its sister disciplines. What justifies its institutionalisation in separate university departments is purely pragmatic. Such are the demands of 'relevance' and the constraints of funding that if anthropology departments specialising in the study of societies outside the Euro-American world did not exist, they would hardly get studied at all. That would exclude most of humanity, both past and present (Houtman 1988). Yet despite Bloch's determination to downplay the differences between the kinds of societies on which sociologists and anthropologists have traditionally specialised, and despite his militant comparativism, it is striking that he rarely calls on comparative examples from the modern West and nowhere does he do so in a sustained way. It is, again, a point I will return to. The neglect of the 'advanced' industrialised world in general allows us to beg some crucial questions posed by his theory of ideology.

That theory, and here I jump ahead of myself to make a limited point about fieldwork, is premised on an insistence on the heterogeneity of human knowledge and on the different generative mechanisms that produce it. The central distinction is between ideological representations and the concepts and categories that people deploy in their everyday lives. While the former are a refraction of the social order, tend to be culturally specific and therefore mark difference, the latter are acquired through a more individualistic process of learning, are of a more universalistic kind and, therefore, reveal strong similarities between cultures. This distinction was first explicitly elaborated in a Malinowski lecture delivered in 1976 (1989a: ch.1), and with certain refinements and modifications has been a central theme in Bloch's work ever since. Much of it has concentrated on the way in which ideological knowledge is constructed through ritual, which underwrites social hierarchy in pre-capitalist societies. The more you have of one, the more you have of the other.

In the essays reprinted in *How we think they think* (1998), however, the focus shifts to the more everyday forms of knowledge, which are recognised as having been under-theorised in earlier work. A large proportion of this knowledge is implicit and is seldom, if ever, verbalised – either because 'it goes without saying' or because (like knowing how to drive a car) it is stored in a non-linguistic form that makes it difficult to put into words. The key questions concern the relationship between this implicit and often unconscious kind of knowledge on the one hand, and knowledge that is explicit and conscious on the other. The key proposition is that culture consists in much more than that which is consciously cognised, and that implicit knowledge is 'perhaps more fundamental' to it. What people say is not the same as what they know; and the most important things they know are often unspoken. Real knowledge of Zafimaniry culture is not contained in their linguistic statements, but in all sorts of practices and unverbalised assumptions that concern, for example, the house and the nature of wood.

How, then, is the anthropologist to access such knowledge? The most important part of the answer is perhaps surprisingly traditional: through the tried and tested anthropological technique of long-term participant observation. The ethnographer must learn as the people studied have learned, by a prolonged and sometimes painful process of socialisation that will (to some degree at least) enable him or her to see the world through their eyes. Though impatient with the fetishisation of fieldwork as an end in itself, Bloch himself has proved a highly committed, and remarkably insightful, ethnographer who – unlike many armchair-bound senior professors – has regularly returned to the field throughout his career.

A good example of the pay-off is a paper entitled 'Time, narratives and the multiplicity of representations of the past' (1998: ch.7) in which he discusses Zafimaniry historical memory and narrative genres. Its centrepiece is an account of the ways in which the inhabitants of the village in which he subsequently lived talk of the terrors and deprivations they experienced in the aftermath of the 1947 rebellion against the French colonial forces. What emerges is a striking contrast between two narrative styles. The first is the 'official' account told in formal public contexts. In this, events are subordinated to 'a well-honed cultural pattern' and made to accord with timeless values and beliefs. Events are subordinated to structure (in the manner of Sahlins 1985) and the Zafimaniry might be taken as an exemplar of Lévi-Strauss's category of 'cold' societies that represent themselves as living outside history. One might even suppose that they have a static and non-cumulative conception of time. But Bloch also recounts an occasion on which he and his adoptive father were caught for some hours in the pouring rain in a small field hut overlooking the landscape on which the villagers' drama had been enacted. The narrative elicited now was of a very different character. Events were presented as contingent, the account itself was open to question and puzzled reflection, and from it one would have concluded that the Zafimaniry inhabit a 'hot' society that locates itself in the mid-stream of history. Nor are these the only narrative styles in their repertoire. It would therefore be plainly absurd to suppose that any one type of narrative 'can be equated with Zafimaniry cognition of the past', or to claim on that basis that they have a view of time and history that is exotically different from our own. Conclusions of that kind are an artefact of the limited type of data (literary representations, theological texts or historical documents) on which those who have proposed them have focused (Sahlins and Ricoeur being singled out). It's a cautionary tale for anthropologists who, by emulating literary critics, philosophers and historians, sell their birthright (as participants and observers in everyday life) 'for a mess of quasi-literary thin gruel'. It is also as powerful a demonstration as one might find of the advantages of the 'field view' over the 'book view' of society (to borrow M.N. Srinivas's contrast).

But behind Bloch's preference for the 'field view' there is, as I see it, not only a judgement on method. There is also a question of temperament, even of moral choice. Anthropology matters because it is the most consistently 'democratic' of the social science disciplines, the one that has shown the greatest commitment to trying to understand the daily existence of ordinary people in their total context (rather than focus more narrowly on their political, economic or religious lives). In a brief note on 'intellectual roots' (in Borofsky 1994: 283), Bloch records his continuing conviction (a legacy from childhood influences) that 'the dominated are more interesting and valuable than the dominators'. It was a French children's book about the sufferings of a Muslim boy under colonialism that first made him want to study the lives of the colonised; and amongst the most formative *intellectual* influences on his anthropological thinking were several Malagasy villagers. True, his theory of ritual shares something with that of Radcliffe-Brown and other 'functionalists', in that the authoritative interpretation is that of the anthropologist and the 'real' meaning is, for the most part, hidden from the participants. But on the other hand, the fundamental questions of the discipline are 'Zafimaniry questions' – questions about which ordinary people all over the world are likely to speculate. Nor is it unimportant that he has consistently avoided the cliquish private argot that makes some anthropological writing seem gobbledegook to non-specialist readers (and to not a few anthropologists as well). Bloch's own writing is direct, clear and entirely without unnecessary obfuscation. A deeply 'democratic' impulse inspires his methodological commitments, the fundamental questions to which he wants answers, the kind of analysis he favours and the style in which he addresses his readers.

* * *

The present volume was never conceived as a conventional Festschrift for Bloch, though it is intended as an affectionate and admiring tribute to him. Contributors were invited to follow his lead in starting from their own field experience to raise some general question of a 'Zafimaniry' kind that might be of interest not only to their professional colleagues but also to a student and non-anthropological audience. This was to be addressed in an, at least implicitly, comparative framework, and in as 'democratically' accessible a way as possible. In deference to Bloch's own impatience with the kind of self-referential anthropology that is more interested in the theorist than in the real world situation to which the theory supposedly relates, our authors were also discouraged from directing themselves to the thoughts and writings of Bloch himself, being asked to focus, instead, on the sorts of question that he is concerned to ask. Apart from this Afterword, the only chapter that has devoted any significant space to his work is the one by Cannell, who has as an alibi in that she is writing on a topic so central to it. In any case, in a volume inspired by Bloch some resistance to authority must be expected, and readers will judge for themselves how far the editors' brief has been met.

With the exception of Lambek and myself, and though from a range of age-sets, all of the contributors were taught by Bloch as students, and all but one of these completed doctorates under his supervision. That perhaps makes it necessary to reiterate the point made in the Preface that there is no 'party line' that runs through this collection. I doubt, for example, that all of our authors would unreservedly sign up to his recent manifesto-style statement about the study of human nature being the only centre that anthropology can have. Each of their essays speaks clearly for itself, and it is not my intention to review them all here. But by briefly – and perhaps invidiously – picking on three, I aim to emphasise that they sometimes take very different theoretical positions, both from each other and from Bloch.

Cannell confronts him directly for developing a theory of ritual that downplays the significance of religious experience and of the emotion that ritual engenders. These, as she shows, are central to the way in which her Bicolano Catholic and US Mormon informants talk about ritual, and to how it matters to them. That granted, however, it, to me, remains unclear how emotions would help us explain either the structure or the symbolic content of the rite – why, for example, the Merina elders blow *water* in blessing, and what logic connects their blessings with the fertility of the land and the descent group.

But, be that as it may, the more general claim that Cannell wants to make is that Bloch's general model of ritual is not general at all. It is an unconscious product of (Protestant) ascetic Christianity that stresses the opposition between body and spirit, and that purifies the soul by mortifying the flesh in a quest for transcendence of the mundane world.[2] The violent transcendence of the body, and the hostility to physical life, that is built into Bloch's model is, in reality, nothing more than a vision of the world derived from a particular, and not at all representative, strand of Christianity. This is now peddled as an analysis of ritual (and indeed of religion) in general; but not without first being filtered through Althusserian Marxism, and inverted. It is, now, not the physical material world that is the enemy, but rather the 'spirit' and the transcendent world, which are revealed as instruments of domination and oppression. Bloch is, however, not the only anthropologist to fall into this kind of trap. Cannell also instances Evans-Pritchard's disregard of emotion, which she sees as stemming from the same source; and it is perhaps worth remembering that Bloch himself (2005: ch.7) has chided Sperber and Boyer for unconsciously basing their arguments about the counter-intuitive (and therefore attention-grabbing) character of religious beliefs on a Christian view of religion.

The implications, as Cannell suggests, are radical. Bloch's model of ritual is no less an 'ideological production' than the Mormon and Bicolano understandings she has discussed. Anthropological writing about religion has proved incapable of transcending Christianity. What she does not acknowledge, however, is that some of this writing – including much that is highly distinguished – has for many decades been produced by anthropologists who do not come from cultural milieus that are Christian. Though it *might* make sense to argue that Srinivas's analysis of Coorg religion (1952) was unable to escape a Brahmanical view of Hinduism, it makes none to suggest that he unconsciously filtered it through a sieve of Christian theology. If the first of these claims were admitted, however, it would certainly support Cannell's more far-reaching (and depressing) conclusion. What is most fundamentally at stake is the very possibility of the kind of secular social science to which Bloch, as heir to an Enlightenment ethic, has been committed.

Of all the papers in this volume, Astuti's discussion of Vezo ideas (we are back in Madagascar) about what happens to people after death is probably most congenial to Bloch's recent preoccupations. I want to suggest, however, that it also raises some of the most difficult questions for his general theory. Summarised baldly, Astuti's interest is in how the Vezo manage to simultaneously hold in their heads and articulate two, apparently contradictory, notions about post-mortem existence – that some aspect of the person survives, and that life is extinguished and 'you are dead when you are dead'. What her data – based on an experimental methodology borrowed from cognitive psychology – seem to show is the extreme fragility of the more 'theological' view that life continues beyond death, and its high degree of dependence on context. Children learn this theory well after they have learned that death is the end of all sentient life; and it seems that it is this latter understanding that 'continues to act as a default, which can be successfully challenged and overcome only in limited contexts'. These are pre-eminently ritual ones, when what counts is to properly perform the ritual prescribed. In line with Bloch, and at odds with the two cases Cannell discusses, what people think and feel at the time is irrelevant and it really does not matter whether they have different ideas about the afterlife. During the ritual they stop speculating, suspend disbelief and defer to custom. As long as they do that, Astuti concludes, 'the dead will continue to find a space to live on in the minds of their living descendants'.

In relation to Bloch's wider theory of ritual, two issues trouble me. The first is that that theory supposes that ritual is the crucible in which ideology is forged. Ritual is, therefore, the domain in which hierarchy is legitimated and political domination is 'naturalised'. But if ritual representations are really as fragile as Astuti's material suggests, and if people so readily revert – once outside that frame – to the default position that 'you are dead when you are dead' (and that ancestors do not, therefore, really exist), we must surely wonder how well ideology really serves power. To deserve the name, domination must surely work in the everyday world; but the ideas and values that underwrite it appear to fade very rapidly.

It is, of course, true – and this brings me to a related question – that Vezo society is less hierarchical than that of the Merina. Following Bloch's theory, one would therefore expect its ritual life to be less elaborated and less ideologically overpowering (and this does indeed seem consistent with the ethnography). But that suggests the possibility that Astuti's results are significantly inflected by what one might call 'social structure', 'political economy' or even 'society'. Were she to repeat her experiment amongst the Merina, the 'default position' might be shown to be set at a much higher threshold (to be, that is, considerably weaker). It is even perhaps possible that if she tried it out on Banarasi Brahmans, the majority fallback response would include details of the precise dimensions of the ('needle-sized') mouths of ghosts. It is, in short, possible that Astuti's results tell us at least as much about the nature of *Vezo society* as about the invariant cognitive nature of human beings and their propensity to return, by default, to a no-nonsense pragmatic view of the world that is uncontaminated by ideology.[3] Even if we agree that knowledge of that kind exists (and not all of Bloch's critics would do so), his own theory seems to suggest that the amount of mental space it is allowed to occupy must vary considerably between societies of different sorts.

Not only in that light, but also on more general grounds I am about to come to and that have to do with its importance in Bloch's earlier work, it is striking that 'society' (including 'social structure' and 'organisation'), to say nothing of 'political economy', makes only an occasional and fleeting cameo appearance in these essays offered in his honour. The most obvious exception is the chapter by Rival that, at various points, clearly attempts to relate the ideas and practices she describes (in this case surrounding sexuality) to the structure of (Huaorani) society. More importantly, it is the one that most obviously begins to put the comparative issue in the context of a consideration of the different forms of social organisation found in the other two (Amazonian) groups she discusses. In the end, however, Rival's central interest, too, is in invariant cross-cultural continuities (in similarities across societies of very different sorts in the way in which sexuality is expressed in everyday 'domestic' contexts).

What makes this relegation of considerations about social structure and political economy to the background surprising is that Bloch was the editor of *Marxist analyses and social anthropology* (1975b) and the author of *Marxism and anthropology* (1983). His first monograph (1971) devoted detailed attention to the way in which dispersed members of the Merina descent group attempted to deal with the precariousness of their political and economic lives. These conditions encouraged them to sustain an idealised and unchanging image of the descent group, which centrally involved the re-incorporation of their dead into ancestral tombs located on ancestral land. Amongst his influential early essays are ones dealing with the relationship between the morality of kinship and the demands of economic interest (1973), and with the close fit between the conceptual and symbolic worlds of the Merina and the Zafimaniry and their modes of production (1975a and 1980). In later work, however, Bloch has himself been concerned to downplay that fit, and to emphasise the relative autonomy of the symbolic order. Political economy and social organisation and structure seem to have faded into the background in the quest for cognitive universals. In the space that remains to me I want to look in more detail at this trajectory, and to try to suggest that *some* of the questions of anthropology that are still most worth asking are the ones that were more directly addressed in Bloch's earlier writings.

* * *

It would not be difficult to construct a story of almost seamless continuity and development in Bloch's thinking from *Placing the dead* (1971), through his major writings on ritual, to his more recent essays on implicit knowledge and 'partial recurrences'. The central theme of that first monograph was the negation of history and the construction, through ritual, of a timeless social order that is at radical odds with everyday life. In theoretical essays that followed, this contrast between the ideal order and the one that actually obtains is associated with different types of knowledge. Initially these were distinguished as 'ritual discourse', which is socially determined, mystifies reality and legitimates inequality; and 'practical discourse', which is based on cognitive universals, allows people to apprehend the world as it 'really' is, and – in the right politico-economic circumstances – provides them with an intellectual resource for criticising and perhaps even changing their society ([1977] 1989a: ch.1). The next crucial step ([1985] 1989a: ch.5) was to look more closely at the way in which these disparate modes of thought are interrelated, and to develop a model of the way in which ritual transforms cognition ('practical discourse') into ideology ('ritual discourse'). Drawing heavily, also, on ideas about the distinctive nature of ritual communication that had been worked out in an earlier paper ([1974] 1989a: ch.2), and that reflected Bloch's engagement with the recent literature in linguistics, this model was then applied – in *From blessing to violence* (1986a) – to a detailed case study of Merina circumcision rituals over a two-hundred-year span of history. It was then ambitiously generalised in *Prey into hunter* (1992), where it was applied in a variety of different ethnographic settings to a variety of different types of ritual (initiation, sacrifice, marriage and mortuary rites amongst others). Despite their surface heterogeneity, the form that these rituals take turns out to be almost monotonously familiar. The reason is that they all attack – with the same limited symbolic armoury – the same fundamental problem: that of constructing an enduring and transcendent social order in the face of the fact that the human elements of which it is composed are transient biological beings. We are already dealing with 'partial recurrences', other examples of which are explored in more recent essays, and which are again related back to constants in the human condition.

What this picture of smooth consistency conceals, however, is some significant shifts of emphasis. The one to which I want to draw particular attention is in the way the relationship between representations and political economy is conceptualised.

In his brief but insightful history of the relationship between Marxism and anthropology (1983), Bloch argued that a worthwhile Marxist anthropology was something still to be *developed* through the application of methods and insights that the founders of Marxism had deployed in their analysis of capitalism, rather than something to be *recovered* from their now obsolete writings on pre-class societies. The enduring value of these is vitiated by the rhetorical use to which Marx and Engels had put the limited ethnographic materials at their disposal to show that there is nothing eternal about the institutions of bourgeois society. 'Primitive' societies were supposedly classless societies characterised by the absence of private property, exploitation, the family and the state. Not only were significant parts of that picture wrong, but it also deprived them of everything distinctive in their analytical armoury when it came to such societies. Recent work by French anthropologists had, however, shown the way out of this impasse by showing how a class analysis might be fruitfully applied in such contexts.

What, surprisingly, did not appear to trouble him was that much of this work – Terray (1975) is a good example – sets out to demonstrate that in this kind of world 'classes in themselves' were unlikely to become 'classes for themselves' conscious of their interests in opposition to those of other classes. Since in Marxian theory it is class conflict that provides its dynamic, that leaves such societies stranded by history. Marxian tools are made to serve structural-functionalist ends: the analysis centres on the way that they reproduce themselves.

Though Bloch's own work also centred on reproduction, its focus was not in fact on the detailed, on the ground, reality of relations between classes. What he, more crucially, took from Marx was the handle that the concepts of ideology, alienation and commodity fetishism could provide for an understanding of Merina *representations* of society. These were shown to be a kind of back-to-front picture of the world that masks reality, makes the image of society constructed in ritual seem natural and unquestionable, and thereby legitimises inequality. The powers and creativity that belong to the living are alienated to the ancestors, the ancestral land and the tombs. Human labour is devalued; the tombs take on the role that capital and money possess in the ideology of capitalism (e.g. Bloch 1989b). They are the 'real' source of increase and productivity. In fact, they go one better than capital in that they are not only the ultimate guarantors of material production but of human reproduction as well.

Where does this mystification come from? In earlier papers the answer seems clear: from the critical role that slavery played in the political economy. Though they had earlier held slaves (mostly other Merina) on a comparatively small-scale, their direct and heavy involvement in the international slave trade dramatically took off towards the end of the eighteenth century. By now, most of these slaves were captives from other groups, and most were traded with Europeans for guns. It was an upward spiral: guns meant more slaves meant more guns... But at the same time, the Merina agrarian economy was, itself, becoming increasingly dependent on their labour. By the mid-eighteenth century (Berg 1986), the Merina state had embarked on large-scale irrigation and hydraulic works to which slave labour was crucial. Moreover, as the state expanded and more and more free Merina were drafted as soldiers or employed in its administration, more and more slaves were required to replace their labour on descent group land. When the international trade in slaves was eventually suppressed, domestic consumption shot up. Demand remained high; and supply was guaranteed by the fact that, for reasons of realpolitik (and despite the self-denying ordinance that precluded the acceptance of slaves in lieu), the British continued to provision the Merina with modern weapons. In fact, they now had a more complete monopoly on them since their competitors could no longer acquire guns for slaves. By the end of the nineteenth century, more than half the population in the Merina heartlands were probably slaves, and the dominant relation of production was between freemen and slaves. For present purposes, however, the crucial point is that the growing importance of slavery changed the way in which production was ideologically represented. Labour was radically devalued and free Merina *no longer* represented reproduction as the product of it, but rather of 'an ever more mystical and abstract relation to their ancestral lands' (Bloch 1980: 131). In short, the representations of fertility and increase radically changed. Before slavery really took off, they were (correctly) understood to come from labour; and only subsequently from the now fetishised land and tombs. The ideas appear to be an epiphenomenon of material conditions and to change in direct response to politico-economic circumstance.

Much the same argument was elaborated in an earlier paper (1975a) that correlated differences in the property and kinship systems of the Merina and the Zafimaniry with differences in their modes of production. Though on a less ambitious scale, its general thesis anticipated Goody (1976) by a neck. The broad character of the productive regime (Zafimaniry swidden agriculture versus Merina irrigated rice cultivation) is causally related to the very different way in which property relations are represented in the two groups (as a relationship between people in the first case, and in the mystified form of a relationship between people and things in the second). These different property systems in turn generate crucial differences in the kinship and marriage systems (even though the two groups operate with almost identical kinship terminologies). As with Goody, gross differences in the systems of agricultural production are associated with differences in the system of property rights, which are in turn correlated with differences in kinship and marriage.

As with Goody also – consider, for example, his discussion of the symbolic antagonism between horses and the shrines of the earth throughout the savannah grasslands of West Africa (1971: ch.4) – past politico-economic realities linger on in contemporary ideological representations. Thus slavery as the dominant relation of production in the fairly recent Merina past is what allows labour to be ideologically disregarded, and the ancestral land – and the tombs that root the descent group in it – to be fetishised. And it is 'this false representation of production [that] reproduces Merina social organisation' (Bloch 1975a: 208). It explains, for example, the premium that is put on descent group endogamy (lest, given bilateral inheritance, land be lost to it). It also explains why the domestic unit (with its individualised property interests) is seen as a threat to the unity of the descent group (and its collective rights in the land), and why the former is subjected to symbolic assault and denigration in many Merina rituals. In the Zafimaniry case, by contrast, production is properly understood to be the product of labour, and the domestic unit is not seen as a threat to anything. Until, at least, the Zafimaniry turn to irrigated rice cultivation (as some have been forced to do). When that happens the kinship and marriage system begins to metamorphose into something very like that of the Merina.[4]

Compare all this with the subsequent analysis of Merina circumcision rituals (1986a). No longer a reflection of the mode of production, what is now emphasised is the autonomy of the symbolic order – at least in terms of its content – from the world of material production. Despite major changes in political economy over the same period, the symbolism of these rites and their basic structure had hardly changed between the earliest account we have of them from the beginning of the nineteenth century[5] to Bloch's own field observations of the 1960s and early 1970s.

In broad-brush terms, these rituals construct an image of an ideal order, free from time and death. They do so by negating and devaluing the ordinary everyday world, physical life and biological processes. This involves violent symbolic assaults on the household, women and the powers of the wild, represented pre-eminently by *vazimba* spirits. The problem that ritual has to recognise, however, is that in the workaday world the vitality that these represent cannot be dispensed with entirely. It is not quite possible to transcend that world until you are dead. The *vazimba*, and all that they stand for (including matrilineal descent), must first be dramatically driven out, but are then recovered under violent control. The rituals thus proceed in three stages. The everyday world that must be transcended is represented in a heightened and exaggerated form. The boy to be circumcised is portrayed as the progeny of his mother alone, the product of purely matrilineal descent. This world is then subjected to violent and chaotic assault. The third phase restores order by revealing that the boy is 'really' the fruit of ancestral blessings, reincorporates the vitality that had earlier been driven out in a subdued and subordinated form, and turns the initiand himself into one of the vanquishers. It is supposedly an illustration of the way in which ritual transforms ordinary everyday knowledge into ideology. It is not, however, obvious that this is quite what occurs. Babies aren't really born without the intervention of men, and the way in which the world is represented in the initial phase of the ritual is already ideologically constructed. It is not so much a matter of ideology emerging out of 'practical discourse' as of one ideology trumping another.

However that may be, the central claim that the *symbolic content* of the ritual has remained remarkably constant over a considerable period is meticulously substantiated (even if – as I will shortly suggest – it would be unwise to assume that this symbolic stasis goes back any further than the documents show). The influence of politico-economic developments on it was negligible. When it comes to the *scale* and *functions* of the ritual, however, these developments are shown to have been crucial. At some historical junctures, circumcision was an almost furtive domestic rite that could hardly have buttressed the authority of more than a handful of elders in the local arena. At others it became a massive state ritual that pivoted around the ruling monarch, involved the army in crucial roles, represented the whole kingdom as one giant descent group, and played up the symbolic conquest of savage external powers. It became, that is, 'a celebration of Merina aggression towards neighbours and outsiders' (Bloch 1986b: 352). In short, at different times the ritual is appropriated to the purposes of different types of authority figure and used to legitimate different forms of domination. It can do that only, Bloch argues, because of the distinctive nature of ritual communication which makes it impossible to argue with its vague and mystical assertions about the nature of the world, which protects these assertions from sceptical scrutiny and which prevents their counter-intuitive character from coming to the fore. It is also this that gives the content of ritual its remarkable durability through time.

When this model is then generalised in *Prey into hunter*, the disjunction between symbolic content and political function must necessarily emerge even more sharply for the obvious reason that the societies to which it is applied are so different. Representations that were the product of political economy in earlier essays now reflect constants in the human condition.

But there is, perhaps, still something to be said for the first of these views. In his *Current Anthropology* comment on *From blessing to violence*, the historian of Madagascar, Gerald Berg (1986), had suggested as much. By the middle of the eighteenth century, large-scale irrigation had begun to bring about a major transformation in Merina land ownership. The rights of individual households were progressively appropriated by the descent group hierarchies that constructed and maintained the irrigation systems. Over time, too, Merina monarchs assumed an increasingly 'dominant position in the ordering of land use'. Rather than there being any clear disjunction between the symbolic order and politico-economic reality, there was in fact a close fit between them. The ritual devaluation of the domestic unit and the exaltation of the descent group hierarchy are entirely consistent with what had gone on with regard to land rights.

Bloch's response was robustly dismissive (1986b). He doubted that evidence could be found to show that the anti-household symbolism of the rituals was a response to these changes; and it is, anyway, so widespread in Madagascar that it is not satisfactory to account for it in terms of Merina specificities. If, moreover, the symbolism is explained in that way, it is difficult to see why it should have persisted when politico-economic circumstances changed yet again. But this rebuttal was perhaps inconclusive. Even in the absence of direct evidence, Berg's suggestion seems just as convincing as Bloch's no better-substantiated, but still highly plausible, argument that the fetishisation of the land and the tombs was a consequence of slavery. As to the anti-house symbolism, it was Bloch himself who had shown that for politico-economic reasons this made no sense in the Zafimaniry context. And on his own evidence again, it is not at all hard to imagine why that symbolism persists in the modern world. An ideologically undivided descent group provides its highly dispersed membership with a network of crucial links with the administration and with business all over the island (1971, 1980), and this social capital is plainly jeopardised if people's loyalties contract in on the household.

Berg's line of argument might be extended. The wild untamed power that the *vazimba* represent, and that is subdued and appropriated during the course of the ritual, seems like a fairly transparent allegory of the real dependence of Merina society on slaves raided from neighbouring peoples. In the founding myth of the ritual, the king who originates it is able to vanquish the *vazimba* by virtue of his superior technology (in the myth – iron; in history – guns). His own mother was a *vazimba* queen and is described as small, dark and curly-haired – which is just how contemporary Merina picture people of slave descent (1986a: 106; 1971: 3–4). In the ritual, the plants that represent *vazimba* power must (like slaves) be violently stolen; and are of species that reproduce parthogenetically, and that are, therefore, considered to be matrilineal. The logic of free Merina representations would suggest that so, too, are slaves since they do not have 'proper' descent groups or ancestors. Nor presumably, since slaves might be sold, did they have proper descendants – which is one definition of *vazimba* (ibid., p.42). What I am suggesting, then, is that *vazimbas* are the mystical counterparts of the victims of Merina slavery and that their ritual treatment is an accurate reflection of the reality on which the expansionist Merina state was founded. It is, therefore, significant that the earliest account of the ritual that Bloch has to call on post-dates the rapid expansion of its role in the slave trade. Though we cannot be sure, it seems likely – as Bloch himself acknowledges (ibid., p.113) – that the royal decree on which this account was supposedly based had instituted significant innovations in the form of the ritual. What is certainly the case is that it became a major state cult at precisely the point at which the Merina army 'was killing, pillaging and enslaving on a terrifying scale and with horrible brutality' (ibid., p.192).

In her paper for this volume, Cannell wonders whether Bloch's model of ritual really derives from 'traditional' Merina religion, from Merina Christianity or from the unconscious impact of Christian teaching on Bloch himself. To me it seems likely that its *ultimate* source is Merina slavery. But for the model to be made ready for export, its connection with such circumstances had to be severed. The quest for generality, and the Holy Grail of human universals, requires their relegation into the long grass of penumbral factors that explain only the uses to which the ritual is put and the incompleteness of 'incomplete regularities'.

To summarise: I have tried to identify a significant shift in Bloch's thinking between his earlier and later writings, with *From blessing to violence* as the crucial watershed. In the earlier Bloch, the symbolic order tended to be portrayed as more or less directly responsive to politico-economic circumstance. Thus, with the rapid growth of slavery, the Merina '*no more*' saw labour as the source of reproduction but attributed it rather to the fetishised land and the tombs. Thus, it is a particular productive regime, through the mediation of a particular representation of property rights, that gives rise to the way in which the Merina household is depicted in ritual as anti-social. In emphasising this 'functionalist fit', however, I certainly do not intend to accuse Bloch of the functionalist error he had so effectively criticised in one of his earliest articles – the error of assuming that 'the cause of social facts is the uses to which they are put' (Bloch 1973). The authority of the elders is a *consequence* of the fetishisation of the land and the tombs, not the cause of it (for which it was the rise of slavery that was the crucial necessary condition). By the time we get to the watershed monograph on Merina circumcision ritual and to *Prey into hunter,* however, the position has changed. The core symbolic elements of which the ritual is made must somehow have been 'always' there since they are products of perennial human problems of a universal nature. Though politico-economic circumstances may tell us almost everything we need to know about how these symbolic sequences are picked up and used, they tell us almost nothing about their content or how they are constituted. My argument has been that Bloch's own ethnography provides reason to doubt this, and that there is much to be said for the earlier view. That lays me wide open, I recognise, to the charge of retreating into what might be pejoratively dismissed as a species of 'easy functionalism' that searches for a 'fit' between the two orders, and from which Bloch has been concerned to distance himself. But as I will suggest in a moment, that fit sometimes seems closer and more plausible than that postulated between some putative cognitive universal and the symbolic practices it is held to illuminate.

The ritual domain has been central to so much of Bloch's work because of the fundamental place he sees it as having in pre-industrial society. It is the principal locus for the production of ideology, and thus performs the role played in industrial societies by Althusser's ideological state apparatuses – the educational system, the church, the mass media and so forth (e.g. Bloch 1989a: ch.5). So great, in fact, is the ideological influence that is attributed to it that the unwary reader is liable to be seduced into almost forgetting the more secular sources of domination that buttress its message – the land, the guns, the slaves and the standing army. At a number of points, Bloch draws direct inspiration from Marx and Engels on *The German ideology* (1947). But at a number of points, too, he seems to come uncomfortably close to ignoring their main message – that 'primary causes' do *not* lie in the realm of ideas.

What his theory of ritual brilliantly provides is a powerful purchase on the way in which ritual communication makes its ideological message seem – within the ritual frame itself – unquestionably authoritative. Where it is, in my view, less compelling (as I have already indicated) is in explaining how that ideology continues to persuade in the everyday world in the face of the resistance it meets from other forms of knowledge. For ritual to have the significance that Bloch claims for it, it must clearly do that, and again one wonders what part other non-ritual sources of persuasion might play in the process. If domination requires rituals to legitimate it, it is equally the case that rituals require domination to make them authoritative (cf. Asad 1979).

In line with either proposition, it is not surprising that when Bloch writes on the Merina, ritual is a central preoccupation; but when it comes to the less hierarchical Zafimaniry he has relatively little to say on the subject. The focus is, rather, on more everyday symbols and practices as providing a privileged window on their world – the house (1998, 2005) and the naming system (2006), for example. Zafimaniry understandings of these matters are plainly socially constructed (rather than manifestations of 'practical discourse' based on cognitive universals). Presumably, they should, therefore, be regarded as 'ideological', though the point is not explicitly addressed. Either way, however, they certainly seem to be an important part of what is called 'culture', and their centrality in it does not appear to be produced in ritual. That seems to suggest that ritual may not, after all, be so important in creating non-intuitive knowledge in many pre-industrial societies.

In industrial societies, we can infer, it is *relatively* unimportant. 'Ideological state apparatuses' do the job instead.[6] But whether these are really analogous mechanisms is not discussed. The implication, however, is that they differ significantly. In the pre-industrial world, ideology is forged in ritual; and the nature of ritual communication makes it uniquely immune to change and to challenge. But what then of the industrial world where ritual is no longer the principal locus for the production of ideology? Are we to conclude that ideology must work very differently, and is less 'arthritic' and inflexible? And if that is the case, would it not in some measure justify the stress on difference between 'modern' and 'traditional' societies that Bloch is so suspicious of? It was with such issues in mind that I earlier suggested that his lack of comparative attention to the modern industrial world results in an evasion of crucial issues raised by his theory.

Questions of this kind concern difference; but – as we have seen – the focus of Bloch's attention in his recent work is on regularities, and his agenda for anthropology is that it should return to its roots as the study of human nature in general. But as my comments on Astuti's contribution to this volume were intended to suggest, it is often difficult to be sure how much of what anthropologists observe can be attributed to this source.

An illustration of this is the paper by Bloch and Sperber that I referred to earlier. This deals with the 'privileged aggression' that, in a number of patrilineal systems, the sister's son is expected to display towards his mother's brother, whose property he snatches. To recapitulate, this was interpreted as a surface expression of an underlying contradiction between the universal propensity postulated by socio-biological theory to recognise kinship bilaterally, and a rule of patrilineal descent that precludes inheritance from the mother's group. This contradiction makes it possible for such a custom to 'take' and become institutionalised. It by no means makes it inevitable. But in what proportion of cases does it 'catch'? Bloch and Sperber ignore the issue, though it's surely crucial? If that proportion is small, the influence of the universal propensity would appear rather limited and we might wonder how much explanatory value it actually has; even whether it really exists (since the recurrence might be explained by other factors). One might, more importantly, wonder how securely this alleged propensity is established.[7] It, a priori, seems equally likely that human beings everywhere are predisposed to distinguish between male and female offspring. In that case, unilineal descent systems might appear uncontradictory; bilateral ones as creating a problem. And if both propensities could be shown to exist, they might be expected to counteract each other. The vague correlation between the postulated cognitive universal and the complex customary behaviour seems a little too tenuous for us to be confident that the two are actually related. If there are dangers in 'easy functionalism', the perils of hasty universalism seem no less great.

That is not, of course, reason enough for abandoning the whole enterprise or for rejecting Bloch's vision of what anthropology might be. His recent essays on 'partial recurrences' raise fundamental questions that most anthropologists are too timid to address, and offer answers that are invariably bold and challenging. 'Most anthropologists', but not all; and I find it instructive to think of his work in relation to that of two others who have also kept faith with a vision of anthropology as a grand comparative enterprise – though one that is perhaps closer to the earlier Bloch than the later.

The first is Jack Goody, whose work has a breadth and ambition that makes him another direct heir to the founders of the discipline. Like Bloch, he has been concerned to account for very broad similarities and differences between human populations, though his analytical strategy is very different from that of Bloch in his more recent work. Bloch, as we have seen, explains the similarities by reference to human nature and to problems of an existential nature that human beings everywhere confront, and the differences by reference to political economy and history. Goody understands *both* in terms of the possibilities that different types of technology provide for the development of society – the technology of warfare (e.g. Goody 1971), the technology of agricultural production (e.g. Goody 1976) and 'the technology of the intellect' (that is, literacy [e.g. Goody 1977]). The second is Sherry Ortner in her writings on gender. These initially set out to explain an apparently universal phenomenon – the subordination of women – by reference to invariant aspects of the human existential condition (Ortner 1974). The next step, however, is to try to account for the fact that that subordination is more marked in some kinds of societies than in others. This is explained by reference to broad differences in wider patterns of social inequality and in the nature of kinship systems (Ortner 1981). In short, what Ortner succeeds in combining is an analysis of what appears to be a human universal with one that clearly relates its relative salience to differences in social structure.

As with Bloch, it is a measure of the impact that both of these authors have had that their ideas have been subject to copious comment and criticism. But it is not so much the content of their arguments that is at issue here as their conception of what anthropology should be, and what kinds of question it should ask. In the end we are a natural science, claims Bloch. But of what? His answer is spelled out in the 2005 manifesto statement with which I started. Human nature is the *only* centre our subject can have. It should be remembered, however, that a later generation of anthropologists to the one whose vision Bloch hopes to restore had a rather different formulation – anthropology should aspire to be 'a natural science of *society*'. In subsequent generations, any claim to the status of a natural science has made many anthropologists cringe. But if we re-formulate the project a little less tendentiously as 'the comparative study of society', then it seems to me that it has been brilliantly carried forward by the two authors to whose work I have just referred, as well as in many of Bloch's own writings. What concerns me about his recent return to roots is that there is some danger in his formulation of our disciplinary objectives that the subject will drift even further away from a proper concern with political economy (that is so central in Goody); and with the structure of society (that Ortner manages to combine so fruitfully with a bold attempt to grapple with universals). The questions of ('Zafimaniry') anthropology to which ordinary people want answers are surely as much about these as about the general properties of human nature. It would be a mistake to let the second kind of enquiry eclipse the first.

NOTES

1. Malinowski was explicit about his 'general bias towards' and 'greater interest' in 'underlying sameness' (Young 2004: 76), and it emerged especially clearly in the polemic he directed at the Durkheimians in *Crime and custom in savage society* (1926). With regard to the concept of the person, the contrast between Malinowski and Mauss is (very much to the advantage of the former) well drawn out by Béteille (1991), who stresses 'the artifice of inversion' that informs Mauss's celebrated essay on the subject. '...if the individual was to count for everything in the most advanced society, as both (Durkheim and Mauss) believed and hoped, then it stood to reason that he should count for nothing in the most primitive ones.' As Bloch (1983) himself shows, and I return to this point below, Marx also adopted that artifice in constructing an image of 'primitive' society as an inversion of the modern capitalist order.
2. Hermits and anchorites on desert pillars might perhaps make one wonder about this equation between Protestant and ascetic Christianity. Though it does not, of course, refute the possibility of a Protestant influence, it is in fact the case that Bloch's main exposure to Christianity was through a partly Catholic upbringing. Evans-Pritchard, whom Cannell sees as similarly influenced, was a Catholic convert.
3. Not that Astuti explicitly excludes the first possibility, though I infer that it is the second that really interests her.
4. For complex reasons, not strictly relevant here, Bloch argues that a reverse transformation – when Merina are forced to 'revert' to slash-and-burn agriculture – does not occur.
5. This was probably written after 1810 but purports to record a royal speech laying down the correct manner of performing the ritual that had been delivered during the previous reign and therefore dates from somewhere around the turn of the century. The dating is of some significance for the argument that follows, as is Bloch's observation (1986a: 113) that we can be 'reasonably certain' that the royal decree 'represent[ed] a certain degree of innovation'.
6. This is not, of course, to deny that religious ideology and ritual are of real significance in *some* industrial societies. That is not, however, the issue here. This, rather, concerns the different ways in which ideology might work when it is reproduced through ritual, or through other means.
7. The authors themselves seem uncertain and treat it as a hypothesis rather than as an established fact.

REFERENCES

Asad, T. 1979. 'Anthropology and the analysis of ideology', *Man* 14(4): 607–27.

Berg. G. 1986. Review of *From blessing to violence: history and ideology in the circumcision ritual of the Merina of Madagascar*, *Current Anthropology* 27(4): 354–5.

Béteille, A. 1991. 'Individual and person as subjects for sociology', in A. Béteille, *Society and politics in India: essays in a comparative perspective*, London: Athlone Press.

Bloch, M. 1971. *Placing the dead: tombs, ancestral villages, and kinship organization in Madagascar*, London: Seminar Press.

—— 1973. 'The long term and the short term: the economic and political significance of the morality of kinship', in J. Goody (ed.), *The character of kinship*, Cambridge: Cambridge University Press.

—— 1975a. 'Property and the end of affinity', in M. Bloch (ed.), *Marxist analyses and social anthropology*, London: Malaby Press.

—— (ed.) 1975b. *Marxist analyses and social anthropology*, London: Malaby Press.

—— 1980. 'Modes of production and slavery in Madagascar: two case studies', in J.L. Watson (ed.), *Asian and African systems of slavery*, Berkeley: University of California Press.

—— 1983. *Marxism and anthropology: the history of a relationship*, Oxford: Clarendon Press.

—— 1986a. *From blessing to violence: history and ideology in the circumcision ritual of the Merina of Madagascar*, Cambridge: Cambridge University Press.

—— 1986b. 'Author's précis' and 'Reply', *From blessing to violence: history and ideology in the circumcision ritual of the Merina of Madagascar*, *Current Anthropology* 27(4): 349–53, 359–60.

—— 1989a. *Ritual, history and power: selected papers in anthropology*, London: Athlone Press.

—— 1989b. 'The symbolism of money in Imerina', in J. Parry and M. Bloch (eds), *Money and the morality of exchange*, Cambridge: Cambridge University Press.

—— 1992. *Prey into hunter: the politics of religious experience*, Cambridge: Cambridge University Press.

—— 1998. *How we think they think: anthropological approaches to cognition, memory, and literacy*, Boulder, Colorado: Westview Press.

—— 2000. 'Postmodernism – The nature/culture debate in just another guise?', *Irish Journal of Anthropology* 5(1): 111–5.

—— 2005. *Essays on cultural transmission.* Oxford: Berg.

—— 2006. 'Teknonymy and the evocation of the "social" among the Zafimaniry of Madagascar', in G. vom Bruck and B. Bodenhorn (eds), *The anthropology of names and naming*, Cambridge: Cambridge University Press.

Borofsky, R. 1994. *Assessing cultural anthropology*, New York: McGraw-Hill Inc.

Dumont, L. 1970. *Homo Hierarchicus: the caste system and its implications*, London: Weidenfeld and Nicolson.

—— 1986. *Essays on individualism: modern ideology in anthropological perspective*, Chicago: Chicago University Press.

Geertz, C. 1975. *The interpretation of cultures*, London: Hutchinson.

—— 1980. *Negara: the theatre state in nineteenth century Bali*, Princeton: Princeton University Press.

Goody, J. 1971. *Technology, tradition, and the state in Africa*, London: Oxford University Press.

—— 1976. *Production and reproduction: a comparative study of the domestic domain*, Cambridge: Cambridge University Press.

—— 1977. *The domestication of the savage mind*, Cambridge: Cambridge University Press.

Houtman, G. 1988. 'Interview with Maurice Bloch', *Anthropology Today* 14(1): 18–21.

Malinowski, B. 1926. *Crime and custom in savage society*, London: Kegan Paul, Trench, Trubner and Co.

Marx, K. and F. Engels. 1947. *The German ideology*, New York: International Publishers.

Ortner, S. 1974. 'Is female to male as nature is to culture?', in M. Rosaldo and L. Lamphere (eds), *Woman, culture and society*, Stanford: University Press.

—— 1981. 'Gender and sexuality in hierarchical societies: the case of Polynesia and some comparative implications', in S. Ortner and H. Whitehead (eds), *Sexual meanings: the cultural construction of gender and sexuality*, Cambridge: Cambridge University Press.

Sahlins, M. 1985. *Islands of history*, Chicago: Chicago University Press.

Srinivas, M.N. 1952. *Religion and society among the Coorgs of south India*, Oxford: Clarendon Press.

Terray. E. 1975. 'Classes and class consciousness in the Abron kingdom of Gyaman', in M. Bloch (ed.), *Marxist analyses and social anthropology*, London: Malaby Press.

Tylor, E.B. 1910. 'Anthropology', *Encyclopaedia Britannica* (11th edition) 2: 108–19, New York: Encyclopaedia Britannica Inc.

Young, M. 2004. *Malinowski: odyssey of an anthropologist, 1884–1910*, New Haven: Yale University Press.

CONTRIBUTORS

Catherine Allerton teaches anthropology at the London School of Economics. She is the author of a number of articles on Manggarai housing, marriage, sarongs and cosmetic use. She is currently completing a book manuscript on landscape, everyday life and modernity in Flores.

Rita Astuti teaches anthropology at the London School of Economics. She is the author of *People of the sea* (1995, Cambridge) and *Constraints on conceptual development* (with G. Solomon and S. Carey, 2004, Blackwell).

Fenella Cannell teaches anthropology at the London School of Economics. She is the author of *Power and intimacy in the Christian Philippines* (1999, Cambridge), and editor of *The anthropology of Christianity* (2006, Duke).

Janet Carsten teaches anthropology at the University of Edinburgh. She is the author of *After kinship* (2004, Cambridge) and editor of *Cultures of relatedness* (2000, Cambridge) and *Ghosts of memory: essays on remembrance and relatedness* (forthcoming, Blackwell).

Luke Freeman teaches anthropology at the London School of Economics. He is the author of a number of articles on Madagascar, focusing especially on the social, ritual and economic implications of formal education.

Olivia Harris teaches anthropology at the London School of Economics. Among her publications are *To make the earth bear fruit* (2000, Institute of Latin American Studies) and *Qaraqara-Charka: historia antropologica de una confederacion aymara, siglos XV–XVII* (2006, Ediciones Plural).

Eva Keller is a Research Fellow in the Institute of Anthropology at the University of Zurich. She is the author of *The road to clarity: Seventh-day Adventism in Madagascar* (2005, Palgrave).

Michael Lambek teaches anthropology at the London School of Economics as well as at the University of Toronto where he holds a Canada Research Chair. He is the author of *The weight of the past* (2002, Palgrave-Macmillan) and has edited several collections, including *Illness and irony* (with Paul Antze, 2003, Berghahn).

Jonathan Parry teaches anthropology at the London School of Economics. He is the author of *Death in Banaras* (1994, Cambridge), and co-editor of *Money and the morality of exchange* (with M. Bloch, 1989, Cambridge) and *Institutions and inequalities* (with R. Guha, 1999, Oxford).

Laura Rival teaches anthropology at the University of Oxford. She is the author of *Trekking through history: the Huaorani of Amazonian Ecuador* (2002, Columbia).

Charles Stafford teaches anthropology at the London School of Economics. He is the author of *Separation and reunion in modern China* (2000, Cambridge) and the editor of *Living with separation in China* (2003, RoutledgeCurzon).

Michael Stewart teaches anthropology at University College London. He is the author of *The time of the gypsies* (1997, Westview) and co-editor of *Lilies of the field: marginal people who live for the moment* (1999, Westview).

Christina Toren teaches anthropology at the University of St Andrews. She is the author or *Making sense of hierarchy: cognition as social process in Fiji* (1990, LSE Monographs on Social Anthropology) and *Mind, materiality and history* (1999, Routledge).

INDEX